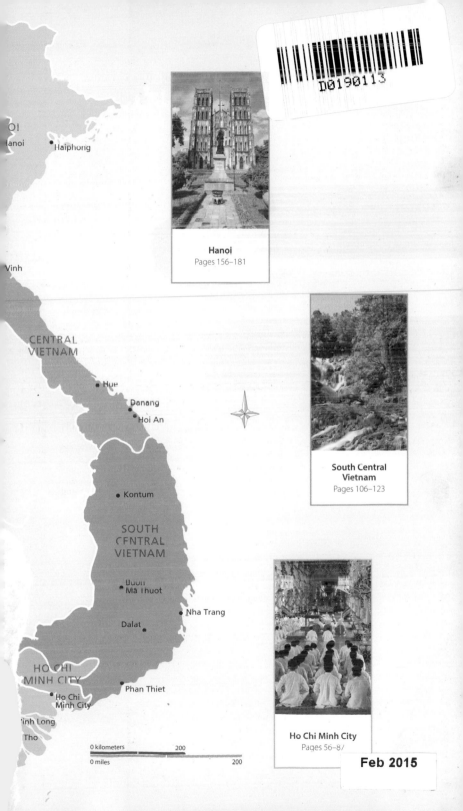

OI
Hanoi
Haiphong

Vinh

CENTRAL
VIETNAM

Hue
Danang
Hoi An

Kontum

SOUTH
CENTRAL
VIETNAM

Buon
Ma Thuot

Nha Trang

Dalat

HO CHI
MINH CITY

Ho Chi
Minh City

Vinh Long

Tho

Hanoi

**South Central
Vietnam**

Ho Chi Minh City

0 kilometers   200

0 miles   200

Feb 2015

D0190113

VIETNAM
& ANGKOR WAT

EYEWITNESS TRAVEL

VIETNAM
& ANGKOR WAT

LONDON, NEW YORK,
MELBOURNE, MUNICH AND DELHI
www.dk.com

Managing Editor Aruna Ghose
Design Manager Priyanka Thakur
Project Editor Shahnaaz Baksh
Project Designer Kavita Saha
Editors Arunabh Borgohain, Jyoti Kumari,
Jayashree Menon, Asavari Singh
Designer Shipra Gupta
Cartogrophy Manager Uma Bhattacharya
Senior Picture Researcher Taiyaba Khatoon
Picture Researcher Sumita Khatwani
DTP Designer Vinod Harish

Contributors
Claire Boobbyer, Andrew Forbes, Dana Healy, Richard Sterling

Consultants
Claire Boobbyer, Dana Healy

Photographers
Demetrio Carrasco, David Henley, Chris Stowers

Illustrators
Gary Cross, Surat Kumar Mantu, Arun Pottirayil,
Gautam Trivedi, Mark Warner

Printed in Malaysia by Vivar Printing Sdn. Bhd.

First American Edition, 2007
14 15 16 17 10 9 8 7 6 5 4 3 2 1

Published in the United States by DK Publishing,
345 Hudson Street, New York, New York 10014

Reprinted with revisions 2009, 2011, 2015
Copyright © 2007, 2015 Dorling Kindersley Limited
A Penguin Random House Company

All rights reserved. Without limiting the rights under copyright reserved above, no part
of this publication may be reproduced, stored in or introduced into a retrieval system, or
transmitted in any form or by any means (electronic, mechanical, photocopying,
recording or otherwise), without the prior written permission of both the copyright
owner and the above publisher of the book.
Published in Great Britain by Dorling Kindersley Limited.

A catalog record for this book is
available from the Library of Congress.

ISSN 1542-1554

ISBN 978-1-4654-1210-2

Floors are referred to throughout in accordance with American usage; ie the first floor is
at ground level.

MIX
Paper from
responsible sources
FSC™ C018179
www.fsc.org

**The information in this
DK Eyewitness Travel Guide is checked regularly.**
Every effort has been made to ensure that this book is as up-to-date as possible at
the time of going to press. Some details, however, such as telephone numbers,
opening hours, prices, gallery hanging arrangements, and travel information are
liable to change. The publishers cannot accept responsibility for any consequences
arising from the use of this book, nor for any material on third party websites, and
cannot guarantee that any website address in this book will be a suitable source of
travel information. We value the views and suggestions of our readers very highly.
Please write to: Publisher, DK Eyewitness Travel Guides, Dorling Kindersley, 80
Strand, London, WC2R 0RL, UK, or email: travelguides@dk.com.

Front cover main image: Ha Long Bay, North Vietnam

◀ Beautiful golden rice field in Vietnam

Contents

Spirals of incense burning, Thien Hau
Pagoda (see p74)

Introducing
Vietnam

Fishermen working in the waterways of the
Mekong Delta

Wooden stilt huts amid the flooded paddy fields around Son La

Sculptures in Thien Hau Pagoda

Sculpture in Dieu De Pagoda

Unusual mix of architecture at the Cao Dai Holy See *(see pp78–9)*

INTRODUCING VIETNAM

DISCOVERING VIETNAM

The following tours have been designed to take in as many of the country's highlights as possible in a limited time. The first itineraries outlined here are two 2-day tours of Vietnam's major cities: Hanoi and Ho Chi Minh City. Additional suggestions are included in case visitors want to spend more time in either city. Next is a two-week tour that includes all the main attractions between these two cities along Highway 1 from north to south. The trip begins in Hanoi and takes in several UNESCO World Heritage sites, including Halong Bay, Hue, and Hoi An, as well as the beach resorts of Nha Trang and Mui Ne, before ending in Ho Chi Minh City. Choose and combine tours or dip in and out and be inspired.

Halong Bay
A boat trip on this stunning bay, peppered with pinnacles rising out of the sea, makes a memorable experience.

Two Weeks from Hanoi to Ho Chi Minh City

- Marvel at the other-worldly landscapes created by limestone outcrops in **Halong Bay**.

- Explore the legacy of the Nguyen Dynasty at the Imperial City in **Hue**.

- Stroll the narrow lanes of the Old Quarter in **Hoi An** and indulge in a tailor-made outfit.

- Wander round the Cham ruins at **My Son** and admire the intricate sculptures crafted by this ancient civilization.

- Enjoy a seafood feast and saunter around deserted beaches near **Quy Nhon**.

- Join a boat trip to offshore islands and lounge on the sand at **Nha Trang**, the country's main beach resort.

- Go kitesurfing and "sand-sledding" at the hip resort of **Mui Ne**.

Key

— Two weeks from Hanoi to Ho Chi Minh City

Hue
Celebrated for its rich culture and heritage, the city of Hue is home to the evocative remains of numerous palaces, tombs, and temples.

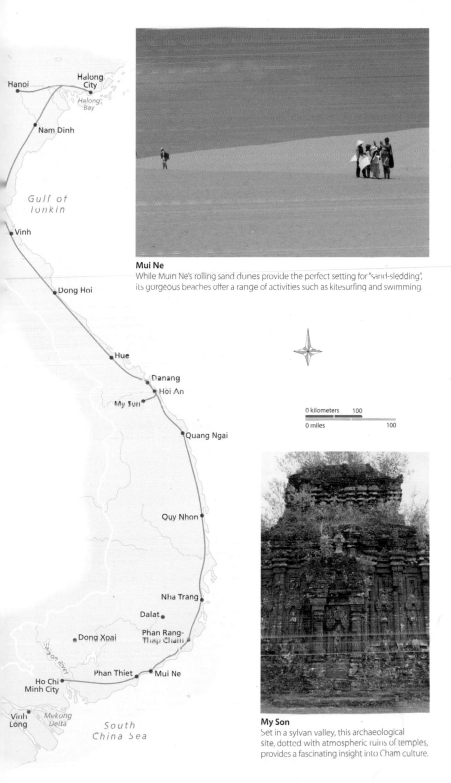

Hanoi

Halong
City

*Halong
Bay*

Nam Dinh

*Gulf of
Tonkin*

Vinh

Dong Hoi

Hue

Danang
Hoi An
My Son

Quang Ngai

Quy Nhon

Nha Trang

Dalat

Dong Xoai

Phan Rang-
Thap Cham

Phan Thiet
Mui Ne

Ho Chi
Minh City

Vinh
Long

*Mekong
Delta*

Saigon River

*South
China Sea*

0 kilometers   100

0 miles   100

Mui Ne
While Mui Ne's rolling sand dunes provide the perfect setting for "sand-sledding",
its gorgeous beaches offer a range of activities such as kitesurfing and swimming.

My Son
Set in a sylvan valley, this archaeological
site, dotted with atmospheric ruins of temples,
provides a fascinating insight into Cham culture.

Two Days in Hanoi

Hanoi's attractions are conveniently clustered in a few key areas – the Old Quarter, the French Quarter and Ba Dinh Square – making it easy to explore the city's temples, museums, and markets on foot.

- **Arriving** Hanoi's Noi Bai Airport is located 22 miles (35 km) north of the city. A taxi takes about 45 minutes to reach the city center, while minibuses and regular buses take an hour or more.

- **Moving on** Regular domestic flights connect Hanoi with Ho Chi Minh City and other major towns.

Day 1

Morning Begin the day early with a trip to **Hoan Kiem Lake** *(see p164)*. Cross the bright red The Huc bridge to Den Ngoc Son, which stands on an island at the northern edge of the lake, and watch locals lighting incense at the temple altars. Then stroll around the lake, past graceful Tai Chi practioners, and youngsters painting landmarks such as Thap Rua, or Turtle Tower. Walk north to the bustling **Old Quarter** *(see pp160–61)*, where it is easy to find a number of important sights with the aid of a map. These include the interesting Memorial House Museum,

The charming One Pillar Pagoda in the middle of a lotus pond, Hanoi

the elegant **Bach Ma Temple** *(see p162)*, devoted to the city's guardian spirit, the Quan Chuong Gate, and **Dong Xuan Market** *(see p162)*, the oldest and largest market in the city.

Afternoon Head for the **Sofitel Metropole Hotel** *(see p166)*, the city's most celebrated residence with whitewashed walls and green shuttered windows, before walking round the corner to see the imposing façade of the **Opera House** *(see p166)*. The architectural theme continues with the **National Museum of Vietnamese History** *(see pp166–7)* nearby, where the striking exterior is almost as impressive as the extensive collection of artifacts inside. Spend at least an hour or two here before moving

on to **Hoa Lo Prison Museum** *(see p165)*, once known to American PoWs as the "Hanoi Hilton". After about an hour of exploring this haunting place, if there is still time, the **Ambassador's Pagoda** *(see p165)*, home to many Buddha statues, is only a short walk away.

Day 2

Morning Start off with a visit to the **Ho Chi Minh Mausoleum** *(see p169)* in Ba Dinh Square to pay respect to Vietnam's greatest hero. The severe stone blocks of the mausoleum are in stark contrast to the nearby **Stilt House** *(see p169)* that was Ho's home for over a decade. Next, make a short stopover at the lovely **One Pillar Pagoda** *(see p169)*, which stands in a small lotus pond, but reserve plenty of time to explore **Hanoi Citadel** *(see p172)* that has only recently opened to the public. After learning about the city's 1,000-year long history, go round the corner to visit either the **Military History Museum** *(see p168)* or the **Fine Arts Museum** *(see p168)*.

Afternoon Enter the grounds of the **Temple of Literature** *(see pp170–71)*, which is Hanoi's oldest and most popular attraction, and is usually bustling with tour groups. Spend time admiring the beautiful structures such as the Khue Van Cac, or Constellation of Literature, and the Temple of Confucius in the heart of the compound. From here, take a cab to the **Museum of Ethnology** *(see p176)* to learn about the country's various ethnic groups. Alternatively, head for the enormous **Ho Tay** or **West Lake** *(see p172)* to see the Quan Thanh Temple and the Tran Quoc and Kim Lien pagodas, all of which sit on the shores of the lake.

> **To extend your trip...**
> Take a half- or full-day trip west of the city to the ancient **Thay** and **Tay Phuong** pagodas *(see p177)*, famed for religious statues and wood carvings.

Austere façade of Ho Chin Minh Mausoleum, Hanoi

Two Days in Ho Chi Minh City

Still called Saigon by most inhabitants, Ho Chi Minh City is the powerhouse of the Vietnamese economy. This bustling city has a curious mix of Chinese, French, and American cultural influences.

- **Arriving** Tay Son Nhat Airport is just 4 miles (7 km) north of the city center. A taxi takes half an hour to reach the center, however, it could take longer during rush hour.

- **Moving on** Ho Chi Minh City is connected by domestic flights with Hanoi and all other main towns in Vietnam.

Intricately detailed ceramic-tiled roof of the Quan Am Pagoda, Ho Chin Minh City

Day 1

Morning Begin the day in Lam Son Square, in the heart of Saigon, where stands the Neo-Classical **Municipal Theater** *(see p62)* between the city's most famous hotels: the **Continental** *(see p62)* and the **Caravelle** *(see p62)*. From here, walk one block west to admire the elaborate façade of the **People's Committee Building** *(see p63)*, formerly known as the Hôtel de Ville. Just two blocks north of here, the **Notre Dame Cathedral** *(see p64)* with its iconic twin spires is probably the city's best-known landmark. Spend the rest of the morning in the sprawling **Reunification Palace** *(see p65)*, reliving the days before tanks crashed through the gates to end the Vietnam War in 1975.

Afternoon Take a deep breath and enter the **War Remnants Museum** *(see p69)*, which recounts the horrors of the Vietnam War, particularly the country's conflict with the US. Most visitors leave the place lamenting the inhumanity that war engenders. To cheer up, head for **Ben Thanh Market** *(see p70)* for some shopping. Pick up souvenirs such as

lacquerware or ethnic fabrics, but nothing too bulky, as it will be grueling to cart them to the top of the **Bitexco Financial Tower** *(see p63)* for the day's last stop, the **Saigon Skydeck**. Soak up the panoramic views from here, and see how many of the city's main sights you can spot.

Day 2

Morning Head north of the city center to the **Jade Emperor Pagoda** *(see pp66–7)*, which packs a lot of attractions into a small space. These include the Hall of Ten Hells, a Women's Room, and a tortoise shelter. While in this part of town, stop by the **Le Van Duyet Temple** *(see p68)* dedicated to General Le Van Duyet, one of Vietnam's many national heroes. On the way back towards the center, check out the **Museum of Vietnamese History** *(see p65)* to find out about the country's complex past. Afterwards, stretch your legs in the **Botanical Gardens and Saigon Zoo** *(see p65)* next door.

Afternoon Make your way to District 5 of the city, also known as **Cholon** *(see pp72–3)*, or big market, the largest Chinatown in Vietnam. Dive straight into **Binh Tay Market** *(see p75)* for a taste of frenetic commercialism before heading to its ancient and atmospheric temples in the backstreets.

Don't miss **Quan Am Pagoda** *(see p74)*, home to a plethora of deities, or **Thien Hau Pagoda** *(see p74)*, decorated with intricately carved friezes and tableau. Round off the day with a visit to District 11 and the tranquil **Giac Vien Pagoda** *(see p75)*, one of Ho Chi Minh City's oldest places of worship.

> **To extend your trip...**
> Join a day trip to the **Cu Chi Tunnels** *(see p70)*, a classic example of Vietnamese ingenuity, and the **Cao Dai Holy See** *(see pp78–9)*, a mind-boggling amalgam of religious icons.

The imposing Notre Dame Cathedral, Ho Chin Minh City

Two Weeks from Hanoi to Ho Chi Minh City

- **Airports** Arrive at Noi Bai Airport in Hanoi and depart from Tan Son Nhat Airport in Ho Chi Minh City.

- **Transport** Join a tour from Hanoi to Halong Bay, then rent a car and driver for rest of the itinerary. While the train covers the route from Hanoi to Ho Chi Minh City and stops in major towns such as Hue and Nha Trang, it does not halt in places like My Son and Mui Ne.

Day 1: Hanoi
Stroll around the narrow streets of Hanoi's **Old Quarter** (see pp160–61), where colorful shop displays, exotic aromas and vibrant calls from street vendors create a heady mix. Pop in to the Memorial House Museum to see the layout of a typical tube house, then check out the area's streets specializing in particular products, such as the Hang Gai Street, or Silk Street. After a leisurely lunch, wander south to **Hoan Kiem Lake** (see p164), pausing for a look at the bright arc of The Huc Bridge and Thap Rua, which stands on a tiny island in the lake. Next, delve into the leafy boulevards of the French Quarter, where sights such as the **Opera House** (see p166) and the **National Museum of Vietnamese History** (see p166) testify to the city's colonial past.

Days 2 and 3: Halong Bay
Join a tour from Hanoi to **Halong Bay** (see pp186–7) and spend a night in this magnificent landscape of limestone pinnacles that rise vertically from the emerald-green waters of the bay. Paddle a kayak, explore illuminated caves and take lots of pictures.

Days 4 and 5: Hue
Devote a day to exploring the **Imperial City** (see pp144–7) in the heart of the Hue Citadel, which was Vietnam's capital from 1802 to 1945. Don't miss the Thai Hoa Palace with its splendidly decorated throne

hall, the beautifully restored The Mieu and the Nine Dynastic Urns, each of which weighs more than 2 tons (2 tonnes). End the day with a sumptuous multicourse meal of Imperial cuisine. On the second day, take a boat trip along **Perfume River** (see p152) and, later, visit a few of the **Royal Tombs** (see p149), which are all lavishly decorated and set in delightful gardens. The most impressive are the tombs of Tu Duc and Minh Mang.

Day 6: Danang
Head for the Marble Mountains, just south of **Danang** (see p138), in the morning to enjoy views along the coast and explore atmospheric shrines sheltered in huge caves. Then go back to the city to visit the Museum of Cham Sculpture (see p138), which contains some exquisite examples of stone carvings created by the Cham civilization. In the evening, take a stroll by the Han River and admire the new Dragon Bridge, which actually breathes fire.

Day 7: Hoi An
For many visitors to Vietnam, a walk around Hoi An's **Old Quarter** (see pp130–32) is the highlight of their trip. The area boasts a combination of ornate pagodas, evocative museums and ancient houses. Be sure to get a custom-made outfit at one of the town's stylish boutiques, and try the gastronomic delights served at its restaurants.

Steps leading to the octagonal The Mieu Tower, Hanoi

Day 8: My Son
Spend the day exploring **My Son** (see pp134–6), once the most important religious centre of Cham culture. The ruins here are reminiscent of Angkor Wat, in Cambodia, although American bombs destroyed much of the site during the 1960s. Many of the brick towers are overgrown, lending the place an irresistible mystique, but restoration work is ongoing. Check out groups B and C, which comprise the best-preserved remains, while several evocative sculptures can be seen displayed in buildings D1 and D2.

Day 9: Quy Nhon
A large port town with a broad swathe of beach, **Quy Nhon** (see pp122–3) offers the

View of the Thap Rua tower in the middle of the Hoan Kiem Lake, Hanoi

Flower beds fronting the elegant Nha Trang Cathedral, with the clock tower dominating the skyline

opportunity to experience the real Vietnam without being hassled by hawkers. Visit the **Thap Doi Cham** (see p123), or Double Cham Towers, on the western edge of town, sample scrumptious seafood and take a ride along the coast road south of town to see picture-postcard beaches lapped by azure waters.

Days 10 and 11: Nha Trang

Vietnam's premier beach resort, **Nha Trang** (see pp112–15), has a few sights that can be visited in a morning. Begin at the Gothic-style **Nha Trang Cathedral** (see p112), before heading for the hilltop **Long Son Pagoda** (see p112). Later, go to the **Oceanographic Institute** (see p114) in Cau Da to see displays of diverse marine life, and then stop by the well-preserved **Po Nagar Cham Towers** (see p113). Spend the afternoon hours lounging at the beach, and wait for strolling vendors to tempt you with fresh seafood, ice-cold drinks or a soothing massage. After dark, check out a few of the bars that stay open most of the night.

On the next day, take a boat trip to the islands (see p114), which lie just offshore, for a day of snorkelling and sunbathing. Round off the day with a visit to the aquarium, free lunch and drinks at a floating bar.

Days 12 and 13: Mui Ne

In less than two decades, **Mui Ne** (see pp110–11), with its 12-mile (20-km) long beach, has developed from a tiny fishing village to a sophisticated beach resort that rivals Nha Trang. Spend the morning windsurfing and kitesurfing; there are several places that offer instruction for beginners. Afterwards, take off for the enormous sand dunes on the fringes of the resort, where "sand sledding" is a fun way to pass the time. Devote the rest of the day to snoozing on the beach, relishing fresh seafood, or pampering your body at a spa.

Elaborately carved exterior of one of the Po Nagar Cham Towers, Nha Trang

Day 14: Ho Chi Minh City

Begin at the **Reunification Palace** (see p65) and learn about the last days of the Vietnam War. From here, head to **Dong Khoi** (see pp60–61), the city's main street, to see the **Notre Dame Cathedral** (see p64) and **General Post Office** (see p164), which serve as reminders of the city's colonial past. Walk down the Dong Khoi area towards Saigon River, making a brief diversion to look at the ornate **People's Committee Building** (see p63). Pick up a few distinctive souvenirs in the shops at Dong Khoi and take time out in one of the many elegant restaurants along here for a leisurely lunch. That done, go up to the 49th floor of the **Bitexco Financial Tower** (see p63), where the **Saigon Skydeck** offers a bird's-eye view of the city center. End the day with a sundowner at the Saigon Saigon Bar of the **Caravelle Hotel** (see p62).

> **To extend your trip...**
> Sign up for a tour of the **Mekong Delta** (see pp88–105) and spend anywhere between a day and a week exploring floating markets, fruit orchards, bird sanctuaries and Khmer pagodas.

Putting Vietnam on the Map

Extending along the Indochinese peninsula, Vietnam lies within the tropics, 11 degrees north of the equator. Bordering China, Laos, and Cambodia, it is approximately 128,000 sq miles (331,000 sq km) in area, with a coastline stretching for 2,040 miles (3,260 km) from the South China Sea to the Gulf of Tonkin. With a diverse population of about 92 million people, Vietnam is divided into 58 *tinh* or provinces and 5 *thu do* or municipalities. Although Hanoi is the capital, Ho Chi Minh City dominates the national economy.

Southeast Asia

Key
Highway
Main road
Railroad
International border

A PORTRAIT OF VIETNAM

Lush green mountains, scenic beaches, ancient pagodas, and the allure of a fascinating culture attract millions of visitors to Vietnam each year. The country emerged from the 1990s as an increasingly prosperous nation, with a strong tourism industry, largely due to economic reforms and an effort by its people to rebuild after the war and move further away from Communist principles that have stifled the nation.

Bounded by the warm waters of the South China Sea, Vietnam is in the southeastern corner of the Indochinese peninsula. To the country's west are Laos and Cambodia, separated from Vietnam by the Annamite Mountains or the Truong Son Range, while to the north lies the great bulk of China. Vietnam itself is long and thin – just 31 miles (50 km) wide at its narrowest – with an extensive coastline stretching from the Gulf of Tonkin in the north to the Gulf of Thailand in the south.

The Vietnamese generally divide their country into three regions. In the north, dominated by the charming capital Hanoi and hemmed in by mountains on three sides, is the fertile Red River Delta. The long central part of Vietnam is marked by several scenic beaches, the former imperial city of Hue, the mercantile town of Hoi An, and the large port city of Danang, along with remnants of the Demilitarized Zone (DMZ). In its lower half, it broadens and is home to the highlands around Pleiku and Dalat. In the far south lies burgeoning Ho Chi Minh City, Vietnam's commercial hub, and the Mekong Delta. Characterized by palm trees and numerous canals, this bucolic region is the country's largest rice-producing belt.

Vietnam's geographical diversity is reflected in its people, and the nation is home to 54 recognized ethnic groups. The largest, Viet or Kinh, constitute 86 percent of the nation's 92 million people and live mainly on the coastal plains and in the delta

The Yen River winding its way to the Perfume Pagoda *(see pp196–7)*

◀ Street vendors setting up a makeshift kitchen to prepare hot snacks, Hoi An *(see pp128–33)*

Hmong minority of the northern highlands

regions. Most of the ethnic minorities inhabit the northern and central highlands and are distinguished by their unique history, culture, and language. The ethnic Chinese, or Hoa, by contrast, are mostly based in the lowlands and major cities, while the Cham and Khmer are settled in the southern coastal plains and the Mekong Delta.

Culture

The traditional structure of Vietnamese society has always been hierarchical and patriarchal. Drawing heavily from the Confucian model, family and filial duties are upheld as cardinal virtues. Elders are given respect and education is highly esteemed. The role of women has changed since their emancipation by the Communist regime. Today, although women have gained equality in the public sphere, the home is usually still "run" by a woman.

Vietnam's culture is made more fascinating by the foreign influences it has assimilated over the centuries. Nearly 1,000 years of Chinese occupation has left its mark on the Vietnamese, who have selected and adopted those customs, traditions, beliefs, and architecture most suited to their culture. It is, however, a love-hate relationship, with Vietnam emulating Chinese culture while rejecting any form of political domination by its northern neighbor. The impact of the French, who attacked Saigon after a wave of Catholic executions in the 19th century and went on to conquer the country, is less comprehensive. The colonial power's influence is most visible in the distinctive architecture of the cities and, to some extent, in the food.

Some overseas Vietnamese, or *Viet Kieu*, who fled the country as refugees from the communist North in the 1950s and from the South after 1975, are now returning and bringing Western cultural influences with them. While members of the older generation refuse to visit their former homeland, still ruled by the very people who forced them into exile, others are coming back to set up businesses or discover their "roots."

French-style baguettes for sale

Tourism and the media have also played a role in the Westernization of the culture, which is evident among urban youngsters. Everyone is learning English, iPhones are coveted, and jeans and designer clothing are common. During the 1990s Vietnam was known for its austere fashions, but today it is an emporium for purchasing clothes, accessories, and homeware in luxurious fabrics and funky designs. Western-style clothing is common among young women, but the traditional *ao dai* or trouser dress, is still worn on special occasions, in schools, and in formal settings.

A Vietnamese woman in the traditional *ao dai*

Flamboyantly carved dragon pillars adorning Quan Am Pagoda in Ho Chi Minh City *(see p74)*

Religion

During the communist years, atheism was officially promoted, but in the modern era of pragmatism, old faiths and traditions flourish. Vietnam has long embraced a mélange of faiths based on Tam Giao or the Triple Religion of Buddhism, Taoism, and Confucianism, to which has been added ancestor worship, indigenous spirit beliefs, and even Hindu traditions from ancient Champa. The country is also home to a large Catholic population, and idiosyncratic faiths such as Cao Daism *(see p27)* and Hoa Hao. These are all tolerated, provided they do not threaten the Communist Party's hold on power.

Buddhist monk at prayer

Language and Literature

Vietnamese, or *tieng Viet*, is the national language of Vietnam, spoken by around 87 per cent of the population as their first language. Until about AD 1000, there was no written form of Vietnamese, but in the 11th century, a system called *chu nom* was introduced, using adapted Chinese characters. In the 17th century, a Romanized script, *quoc ngu*, was developed by European missionaries, which has become the accepted script. However, there are regional and intra-regional variations in dialect throughout the country.

Vietnam has a rich literary heritage, written in Chinese, *chu nom*, and *quoc ngu*. The epic poem, *The Tale of Kieu*, written by mandarin and scholar Nguyen Du (1766–1820), is a classic morality tale widely regarded as the greatest work in Vietnamese literature. Also famous are the poems of high-ranking concubine, Ho Xuan Huong (1772–1822), known for her witty verse. Today, as a result of gradual political liberalization, a new style of writing has emerged that explores "forbidden issues," and focuses on the plight of the individual. Bao Ninh is a popular writer whose novel *Sorrow of War* is a powerful account of the Vietnam War. Some contemporary names include Pham Thi Hoai, Nguyen Huy Thiep, and Duong Thu Huong.

Economic Development

Once among the poorest nations of the world, Vietnam experienced an economic boom in the 1990s and early 2000s. The credit for this initially went to the introduction of *doi moi* (economic reforms) in 1986, which permitted the setting up of free market enterprises, abolished the practice of collectivized farming, and set the stage for political liberalization.

In 1993, the World Bank declared 58 percent of the population to be living in poverty. By 2008, this figure was less than 16 percent. Agriculture remains the most important element of the economy, forming a major portion of the country's exports sector and employing nearly 65 percent of the population.

Motorbikes and modern buildings in Ho Chi Minh City

Today, Vietnam is the world's second-largest exporter of rice – an astounding feat for a nation facing famine in the 1980s.

The industrial sector has shown immense improvement and expansion as well. Mining continues to be an integral part of the economy, and oil, gas, and coal production account for more than 25 percent of industrial GDP. The tourism industry is one of the largest earners of foreign currency in the country. Vietnam has also made great strides on the international stage. In 1995, it became a full member of ASEAN, and of the WTO in 2006.

Beginning in 2008, Vietnam saw a retraction in its economy, largely due to an unwillingness of Communist Party cadres to implement further reforms. State-owned enterprises, in particular, began to fail across the country.

Government and Politics

Vietnam is a one-party country run by the Vietnamese Communist Party. Currently, Nyugen Tan Dung and Troung Tan Sang are the prime minister and the president of the Republic of Vietnam respectively. They were chosen by the National Congress which meets every five years. Authoritarian in essence, the party opposes political dissent; many who have expressed disagreement with the regime have been punished. However, since the adoption of limited free market capitalism, the party has taken several steps towards reforming. At the same time, though, it is plagued with corruption, slowing down the process of any political change. As a result, while economic reform speeds along, political rights and freedoms continue to lag behind. In 2009, Hanoi began blocking social networking sites. Several foreign journalists were detained and expelled due to reports on human rights. Then in 2012, the plight of citizens in re-education and work camps were made public. Yet the desire for change amongst the Vietnamese is great, and the populace recognizes that an increased say in politics is not only desirable, but essential for continued development.

Conservation

Despite its increasing wealth, Vietnam remains a poor country with a rapidly expanding population and limited land resources. By 2020, Vietnam is projected to have around twice the population of Thailand, but with less than half the arable land. According to the World Conservation Monitoring Center, at present around 74,000 acres (30,000 ha) of forest is lost annually. Both plantlife and wildlife have suffered at the hands of hunters and farmers, but the government's relocation and collectivized

Farming Vietnam's most important crop, rice

farming programs have perhaps had the greatest long-term impact on the environment. In the 1980s, large tracts of arable land were cleared for futile farming efforts that never saw fruition.

Fortunately, the outlook for Vietnam's nature is improving now. Laws protecting forests and endangered species are being introduced every year, in keeping with Ho Chi Minh's 1962 pronouncement that "forest is gold." Tourism has indirectly had a positive impact on the environment by providing a new source of income that can prove far more profitable than hunting and logging.

Shop selling a wide variety of handicrafts, Hoi An

Tourism

When Vietnam first opened to tourism in the early 1990s, many visitors were drawn by images of a war-torn nation. The Viets have since done their best to change this view, emphasizing the country's beauty instead. Historic pagodas and French-Colonial buildings have been restored, while most hotels and restaurants have now returned to the private sector, allowing proprietors to strive for excellence in an increasingly competitive industry. The country's road and rail transport infrastructure needs major upgrading, but its airports and national airline now offer a high standard of service.

The tourism industry has grown at almost 20 percent annually, although it began to slow in 2008. Each year, millions of visitors are drawn to the country by its ancient monuments, scenic beaches, sophisticated cuisine, excellent shopping opportunities, and the warmth of the Vietnamese people. Another positive outcome of the tourist boom has been the resurgence of traditional culture, including music, dance, and drama. Old festivals are being re-established, and arts such as water puppetry are flourishing.

Hien Lam Pavilion in the Hue Citadel, one of the country's premier tourist attractions *(see p147)*

Landscape and Wildlife

Vietnam is one of Asia's most ecologically diverse countries. Habitats range from the cool mountains of the northwest, through the narrow coastal plains and highland plateaus of the center, to the delta regions of the Red and Mekong Rivers. Especially noteworthy for wildlife enthusiasts are the expansive national parks of Northern Vietnam, filled with fascinating flora and fauna *(see p205)*. For sightings of indigenous and migratory birds, the Mekong Delta offers some of the best opportunities *(see p101)*, while offshore are numerous islands, some with pristine coral reefs *(see p194)*.

Key

The Deltas

Central Highlands

Central Coastline

Northern Mountains

The Deltas

The broad and fertile Red River Delta forms the heartland of Northern Vietnam, while Southern Vietnam is dominated by the rich alluvial lands of the Mekong Delta. Most of Vietnam's rice is produced in these belts. However, while the Red River Delta is almost completely given over to agriculture, the Mekong Delta is also home to wildlife-rich marshlands and mangrove forests.

Central Highlands

Embracing the southern reaches of the Truong Son Range, the topography of the Central Highlands varies between craggy mountains to the far west, and fertile plateaus towards the interior. The red volcanic soil around Pleiku and Kontum supports coffee, tea, and rubber plantations, while the mountains are home to jungles with many species of flora and fauna.

Red mangroves are distinctive for their supporting roots, which arch above the water level, providing a secure environment for many species of small fish, birds, and reptiles.

Asian elephants were widely used in forestry work, but are increasingly threatened today. Yok Don National Park *(see p122)* is an important conservation site.

The endangered red-headed crane, also known as the *Sarus crane*, is found almost exclusively in the grasslands of the Mekong Delta, with the largest concentration at the Tam Nong Bird Sanctuary.

The paulownia, a deciduous tree indigenous to Vietnam and southern China, produces a purple, foxglove-like flower during the early spring.

The clouded leopard is named for the ellipses marking its tawny coat. It has short legs, a bushy tail, and is related to the extinct saber-toothed cat.

The big-eyed pit viper is a small, arboreal predator, which stuns rodents, lizards, and small birds with its toxic venom before eating them.

Butterflies of Vietnam

Vietnam is filled with the fluttering colors of butterflies – from elegant, broad-winged giants on azaleas in city parks, to the innumerable clouds of multicolored purple sapphires and knights at Cuc Phuong National Park (see p197) each April and May. At Tam Dao National Park in the north, more than 300 species have been identified, while at Cat Tien National Park (see p81), the count stands at 440 species. The butterflies' names are generally as evocative and beautiful as their colorful wings. Some of the best-known species are the white dragontail, red lacewing, and jungle queen.

Swallowtail

Red lacewing

Peacock pansy

Red Jezebel

Central Coastline

The upper center comprises a very long and comparatively narrow strip of coastal flatland running along the choppy waters of the South China Sea. While the land is not as productive as the delta regions, it is home to some beautiful beaches, especially around Nha Trang (see p115) in the lower half of the central coastline.

The Northern Mountains

The Northern Mountains all but encircle the Red River Delta on three sides. Sharp, jagged peaks rise above long mountain valleys, forming the most inaccessible part of the entire country. The forest-clad slopes of the northwest once provided a safe retreat for flora and fauna, but today new roads, logging, and human settlement pose an increasing threat to the area's natural beauty.

The three-striped box turtle is a critically endangered species, indigenous to the waterways of Central and Northern Vietnam.

The white-breasted kingfisher is twice the size of the common kingfisher and makes its presence known by its loud sharp call. It has a large red beak, and its striking blue wings and tail are set in contrast against a white throat.

The rhododendron campanulata, a wild plant, flourishes on the stony slopes of the highest and remote reaches of the Truong Son Range. The flowers are beautiful but poisonous.

The Asiatic black bear is a nocturnal omnivore, distinguished by its coat of smooth black fur and the v-shaped patch of white fur on its chest. It is now rarely sighted in Vietnam.

The coconut palm is ubiquitous in Vietnam. It provides many products, including food from its nutritious fruit, wood for boat building, palm fronds for thatch, and coir for mats and handicrafts.

The stump-tail macaque is a sturdily built primate found in Northern Vietnam. It weighs up to 22 lb (10 kg) and can live for more than 30 years.

Peoples of Vietnam

Vietnam is home to a diverse mix of more than 54 officially recognized ethnic groups. Of these, the Kinh or ethnic Viet of southern Chinese origin, make up around 86 percent of the population. Settled along the coast and in the Red River and Mekong Deltas, they share the plains with the Hoa or ethnic Chinese, as well as the Khmer and Cham. A further 50 ethnic groups live scattered across the Northern and Central Highlands, all with their own distinctive customs, clothing, and languages. While the northern groups, such as Thai and Hmong, have mostly migrated from China, those of the Central Highlands are mainly indigenous.

Viet Kinh bride and groom in silk *ao dais*, the traditional Viet costume

The Khmer are of Cambodian origin and still follow many of their customs and traditions. One of these is the Prathom Sva Pol or the Monkey Dance, which is performed during the Oc Om Boc Festival *(see p37)* when dancers in masks portray the spirit of monkeys.

The Bahnar people of the Central Highlands center their cultural activities around *nha rong* or communal houses. With distinctive upward tapering roofs, these buildings are inaugurated with gong music, dancing, and jars of rice wine.

Baby carriers are used by mothers, almost from the time they give birth, to take their infants everywhere.

Distribution of Ethnic Groups

Key

1 Khmer
2 Cham Balamon
3 Cham Bani
4 K'ho/ Lat
5 Ede/ Rhade
6 Jarai
7 Bahnar
8 Mnong
9 Bru
10 Muong
11 Black Thai
12 Flower Hmong
13 Red Dao

Viet Kinh make up around 86 per-cent of the country's population

Cham Muslims or Cham Bani follow an indigenous form of Shiite Islam. Friday prayers are chanted by a group of about 50 priests, who dress in white sarongs and cover their shaved heads with a ceremonial turban.

The Bru live in the Central Highlands and belong to the Mon-Khmer group. They rely on wet-rice farming and enjoy lively folk music for entertainment. A common habit among the Bru is smoking tobacco and adults, as well as children, can be seen with a pipe in their mouth.

Mnong tribesmen, once acclaimed elephant catchers and trainers, have long enjoyed communal smoking of tobacco through water pipes. Today, both men and women of this matrilineal society are known for their skills at basket weaving, textile printing, and jewelry making.

The distinctive headgear of Black Thai women consists of a black turban embellished with bright embroidery.

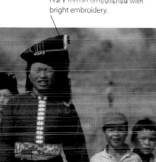

Thai Community

The second largest ethnic minority in Vietnam, the Thai are divided into Black, White, and Red subgroups based on the color of their clothing, as well as on the basis of their early settlements around the Black and Red Rivers respectively. The Black Thai are the most industrious and prosperous of all the subgroups, farming rich rice paddies in the uplands of the northwest. Although a high value is set on education, they are faithful to their cultural heritage. They continue to perform spirit worship, and have kept their ancient folk songs and dances alive and unchanged through the centuries.

Flower Hmong women are among the most distinctive of all minority groups. They dress elaborately with layers of colored cloth, and devote much of their time to the exquisite embroidery for which they are famous (see pp202–3).

The costume favored by Thai women consists of a narrow tube skirt accompanied by a sash and a tight blouse with silver buttons down the front.

The Muong are justly celebrated for their weaving skills. They usually place their bamboo loom in the shady space under their thatched stilt houses.

The Red Dao subdivision of Northern Vietnam's Dao minority group derives its name from the brilliant red turbans worn by the women, who beautify themselves by shaving off their hair and eyebrows. Arguably the most enterprising of the highland peoples, the Dao make a living farming, weaving, and paper making. They also have a rich literary heritage, which is written in a variation of the Chinese script.

Religions of Vietnam

The three most prominent strands in Vietnam's religious tradition are Buddhism, Taoism, and Confucianism, known collectively as Tam Giao, Three Teachings, or Triple Religion. Added to this are the indigenous customs of spirit worship, ancestor veneration, and the deification of Vietnam's patriotic heroes – all practiced widely. Cao Dai is a recent syncretic religion based in the south. Vietnam also has a large population of Christians, and a smaller section of Hindu and Muslim Cham.

Confucius, the Buddha, and Laozi – three great religious teachers

Tam Giao

In Vietnam, Mahayana Buddhism has become closely linked with Confucianism, an ethical system originating in China, and Taoism, also from China. The three Sinitic teachings are known as Tam Giao. Vietnamese follow both Mahayana and Theravada Buddhism.

Boddhisattvas idolized by Mahayana Buddhists include Dai The Chi Bo Tat, God of Power; Thich Ca, the Historical Buddha; and Quan Am, Goddess of Mercy.

Theravada Buddhism claims to rely more strictly on the tenets of the Buddha, and was brought to Vietnam by traders from India. The monks wear saffron robes and chant scriptures from the Tripitika, which is a part of the Buddhist canon.

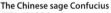

The Chinese sage Confucius *(551–479 BC)* has been revered for centuries. His teachings outline a code of ethics that includes loyalty to the state and the family. Confucian ideas have led to complex hierarchies in Vietnamese families, extending respect, cooperation, and submission to even the most distant cousins.

Incense burning, originally a Buddhist practice, is an integral part of religious life in the Tam Giao pantheon, ancestor worship, Cao Dai temples, and even in Catholic churches.

Groups of family tombs can be seen in paddy fields everywhere. Viet religion is family-oriented and this proximity to ancestors is at once comforting and reassuring of continuity. This custom evolved from Confucianism.

Laozi, a Chinese philosopher of 6th century BC, identified Tao or The Way as the natural source of everything in the world and the guarantor of stability. Taoism focuses on following The Way to live in harmony with the universe.

Cao Daism

*Founded by Ngo Van Chieu, a Vietnamese civil servant,
Cao Dai or Supreme Spirit reinterprets aspects of Tam Giao.
A cornerstone of this unusual religion is a belief in "Divine
Agents" who make contact with priests during seances. Patron
saints include Joan of Arc, Louis Pasteur, and Charlie Chaplin.
Initially condemned by the Communists, Cao Dai is now
tolerated and has about three million followers.*

Cao Dai priests wear yellow, blue, and red
robes to symbolize Buddhism, Taoism,
and Confucianism, and don tall, square
miters bearing the Divine Eye symbol.

Cao Dai services at the Holy See
(*see pp78–9*) are remarkably colorful,
as the elaborate costumes of the
worshippers blend and mingle
with dragon-entwined pillars.

The all-seeing Divine Eye first appeared to
Ngo Van Chieu in a vision and is the iconic symbol of Cao Daism. Framed in a triangle, its image
features prominently in all Cao Dai temples.

Ancestor Veneration and Spirit Worship

*Practiced almost universally in Vietnam, ancestor and spirit worship
effectively make up a fourth, unacknowledged strand to Tam
Giao. While ancestor veneration is derived from Chinese culture,
spirit worship is an indigenous Southeast Asian tradition. Buddhism
and Confucianism officially disapprove of spirit worship, but have
never been able to eliminate it from Viet tradition.*

Ancestral tablets, based on
the Confucian tradition of
filial devotion, are found in
most homes as well as in
temple altars. The memorial
tablets are complete with
pictures and descriptions of
the deceased, set alongside
offerings of fruit, flowers,
incense, tea, and even
cigarettes and alcohol.

Ghost money, often in the form
of fake US dollars, is sent to
ancestors in the spirit world by
burning it along with other
useful items made of paper, such
as cars, TV sets, and houses.

Animism is based on
the belief that guardian
spirits exist in stones,
fields, forests, and many
other inanimate items.
The Vietnamese, partic
ularly the hill tribes,
make small houses in
order to appease these
entities, and often leave
offerings at shrines.

Other Religions

Vietnam's ethnic diversity is matched by
an equally eclectic range of religions and
belief systems. Chiefly through the efforts
of European missionaries from the 16th
century on, the country is home to about
nine million Christians, of which more
than 90 percent are Catholics. A more
obscure religion is Hoa Hao, which is
centered in the Mekong Delta. The sect is
based on a puritanical interpretation of
Buddhism, and was known for its militant
opposition to communism during the
Vietnam War. In addition, variations of
Hinduism and Islam are followed by the
Cham of the central coast and Mekong
Delta respectively.

Cathedrals and churches,
found all over Vietnam,
cater to the interests of the
Christian community.

Traditional Music and Theater

Vietnam has a long and rich heritage of music and theater, combining both indigenous and foreign influences. Its repertoire of musical traditions plays an intrinsic role in the country's many theater forms, and includes folk songs, classical music, imperial compositions, and the unique courtship melodies of various ethnic minorities. This multifaceted legacy is deeply rooted in Vietnamese culture and forms an integral part of all celebrations and festivals.

Musician playing the *dan bau*, a single-stringed instrument

Music in Vietnam

Vietnamese traditional music comprises several genres, including court, religious, ceremonial, chamber, folk, and theater music. Foreign influences have left their mark, with the adoption of operatic traditions from China as well as Indian rhythms through contact with the Cham Empire – all modified to create a distinctive Vietnamese style of music. Another aspect is the use of a five-tone scale in contrast to the eight-tone scale usually used in Western music.

Hat Chau Van uses rhythmic singing and dancing to induce a state of trance in a person who is believed to be estranged from the spirits. This art form originated in the 16th century as an incantation during religious rituals.

Quan Ho are singing contests that originated in the 13th century and are an important part of spring festivals. This popular folk art features groups of young men and women who take turns to sing, alternately challenging and responding to each other in a traditional courtship ritual.

Dan day, a rectangular, long-necked lute, with three strings.

Trong de, a drum played with a hardwood drumstick.

Phach, a wooden instrument that resembles castanets.

Ca Tru (Hat A Dao) or singing for reward is a form of chamber music. In this form of entertainment, women sing and play a *phach* for well-off men. This 15th-century art form suffered a fall in popularity during the communist era. In 2009, it was included in UNESCO's list of Intangible Cultural Heritage in Need of Urgent Safeguarding.

Nhac Tai Tu is a form of chamber music that accompanies *cai luong* theater. Instruments in the picture above are the *dan tranh* (left), a sixteen-stringed zither, the *dan nguyet* (center), and the flute (right).

Musical Instruments

The Vietnamese have a diverse range of indigenous musical instruments made from natural materials such as wood, animal horn, bamboo, stone, and reed. Among the most commonly used are the *dan bau*, in which a single string is stretched over a sound box and plucked by a wooden pick; the *dan nguyet* or moon-shaped lute, used in Vietnam since the 11th century; *dan trung*, a bamboo xylophone; *broh*, a two-stringed bamboo lute; *dan ty ba*, a pear-shaped guitar; and many types of gong (*cong chien*) and drum (*trong*).

Dan trung

Cong chien

Trong

Broh

Theater Styles

Vietnam has a remarkable tradition of performing-arts genres, with music, singing, and dance as an essential aspect of all theater forms. The presentations vary in style and intended audience – cheo is a popular style of theater that traditionally provided moral instruction for rural communities, while roi nuoc (water puppetry) delivers spectacular entertainment at the end of the harvest season. Tuong or hat boi, a more classical form of theater, was developed as entertainment for the king and his court, and cai luong, a modernized form of tuong, was created for urban intellectuals.

Roi nuoc is a unique art that uses water as a stage *(see p163)*. Colorful puppets, guided by hidden puppeteers, enact tales from folklore, mythology, history, and everyday life, accompanied by a musical ensemble, drum rolls, and exploding firecrackers.

Tuong (Hat Boi), Influenced by Chinese opera, uses stylized gestures and symbolism to represent emotion and character. It celebrates Confucian virtues of courage, virtue, and filial piety, and explores themes of loyalty to the king and good overcoming evil.

Elaborate tuong make-up, costumes, and stage settings rely on traditional theatrical conventions. For example, make-up helps to define a character. Hence, a face painted red symbolizes loyalty and bravery, while a white face stands for cruelty and villainy.

Cai Luong (Reformed Theater) emerged in south Vietnam In the early 20th century, and incorporates elements of French theater in the form of spoken scenes. Less stylized than traditional theater, *cai luong* tackles social issues such as corruption, alcoholism, and gambling.

Performers in costumes of the court, Hue

Royal Music and Dance

Entertainment for Vietnam's royal audiences found its main inspiration from the music of the Chinese Imperial Court. *Nha nhac* or court music was introduced in the 13th century and reached its pinnacle under the Nguyen Dynasty *(see p45)*. Performances of this elegant music, accompanied by dances, were held at royal ceremonies, such as coronations and funerals, as well as on religious events and special occasions. With the fall of the monarchy in Vietnam, nha nhac was forgotten, but has been revived in recent years. In 1996, it was added to the syllabus of Hue College of Art, and in 2003, it was recognised as a Masterpiece of Oral and Intangible Heritage by UNESCO.

Cheo (Popular Theater) originated among the rice farmers of the Red River Delta. Performances are usually held outside the village communal house and combine singing, dancing, poetry, and improvization.

Traditional dancers

Architecture

Vietnam's long history of foreign invasions has left a legacy in the form of diverse architectural styles found throughout the country. Indigenous architecture in the shape of "tube houses" and single-story pagodas exist alongside buildings that reveal foreign influences. The ancient buildings of the central coast indicate the Cham influence, while Chinese elements are reflected in the pagodas, especially in Hanoi and Hue. French influence is pervasive in the colonial buildings.

Diep Dong Nguyen House — ancient tube house in Hoi An

Pagodas

Vietnamese pagodas are generally single-story buildings, resting on wooden pillars that support a complex cantilevered structure of timber beams, surmounted by a tiled roof with upswept eaves. The interior consists of a front hall, a central hall, and the main altar hall, usually arranged in ascending levels. Most pagodas have a sacred pond, a bell tower, and a garden. There is elaborate use of symbolism, especially including several Chinese characters.

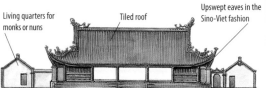

Living quarters for monks or nuns

Tiled roof

Upswept eaves in the Sino-Viet fashion

The Thay Pagoda in Hanoi rests on a stone platform supporting ironwood columns that carry the entire weight of the building. The low, steep-pitched roof features elaborate upswept eaves with dragon finials. Turned wooden grills admit a flow of fresh air.

One Pillar Pagoda in Hanoi was originally built on a single wooden pillar set in a pond, and designed to resemble a lotus flower. Partially burned in 1954, it now rests on a concrete pillar. Fire has long been a hazard for wooden pagodas.

The Tran Quoc Pagoda in Hanoi is an eminent example of a single-story pagoda built around many brick stupas. Considered to be Vietnam's oldest pagoda, it was built by Emperor Ly Nam De in the 6th century AD on the banks of the Red River, but due to heavy erosion, the pagoda was shifted to its present site, Ho Tay *(see p172)*.

Characteristic Chinese-style "flying" eaves

Multi-tiered pagodas are derived from Chinese tradition. They are usually pointed at the top, and the roofs are made of terracotta tiles.

Thanh long or dragon is associated in both Vietnamese and Chinese mythology with imperial power, prosperity, longevity, and good fortune. Dragon motifs are used extensively to decorate both pagodas and temples.

Royal Citadels

Awe-inspiring and imposing, Vietnamese citadels were constructed to provide defense against both physical and spiritual attack. This was achieved by assuming Chinese characteristics of huge, square stone walls topped by battlements, along with elements of feng shui. Military architecture under French influence gave rise to citadels with massive, thick walls, ringed by moats, punctuated by towers, with crenellated ramparts and pentagonal bastions.

Hien Nhon Gate at Hue Citadel is a fine example of Sino-Viet decorative elements combined with French military genius. This Chinese gate has elaborate turrets, as well as two-story platforms to provide vantage points for soldiers.

The Ngo Mon Gate of Hue Citadel, made of thick stone walls and in accordance with the principles of *feng shui*, has five entrances. The central way, used solely by the emperor, is flanked by openings for mandarins of the royal court.

French Architecture

The capital of French Indochina in the 19th century, Hanoi was transformed with the construction of villas in French provincial style, administrative buildings emulating Parisian styles, and even Franco-Gothic structures such as Hanoi Cathedral.

Louvered shutters

Ornate wrought ironwork

Hanoi's State Guest House, once the residence of the French governor, is a beautiful, restored French-Colonial building, with an elaborately upswept wrought-iron entrance.

The Presidential Palace in Hanoi is a perfect example of the French-Colonial style, with a grand staircase, wrought-iron gates, Belle Époque filigree work, and colonnades. Built between 1900 and 1906, it is flanked by extensive gardens and orchards.

Tube Architecture and its Present Adaptation

Interior courtyard for fresh air and to separate work and living areas.

The rear of the house was occupied by the kitchen and bathroom areas.

First built during the Later Le Dynasty (1428–1788), "tube houses" can be as little as 6.5 ft (2 m) wide, but up to 262 ft (80 m) deep. Behind the shopfront are work areas, courtyards, and living rooms. Today, these houses have soared to create tall, thin "rocket buildings," still limited in their ground area by the original land deeds.

Narrow frontage for shop area

Colorful present-day "rocket buildings" lined up in Hanoi

Tet Nguyen Dan

As the country's single most important festival, Tet Nguyen Dan or Festival of the First Day marks the onset of the lunar new year. Celebrated as a time of rebirth and renewal, this spring festival serves as an opportunity for thanksgiving and paying homage to ancestors. Preparations begin a week before Tet, as people clear their debts, clean the family tombs, decorate homes with peach blossoms or kumquat trees, and make offerings to the Jade Emperor *(see pp66–7)*. The three main days of Tet are a purely domestic affair, as families gather for elaborate meals, exchange gifts, and wish each other a happy new year.

Houses are traditionally decorated with kumquat trees during Tet

Ancestor Worship

The Vietnamese veneration of ancestors finds its greatest expression during Tet, when the spirits of deceased family members are believed to visit the living. The ancestors are invoked with prayers, special foods, and symbolic gifts made of paper, such as false money, clothes, and even watches.

Dazzling colorful displays of flowers brighten streets and markets all over Vietnam around Tet. Peach blossom sprigs, symbolizing prosperity and well-being, are popular for decorating houses, shops, and temples.

Offerings of food and drink

Portrait of the deceased

Names of the deceased

Incense sticks

Family chapels or altars are an integral part of almost every household in the country. They display pictures of ancestors along with tablets listing their names, incense, flowers, and offerings of fruit, rice, and alcohol.

Incense sticks play a key role in Tet rites. The scented smoke is said to waft up to the heavens, attracting ancestors to the celebrations on earth. Sticks of all sizes are crafted in small villages and left to dry in the sun before being taken into towns for sale.

Tombs of ancestors dotting cultivated fields are common in Vietnam. During Tet, relatives clean the tombs of their ancestors and make many offerings to ensure that the spirits of the deceased are at peace.

Special Tet Food

Tet is a time of indulgence, and festivities are not complete without an array of delicacies. Families may save all year for the necessary luxuries, but the resulting feast is considered well worth it. Pork, duck, and chicken are on the menu, along with rich soups and mounds of sticky rice. Succulent tropical fruits follow meals, especially dragon fruit and watermelon whose pulp is an auspicious red.

Traditional Tet confectionery consists of candied fruits, coconuts, soursop juice, lotus seeds, or ginger and puffed-rice treats. The markets overflow with bins of sweets the week before Tet.

Banh chung and banh tet are savory treats most closely associated with Tet. They consist of glutinous rice, mung bean paste, and fatty pork, boiled together in small parcels of banana leaves tied with strips of bamboo.

Banh tet ingredients ready for wrapping

Tet Festivities

Lavish, exuberant, and time-honored Tet activities, frowned upon during the years of communist austerity, have made a major comeback in recent years. Entire communities participate in the traditional music, singing, and dancing, as well as fairs, processions, and games played through the centuries. Young people take advantage of this opportunity to meet and flirt.

Human chess, played only during Tet, is a unique game where local people take the place of pawns. Participants should be young, attractive, and have had no recent instances of bad luck in their lives.

Bit mat dap nieu or breaking the pots is a traditional game in which revelers, donning flashy Tet masks as blindfolds, try to break clay pots with wooden clubs.

Vibrant firecracker procession

Tet Firecrackers

Once an essential part of Tet festivities, firecrackers have been banned in Vietnam since 1994 on grounds of public safety, and replica firecrackers are paraded instead. According to lore, loud noises scare off evil spirits, but for the time being, even playing recordings of bursting crackers is forbidden by law.

The dragon dance is an age-old tradition originating in China. To welcome the coming year, costumed young men prance vigorously through the streets, accompanied by wild drumming. The dragon symbolizes good luck, and the dance is said to drive away demons.

VIETNAM THROUGH THE YEAR

Most traditional festivals in Vietnam have close links with Chinese cultural traditions, and follow the lunar calendar, which has only 29.5 days a month. Accordingly, the solar dates change annually, and festivals do not fall on fixed dates. Secular holidays, by contrast, are fixed to the Western calendar, and often associated with the country's recent revolutionary history. Over the past two decades, with the liberalization of the Vietnamese economy and society,

many traditional festivals have also staged a grand comeback, including those related to the imperial dynasties of Vietnam. These are marked by ancestor worship ceremonies, colorful parades, feasts, singing, and dancing. In addition to nationwide events, there are many local festivals as well, especially in the Red River Delta. The ethnic minorities of the north, and the Cham and Khmer of the south celebrate their own festivals.

Spring (Feb–Apr)

A time of renewal and rebirth, spring is the most festive season in Vietnam. Ushered in with the lunar new year, Tet (see pp32–3), it marks a long period of merrymaking all across the country.

1st Lunar Month

Tet Nguyen Dan *(late Jan–Feb)*. Commonly known as Tet, this is the most important festival in the Vietnamese calendar. Homes and streets are decorated with lights and colorful flowers, stalls selling traditional foods are set up, and families exchange gifts and gather for feasts. Officially a three-day holiday, businesses often shut for a week.
Founding of the Vietnamese Communist Party *(Feb 3)*. Commemorates the day on which Ho Chi Minh established the party in 1930.

Tay Son Festival *(early Feb)*, Tay Son District, Binh Dinh Province. Marking the 18th-century Tay Son Rebellion, this week-long revelry features elephant parades, a drumming competition, and martial arts performances.
Yen Tu Festival *(mid Feb–end Apr)*, Yen Tu Mountain *(see p189)*. Honors the founding of the Truc Lam Buddhist sect. Pilgrims climb to the summit to burn incense and meditate at the pagodas here.
Lim Festival *(mid-Feb)*, Lim Village, Bac Ninh Province. Celebrated 14 days after Tet, this festival is best known for its *quan ho* folk songs. Clad in ethnic garb, both men and women sing improvised lyrics to each other, often in the form of witty repartee. Also features wrestling matches and weaving competitions.
Perfume Pagoda Festival *(Feb–May)*, Perfume Pagoda *(see pp196–7)*. The scenic

Traditionally dressed women singing at Lim Festival

surrounds are said to be the Buddha's heaven. Thousands of pilgrims visit the pagoda to celebrate this three-month-long religious festival.

2nd Lunar Month

Hai Ba Trung Festival *(early Mar)*, Hai Ba Trung Temple *(see p167)*, Hanoi. Honors the heroic Trung Sisters. A procession takes their statues from the temple to the Red River for a ceremonial bath.
Ba Chua Kho Temple Festival *(Mar)*, Ba Chua Kho Temple, Co Me, Bac Ninh Province. Worshippers congregate at the temple to petition Lady Chua Kho for good fortune and borrow money from her in a symbolic ritual.

3rd Lunar Month

Thay Pagoda Festival *(Apr 5–7)*, Thay Pagoda *(see p177)*, Ha Tay Province. People gather to worship the patron saint of water puppets, Tu Dao Hanh, who is said to have become a Buddhist at Thay Pagoda. Celebrated over two days, several water puppet shows are staged to mark the occasion.

Street market festooned with brightly colored flowers during Tet

Platters of food offerings to Lady Chua Kho. Ba Chua Kho Temple Festival

Hon Chen Festival (early Apr), Hon Chen Temple (see p152), Hue. Based on an old Cham festival, this biannual event, held in the 3rd and 7th lunar months, pays tribute to the Goddess Thien Y A Na. This event features a procession of boats on the Perfume River, as well as the staging of traditional tableau.

Thanh Minh (early Apr). Dedicated to departed souls, this festival is observed all across Vietnam. Offerings are made to the spirits of the deceased, and ancestral graves are repaired and cleaned properly.

Hung Kings' Temple Festival (Apr), Hung Kings' Temples (see p177), Phu Tho Province. This three-day festival honors the Hung Kings and the celebrations include gaily colored parades that take place around the temples. Various cultural events such as classical opera at Den Ha and xoan song performances are held at Den Thuong.

Liberation Day (Apr 30). Honors the fall of Saigon to communist forces on April 30, 1975.

Summer (May–July)

With the summer solstice celebrated in early June, this primarily hot and wet season is when the country observes some of its most important national holidays.

4th Lunar Month

Labor Day (May 1). Legions of workers parade through cities to mark their solidarity with working people throughout the world.

Ho Chi Minh's Birthday (May 19). Supposedly a secular public holiday, this day has become something of a quasi-spiritual event as Ho Chi Minh achieves the status of a deified hero in Vietnam.

The Buddha's Birthday (May 28). Also known as Le Phat Dan. Lanterns are hung outside temples and homes to celebrate the Buddha's birth, enlightenment, and death.

Tra Co Village Festival (May 30–Jun 7), Hai Ninh District, Quang Ninh Province. Held in far northeast Vietnam, this rural festival highlights events such as pig-breeding and cooking contests, traditional games, and dancing.

Cleaning and decorating a small grave for Thanh Minh

Vietnamese Astrology

The Vietnamese zodiac runs on a 12-year cycle, each represented by a specific animal. Instead of centuries, the Viet lunar calendar is divided into 60-year cycles known as hoi. Each of these consists of five 12 year animal cycles.

Goat (Mui) 2015, associated with creativity and good taste.

Monkey (Than) 2016, versatile and mischievous. Associated with inventors, entertainers, and anything ingenious.

Rooster (Dau) 2017, brave and resilient, but can also be self-absorbed and pretentious.

Dog (Tuat) 2018, is considered lucky, loyal, and likeable.

Pig (Hoi) 2019, is honest, patient, and also associated with virility.

Cat (Meo) 2020, known for being tranquil, realistic, intelligent, and artistic.

Rat (Ty) 2021, welcomed as a bringer of good luck.

Buffalo (Suu) 2022, associated with riches achieved through hard work.

Tiger (Dan) 2023, warm-hearted yet fearsome, and brave in the face of danger.

Dragon (Thin) 2024, imperial symbol, associated with the male element yang.

Snake (Ty) 2025, enigmatic, wise, and likes to live well.

Horse (Ngo) 2026, signifies freedom and confidence.

The dragon, a symbol of royalty, adorns many palaces and tombs

Colorful procession celebrating National Day or Quoc Khanh in Hanoi

5th Lunar Month

Tet Doan Ngo (early Jun). Also known as the "Killing the Inner Insect Festival," Tet Doan Ngo signals the summer solstice. This Taoist festival falls at the hottest time of the year, when fevers caused by insects are at their peak. To ensure good health and wellbeing, offerings are made to the God of Death.

Chem Temple Festival (mid-Jun), Thuy Phuong Village, Tu Liem District, Hanoi. Held in honor of Ly Ong Trong, a great 3rd-century warrior, this festival features elaborate ceremonies such as a dragon-boat race, the releasing of pigeons, and a ritualized washing of the temple's statues.

6th Lunar Month

Dad Xa Village Festival (Jul 9–10), Tam Thanh District, Phu Tho Province. Hosted to honor General Ly Thuong Kiet's victory over the Chinese in AD 1075. The festivities include boat racing on the Song Da or Black River.

Tam Tong Festival (Jul), Vinh Loc District, Thanh Hoa Province. With no fixed date, Tam Tong takes place at times of drought.

Autumn (Aug–Oct)

While the south remains hot and wet, the north becomes cooler and pleasant. As the leaves change color, autumn is a good time to follow the festivals in the north.

7th Lunar Month

Hon Chen Festival (early Aug), Hon Chen Temple (see p152).

Trung Nguyen (mid-Aug). The most important festival after Tet, the Taoist Trung Nguyen also has a Buddhist equivalent, Vu Lan, which takes place during the same time. It is believed that lost spirits leave hell on this day to wander the earth. Paper money is burnt to placate these tortured souls.

Le Van Duyet Temple Festival (late Aug–early Sep), Le Van Duyet Temple (see p68), Ho Chi Minh City. The festival takes place on the anniversary of the death of Le Van Duyet. People flock to his mausoleum to pray for a good harvest, safety, and happiness. Traditional opera and dance recitals are staged.

8th Lunar Month

National Day (Sep 2). Marks Ho Chi Minh's 1945 proclamation of the Declaration of Independence. In Hanoi, the day is celebrated with lively parades in Ba Dinh Square.

Do Son Buffalo Fighting Festival (early Sep), Do Son, Haiphong Province. A procession of six specially trained buffalos are ceremoniously led into the arena, and paired off to fight each other. A winner is declared when one of the buffalos runs away. It is a short respite, as at the end of the day, the animals are slaughtered and eaten.

Trung Thu or mid-Autumn Festival (mid-Sep). Also known as the Children's Moon Festival, Trung Thu is a colorful affair, with much revelry and excitement all around. Children are given new toys and festive masks, and are treated to freshly baked moon cakes. Lantern processions, games, and martial arts demonstrations are all part of the festivities.

Decorated sweet moon cakes for the Trung Thu Festival

Whale Festival (Sep). The worship of whales is an ancient practice likely rooted in the Khmer and Cham cultures. Large processions gather at the temples to make offerings. In Phan Thiet (see p110), the festival also includes

Locked horns at the Do Son Buffalo Fighting Festival, Haiphong

Cham dancers and musicians celebrating the Kate Festival

the Chinese community, with elaborate parades throughout the city.

Kate Festival (Sep–Oct), Po Klong Garai Towers, Phan Rang–Thap Cham (see p111). This lengthy festival follows the Cham calendar, and is the most important celebration for the Cham minority. Droves of devotees in colorful processions, along with traditional musicians, make their way up to the towers to pay homage to the Cham deities, rulers, and revered national heroes.

9th Lunar Month

Keo Pagoda Festival (mid-Oct), Vu Nhat Village, Thai Binh Province. The anniversary of the death of Buddhist monk Duong Khong Lo is remembered over three days. Events include a lavish procession and religious rituals, as well as cooking and duck-catching competitions, and a trumpet and drum contest.

Confucius' Birthday (late Oct/ early Nov). Confucianism, as a system of state administration, may have disappeared under the communist regime, but Confucius is still venerated. The date has been declared Teacher's Day, and the sage is offered incense and prayers in many temples.

Winter (Nov–Jan)

By now it is cold and rainy in the north, the traditional Viet homeland where most festivals originated, so there are fewer celebrations during this season.

10th Lunar Month

Oc Om Boc Festival and Ngo Boat Races (mid-Nov), Soc Trang (see p100). This Khmer festival is dedicated to the moon. Villagers deposit trays of rice, bananas, and coconuts in temples in the hope of abundant crops and plentiful fish. The main event has a series of ngo or canoe races, with competitors from Vietnam and Cambodia. Each boat is carved from a single tree.

Nguyen Trung Truc Temple Festival (late Nov), Long Kien Village, Cho Moi District, An Giang Province. This temple is dedicated to the deified national hero, Nguyen Trung Truc (1837–68), renowned for leading the anti-French movement in southern Vietnam. Boat racing competitions and chess matches are enjoyable components of the revelries, along with the re-enactment of the sinking of the French ship, Esperance, at the hands of Nguyen Trung Truc and his partisans.

Festive array of incense sticks, candles, and spirit money

11th Lunar Month

Dalat Flower Festival (Dec), Dalat (see pp118–20). Held by the shores of Xuan Huong Lake, this festival showcases the many beautiful species of flowers that thrive in the cool uplands around Dalat. Along with the array of flowers, there is music and dancing, as well as displays of colored lanterns.

Trung Do Festival (late Dec). This festival honors the Viet patriot Ly Bon who led a successful revolt against the Chinese in AD 542, later proclaiming himself as the Emperor Li Nam De. Traditional ball games known as phet are played during the boisterous celebrations.

Christmas (Dec 25). Although predominantly a Buddhist country, Vietnam has a large Christian community as well. As such, Christmas is celebrated with enthusiasm, especially in the big cities where streets and stores are decorated with lights, fake snow, shiny baubles, and ornaments.

12th Lunar Month

New Year's Day (Jan 1). No special events are associated with this recent addition from the Western calendar, but this day is officially recognized as a public holiday, and its status is gaining recognition. Still, it is nowhere close to attaining Tet's status.

Public and other Holidays

New Year's Day Jan 1

Tet Nguyen Dan Feb 19–21 (2015)

Founding Day of the Communist Party of Vietnam Feb 3

Hung Kings Day Apr 28 (2015)

Liberation Day Apr 30

Labor Day May 1

Ho Chi Minh's Birthday May 19

National Day Sep 2

The Climate of Vietnam

Though Vietnam has a tropical climate, there is considerable diversity from north to south and from coast to highlands. In general, the seasonal monsoons bring heavy rains between May and October, while it remains relatively dry from November to February. The hot season between February and April can be uncomfortable, with temperatures reaching up to 35°C (95°F), and humidity rising to a sticky 80 to 100 per cent.

Regionally, the south is consistently warm and humid, with frequent downpours during the rainy season. The central coast suffers typhoons between July and November, but winters are often rainy and cool. The north experiences cold and wet winters between November and March, with occasional snowfall on Mount Fansipan. Summers in the north are warm and humid.

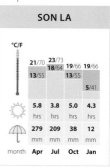

KEY

- Hot wet summer, cold dry winter with occasional frost
- Mild wet summer, cold rainy winter, with snow on higher belts
- Cool rainy summer, chilly dry winter with some rain
- Warm wet summer, cool winter with occasional rain
- Hot dry summer, cool rainy winter
- Moderate dry climate all year, with a brief winter monsoon
- Warm summer with heavy rainfall, cool dry winter
- Hot wet summer, warm dry winter with some rain
- Hot summer with heavy rainfall, warm wet winter

0 kilometers 200
0 miles 200

LAO CAI

°C/F	Apr	Jul	Oct	Jan
	30/86	33/91	28/82	
	23/73	25/77	20/68	21/70
				13/55
hrs	5.2	4	4.5	4.7
mm	52	38	81	20
month	Apr	Jul	Oct	Jan

SON LA

°C/F	Apr	Jul	Oct	Jan
	21/70	23/73	19/66	19/66
	13/55	18/64	13/55	
				5/41
hrs	5.8	3.8	5.0	4.3
mm	279	209	38	12
month	Apr	Jul	Oct	Jan

CHAU DOC

°C/F	Apr	Jul	Oct	Jan
	35/95	32/90	30/86	31/88
	24/75	23/73	24/75	21/70
hrs	5	4	7	8
mm	70	190	230	10
month	Apr	Jul	Oct	Jan

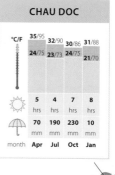

Cai Rang Floating Market in the early morning, Can Tho

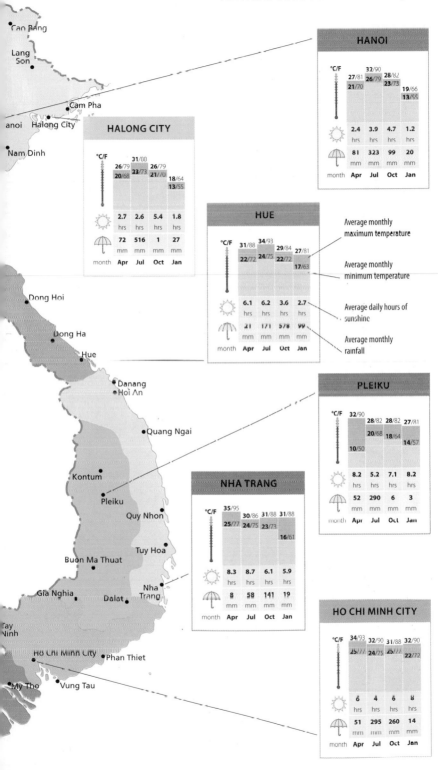

HANOI

°C/F				
	27/81 21/70	32/90 26/79	28/82 23/73	19/66 13/55
☀	2.4 hrs	3.9 hrs	4.7 hrs	1.2 hrs
☂	81 mm	323 mm	99 mm	20 mm
month	Apr	Jul	Oct	Jan

HALONG CITY

°C/F				
	26/79 20/68	31/88 23/73	26/79 21/70	18/64 13/55
☀	2.7 hrs	2.6 hrs	5.4 hrs	1.8 hrs
☂	72 mm	516 mm	1 mm	27 mm
month	Apr	Jul	Oct	Jan

HUE

°C/F				
	31/88 22/72	34/93 24/75	29/84 22/72	27/81 17/63
☀	6.1 hrs	6.2 hrs	3.6 hrs	2.7 hrs
☂	21 mm	171 mm	578 mm	99 mm
month	Apr	Jul	Oct	Jan

Average monthly maximum temperature

Average monthly minimum temperature

Average daily hours of sunshine

Average monthly rainfall

PLEIKU

°C/F				
	32/90 10/50	28/82 20/68	28/82 18/64	27/81 14/57
☀	8.2 hrs	5.2 hrs	7.1 hrs	8.2 hrs
☂	52 mm	290 mm	6 mm	3 mm
month	Apr	Jul	Oct	Jan

NHA TRANG

°C/F				
	35/95 25/77	30/86 24/75	31/88 23/73	31/88 16/61
☀	8.3 hrs	8.7 hrs	6.1 hrs	5.9 hrs
☂	8 mm	58 mm	141 mm	19 mm
month	Apr	Jul	Oct	Jan

HO CHI MINH CITY

°C/F				
	34/93 25/77	32/90 24/75	31/88 25/77	32/90 22/72
☀	6 hrs	4 hrs	6 hrs	8 hrs
☂	51 mm	295 mm	260 mm	14 mm
month	Apr	Jul	Oct	Jan

THE HISTORY OF VIETNAM

The early history of Vietnam is obscured in the mists of time and legend, but tracing its journey through the centuries of recorded history tells the story of a nation constantly besieged by foreign invasions and civil wars. This historical narrative – from the reassertion of independence in AD 979, after 1,000 years of Chinese occupation, to Reunification in 1975 – also reveals the unflinching Viet determination for autonomy and freedom.

It is believed that more than 5,000 years ago, the Viet people learned to cultivate rice, and settled in the fertile lands around present-day Guangxi and Guangdong in China. Their neighbors to the north, the Han Chinese, forced them to flee southwards, where the Viet leader proclaimed himself Viem De, the "Red Emperor of the South," and established a kingdom called Xich Qui in the Red River Delta. This period represents the earliest mythical Viet state as well as the first recorded separation from China.

Legend has it that King De Minh of Xich Qui married a mythical mountain fairy, and their son, Kinh Duong, married the daughter of the Dragon Lord of the Sea. This union gave birth to Lac Long Quan, considered to be the first Vietnamese king. To maintain peace with the Chinese, he married Princess Au Co, a beautiful Chinese immortal, who bore him 100 sons. Lac Long Quan then sent his wife with 50 of their sons to the mountains and remained by the sea with the other 50. Thus, the Viet race came into being, with half of them living in the highlands, and the other half in the Red River Delta. Lac Long Quan raised his eldest son to be king of the Kinh or Viets, and gave him the regal name Hung Vuong. He became the first of a line of legendary Hung Kings, whose dynasty, Van Lang, was based at Phu Tho on the left bank of the Red River, about 50 miles (80 km) northwest of present-day Hanoi. It is widely believed that the ancient bronze drums, excavated in Northern Vietnam and southern China, and attributed to the Dong Son civilization, were associated with this important dynasty.

The Era of Hung Kings

According to folklore, the 18 Hung kings' combined rule lasted for 150 years. By the 3rd century BC, Van Lang was in decline. In 258 BC, Thuc Phan, ruler of Au Viet, a rival kingdom to the north, overthrew the Hung and founded a new state called Au Lac, with its capital at Co Loa near Hanoi. Scholars regard this as the first Viet state, which flourished under Thuc Phan, who ruled as An Duong Vuong.

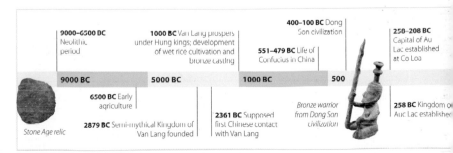

| 9000–6500 BC Neolithic period | 1000 BC Van Lang prospers under Hung kings; development of wet rice cultivation and bronze casting | | 400–100 BC Dong Son civilization | 258–208 BC Capital of Au Lac established at Co Loa |
| | | | 551–479 BC Life of Confucius in China | |

| 9000 BC | 5000 BC | 1000 BC | 500 | |

| | 6500 BC Early agriculture | | | Bronze warrior from Dong Son civilization | 258 BC Kingdom of Au Lac established |
| Stone Age relic | 2879 BC Semi-mythical Kingdom of Van Lang founded | 2361 BC Supposed first Chinese contact with Van Lang | | |

◄ The French use anchored balloons for reconnaissance purposes at the capture of Hong Hoa in Indochina, 1884

The Chinese Connection

Through the ages, Vietnam's development has been marked by its proximity to China. In 207 BC, a renegade Chinese general, Trieu Da, conquered Au Lac and unified it with his own territories in southern China. Nam Viet, the kingdom he founded, had its capital at Fanyu in what is today Guangdong province in China. Trieu Da's rule marked the beginning of almost 1,000 years of Chinese occupation that made Vietnam a unique outpost of Chinese civilization in Southeast Asia.

Nam Viet was probably as much Viet as it was Chinese. Although the ruling Western Han Dynasty (206 BC–AD 9) regarded the area south of the Yangtze River as on the fringes of Han civilization, Chinese ways and cultural values were increasingly imposed on Nam Viet. The kingdom became a tributary state of the Western Han in 111 BC when Trieu Da's successors acknowledged the suzerainty of Emperor Wudi (r.141–87 BC). With the establishment of Han authority, the Viet territories became the Chinese province of Giao Chi.

Statue of a Han warrior

During the first centuries of Chinese rule, many attempts were made to Sinicize the Viets, but with limited success. While the Viets embraced many facets of Chinese culture, from education to Confucianism, Taoism, and Buddhism, they resolutely refused to become a part of China, and resistance and rebellions continued throughout the long years of Chinese rule.

In AD 40, two Viet noblewomen, the Trung Sisters *(see p167)*, led the first and most famous bid for freedom. They proclaimed themselves queens of an independent kingdom, with their capital at Me Linh. However, just three years later, the Han re-established Chinese control over the region.

Despite repeated revolts, Chinese rule remained secure for the next nine centuries. By AD 679, Vietnam had become an appendage of the Tang Dynasty (AD 618–907) under the name An Nam or Pacified South, with its capital at Tong Binh on the banks of the Red River near present-day Hanoi.

The Creation of Dai Viet

The millennium of foreign occupation ended in AD 938 when one of Vietnam's most celebrated national heroes, Ngo Quyen, ingeniously destroyed a Chinese fleet attempting to sail up the Bach Dang River near Haiphong by planting a barrier of iron-tipped stakes in the bed of the river. Following this triumph, he proclaimed himself King Ngo Vuong of Dai Viet, and transferred his capital from Dai La, the Tong Binh fortress, back to Co Loa, capital of the first free Viet Kingdom, Au Lac.

Painting depicting the Trung Sisters battle against the Chinese

208 BC Capital moved to Fanyu in Guangdong

AD 1 Han overlords impose Chinese culture in Vietnam

40 Trung Sisters Uprising

100s Cham Kingdom established

Cham sculpture

| 200 BC | 100 BC | 0 | 100 AD | 200 | 300 |

111 Nam Viet conquered by Han Emperor Wudi

43 Chinese reconquest

AD 1 Kingdom of Funan is established

300s Cham capital at Singhapura

Funan jewelry

Architectural ruins at My Son (*see pp134–6*), the Cham religious capital between the 4th and 13th centuries

Funan and Champa

Even as the Chinese-influenced Viet culture evolved in the heart of the Red River Delta, the south saw the emergence of two Indic kingdoms – Funan and Champa. A precursor to the great Khmer Empire, Funan is believed to have been established in the Mekong Delta in the 1st century AD. At the height of its power, its influence extended across much of Cambodia and along the east coast of Thailand. It was probably founded by a merchant from India who, legend says, wed the daughter of a naga (serpent) deity and established the dynasty.

Between the 2nd and 6th centuries, Funan's rulers increased their wealth largely through commerce. There is evidence that they traded with China, India, and even the Roman Empire. But by the end of the 6th century, Funan was supplanted by a new Khmer power, the kingdom of Chen La. Located farther inland, it was less subject to Javanese attacks and disastrous floods.

Statue from the Oc Eo era

Today, little of Funan remains beyond the ruins of the port-city of Oc Eo near Rach Gia, and some artifacts in museums at Hanoi, Ho Chi Minh City, and Long Xuyen.

The earliest records of the Kingdom of Champa date from AD 192, when settlements of the Cham, believed to have originated in Java, began to appear along the central coast of Vietnam. At the peak of their power, they controlled the lands stretching from Vinh to the Mekong Delta, and excelled at maritime trade, their main exports being slaves and sandalwood. By about AD 800, Champa found itself increasingly threatened by the newly powerful Khmer kingdom of Angkor and the Viet expansion toward the south. The situation worsened over the centuries, and in 1471, the Cham suffered a terrible defeat at the hands of the Viet. Champa was reduced to a small piece of territory from Nha Trang south to Phan Thiet, which survived until 1720, when the king and many of his subjects fled to Cambodia rather than submit to the Vietnamese.

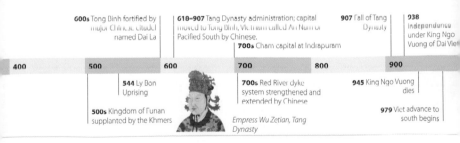

600s Tong Binh fortified by major Chinese citadel named Dai La

618–907 Tang Dynasty administration; capital moved to Tong Binh, Vietnam called An Nam or Pacified South by Chinese.

700s Cham capital at Indrapuram

907 Fall of Tang Dynasty

938 Independence under King Ngo Vuong of Dai Viet

400   500   600   700   800   900

544 Ly Bon Uprising

500s Kingdom of Funan supplanted by the Khmers

700s Red River dyke system strengthened and extended by Chinese

Empress Wu Zetian, Tang Dynasty

945 King Ngo Vuong dies

979 Viet advance to south begins

Temple of Literature, Hanoi, a center of learning

The Consolidation of Dai Viet

In AD 945, Ngo Vuong died, and Viet independence was threatened once again as control was divided between competing fiefdoms. Fortunately, in 968, Dinh Bo Linh, the most powerful lord, reunified the country, calling it Dai Co Viet. He took the name Tien Hoang De and founded the short-lived Dinh Dynasty (968–980). He also re-established a tributary relationship with China to stave off further invasions. Then, in 979, the throne was seized by Le Dai Hanh, who founded the Early Le Dynasty (980–1009) and continued the conquest of Champa.

The Ly Dynasty

Held to be the first completely independent Vietnamese dynasty, the Ly Dynasty (1009–1225) was established by the learned and brave Ly Thai To. In 1010, he moved the capital back to Dai La in Tong Binh, giving it the auspicious name, Thang Long (*see p164*) or Ascending Dragon. Thang Long would remain

Vietnam's capital for the next 800 years. Buddhism became the state religion, while Confucianism was adopted for state administration during Ly Thai To's rule. Under this dynasty, Vietnam began to evolve as a powerful autonomous state, though it remained very much in China's cultural orbit. It followed a system of strong centralized government, with a national tax system, a codified legal structure, and a professional army. At the head stood the king who was absolute monarch and mediator between Heaven and Earth.

The Tran Dynasty

The Tran Dynasty (1225–1400) introduced land reforms and defended Vietnam from Mongol attacks. In 1288, the national hero Tran Hung Dao defeated a major Mongol invasion at the second Battle of the Bach Dang River by using Ngo Quyen's tactics of planting metal stakes in the bed of the river. At the same time, Vietnam continued its southward advance, absorbing Cham territory as far as Hue.

Nguyen Trai, advisor to Tran Hung Dao

The Later Le Dynasty

In 1407, the Ming invaded Vietnam but were ousted in 1428 by the nationalist leader Le Loi during the turbulent Lam Son Uprising. The Chinese were forced to recognize Dai Viet's autonomy after this victory, and Le Loi founded the Later Le Dynasty (1428–1788). His successor, Le Than Ton, inflicted a crushing defeat on Champa in 1471, pushing the frontier south of Qui Nhon. By this time Vietnam had become a major power on the Southeast Asian mainland.

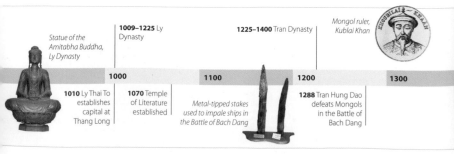

Statue of the
Amitabha Buddha,
Ly Dynasty

1009–1225 Ly Dynasty

1225–1400 Tran Dynasty

Mongol ruler,
Kublai Khan

1000 | **1100** | **1200** | **1300**

1010 Ly Thai To establishes capital at Thang Long

1070 Temple of Literature established

Metal-tipped stakes used to impale ships in the Battle of Bach Dang

1288 Tran Hung Dao defeats Mongols in the Battle of Bach Dang

A Nation Divided

As the Le Dynasty extended its domain, it incurred the wrath of local fiefdoms. In 1527, Mac Dang Dung, an opportunist in the Le court, seized the throne. However, from 1539 onward, real power was divided between two warlord families, the Trinh and the Nguyen. For more than two centuries, the nation would remain divided, with the Nguyen developing their capital at

A shrine to Quang Trung, leader of the Tay Son Rebellion

Hue to rival the Trinh capital at Thang Long. Under the Nguyen, the Viet conquest of lower Cambodia and the Mekong Delta began with the absorption of the Khmer settlement of Prey Nokor, later renamed Saigon.

Early European Influences

In 1515, the Portuguese established the first European factories in Vietnam. At first, they helped the Nguyen lords develop a foundry and weapons, but later, also aided the Trinh so they could benefit from the spice trade. The Dutch, followed by the French, replaced the Portuguese as leading traders in the 17th century. Christian missionaries also made inroads, the most important figure being Alexandre de Rhodes (1591–1660), a French Jesuit who converted thousands of locals to Christianity, leading to his expulsion. However, this led to the beginning of a French interest in the area for its wealth.

Tay Son Rebellion

In response to the years of civil war and harsh government under the Trinh and Nguyen lords, the Tay Son Rebellion broke out in 1771. Supported by merchants and peasants, it was led by three brothers who overthrew the Nguyen in 1783. The last lord, Nguyen Anh, fled abroad and sought French assistance. In 1786, the Tay Son overthrew the Trinh, provoking a Chinese invasion. The greatest of the Tay Son brothers crushed the Chinese and proclaimed himself Emperor Quang Trung. He died in 1792, leaving behind a much weakened Tay Son.

Triumph of the Nguyen Dynasty

In 1788, Nguyen Anh returned home and seized control of Saigon with the help of French missionary, Pigneau de Behaine (1741–99). Following Quang Trung's death, Nguyen Anh easily defeated the Tay Son in the north. In 1802, he declared Hue the new national capital and himself the first ruler of the Nguyen Dynasty.

Ngo Mon Gate, Hue Citadel, was built by Nguyen Emperor Gia Long

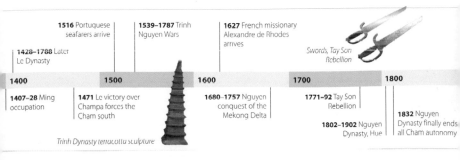

1516 Portuguese seafarers arrive

1539–1787 Trinh Nguyen Wars

1627 French missionary Alexandre de Rhodes arrives

Swords, Tay Son Rebellion

1428–1788 Later Le Dynasty

1400

1407–28 Ming occupation

1471 Le victory over Champa forces the Cham south

Trinh Dynasty terracotta sculpture

1500

1600

1680–1757 Nguyen conquest of the Mekong Delta

1700

1771–92 Tay Son Rebellion

1802–1902 Nguyen Dynasty, Hue

1800

1832 Nguyen Dynasty finally ends all Cham autonomy

French troops arriving in the Bay of Haiphong, 1884

Establishment of French Control

Nguyen Anh gave himself the title of Gia Long, deriving it from Gia Dinh and Thang Long, the old names of Ho Chi Minh City and Hanoi, and thus representing the unification of Vietnam. A strong ruler, he died in 1820.

Minh Mang (r.1820–41), the son of Gia Long, inherited the throne as well as a legacy of French involvement in Vietnamese affairs. Unlike his father, he felt no gratitude to the French. On the contrary, he was hostile to them and issued decrees prohibiting the spread of Catholicism. His son, Thieu Tri (r.1841–7) pursued similar policies, as did Tu Duc (r.1847–83) who denounced converts as "fools seduced by priests."

These anti-French measures instigated the imperialist faction in France to implement a "civilizing mission," which led to the loss of national independence for almost 100 years. In 1858–9, ostensibly responding to the execution of missionaries, France briefly occupied Danang. Two years later, it

seized Saigon and, in 1865, forced Tu Duc to form Cochinchina, a French colony. By 1883, France controlled the whole country, making Annam (the north) and Tonkin (the center) into protectorates. Tu Duc died the same year and his successors were reduced to being puppets of the French. Meanwhile, France occupied Cambodia and Laos, and in 1887, created the Indochinese Union, with its capital at Hanoi.

The Colonial Period

Paul Doumer, the French Governor of Indochina (1897–1902), invoked the An Nam or Pacified South of the 7th century, saying "when France arrived in Indochina, the Annamites were ripe for servitude." He would eventually be proved wrong, but for many decades, Vietnam suffered under the French imposition of heavy taxation, state monopolies on salt, alcohol, and opium, and enforced labor known as *corvée*. The French also profited from coffee and rubber plantations as well as Vietnam's extensive mineral resources. All this changed in 1940, when Nazi Germany occupied France and established the puppet Vichy regime. In Indochina, the Vichy authorities collaborated with Germany's Axis partner, Japan, and Vietnam fell under a new, brutal colonial yoke.

Paul Doumer, Governor of French Indochina

The Rise of Socialist Resistance

From the early 20th century, several nationalist movements began to emerge across Vietnam. The 1911 Revolution in China inspired the Viets, and the Viet Nam National Party (VNQDD) was formed in emulation of the

1820–41 Emperor Minh Mang issues anti-French edicts

1858–59 France seizes Danang

1887 France creates Indochinese Union of Vietnam, Laos, and Cambodia

1865 Cochinchina declared a French colony

1820   **1835**   **1850**   **1865**   **1880**

1832 Last principalities of Champa extinguished

1883 France establishes protectorate over Annam and Tonkin

1890 Birth of Ho Chi Minh near Kim Lien

Emperor Minh Mang

Chinese nationalist Kuomintang. In 1930, the French sent Nguyen Thai Hoc, the VNQDD chairman, to the guillotine along with 12 of his colleagues. In 1941, Ho Chi Minh *(see p173)*, the architect of Vietnam's independence, returned to Vietnam after many years. He formed the Vietnamese Independence League or Viet Minh, and began organizing a nationalist movement against the French and Japanese. In March 1945, faced with imminent defeat in the Pacific War, Japan took over direct administration from the Vichy regime. However, Ho Chi Minh and his Viet Minh forces had already liberated parts of the far north and were fast advancing on Hanoi. The Japanese surrendered on August 15, 1945, and on September 2, Ho Chi Minh declared national independence at Hanoi's Ba Dinh Square.

Ho Chi Minh (left) with military planners at Dien Bien Phu, 1953

The First Indochina War

Following France's liberation from Germany, General Charles De Gaulle and senior military officials were determined to restore their hold on Indochina, and reinstated French troops in Vietnam. This led to an uprising in Hanoi in 1946 and the outbreak of the First Indochina War. From their stronghold in Viet Bac, the Viet Minh forces, directed by General Vo Nguyen Giap, fought back, taking over broad swathes of the country. The French retained control of Hanoi, Saigon, and most large towns, but could not win.

As Ho Chi Minh warned the French in 1946, "you can kill ten of my men for every one I kill of yours. But even at those odds, you will lose and I will win." By 1954, the Viet Minh inflicted their final defeat on the French at the Battle of Dien Bien Phu *(see p199)*. However, the United States, frantic to curb communism, had already been funding as much as 80 percent of the French war effort, and the stage was set for the Vietnam War.

Prelude to the Vietnam War

The Geneva Conference was held in 1954, where France, Britain, the US, and the USSR decided to partition Vietnam at the 17th parallel, pending general elections in 1956. These elections were never held, and the partition became permanent. The North became the Communist Democratic Republic of Vietnam, with its capital at Hanoi under Ho Chi Minh, and the South became the anti-communist Republic of Vietnam, with its capital at Saigon under the US-allied and fervently Catholic Ngo Dinh Diem.

Viet Minh soldiers attack French military base, Dien Bien Phu

1911 Ho Chi Minh travels to Paris. Joins French Communist Party in 1920

1924 Ho Chi Minh becomes an agent of Comintern

1940 France occupied by Nazi Germany, Vichy regime

1945 Nguyen Emperor Bao Dai abdicates; Ho Chi Minh declares Independence

Bao Dai (right) with General Navarre

| 1895 | 1910 | 1925 | 1940 | 1955 |

French Indochinese postcard

1930 Ho Chi Minh forms Indochinese Communist Party in Hong Kong

1945 March 9, Japanese coup against the French; August 15, Japan capitulates

1954 France suffers crushing defeat at Dien Bien Phu

1946 First Indochina War begins as French seek to reimpose their rule

The Vietnam War

From 1954, South Vietnam, under the leadership of President Diem, was propped up politically and financially by the US. Under Diem, communists and Buddhists were persecuted, whereas the North was hostile to Catholics, many of whom fled to the South. The entire nation was reeling with unrest and strife, and the time was ripe for an intervention by the US. In the meantime, the North allied with China and the USSR, and in 1960, the National Liberation Front (NLF) or Vietcong was formed with the mission of unifying the country. In 1960, US military advisors arrived in the South, thus initiating the 15-year war known to the Vietnamese as the "American War" and to the Americans as the "Vietnam War."

Guerrilla Warfare
Both the NLF and the allied North Vietnamese Army (NVA) were adept at preparing simple but deadly booby traps.

US Soldiers in Paddy Fields, Mekong Delta

By 1967, there were half a million American soldiers in Vietnam, many of them one-year conscripts. Most were inexperienced and unmotivated, and had to fight in unfamiliar and difficult terrain, wading through rice paddies and swamps in search of their elusive opponents. More professional, specialist American forces mounted LRRPS or Long Range Reconnaissance Patrols, staying in deep jungle or marshland on dangerous five-day missions.

Gulf of Tonkin Incident (1964)
The US accused NLF torpedo boats of launching unprovoked attacks on the USS *Maddox.* Lyndon Johnson used this incident as his reason for bombing the North and for sending American troops to Vietnam.

Death from the Air
The US Air Force (USAF) and its South Vietnamese allies used a wide range of chemical warfare, including white phosphorus, on enemy positions. Here, a US aircraft is bombing Danang, 1966.

Ho Chi Minh Trail
With its hidden narrow paths and frail bridges, the Ho Chi Minh Trail *(see p155)* was used by communist troops to travel from North Vietnam to Saigon.

South Vietnam's President Ngo Dinh Diem, 1958

1954 Treaty signed at Geneva Convention, sanctioning Vietnam's partition

1960 Communists form the National Liberation Front in South Vietnam

1965 First US combat troops arrive; USAF bombing of North Vietnam begins

1955

1960

1965

Buddhist monk self immolates in protest against Diem's government, 1963

1963 Diem is assassinated, allegedly by South Vietnam generals

1964 North Vietnamese torpedo boats allegedly attack US destroyers in Gulf of Tonkin

The Tet Offensive (1968)
The longest and bloodiest battle was the January Tet Offensive, when communist forces seized the old imperial capital of Hue and held it against massive counterattacks for 25 days. Both sides suffered heavy losses.

Hamburger Hill (1969)
On May 10, the US 101st Airborne battalion attacked forces holding Ap Bia Mountain, near Laos. In ten days, 46 US soldiers were dead and 400 wounded, earning the peak the notorious epithet, "Hamburger Hill."

Napalm Bombings
A vicious but effective compound of jellied petroleum, napalm killed many thousands of people. When this infamous picture of young victims was beamed across the world in June 1972, US public opinion turned against the war.

Anti-War Protests
In the late 1960s and 70s, the anti-war movement grew in strength everywhere, including the US. These demonstrators are outside the American Embassy in London's Grosvenor Square.

Paris Peace Accords (1973)
Henry Kissinger and Le Duc Tho signed the treaty on January 23. US forces withdrew from Vietnam and the North released almost 500 US POWs.

April 29, 1975
The last remaining American personnel in Saigon were evacuated by helicopters to US Naval vessels in the South China Sea, even as the city was falling to victorious communist forces.

My Lai Massacre memorial

1968 Tet Offensive is launched in Jan–Feb; in March, the My Lai Massacre *(see p123)* shocks the country

1973 Ceasefire agreement is signed; US troops leave Vietnam

Anti-war badges worn during the 1970s

1970

1975

1969 Ho Chi Minh dies; Nixon proposes peace talks

1972 Americans bomb Haiphong Harbor

1971 *New York Times* prints extracts from Pentagon Papers exposing US involvement in Vietnam War

1975 South surrenders to North; provisional government installed

1971, Anti-war protestor atop a statue near Capitol Hill waves a Vietcong flag

Reunification and Isolation

Following the overwhelming victory of
the North in 1975, Le Duan, the general
secretary of the Communist Party after Ho
Chi Minh's death, came into power. It was
his doctrinaire government's policies that
shaped the next decade. In July 1976,
Vietnam was officially reunified and the
Socialist Republic of Vietnam proclaimed. Six
months later, at the Fourth Party Congress,
a decision was taken to press ahead with
forced collectivization of industry, commerce,
and agriculture in the south. Officials of the
former southern regime were severely
persecuted, many being sent for long
periods of re-education in undeveloped
border areas, a policy which denied Vietnam
the services of thousands of skilled and
educated citizens. To compound matters,
Saigon was renamed Ho Chi Minh City – a
designation never fully accepted in the South.
In Cholon *(see pp72–3)* and across the south,
persecution of the merchant class rapidly

Vietnamese troops leaving Cambodia in 1989

stopped businesses, a move that angered
China as most commerce was controlled by
the ethnic Chinese or Hoa. By 1977, great
numbers of refugees, known as "boat people,"
had started to flee abroad, further depleting
human resources. Also, a harsh trade
embargo imposed by the US after 1975
added to Vietnam's economic disintegration.

Matters deteriorated on the regional front
as well. In 1976, Pol Pot's Democratic
Kampuchea (Khmer Rouge of Cambodia),
supported by China, launched cross-border
attacks on Vietnam. Vietnam responded by
signing a security pact with the Soviet Union
in 1978, and overthrowing Pol Pot later in
the same year. Early in 1979, China retaliated
by invading the north and destroying
several provincial capitals before withdrawing unilaterally. Hanoi, execrated by
China and most of the West, was forced into
a closer alliance with the USSR. By the early
1980s, impoverished and isolated, Vietnam
was well on the way to starvation and
economic collapse.

Renovation

The death of Le Duan in 1986 brought about
change. Nguyen Van Linh, a southerner,
became party leader, and a policy of *doi moi*,

Refugees, or boat people, sailing to Manila, 1978

1975 Reunification
of North and South
under a communist
government

1979 China
invades
Northern
Vietnam

*Pol Pot – the
Cambodian
dictator*

1989 Vietnamese
troops withdraw
from Cambodia

1994 US
embargo lifted

| 1976 | 1980 | 1984 | 1988 | 1992 | 1996 |

1978 Vietnam invades Cambodia
and overthrows Khmer Rouge

1986 Death of
Le Duan;
introduction of
doi moi

Le Duan

1995 Vietnam
joins ASEAN;
diplomatic
relations with
USA instated

1976 Socialist Republic of
Vietnam established

or economic reforms, was adopted at the Sixth Party Congress, opening the way to gradual economic and social reform under the Communist Party. The liberalization policy was accelerated by the collapse of the USSR and the end of the Cold War in 1991. Vietnam lost its ally and financial patron, and was forced to mend fences with China, establish closer links with its Southeast Asian neighbors, and open increasingly to the West.

As a result, in 1994, the US lifted its trade embargo, and in 1995, restored full diplomatic relations with Hanoi. In the same year, Vietnam became a full member of the Association of Southeast Asian Nations (ASEAN). In 1997, the policy of continuing economic reform was confirmed with the election of the forward-looking Tran Duc Luong as president and Phan Van Khai as prime minister.

Tran Duc Luong with US president Bill Clinton, 2000

Rebirth

Since the turn of the 20th century Vietnam has seen a remarkable turnaround. In 2000, US President Bill Clinton's visit was indicative of fast improving relations between the two former enemies. In 2001, this was followed by the normalization of trade relations between Washington and Hanoi, and the election of Nong Duc Manh as Secretary General of the Communist Party – the most powerful position in Vietnam followed by the prime minister and president. Widely regarded as a modernizer, Nong Duc Manh promised on his election that he would focus on economic development and fight

corruption and unnecessary red tape. In 2006, Nguyen Tan Dung, the country's youngest prime minister, was confirmed by the National Assembly. The first leader of post-war Vietnam with no experience of the independence struggle, he has vowed to strive for development and to "pull the nation out of backwardness." For the next two years Vietnam continued to prosper economically. The country has since been one of the fastest-growing economies in Asia. In 2010 there was an influx of foreign brands and construction of many modern skyscrapers in Ho Chi Minh City. The unwillingness to continue reforms, however, led to a contraction of the economy and social tensions. In 2011, a number of riots and protests occurred in response to police brutality and large-scale government land grabs, leading to embarrassment and censure of top leaders. Despite this, most Vietnamese enjoy more freedom than their forefathers did at any time in their country's history.

View across Ho Chi Minh City

VIETNAM AREA BY AREA

Vietnam at a Glance

A long and narrow country with amazingly diverse terrains, Vietnam encompasses the magnificent and remote valleys of the northwest, the high peaks and plateaus of its mountainous spine, and the pristine beaches and warm tropical waters of the southern coasts. The mighty Red River in the north and Mekong River in the south give rise to two immensely fertile deltas, lush forests, meandering canals, and vast paddy fields. Apart from its scenic wealth, Vietnam is a treasure trove of art and culture, evident in the museums and exquisite French architecture of Hanoi, the royal palaces of ancient Hue, and the elegant restaurants and vibrant nightlife of Ho Chi Minh City. This guide divides Vietnam into six regions; each area is color-coded as shown here.

Ha Giang

Sapa

NORTHERN VIETNAM *(see pp182–205)*

Dien Bien Phu

HANOI *(see pp156–81)* Han

Tuong Duong

Th. Ho

Vin

Sapa *(see pp200–201),* located in a remote part of Northern Vietnam, is known for its breathtaking beauty. Its landscape is marked by rice fields that rise in steep terraces along the flanks of the Hoang Lien Mountains, and has been farmed for centuries by the region's ethnic minorities.

| 0 kilometers | 200 |
| 0 miles | 200 |

The Old Quarter *(see pp160–61)* is Hanoi's unique commercial district. Originally known as 36 Streets, this center used to cater to the needs of the palace in the 13th century. Today, this colorful, bustling market is a treasure house of silk, freshly ground coffee, lanterns, and more.

Tra Vinh *(see p93)* is a fertile delta town, featuring several narrow canals winding through dense foliage, coconut palm trees, and fruit orchards. Known for its religious diversity, Tra Vinh is home to a large number of Khmer Buddhists and Christians.

Chau Doc

Can Tho

MEKONG DELTA AN¦ SOUTHERN VIETNAM *(see pp88–105)*

Ca Mau

◄ View of Ho Tay or West Lake at dusk, Hanoi

Hien Lam Pavilion in the Hue Citadel *(see pp144–7)* is also known as the Pavilion of Splendor. This exquisite triple-roofed temple is situated within the Yellow Enclosure of the Imperial City and presides over the massive Nine Dynastic Urns.

The Po Nagar Cham Towers *(see p113)* were built in the 8th century and are among the most important Cham sites in Vietnam. Located in Nha Trang, these magnificent ruins provide an excellent insight into the architectural styles of the once mighty Cham Empire.

CENTRAL VIETNAM
(see pp124–55)

Hue

Hoi An

Quang Ngai

Plei Kan

SOUTH CENTRAL VIETNAM
(see pp106–23)

Quy Nhon

Buon Ma Thuot

Nha Trang

Dalat

HO CHI MINH CITY
(see pp50–87)

Ho Chi Minh City

Haiphong

Mui Ne Beach *(see p110)* stretches for 12 miles (20 km) and is one of the best beaches south of Nha Trang. Its windy weather between October and February is ideal for surfing. Mui Ne Village comes to life in the morning when the fish merchants are in action.

The Rooftop Garden of the Rex Hotel *(see p64)* is one of Ho Chi Minh City's most popular restaurants, offering spectacular views across the bustling and atmospheric streets of the city's downtown district.

HO CHI MINH CITY

The largest city in Vietnam is also its commercial capital and is fast becoming the nation's window to the world. Buzzing with frenetic activity, cosmopolitan Ho Chi Minh City looks outward, listens to pop music, and drinks French wine. Existing alongside the high-rise hotels, shopping malls, and chic restaurants are ancient pagodas and colonial buildings, recalling a checkered but vibrant past.

Originally established as a Khmer trading post, centuries ago, Ho Chi Minh City was destined for greater things. By the 18th century, the city, then named Saigon, had become the provincial capital of the Nguyen Dynasty. However, in the second half of the 19th century, control over the city passed to the French, and Saigon became the capital of French Cochinchina This was a period of much infrastructural and architectural development, during which Saigon earned the epithet "Paris of the Orient." Many buildings of this era are in good condition even today. In 1954, the city was proclaimed the capital of South Vietnam (see p47). The ensuing war between the US and the Communist North lasted until 1975, when North Vietnam took over Saigon and renamed it Ho Chi Minh City.

Today, under growing economic and cultural liberalization, the city has entered a period of modernization and is constantly evolving and reinventing itself. Populated by an estimated seven million people, the city has long been the hub of manufacturing, entertainment, and cuisine in Vietnam. Upscale restaurants and cafés offering a range of international delicacies are opening every day, while bars, clubs, and discos are at the center of a thriving nightlife. The best place to catch the action is Dong Khoi (see pp60–61) and the rest of District 1. Attracting many tourists, the area is home to historical buildings and museums, sophisticated shops, and roadside cafés, as well as people of all ages zipping around noisily on motorbikes and causing gridlock.

Large portrait of Ho Chi Minh presiding over the hallway of the General Post Office

◀ Meditating followers of the Cao Dai religion in the temple Cao Dai, South Vietnam.

Exploring Ho Chi Minh City

The most prominent area in the city is around Dong Khoi Street in District 1, boasting fashionable shops, museums, and fine dining. It also features examples of French-Colonial structures, such as the Municipal Theater, Notre Dame Cathedral, and the General Post Office. To the north are sprawling residential areas and the historic Jade Emperor Pagoda, known for its exquisite architecture and ornate carvings. To the west lies Cholon, or Chinatown. Home to the ethnic Chinese, or Hoa, this is the best place to find herbs, traditional Chinese medicines, and other goods, as well as some of the city's most ancient pagodas.

0 meters	800
0 yards	800

Sights at a Glance

Churches, Temples, and Pagodas

8 Notre Dame Cathedral
12 *Jade Emperor Pagoda pp64–7*
13 Le Van Duyet Temple
14 Vinh Nghiem Pagoda
17 Xa Loi Pagoda
18 Mariamman Hindu Temple
21 Nghia An Hoi Quan Pagoda
22 Thien Hau Pagoda
23 Quan Am Pagoda
25 Phung Son Pagoda
26 Giac Vien Pagoda
27 One Pillar Pagoda of Thu Duc
30 *Cao Dai Holy See pp78–9*

Historic Sights and Buildings

4 People's Committee Building
6 Bitexco Financial Tower
9 General Post Office
28 Cu Chi Tunnels

Theaters

2 Municipal Theater

Museums and Palaces

5 Ho Chi Minh City Museum
10 Reunification Palace

11 Museum of Vietnamese History
15 Women's Museum of Southern Vietnam
16 War Remnants Museum
20 Fine Arts Museum

Beaches, Springs, Nature Reserves, and Mountain

29 Nui Ba Den
33 Ho Coc Beach
34 Binh Chau Hot Springs
35 Cat Tien National Park

Towns and Markets

19 Ben Thanh Market
24 Binh Tay Market
31 Vung Tau
32 Long Hai

Hotels

1 Caravelle Hotel
3 Continental Hotel
7 Rex Hotel

DISTRICT 11

DISTRICT 6

DAM SEN PARK

Mien Tay Bus Station

Cholon Station

Getting Around

The areas of Dong Khoi and Cholon are small enough to be explored comfortably on foot. However, the most popular mode of transport is the Honda om, or motorbike taxi. A ride to anywhere in town should cost no more than a few dollars. Radio-dispatched, metered taxis are also common now. Most travel agencies will arrange trips to the outlying areas of the city.

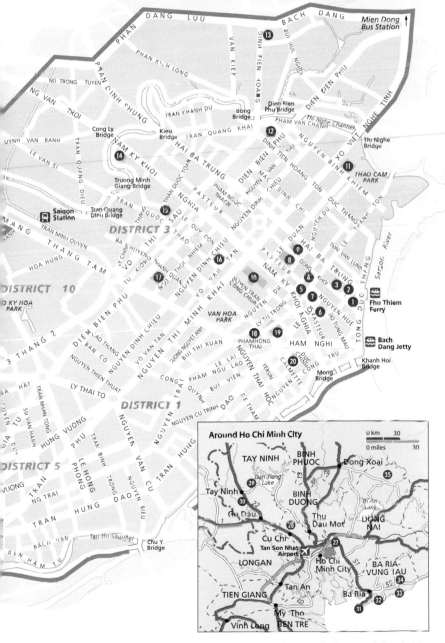

Street-by-Street: Dong Khoi

Arguably the liveliest part of the city, the area around Dong
Khoi Street is the very nerve center of Ho Chi Minh City.
Dong Khoi Street itself became famous during the French
era, and was then known as the Rue Catinat. Home to stately
hotels, elegant boutiques, and cozy cafés that coexisted with
bars and brothels, it was at the center of most of the action in
Graham Greene's novel, *The Quiet American*. The subsequent
communist regime shut down most of these establishments,
but Vietnam's economic liberalization in 1986 gave the area
a new lease on life as smart hotels, restaurants, and shops
slowly made a reappearance. Today, Dong Khoi's vibrance is
unparalleled in the country, and it does justice to the city's
old nickname "Paris of the Orient."

View of Dong Khoi from Diamond Plaza *(see
p255)*

❾ ★ General Post Office
One of the most handsome
French-Colonial buildings in
the city, the cavernous interior
of this massive structure, with
its comfortable benches,
provides a cool respite from
the heat outside.

**The Metropolitan
Building** is home to
HSBC's headquarters
and is a popular
café spot.

**❽ ★ Notre Dame
Cathedral**
This tall, late 19th-century
cathedral is built of locally
quarried stone and
covered with red ceramic
tiles shipped in from
France. The statue of the
Virgin Mary was added to
the lawns in front of the
building in the 1950s.

❹ People's Committee Building
The erstwhile Hôtel de Ville now houses
the office of the People's Committee of
Ho Chi Minh City. It is one of the most
magnificent and photogenic colonial
buildings in the entire city.

NGUYEN D

NGUYEN DU

Pasteur

LY TU TRONG

Lower Dong Khoi

This area has become one of Saigon's most fashionable spots for boutique shopping. Local brands such as Khai Silk can be found here, alongside well-known international brands such as Louis Vuitton (left).

| 0 meters | | 150 |
| 0 yards | | 150 |

Locator Map

❸ Continental Hotel

Constructed in classic French Colonial style, this elegant hotel is a serene haven amid the bustle of the city. The central atrium is popular for afternoon tea and the patio offers al fresco dining in summer.

Key

— Suggested route

The Vincom Shopping Center (Vincom Towers) is one of the largest modern shopping centers in Vietnam, selling a variety of imported brands.

DONG KHOI

LE THANH TON

NGUYEN HUE

LE LOI

→ Caravelle Hotel

❷ ★ Municipal Theater

This lovely Neo-Classical building, known as the Opera House in colonial times, was once the heart of French high society

❼ Rex Hotel

A popular base for several journalists during the Vietnam War, the Rex is one of the best known landmarks in the city. The hotel's rooftop bar offers superb views of the street below.

❶ Caravelle Hotel

19 Lam Son Sq, District 1. **Map** 2 F3.
Tel (08) 3823 4999. **Open** daily. 🖉
🖥 🏠 **W** caravellehotel.com

When it opened on Christmas Eve in 1959, the Caravelle Hotel, at ten stories, was the tallest building in the city. At its gala launch, the hotel was praised by the local press for its central air-conditioning system and bulletproof glass. Its designers were considered almost prescient as the hotel became a central headquarters for diplomats and journalists during the Vietnam War *(see pp48–9)*. Both Australia and New Zealand maintained embassies here, while the *Washington Post*, *New York Times*, *Associated Press*, and many other news agencies established bureaus in the hotel. Reporters would joke that they could cover the entire war without leaving their seats at the rooftop bar. The glamor faded after the fall of Saigon in 1975, when the hotel was taken over by the government. In 1998, however, it was reopened after extensive renovations.

Today, with its soaring, new marble-lined tower, Caravelle is one of the city's most luxurious hotels. While old-timers may have trouble recognizing it, the rooftop bar, with its curved balconied corners, still tops the old wing and there are few better places for an evening cocktail.

❷ Municipal Theater

7 Lam Son Sq, Intersection of Le Loi and Dong Khoi sts, District 1.
Map 2 F3. **Tel** (08) 3829 9976.
Open varies. 🖉 🖥

A superb, French-Colonial style building, the Municipal Theater or Nha Hat Thanh Pho was built in 1899 as a concert hall for the French. Still referred to as the Opera House, the hall temporarily served as the headquarters of the South Vietnam National Assembly in 1956. A graceful staircase leads up to the entrance, which

Finely carved figures on the rooftop of the Municipal Theater

is flanked by two huge columns shaped like Greco-Roman goddesses. Winged figures and exquisite scrollworks grace the eaves below the roof, and the grounds are speckled with lovely fountains and statues.

While the interior is not as ornate, it is a fine setting for performances that include everything from traditional Vietnamese theater and Western classical music to rock concerts and gymnastics. Program details are posted on the box office billboards.

Diners relaxing in the Continental Hotel's courtyard garden

❸ Continental Hotel

132–134 Dong Khoi St, District 1. **Map** 2 F3. **Tel** (08) 3829 9201. **Open** daily. 🖉 🖥 **W** continentalsaigon.com

With its stately façade, the Continental is the grande dame of hotels built during French rule. The hotel is set around a courtyard, which is well-shaded with frangipani trees, while inside, the red-carpeted staircases retain their original tropical hardwood. The structure, for the most part, has been spared the "modernization" visited upon some other historic buildings in the city, and the hotel wears its patina of age well.

The hotel has also earned a place in the annals of history for attracting illustrious visitors since its completion in 1886. During the Vietnam War, top-flight journalists, including Walter Cronkite (1916–2009), would stay here and spend hours on the famous terrace bar, which they dubbed "The Continental Shelf." Writers André Malraux (1901–76) and W. Somerset Maugham (1874–1965) are other guests of note, but it is Graham Greene (1904–91) who immortalized the Continental in his novel *The Quiet American* (1955). It is no surprise that he captured the spirit of the time and place so well, since he lived in the hotel for several months.

The plush lobby of the Caravelle Hotel decorated with Christmas wreaths

For hotels and restaurants see pp236–41 and pp246–53

➍ People's Committee Building

Intersection of Le Thanh Ton and Nguyen Hue sts, District 1. **Map** 2 E3. **Closed** to the public.

Designed by French architect P. Gardes and completed in 1908, the People's Committee Building, once known as the Hôtel de Ville, is probably the most photographed building in the city. It was outside this building in 1945, that thousands of people congregated to establish the Provisional Administrative Committee of South Vietnam. Still the house of the city government, it sits regally at the city's center. Contrary to popular belief, this striking building has never been a hostelry, nor is it open to the public. Modeled on the City Hall in Paris, it comprises two stories, with two wings off a central hall and a clock tower. It is capped with a red-tile roof, and its fanciful yellow-and-cream-colored façade is most often described as "gingerbread." Despite its obviously Parisian appearance, the building fits in well with the cityscape, especially at night when it is gorgeously floodlit. Unfortunately, there is no way for the general public to see the chandelier-bedecked interior today. However, the square in front of the hall, featuring a statue of Ho Chi Minh cradling a child, is a popular vantage point to admire the structure.

The imposing façade of the French-Colonial People's Committee Building

Picture taken during the fall of Saigon (1975) at Ho Chi Minh City Museum

➎ Ho Chi Minh City Museum

65 Ly Tu Trong St, District 1. **Map** 2 E4. **Tel** (08) 3829 9741. **Open** 8am–5pm. 🏠 🏛 🌐 **hcmc-museum.edu.vn**

Once the French governor general's residence, this, like many of the city's buildings, looks as if it were shipped in pieces from France and reassembled here. Light grey with white trim and a colonnade, it strikes a commanding presence. The spacious halls, with high ceilings and chandeliers, are a much sought-after venue for wedding photographs.

Spread over two rambling floors, the museum purports to represent 300 years of the city's history. However, its original name, Revolutionary Museum, is a more accurate indicator of what to expect. The first floor has somewhat scattered displays of pictures of Saigon during the French rule, old maps, and crumbling documents from the time the city was founded in the 17th century. Also here are relics from Vietnam's natural history and ethnic wedding costumes. The second floor is devoted to Vietnam's struggle against imperialism. Weapons such as AK-47 rifles and improvised bombs are showcased here, along with photographs of soldiers, letters from the front, and political manifestos. Many obligatory engines of war, including a Huey helicopter, a jet fighter, and an American-built tank can be seen on display outside. The museum also has an extensive collection of Vietnamese currency.

➏ Bitexco Financial Tower

2 Hai Trieu St, District 1. **Map** 2 F4. **Tel** (08) 3915 6868. **Open** 9:30am–9:30pm daily. 🏠 🏛 🌐 **saigonskydeck.com**

In just a few years since opening in 2010, this building has become Saigon's newest icon and an emblem of the city's rejuvenation. Its slender, tapered shape with a helipad jutting near the top is visible from everywhere in the city center. The interest for visitors lies on the 49th floor, where the Saigon Skydeck offers panoramic views of the city center and the Saigon river flowing through it. The observatory provides information about the history and culture of the city.

It has binoculars fitted in the glass walls of the observatory for viewing. There are many high-end shops for the shopping enthusiasts along with a wide range of fine restaurants and cafés. From this vantage point 584 ft (178 m) above the ground, many of the city's sights are visible, including the Municipal Theater, the People's Committee Building, and Ben Thanh Market. The bird's eye view also gives an idea of the frantic pace of the city's development, with new high-rise blocks appearing all around.

Rose Garden Restaurant, Rex Hotel

❼ Rex Hotel

141 Nguyen Hue Blvd, District 1.
Map 2 E4. **Tel** (08) 3829 2185.
Open daily. 🚗 🖥 📷
🅦 rexhotelvietnam.com

Located in the center of the city, the Rex Hotel has played an important part in Ho Chi Minh City's history ever since its construction in the 1950s. Originally built by French colonial developers, it quickly became a focus of the social and military activities of American soldiers during the Vietnam War. It was from here that US military officers gave the daily press briefings that became known as "The Five O'Clock Follies," recognized for their blatantly self-serving nature.

Today, with its very popular rooftop bar, the Rex still serves as an important gathering place. Corporate conclaves are held here, gamblers flock to its bingo parlor, and innumerable weddings are celebrated in the central court.

❽ Notre Dame Cathedral

1 Cong Xa Paris Sq, District 1.
Map 2 E3. **Open** 8–10:30am, 3–4pm Mon–Sat; services on Sun. ♿

The basilica-style Notre Dame Cathedral, or Nha Tho Duc Ba, is the largest church ever built in the French Empire. When it was completed in 1880, its 40-m (120-ft) spires made it the tallest structure in the city. At first glance it seems to be brick-built, but in fact, the façade is made of red tiles brought over from Marseilles and attached to granite walls. Stained-glass windows from Chartres were installed, but destroyed during WWII and later replaced with plain glass. The interior is relatively unadorned, but the ambient lighting creates a calm atmosphere.

In front of the cathedral is a statue of the Virgin Mary. Made in Rome, it was brought to Vietnam in 1959 and named Holy Mary Queen of Peace, in the hope that she would bring peace to the war-torn country.

While the city's Roman Catholic community is no longer a political force, droves of worshippers still throng the church. The belfry, open on Sundays, affords lovely views.

Virgin Mary, Notre Dame Cathedral

❾ General Post Office

2 Cong Xa Paris Sq, District 1.
Map 2 E3. **Tel** (08) 3829 3274.
Open 7am–8pm daily. 📷

Designed by French architect Gustave Eiffel between 1886 and 1891, Buu Dien Trung Tam or the General Post Office is one of the most attractive buildings in the city. Its massive façade is coral colored with a cream trim and also features carvings of the faces of famous philosophers and scientists, below which are finely engraved inscriptions. In all, the building is no less than a temple to the art of communicating by mail. Strangely evocative of the inside of a railway station, the interior is vaulted and supported by wrought-iron pillars painted green, with gilded capitals. The floor tilework is intricate, especially in the foyer where huge antique maps illuminated by chandeliers depict the city and the region. One of the maps shows the city in 1892, and another portrays the region in 1932. A large portrait of Ho Chi Minh gazes over the daily bustle. Wooden writing benches are available for patrons' use, as is a kiosk selling souvenirs and stamps. The entire hall is cooled by overhead fans.

The cavernous, elongated interior of the General Post Office

For hotels and restaurants see pp236–41 and pp246–53

The stern and imposing façade of Reunification Palace, a unique example of 1960s Vietnamese architecture

⑩ Reunification Palace

135 Nam Ky Khoi Nghia St, District 1. **Map** 2 D3. **Tel** (08) 3822 3652. **Open** 7:30–11am, 1–4pm daily, except during official functions. 🖥 📷 W dinhdoclap.gov.vn

Set on well-maintained and spacious grounds, this historic building is a prominent symbol of the country's political history. During the 19th century, the Reunification Palace was the site of the Norodom Palace, former residence of the French governor general. It was later occupied by South Vietnam's President Ngo Dinh Diem (see p47), and named the Presidential Palace. In 1962, much of the structure was destroyed when Diem's own air force bombed it in a failed assassination attempt. The building was rebuilt soon after, but Diem was killed before he could move in.

It was in this former palace's International Reception Room that succeeding President Van Thieu received potentates and presidents, until he boarded a chopper from the rooftop helipad and fled before North Vietnamese troops took over Saigon. In 1975, the South surrendered to the North, and the palace gates were knocked down by a North Vietnamese Army tank. The photograph of this event (see p63) has become emblematic of the reunification of Vietnam.

Today, the interior remains largely unchanged, with high and wide corridors that open onto cavernous lobbies and reception rooms. The living quarters, built around a sunny atrium, are lavishly furnished with glittering chandeliers and elaborate antiques. Also not to be missed are the elephants' feet in the "presidential gifts display" and the large lacquer-work piece depicting scenes from the Le Dynasty (see p44).

In the basement is a bunker and military operations center, with radio transmitters and maps. Oddly, the third floor also features a gambling room.

Adjoining the Reunification Palace is a park with trees that offers a place to relax.

⑪ Museum of Vietnamese History

2 Nguyen Binh Khiem St, District 1. **Map** 2 F1. **Tel** (08) 3829 8146. **Open** 8–11am, 1:30–4:30pm Tue–Sun. 🖥 📷 🖼 **Saigon Zoo and Botanical Garden** 2 Nguyen Binh Khiem St. **Tel** (08) 3829 3728. **Open** 7am–9pm daily. 🖥 ♿ 🖥

Built in a classic pagoda style, this very attractive museum, also known as Bao Tang Lich Su, contains a vast collection of artifacts, spanning almost the entire history of Vietnam. Relics from

Vase from the Le Dynasty

the beginning of the nation's cultural evolution can be seen in the form of prehistoric implements and tools. These are followed by bronze artifacts from the Hung Kings era (see p41). Stand-out exhibits include bronze drums belonging to the Dong Son civilization, and tokens from the Oc Eo culture, including a 2nd-century AD Roman coin.

Farther on are remnants belonging to the Nguyen Dynasty (see p45), with a rich collection of garments and jewelry. Also on display are numerous Cham and Khmer relics, such as a stone *lingam* and ceramics. A prominent exhibit is that of a mummy dating back to 1869.

Somewhat out of place, although interesting, is the daily scheduled water puppet show (see p163). The museum is set on the expansive and scenic grounds of the **Saigon Zoo and Botanical Garden**, which provide an ideal setting for a relaxing meander.

Visitors interacting with elephants at the Saigon Zoo and Botanical Garden

⑫ Jade Emperor Pagoda

One of the city's most ornate pagodas, this small house of worship honors the King of all Heavens, Ngoc Huang or the Jade Emperor – chief deity of the Taoist pantheon. Built by the Cantonese community in 1909, its pink façade is almost simple, but the tile roof is an intricate work of art, as are the large wooden doors, richly carved with images of gods and men. Most remarkable, however, are the vibrantly colorful and gilded images of Buddhist divinities and Taoist deities inside the temple. Just about every surface is embellished with tiles and carvings, most of which are dense with religious imagery and symbols.

Carved panel depicting one of 1,000 torments in the Hall of Ten Hells

Women's Room
This fascinating enclosure is filled with two rows of six ceramic female figurines. Draped in colorful robes, each woman represents a lunar year, each juxtaposed with a vice or virtue. Kim Hoa, Goddess of Mothers, officiates over the colorful gathering.

KEY

① **The incinerator** is used for burning votive paper offerings. The rising smoke is said to reach the ancestors in heaven.

② **The King of Hell** and his red, life-size horse head the Hall of Ten Hells, which is lined with wood reliefs depicting lurid scenes of damnation

③ **Tortoise Shelter** This small sanctuary is home to several turtles, which are considered symbols of good luck and fortune in Vietnam. However, although images of turtles are common, such shelters are quite rare.

⟋ To the main gate

Outer Courtyard
Shaded with flowering shrubs and an ancient banyan tree, the outer courtyard is a peaceful spot with park benches and a turtle pond.

Traditional Stacked Roof with Green Ceramic Tiles
A pride of dragons, believed to represent a connection to the divine, rise from the jungle of roof peaks, made of elaborate woodwork and ceramic tiles.

★ Main Sanctuary
Attended by guardians and resplendent in flowing robes, the Jade Emperor presides over the main sanctuary

★ Giant Demon Guards
Made from a resilient kind of papier-mâché, the two larger-than-life demon guards are richly painted and robed in finery. One restrains an evil dragon under his foot, and the other a rampant tiger.

★ Mother of Five Buddhas
One of the most unusual altars here is that of Phat Mau Chuan De, Mother of Five Buddhas of the Cardinal Directions. Her Hindu-style effigy is flanked by statues of her five sons.

Religious Significance of the Hearth

Ong Tao or the Kitchen God resides in the family hearth and acts as the Jade Emperor's snitch, as he knows all that transpires in the home. He is portrayed as a droll, fat fellow whose trousers burned off as a result of standing too close to the fire. Most kitchens in Vietnam contain an altar to him, and every year, during Tet (see pp32–3), Ong Tao reports each family's conduct to the Jade Emperor. If there is strife, the family is punished, but if there is harmony, it is rewarded. To get a good report, Ong Tao's altar is never empty of offerings of food, drink, and incense.

Offerings for Ong Tao in a family altar

⑬ Le Van Duyet Temple

1 Bis Phan Dang Luu St, Binh Thanh District. **Tel** (08) 3841 2517. **Open** sunrise–sunset daily. 🖼 Le Van Duyet Temple Festival (late Aug–early Sep).

Dedicated to General Le Van Duyet (1763–1831), this is perhaps the best example of a temple devoted to a national hero rather than to a deity or religion. Le Van Duyet helped suppress the Tay Son Rebellion (see p45), and was lauded by Emperor Gia Long. After Van Duyet's death, he was repudiated by Emperor Minh Mang (r.1820–41), but was restored to favor in the 1840s, and the temple was built to honor him.

The main sanctuary is bereft of any images other than a large portrait of Le Van Duyet, reminding devotees that they are worshipping a mortal. Also inside is a fascinating collection of the general's personal effects, such as crystalware, weapons, and a stuffed tiger. The patrons are mostly locals who come here to meditate, make offerings, or even seal a solemn oath in lieu of the services of a notary public. Over the years, the temple has grown into a complex of interconnected buildings, cloisters, patios, and courts. From the street, a gate leads into a large parkland, with tall trees shading the benches. The temple exterior is remarkable for its mosaic wall panels and reliefs. The outer sanctuary is unique for its lack of embellishment. All the pillars and altars are made of carved and polished wood, as are the giant cranes and the life-size horse seen here. In contrast, the inner sanctum adjoining it is a blaze of color, with red-and-gold dragon pillars.

Le Van Duyet's tomb is also located on the premises and an annual festival is held at the temple to commemorate the anniversary of his death.

⑭ Vinh Nghiem Pagoda

339 Nam Ky Khoi Nghia St, District 3. **Map** 1 B2. **Tel** (08) 3848 3153. **Open** sunrise–sunset daily. 📷

Vinh Nghiem Pagoda's eight-story tower soaring over its surroundings

Completed with aid from the Japan-Vietnam Friendship Association in 1971, this is, by some measures, the largest pagoda in the city. Certainly, its eight-story tower, located immediately to the left of a high gate, is the tallest. Each side of the tower is adorned with an image of the Buddha in high relief. To the right of the gate is a smaller, 16-ft (5-m) high tower, built of

Huge Buddha with swastika, Vinh Nghiem Pagoda

concrete blocks. The concrete is of such quality and color that the structure appears to be made of granite.

Across a 65-ft (20-m) courtyard is the large, squat main building. A steep staircase leads up to the sanctuary where five massive lacquerware doors lead into the vast first room. The walls here are lined with well-executed paintings of scriptural scenes and explanatory notes are posted alongside. Farther in is the main altar with a huge, seated Buddha, flanked by disciples.

Behind the sanctuary lies a solemn room, filled with photographs and memorials to the departed. A statue of the goddess Quan Am sits on the altar here.

On the second floor, a cloister leads into an art gallery where local artists show their works. Rock and topiary gardens flank the building.

The spacious courtyard and richly embellished exterior of Le Van Duyet Temple

⑮ Women's Museum of Southern Vietnam

202 Vo Thi Sau St, District 3. **Map** 1 C3.
Tel (08) 3932 0322 **Open** 7:30–
11:30am, 1:30–5pm daily. 🎥 📷

To bring to light the cultural and military contributions made by South Vietnamese women over the ages, the Women's Museum of Southern Vietnam or Bao Tang Phu Nu Nam Bo was established in 1985. The ten rooms here span three stories and are filled with fascinating displays, ranging from military plaques and medals to a selection of beautiful ethnic costumes.

The tour usually begins from the third floor. The exhibits in this set of rooms are dedicated to women who were involved in the 20th-century communist struggle for independence and unification. Their photographs line the walls, and some of their personal effects are displayed in glass cases, providing a reminder that Vietnamese women were no strangers to combat. The second floor continues the theme, with the addition of statues and large paintings of historical events involving women. There is also a re-creation of the prison cell that once held a national heroine captive.

However, the first floor, with its focus on traditional crafts and customs, is the most colorful. The anteroom, with a mock-up of a temple entrance bedecked with many artifacts, is dedicated to the ancient Vietnamese practice of goddess worship. In the next room, faux terraces feature mannequins dressed in exquisite regional costumes. In a large room to the left is a complex exhibit about the production of cotton cloth and rush mats. These products are woven by women in craft villages of the south.

The museum complex also boasts a movie theater, a small library, and a boutique.

Tank displayed on the grounds of the War Remnants Museum

⑯ War Remnants Museum

28 Vo Van Tan St, District 3. **Map** 2 D3.
Tel (08) 3930 5587. **Open** 7:30am–
noon, 1:30–5pm daily. 🎥 🖥 📷

Located in the former US Information Service building, this exhibition was once known as the War Crimes Museum. The films, pictures, and other items on display here document atrocities committed by American, Chinese, and French soldiers in grim detail. Events are told from a Vietnamese perspective and are both moving and thought-provoking. Among the

Cluster bomb, War Remnants Museum

most disturbing exhibits are the formaldehyde-filled jars containing foetuses deformed as a result of the chemical defoliants used during the Vietnam War. Also displayed here are photographs showing the effects of torture, a video of a prisoner being thrown from a helicopter by Vietnam's aggressors, along with many American weapons, military vehicles, and even a French guillotine.

⑰ Xa Loi Pagoda

89 Ba Huyen Thanh St, District 3.
Map 1 C4. **Tel** (08) 3930 7605.
Open 7–11am, 2–7pm daily.

This was one of the most important pagodas during the communist revolution. Built in 1956, it was a center of resistance to Ngo Dinh Diem's *(see p47)* corrupt and anti-Buddhist regime in the early 1960s. Three of its monks immolated themselves publicly as a gesture of protest, and on one occasion, about 400 worshippers and clergy were arrested. These actions were crucial in galvanizing widespread opposition to the Diem regime, ultimately leading to the coup that resulted in his assassination in 1963.

Today, few traces of these tumultuous events remain as the pagoda's colorful seven-tiered tower rises above the temple complex. The roof soars to 49 ft (15 m), and large painted panels at the top of the walls depict scenes from the life of the Buddha. The monks' quarters are on the first floor of the two storied main building, and the sanctuary, unusual for its spare decor, is above. The ample space is devoid of furnishings, pillars, censers, and displays so that the visitor is drawn to the massive bronze statue of the Buddha seated behind the solitary altar.

Colossal bronze Buddha inside Xa Loi Pagoda

Colorful images of goddesses on the façade of Mariamman Hindu Temple

⑱ Mariamman Hindu Temple

45 Truong Dinh St, District 1. **Map** 2 D4. **Tel** (08) 3823 2735. **Open** sunrise–sunset daily.

Dedicated to Mariamman, an incarnation of Shakti, the Hindu Goddess of Strength, Mariamman Hindu Temple caters not only to the small community of Hindus in Ho Chi Minh City, but also to the many local Vietnamese Buddhists, who worship here either looking for good luck or driven by superstition.

Built in the late 19th century, the temple is quite small but beautiful, and superbly maintained by the government. The bright, coral-colored wall of the façade is surmounted by numerous images of deities, cows, and lions, all painted vividly in pink, green, and blue. Over the entrance, a stepped-pyramidal tower covered with more sculpted images, mostly of female deities, rises from the rooftop.

Inside, an imposing statue of a red-robed lion guards the entrance, which opens into an uncovered portico that surrounds the main sanctuary. Three of the courtyard's walls are inset with altar nooks in which images of various gods and goddesses rest. Set in the center of the portico, the sanctuary itself is slightly raised. Made of stone, it recalls the architectural style of Angkor Wat (see pp216–17), and forms the setting for the multi-armed representation of Mariamman. The goddess is surrounded by many attending deities, including Ganesha, the Hindu Elephant God, as well as two female deities, who stand on either side of her. Two lingam (Hindu phallic symbols) also stand before her.

The altar is surrounded by numerous incense burners and brass figurine oil lamps. Worshippers hold incense sticks in both hands while praying. The rear of the sanctuary has a prayer wall against which the faithful press their heads in the hope that the goddess will be able to hear their prayers clearly.

⑲ Ben Thanh Market

Intersection of Le Loi and Ham Nghi blvds, District 1. **Map** 2 E4. **Open** 6am–5pm daily; later outside.

One of the most recognizable landmarks in the city, this shopping center was built in 1914 by the French, who named it Les Halles Centrales or Central Market Halls. The main structure that houses the market is made of reinforced concrete and occupies an enormous area. Its most famous feature is the massive clock tower that dominates the neighborhood. Home to several hundred shopkeepers, the market offers an amazingly extensive and varied selection of merchandise, ranging from food and leather goods to household items and clothing, as well as hardware and livestock. The atmosphere here is one of high energy and tremendous bustle as products arrive from around the country and, throughout the day, merchants sing out their wares, customers haggle, and tourists wander in search of great deals. On entering through the main portal on Le Loi Boulevard, general merchandise is on the left. To the right is clothing and textiles. Moving farther in, to the right are dry goods, such as tea, coffee, and spices, as well as packaged foods. Halfway in, fresh foods are on the right, and food stalls, where meals are available, to the left. The eateries here are famous for both quality and price. Since the signage is in English as well as Vietnamese, patrons can point to the posted menu to order.

Well-stocked stall at Ben Thanh Market

For hotels and restaurants see pp236–41 and pp246–53

⑳ Fine Arts Museum

97A Pho Duc Chinh St, District 1.
Map 2 E5. **Tel** (08) 3829 4441.
Open 9am–5pm Tue–Sun.

At first sight, this handsome building, painted a burned yellow with white trim, appears typically French. Built on a large scale, the structure features columns and wrought-ironwork on windows and balconies, all topped with a Chinese-style tiled roof.

Inside, the museum is home to three floors of Vietnamese art, which includes ceramics, lacquerware, sculptures, and oil paintings by Vietnamese and foreign artists. The first floor hosts rotating exhibits of contemporary art. The second floor is given over largely to political art, almost all of it related to the Vietnam War. It displays paintings of some of the leading artists of the country. This floor also has a fine selection of ceramics, mostly of Chinese style or origin. The museum's most interesting collection can be found on the third floor. Cham, Funan, Khmer, Chinese, and Indian works of art are well represented here. On display are many antiques, Óc Eo pottery and sculptures, Chinese objets d'art and wood carvings, and Cham statues. A main highlight is a set of wooden funeral statues from the Central Highlands dating from the early 20th century. Unfortunately, there is little in the way of English signage to help understand the exhibits. Two galleries behind the museum also offer pieces of contemporary art for sale. The museum holds exhibitions by local artists very often. There are quite a few private galleries on the courtyard.

War exhibit displaying helmets of unknown soldiers, Fine Arts Museum

㉑ Nghia An Hoi Quan Pagoda

Stone bust, Fine Arts Museum

678 Nguyen Trai St, Cholon.
Map 4 E4. **Tel** (08) 3853 8775.
Open sunrise–sunset daily.

Renowned for its detailed wood-work and intricate carvings, this pagoda is one of the oldest in Ho Chi Minh City. Built in the 19th century, the temple is dedicated to Quan Cong, a deified Chinese general, and Nghia An, his horse's faithful groom.

On entering, to the left are two of the pagoda's most distinctive features – larger-than-life-size wooden statues of Quan Cong's red horse and Nghia An. Devotees pray at these statues, touching them to collect blessings. Of the two, the horse is considered more sacred. Devotees ring the bell around its neck, and crawl under it to the other side, symbolically wiping up blessings along the way.

To the right is a glass encased altar to Ong Bon, Guardian of Happiness and Virtue. The main sanctuary, entered through wooden folding screen doors, features friezes of a tiger and dragon on either side of the hall. The glass cases behind the main altar have images of Quan Cong and his assistants – Quan Binh, his chief mandarin, on the right, and Chau Xuong, his chief general, on the left. On the 14th day of the 1st lunar month, unicorn, lion and dragon dance groups perform in front of the temple. After the worship takes place, numerous artistic activities commence that last for a few nights. These performances and activities are held to demonstrate the admiration of the Hoa community for Quan Cong.

Vietnam on Film

The setting for more Hollywood films than any country in the region, Vietnam features in more than just war-related movies. The first Hollywood movie set here was *Red Dust* (1932) a romantic drama starring Clark Gable, while both versions of Graham Greene's *The Quiet American*, in 1957 with Audie Murphy and in 2002 with Michael Caine, concentrate on politics and ethics. Of course, war movies do abound, with Francis Ford Coppola's allegorical *Apocalypse Now* (1979) and Oliver Stone's realistic *Platoon* (1986) being two of the best known.

Scene from Oliver Stone's *Platoon*

Beyond Hollywood, Regis Wargnier's *Indochine* (1993) is a sensuous romp through the lives of the privileged in colonial Vietnam. French-Vietnamese director Tran Anh Hung's *Cyclo* (1996) – banned in Vietnam – is a grim look at the seedier side of modern life in Ho Chi Minh City. His *Scent of Green Papaya* (1993), however, is a feast for the eyes.

Cholon Walking Tour

Home to Chinese traders and merchants for more than three centuries, Cholon, which means big market, has long been one of Ho Chi Minh City's most vibrant commercial centers. Also known as District 5, its markets are always busy and brimming with a wide range of specialty shops selling everything from silks, spices, and medicinal herbs to hats, jade curios, and ceramics. With much of the city's vast ethnic Chinese or Hoa community concentrated here, Cholon is a religious hub and home to several Chinese-style pagodas and temples. These striking buildings are concentrated on and around Cholon's main street, Nguyen Trai, which runs through the heart of the area. The narrow streets of this bustling district are best traversed on foot.

Spirals of burning incense, Thien Hau Pagoda *(see p74)*

The electronics market is a one-stop destination for a range of products, such as TVs, toasters, air conditioners, and more.

① Phuoc An Hoi Quan Pagoda
The Fujian community built this pagoda in 1902, dedicating it to Quan Cong. The ancient spears displayed before the main altar represent the cardinal virtues.

TAN HUNG

HUNG VUONG

KY HOÀ

CHAU VAN LIEM

LAO TU

NGUYEN TRAI

LUONG NHU HOC

② Quan Am Pagoda
The only temple complex in the city bisected by a street, this pagoda, also known as Ong Lang, has a colorful façade and an exquisitely detailed ceramic-tiled roof *(see p74)*.

Key

••• Suggested route

③ Thien Hau Pagoda
Perhaps the most outstanding feature of this pagoda is the finely carved frieze along its roof, depicting detailed scenes from Chinese legends *(see p74)*.

0 meters 100
0 yards 100

Locator Map

Trieu Quang Phuc Street
Pungent with the herbs from its numerous traditional Chinese medicine shops, Trieu Quang Phuc is one of Cholon's noisiest and busiest streets.

Tips for the Tour

Tour length: 1 mile (1.6 km).
Stopping off points: Xa Tay Market, next to Cholon Mosque, Trieu Quang Phuc Street, and the electronics market are great places to pick up a range of goods at affordable prices. The stretch on Tran Hung Dao has a number of decent, if expensive, eateries.
Road safety: Traffic can be heavy along Hung Vuong, so take care when walking here.

④ **Nghia An Hoi Quan Pagoda**
Lavishly decorated in red and gold, and embellished with elaborate woodwork, the main altar of Nghia An Hoi Quan is dedicated to Quan Cong, a revered Nguyen lord *(see p71)*.

⑤ **Cholon Mosque**
Built in the early 1930s, this unassuming little mosque has a serene charm. Its modest and simple architecture is in contrast to the ornate pagodas in the area.

⑥ **Tam Son Hoi Quan Pagoda**
Dedicated to Me Sanh, the Goddess of Fertility, this 19th-century pagoda is colorfully decorated, with a number of shrines to various deities. Me Sanh's image graces a small altar at the back of the pagoda, and is worshipped by women hoping to conceive.

HUNG VUONG

KY HOA

TRIEU QUANG PHUC

PHU DONG THIEN VUONG

④

NGUYEN TRAI

⑤

TAN DA

TRAN HUNG DAO

㉒ Thien Hau Pagoda

710 Nguyen Trai St, Cholon. **Map** 4 E4. **Tel** (08) 3855 5322. **Open** sunrise–sunset daily. 🎫 Thien Hau Pagoda Festival (Apr).

Also named Hoi Quan Tue Thanh, but commonly known as Chua Ba, or Lady's Pagoda, this temple is dedicated to Thien Hau, Goddess of the Sea and Patroness of Sailors. Built in the early 1800s by the Cantonese congregation, this is one of the most popular and richly embellished temples in the city. The front courtyard is surrounded by high walls, topped by intricate friezes and carved tableau. The entrance ceiling is more complex, with woodwork and gilt reaching halfway down to the floor.

Inside, the atrium, with its exquisite friezes and reliefs, features giant censers billowing fragrant smoke. The spacious central room has a display case of what seem to be brass clubs with Chinese inscriptions. In fact, these are the nozzles of the fire hoses used to extinguish a fire that threatened the temple in 1898. The walls of this room are covered with prayer flags – red strips of paper on which devotees write their prayers. It is believed that as the breeze rustles the paper, the prayers waft to Thien Hau.

Banks of hanging incense coils grace the main sanctuary ceiling, while three statues of Thien Hau, each flanked by two attendants, preside at the altar. Also hanging from the ceiling is

Quan Am, resplendent in white, Quan Am Pagoda

a carved wooden boat that recalls Thien Hau's connection to the sea. To the right is an image of Long Mau, Goddess of Mothers and Newborns.

㉓ Quan Am Pagoda

12 Lao Tu St, Cholon. **Map** 4 D4. **Tel** (08) 3855 3543. **Open** sunrise–sunset daily.

This pagoda, also known as Ong Lang, was built by Chinese merchants in 1816 and honors Quan Am (or Kwan Yin), the Chinese Goddess of Mercy. The unusual pagoda is set in two parts, separated by a street. On the south side is a small plaza that adjoins a grotto set in a fish and turtle pond, while

Incense pot in Thien Hau Pagoda

the north side houses the main temple complex.

The eye-catching roof and entryway are richly adorned with paintings of saints, gilded scrollwork, and carved wooden panels depicting dragons, houses, people, and scenes from traditional Chinese life and stories. Inside, the first altar is dedicated to the Buddha, and leads into the main sanctuary, featuring two rotating lotus-shaped prayer wheels inset with scores of Buddha images. Devotees make a donation to the temple and can then affix a label with their name onto one of the images. With each turn of the column their prayer is heard.

Next to the main altar is a representation of Quan Am, surrounded by the images of several other deities, including Amida, or the Happy Buddha, who represents the future; A Di Da, the Buddha of the Past; and Thich Ca, the Historical Buddha, Siddhartha. On either side of the altar are small incinerators. Paper money is burnt here for the benefit of departed souls. The pagoda maintains a large and unusual collection of live turtles for good luck. In a courtyard behind the sanctuary are more altars and images of gods and goddesses.

The entire complex is filled with oil lamps and votive candles. The latter are small oil-filled glasses with wicks that are regularly refilled and imbue the air with the fragrance of incense.

The elaborately carved sculptures and ceramic friezes along the roof of Thien Hau Pagoda

For hotels and restaurants see pp236–41 and pp246–53

㉔ Binh Tay Market

Thap Muoi St, Cholon. **Map** 3 C5.
Tel (08) 3857 1512. **Open** 8am–5pm
daily. 🅿 📷 🅦 chobinhtay.gov.vn

The literal translation of *cho lon*
is "big market", and Binh Tay
Market justifies the name. This
grand marketplace is a pagoda-
style tribute to trade. Originally
a small collection of open-air
stalls, a Chinese merchant took
the initiative to build a
permanent structure in 1826.
Over time, it evolved into the
huge emporium it is today.

This yellow building has four
wings joined as a square, with a
courtyard and a fountain in the
middle. A tall clock tower looms
in the center of the complex.
Stacked pagoda-like roofs cover
the bustle of commerce.
Primarily a wholesale market, it
is less touristy than Ben Thanh
Market (*see p70*). A wide range
of items and services are
available here, from medicinal
herbs and imported Chinese
toys, to tailors and mechanics,
and even caged birds.

Tempting sweets in rows of glass jars, Binh
Tay Market

㉕ Phung Son Pagoda

1408 3 Thang 2 St, District 11.
Map 3 B4. **Tel** (08) 3969 3584.
Open sunrise–sunset daily.

Also known as Go Pagoda, the
present complex was built
between 1802 and 1820 on
the remains of an ancient site.
Local lore and, more recently,
archaeological findings suggest

Woman praying before a statue at the
entrance of Phung Son Pagoda

that this was once the site of
a complex belonging to the
Funan Empire (*see p43*).
According to legend,
at one time the
temple was to be
moved to a new
site. But, as
valuables were
loaded upon a white
elephant, the animal
stumbled. This was
taken as an omen for
the pagoda to remain
at its present location.

The complex has the monks'
living quarters, while the main
sanctuary is situated to the left
and contains statues of various
Buddhas. Connected to it is an
atrium with images of Quan
Am, Goddess of Mercy, and the
Buddha, as well as a ceremonial
drum and bronze bell.

Swastika on portico, Giac
Vien Pagoda

㉖ Giac Vien Pagoda

161/35/20 Lac Long Quan St, District
11. **Map** 3 A4. **Open** sunrise–sunset
daily. Dam Sen Water Park: 3 Hoa Binh
St, District 11, **Open** 8:30am–6pm
Mon–Sat, 8am–7pm Sun. 🅿 ♿ 🅿
🅦 damsenwaterpark.com.vn

Established by the monk Hai
Tinh Giac Vien in 1744, this
temple is located on the
outskirts of the city, and is one
of the most peaceful places
around. Well known for its
collection of more than 150

wooden statues, the pagoda
seems to serve mainly as a
dedication to the departed.
Several large, beautifully
carved tombs lie to the right
of the entrance, as do some
photographs of the dead. A
columbarium houses funerary
urns. Although the interior is
dark, strategically placed
apertures in the roof allow the
sunlight to pierce the gloom
with an almost cinematic effect.

The sanctuary's altar is a riot
of several Buddha statues in
varying sizes, some gilded,
others plain wood or ceramic.
A large A Di Da Buddha sits
at the back and two small
Bodhisattvas are perched in
front; more than a dozen sit
between. A stepped conical
structure with a multitude of
small Buddhas on every level
fronts the altar, and is lit by
fairy lights. On either
side of the sanctuary
are cloisters filled
with bonsai trees
and grottos.

Close by is the **Dam
Sen Water Park**, a
welcome diversion,
especially enjoyed
by children. Water
slides and rides, an
artificial river and lake, and
shady rest spots all make for
a fun-filled day. The park also
has landscaped gardens with
lagoons, pagodas and several
unusual animal sculptures.

A large gilded Buddha sits at an altar in the
Giac Vien Pagoda

Reconstruction of a kitchen unit inside the Cu Chi Tunnels

㉗ One Pillar Pagoda of Thu Duc

100 Nyugen Van Bi St, Thu Duc District. **Tel** (08) 3896 0780. **Open** sunrise–sunset daily.

This little pagoda, based on the earlier Lien Phai Pagoda in Hanoi *(see p167)*, was built by monks who fled from there after the country was partitioned in 1954. During the Vietnam War *(see pp48–9)*, the temple was used by the Vietcong as an undercover camp. Despite President Diem's efforts to destroy the pagoda, local support provided by the monks kept the structure safe and intact.

Like its Hanoi counterpart, the building can be seen rising from the middle of a lotus pond. A narrow staircase leads from the pond's edge to the porch-like entrance. The façade has many windows, providing an almost unbroken 360-degree view. The interior is simple, with a low altar.

One Pillar Pagoda emerging from the waters of a lotus pond

㉘ Cu Chi Tunnels

25 miles (40 km) NW of HCMC. 🚌 to Cu Chi town, then by taxi. **Tel** (08) 3794 8820. **Open** 7:30am–5pm daily.

The small town of Cu Chi is famous for its elaborate network of tunnels, located at a distance of around 9 miles (15 km) from the town itself. There are two different tunnel systems here. The one at Ben Dinh village was used by the Vietcong during the Vietnam War. The guided tour begins in a briefing room, where maps and charts display the extent of the network. Following an audio-visual presentation on tunnel history, visitors are led to an area set with faux booby traps and mannequins of Vietcong fighters. Close by are trapdoors that lead down into narrow tunnels. Although these have been widened to accommodate Western visitors, many still find them claustrophobic. Deep down in the depths, the chambers have been restored to the way they might have been at the time of war, with beds, stoves, and caches of ammunition.

The second set of tunnels is at Ben Duoc. Created mainly for tourism purposes, the tunnels here are better equipped than the actual ones used by the Vietcong.

Cu Chi town is known for its shooting galleries, but there is also a memorial pagoda, which features murals and a striking sculpture in the shape of a tear. The rather plain war cemeteries all over the area can be seen from the road.

㉙ Nui Ba Den

66 miles (106 km) NW of HCMC on Hwy 22; 10 miles (15 km) NE of Tay Ninh town. 🚌 to Tay Ninh town, then by taxi. **Tel** (066) 382 6763. 🅿 🖭 🎭 Nui Ba Den Festival (Jun).

There are two major attractions in Tay Ninh province, namely Cao Dai Holy See *(see pp78–9)* and Nui Ba Den or the Black Lady Mountain. Despite the proximity of these sights, few visitors visit Nui Ba Den, as it is off the beaten track and cannot be reached directly by public transport. However, those who do make the trip will find it's worth the effort.

Despite the amusement park atmosphere at the base, the real attraction here is the lovely forest-clad mountain itself. Set amid shimmering lakes and a vibrant green landscape, Nui Ba Den rises above the surrounding plains at a steep 3,235 ft (986 m). The summit boasts stunning views, as well as a shrine to Black Lady, a pious woman named Huong, who died while defending her honor. Those who want the exercise can hike up the mountain to visit the temple, but there is also a chair-lift for those who prefer a more relaxed mode of transport.

Once a Vietcong camp, the mountain was bombed and sprayed with deadly chemicals during the Vietnam War. Today, its caves, used as Buddhist sanctuaries, have regained their beauty. Each year, a festival honors the spirit of Nui Ba Den, with offerings, singing, and dancing.

A large, rotund statue holding a cigarette at the base of Nui Ba Den

Tunnel Complexes

Elaborate tunnel complexes, such as those at Cu Chi and Vinh Moc *(see p154)*, have been used by the Vietnamese for centuries. The tunnels were a key part of guerilla warfare during the Vietnam War *(see pp48–9)*, and played a major role in defeating American soldiers. Claimed to extend more than 125 miles (201 km), the tunnels were dug by local people using shovels. Built at many levels, they had living spaces, kitchens, and clinics. Here, the Vietnamese could escape bombings, hide from the enemy, and mount surprise attacks. The American soldiers knew of the tunnels, and used infrared imaging and sniffer dogs in their search for them. They never quite succeeded in finding them since the tunnels were rerouted and enlarged to avoid detection.

Anatomy of the Tunnel System

While most tunnels were fairly small and simple, the major ones had three levels, and could be up to 33 ft (10 m) deep. Nonetheless, they were hot, cramped, and damp, making life underground difficult and unbearable.

Tunnel entrances were so small and well camouflaged with leaves and branches that they were often invisible to enemy eyes. One method attempted by the Americans to find them was by using stethoscopes to listen to subterranean activity.

"Tunnel rats" was the nickname given to the special teams of US soldiers deployed for entering and disabling the tunnels. They wore masks as protection when releasing gases in the tunnels to drive out the Vietnamese.

A cooking area used highly creative ways to keep smoke from rising to the surface.

Bunker for strategy and planning

Well-hidden firing posts helped the Vietnamese shoot at the enemy and then disappear.

Underwater entrance

The infirmary was not only a place to treat the wounded; many babies were also born here.

Ammunition dump

Air-raid shelters, located at the lowest level of the tunnels, protected the Vietnamese from intense bombing.

Cramped and narrow passageways were made as tight and constricted as possible so that the larger American soldiers would find it difficult to pass through the tunnels.

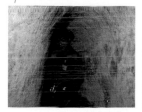

Ingenious booby traps, using everything from bamboo and iron staves to explosives, made the tunnels potential death traps for the unwary.

⑳ Cao Dai Holy See

As the center of Cao Dai religion, which was founded in 1926 (*see p27*), this vast complex draws nearly three million worshippers. The main attraction here is the Great Divine Temple – a massive structure that reflects an unusual mix of Asian and European architectural elements. Amid the vibrant pinks, greens, and yellows of the decor are carvings of writhing serpents and dragons, and a multitude of Divine Eyes gazing from all directions. The prayer services, attended by hundreds of clergy in colorful robes, are held everyday and are a spectacular sight.

Colorful dragon motifs adorn the temple's columns

Maitreya Buddha
Dominating the central tower of the temple's front façade is a statue of the Buddha, reflecting the Cao Dai reverance for Buddhism.

Prayer Hall
This long and garishly colored hall is split into nine levels, representing the nine steps to heaven. Elaborately carved columns and windows featuring the Divine Eye line the passage on either side.

KEY

① **Intricate carvings adorn the pillars**

② **Statues of the Cao Dai pantheon**, including Jesus, the Buddha, and Confucius, dominate the area above the altar.

③ **Prayer hall**

✎ Tomb of Ho Phap

★ Altar of the Eye
The all-seeing Divine Eye, the symbol of Cao Dai, is painted on a large, star-speckled blue globe that adorns the main altar. Decorated with clouds and stars, the dome above represents the achievement of heaven.

VISITORS' CHECKLIST

Practical Information
Long Hoa Village, 2.5 miles (4 km) E of Tay Ninh; 59 miles (96 km) NW of HCMC.
🛈 Tay Ninh Tourist, 210B 30 Thang 4 St, Tay Ninh, (066) 382 2376. **Open** daily. Services: 6am, noon, 6pm, midnight.

★ Phan Cong Tac
One of the founders of Cao Daism, Phan Cong Tac was the chief medium, with the ability to communicate with the holy spirits during seances.

★ The Three Saints
A mural depicts the three Cao Dai saints, Chinese leader Sun Yat Sen, French poet Victor Hugo, and Vietnamese poet Nguyen Binh Khiem as earthly signatories to "Third Alliance Between God and Man."

Vibrant Architecture
The combination of bright colors, ornate carvings, dragon and lotus motifs, and other highly varied elements make this temple one of Vietnam's most photographed structures.

Great Divine Temple

The spiritual centerpiece of the Cao Dai complex, this temple was built between 1933 and 1955. Its vividly decorated three-tiered roof, stained-glass windows, and kaleidoscope of colors make for an unusual, striking building. The presence of the all-seeing Divine Eye represents supreme knowledge and wisdom.

Plan of Cao Dai Holy See

Key
☐ Area illustrated

Key List of Sites
① Great Divine Temple
② Holy Mother's Temple
③ Tomb of Ho Phap
④ Amphitheater
⑤ Meditation Room
⑥ Public Works
⑦ Weaving House
⑧ Information Hall
⑨ Pope's Office
⑩ Lady Cardinal's Office

Fishing boats at Vung Tau harbor, against a scenic mountain backdrop

① Vung Tau

81 miles (130 km) E of HCMC on
Hwy 51. 🗺 250,000. 🚁 helicopter
from HCMC. 🚌 🚢 hydrofoil from
HCMC. 🛈 Vung Tau Tourist, 33 Tran
Hung Dao St, (064) 385 6445.
🇼 vungtautourist.com.vn Bach
Dinh Museum: 4 Tran Phu St. **Tel** (064)
385 2605. **Open** 7–11:30am, 1:30–
5pm daily. 🗺

The peninsula town of Vung Tau
was once a pristine beach
resort, known by the French as
Cap St Jacques. It is still a very
popular seaside getaway, but
now that it is developed and
home to an offshore oil industry,
the quality of the water and
beaches has been somewhat
affected. On weekends it is
crowded, noisy, and expensive.
During the week, however, it is
quieter, and its proximity to Ho
Chi Minh City makes it a
convenient beach destination.
    The two main beaches here
are **Bai Truoc** (Front Beach) on
the west and the long and wide
Bai Sau (Back Beach) on the
east side of the South China Sea
peninsula. Bai Truoc has the
greater concentration of hotels,
bars, and restaurants,
while Bai Sau is less
developed, and
therefore cheaper
and a much
quieter place
to stay.
    In the vicinity
of Vung Tau, two
promontories,
Nui Lon (Big Mountain) and **Nui
Nho** (Little Mountain), are both
worth visiting for splendid views.
Nui Nho features a giant statue

of Jesus; visitors can climb up to
the top in order to take in the
scenery. Alternatively, take a cable
car to the top of Nui Lon. **Vung
Tau Lighthouse**, located about
a mile from the ferry landing also
offers a superb vantage point.
    The local museum, **Bach
Dinh**, or White Villa, was the
residence of Emperor Thanh
Thai while he was under house
arrest by the French. Inside are
many interesting exhibits from
the Chinese Qing Dynasty. The
relics on display were salvaged
from a 17th-century shipwreck.

② Long Hai

81 miles (130 km) E of HCMC on Hwy
19; 30 miles (40 km) NE of Vung Tau.
🚌 from HCMC. 🛈 Vung Tau Tourist,
33 Tran Hung Dao St, (064) 385 6445.
🎭 Fisherman's Festival (Feb/Mar).

While the two cities grew, the
stretch of coastline between
Vung Tau and Phan Thiet was
virtually deserted but a number
of large resorts have now taken
up residence. Home to the
small town of Long Hai, this
area is now rather exagge-
ratedly referred to as Vietnam's
Riviera. Nonetheless, the
beaches are
relatively
unspoiled,
prices are low,
seafood is fresh,
and the atmosphere
is very relaxed.
    A point of interest near
Long Hai is the **Mo Co
Temple**, where
hundreds of boats
from all over the

**Distinctive fishing
boat, Long Hai**

region converge during the
Fisherman's Festival. Farther
east is one of Bao Dai's villas,
now the posh Anoasis Resort
(see p237). The beach is private,
but a small fee allows full use of
its facilities for the day. Although
there is no direct public transport
or hydrofoil from Vung Tau, the
drive to Long Hai offers many
worthwhile sights. A predominantly Catholic area, several
charming churches line the
highway, as do a number of
interesting temples.

③ Ho Coc Beach

118 miles (190 km) E of HCMC; 22
miles (36 km) NE of Long Hai. 🚗 🖥

Ho Coc Beach's relative
seclusion is its best feature.
While popular with the
Vietnamese as a weekend
destination, there is little
public transport, only a few
accommodation options, and
a handful of simple cafés and
restaurants. The beach is superb,
with miles of clean, white sand,
studded here and there with
massive boulders.

Environs
Ho Coc lies adjacent to the **Binh
Chau - Phuoc Buu Nature
Reserve**. The trees come right
up to the beach, and several
trails leading into the wooded
area start from the sand itself.
The preserve was once home
to many large animals, but
most have now been relocated
for conservation and safety
purposes. Nevertheless, the

Thatched shelter on a rock in the sands of
Ho Coc Beach

Choppy South China Sea washing over large boulders, Ho Coc Beach

preserve is still inhabited by several species of monkeys and birds. The greenery and tranquil surroundings are extremely soothing. Guides may be hired for walking tours for a small fee.

❸❹ Binh Chau Hot Springs

93 miles (150 km) SE of HCMC, 31 miles (50 km) NE of Long Hai. ℹ Binh Chau Hot Springs Resort, (064) 387 1131. 🛇 🛇 🖵

With more than a hundred natural hot springs reputed to be imbued with therapeutic properties, Binh Chau is not frequented merely by the rheumatic and arthritic. Although the mineral-rich mud and hot springs are obviously the main attractions here, the place is an amusement center as well.

The Binh Chau Hot Springs Resort here is now a popular holiday destination, boasting a karaoke bar, tennis courts, and snooker tables. Public and private facilities for hot spring baths are on offer as well. The private baths are enclosed by wooden screens for dressing and overhead coverings for shade. These can accommodate two to ten people, and incur a higher charge than the public facilities. The public baths have a swimming pool. The water averages 40 degrees C (86 degrees F) though some pools can reach a boiling 87 degrees C (189 degrees F). As entertainment, baskets of eggs are available for dunking into the pools to cook. People

can boil eggs in the hot springs as well. Large statues of chickens indicate the spots where such a venture is possible. For a relaxing spa experience, therapeutic mud baths are also on offer here.

Amid the springs are verdant marshlands. There are also some well-marked walking trails in the area where visitors can take a stroll.

People boiling baskets of eggs, Binh Chau Hot Springs

❸❺ Cat Tien National Park

100 miles (160 km) NE of HCMC. 🚌 from HCMC. **Tel** (061) 366 9228. 🅿️ 🛇 🛇 🖵 🅦 namcattien.org

Cat Tien is easily one of the most abundant, biologically diverse reserves of its kind. This is remarkable in light of the fact that it was subjected to sustained bombardment by defoliants during the Vietnam War. Even further back in time, it was a place of pilgrimage, as evidenced by the discovery of ancient religious artifacts traced to both the Funan and Champa Empires (see p43).

Today, this 277 sq miles (718 sq km) park is home to a wide range of flora and fauna. There are more than 1,600 varieties of plants, but new ones continue to be discovered. The park where the now-extinct Javan rhinoceros lived continues to be the home of many other animals, including deer, elephants, and over 360 species of birds that attract bird-watchers from all over the world. Colonies of monkeys, including rare douc langurs, populate the trees, while 440 species of butterfly flutter amid wildflowers. Not surprisingly, Cat Tien is one of the most popular adventure destinations in Vietnam. Accommodations in the park are minimal but adequate, and are reached by crossing the Dong Nai River.

Javan Rhinoceros

Of the huge number of species of fauna in Cat Tien National Park, few garnered as much concern as the Javan rhinoceros (Rhinoceros sondaicus). These magnificent beasts that once roamed the forests in large numbers, were nearly hunted out of existence in colonial times. Smaller in size than most rhinos, its skin was very pale, as a result of living under the thick tropical canopy. Sadly, the last Javan rhino was killed by poachers in Cat Tien National Park in 2010, and the species is officially extinct in the country. Vietnam is at the forefront of illegal trade in rhino horn which has led to the problem of rhino poaching in the country.

The rare Javan rhinoceros

HO CHI MINH CITY STREET FINDER

Finding your way around the narrow streets and winding alleys of Ho Chi Minh City can be a challenging experience. The city is divided into 19 *quan*, or urban districts, and five suburban districts. Vietnamese addresses *(see p279)* are usually straightforward but they are more complicated in Ho Chi Minh City because the same street begins new numbering upon entering a new district. On the Street Finder, some words that are common in street names have been abbreviated, such as Nguyen, which appears as Ng. Note that in the south *duong*, meaning street, is usually added to the road name. *Pho* is added to the street name in the north.

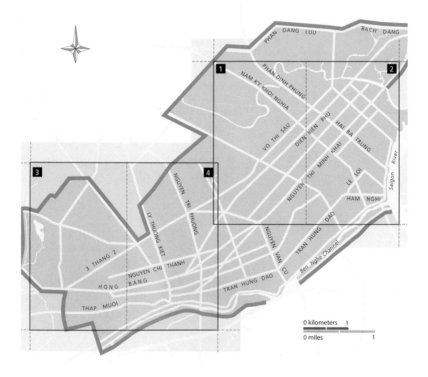

0 kilometers	1
0 miles	1

Scale of Maps 1–2, 3–4

0 meters	500
0 yards	500

Key to Street Finder

- Major sight
- Other sight
- Other building
- 🚊 Train station
- 🚌 Long-distance bus station
- 🛥 Riverboat pier

- 𝒊 Tourist information
- ✚ Hospital
- 🛕 Pagoda/temple
- ✝ Church
- ☪ Mosque

Street Finder Index

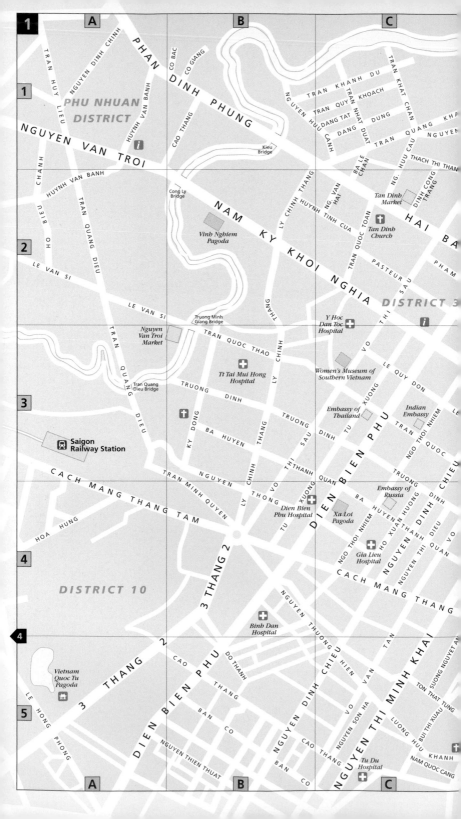

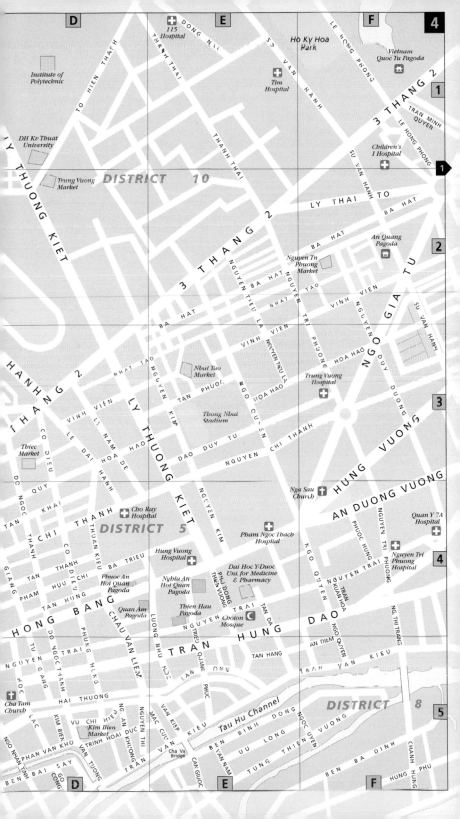

MEKONG DELTA AND SOUTHERN VIETNAM

Life on the delta revolves around the Mekong River, with its green expanses of paddy fields, thick orchards, and intricate patchwork of canals. Floating houses, markets, and fishing boats bob on the rivers, while the islands boast dense forests and beautiful white-sand beaches. Amid the bells, drums, and chanting of the delta's many pagodas, an ancient way of life continues well into the 21st century.

With its origins on the high plateau of Tibet, the mighty Mekong River meanders along for 2,800 miles (4,500 km), gathering silt from China, Myanmar, Thailand, Laos, and Cambodia, before splitting into the distributaries that give the region the name Song Cuu Long or the River of Nine Dragons. These tentacled waterways bestow Vietnam's southern plain with rich alluvial soil that has made it a "rice basket," as well as a "fruit basket" filled with coconut, longan, and mango trees.

The delta has long been laid claim to by Cambodia, and in 1978, the Khmer Rouge orchestrated a savage massacre at numerous villages. Nevertheless, the delta and its people are extremely resilient, having survived the ravages of frequent floods, French and Cambodian occupation, many bombings, and the devastating effects of the chemical defoliant, Agent Orange. Despite this legacy of conflict and upheaval, life on the delta ebbs and flows to an age-old rhythm. Through necessity and tradition, the physical boundaries between land and water are transcended by farmers who row across canals that crisscross their emerald fields. In contrast, commercial towns such as Can Tho and Rach Gia are hurtling towards modernization. Everywhere, however, are attractive Khmer, Vietnamese, and Chinese-style pagodas that reflect the delta's ethnic diversity.

Nature is a major part of the delta's draw. Ha Tien's beaches feature white sand and towering limestone karsts, while the marshland around Bac Lieu is home to a variety of migratory birds. Off Vietnam's southern shore lie Phu Quoc and Con Dao Islands, which boast national parks and are both fast becoming popular as ecotourism destinations.

Lush vegetation overhangs the waterways of Mekong delta

◄ The floating market of Soc Trang in Mekong delta

Exploring Mekong Delta and Southern Vietnam

The Mekong Delta is a unique region where life on the water has remained unchanged for centuries. Closest to Ho Chi Minh City, My Tho is known as a launching pad for boat tours, as is Vinh Long, which lies to its south. Can Tho, the delta's largest city has several lively floating markets in its vicinity. To see some floating architecture, head to Chau Doc, where most people live and work on the water. Khmer culture is prominent in Soc Trang and Tra Vinh, while nature lovers will delight in Con Dao National Park. The shores of Phu Quoc Island boast beautiful coral reefs, and Ha Tien offers secluded beaches.

Well-stocked fruit stall at a local market, Ben Tre *(see p93)*

Sights at a Glance

Towns and Cities

1 My Tho
3 Ben Tre
4 Tra Vinh
5 Vinh Long
6 Cao Lanh
7 Can Tho
8 Soc Trang
9 Bac Lieu
11 Rach Gia
12 Chau Doc
13 Ha Tien

Islands

2 Phoenix Island
10 Con Dao Islands
14 Phu Quoc Island

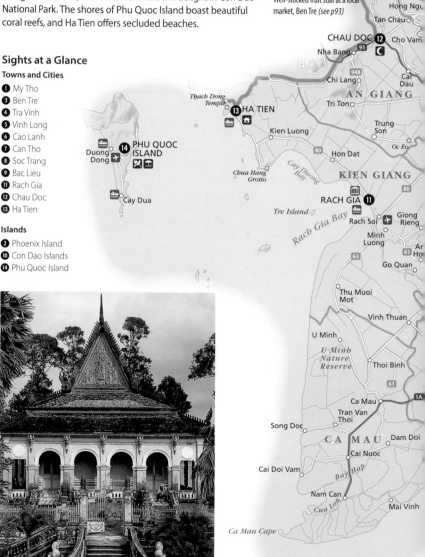

Colonnaded façade of the Khmer-style Ong Met Pagoda, Tra Vinh *(see p93)*

For hotels and restaurants see pp236–41 and pp246–53

Farmers in conical hats harvesting rice in a paddy field

Sa Rai

Vinh Hung

Tan Hung

Moc Hoa

Dong Thanh

Hau Nghia

Duc Hoa

Ho Chi Minh City

Tram Chim

Thanh Hoa

LONG AN

Thanh Hoa

Thu Thua

Ben Luc

Tan An

Can Duoc

DONG THAP

Thanh Binh

Tan Thanh

My An

Tan Thanh

6 CAO LANH

TIEN GIANG

Cai Lay

Dong Tam Snake Farm

1 MY THO

Go Cong

Long Xuyen

Cai Lay

Cai Be

PHOENIX ISLAND 2

Vinh Binh

Tan Hoa

Sa Dec

5 VINH LONG

Cua Tieu

My Tho

ot Not

3 BEN TRE

BEN TRE

Co Do

O Mon

VINH LONG

Vung Liem

Mo Cay

Giong Trom

Binh Dai

Thoi Lai

Cai Rang

7 CAN THO

Cang Long

Ba Tri

CAN THO

Tra On

TRA VINH 4

Thanh Phu

Vi Thanh

Phung Hiep

Tieu Can

Hang Pagoda

Chau Thanh

Cau Ngang

lang Mau

Ke Sach

Cau Quan

TRA VINH

Long My

SOC TRANG

Tra Cu

Ba Dong

Ngan Dua

SOC TRANG 8

Long Phu

Duyen Hai

Phuoc Long

Phu Loc

My Xuyen

Chau Thanh

Huynh Ky

BAC LIEU

Hoa Binh

Vinh Chau

Gia Rai

9 BAC LIEU

Ho Phong

Bac Lieu Bird Sanctuary

Ganh Hao

Getting Around

Once considered a remote backwater, the Mekong Delta now has airports in Can Tho, Con Dao, Rach Gia, and Phu Quoc. While highways are quite reliable, rural roads usually offer bumpy rides in erratically scheduled buses. Many travel agents in the delta and in Ho Chi Minh City organize trips throughout the south by coach and car. However, the best way to experience the delta is by boat. With more than 1,740 miles (2,800 km) of canals, the waterway system is very well developed. The public transportation system is adequate although private boat tours offer more comfort. Bicycles and motorbikes are available to rent everywhere.

Key

- ▬▬ Highway
- ═══ Major road
- ▬ Minor road
- ▬▬ International border
- ▬▬ Provincial border

Con Dao

10

CON DAO ISLANDS

0 kilometers 25

0 miles 25

❶ My Tho

Road Map B6. 45 miles (72 km) SW of HCMC on Hwy 1. 🚍 230,000. 🚌 from HCMC. 🛥 ℹ️ Tien Giang Tourist, 8, 30 Thang 4 St, (073) 387 3184.

Because of its proximity to Ho Chi Minh City, My Tho, on the northernmost tributary of the Mekong River, is the most popular day-trip destination in the delta. It is an ideal base from which to hire a boat and cruise along the canals, stopping along the way to explore the surrounding islands.

A stroll through My Tho's wide tree-lined boulevards and waterfront market is almost a walk back in time. Wooden boats and barges crowd the shore, as vendors sell an impressive array of goods, from food to hardware and domestic items such as the giant earthenware urns used for bathing. The pungent aroma of dried fish and the fragrance of pineapple and jackfruit fill the air.

In addition to commerce, My Tho is also a religious center, with **Vinh Trang Pagoda** being one of its most noteworthy edifices. The temple's façade is embellished with mosaics made from broken pottery, a custom followed throughout Southeast Asia. Lily ponds and stone tombs surround the beautiful complex, and an image of the Buddhist goddess Quan Am is set into the heart of a banyan tree.

Blackened funerary urn resting on a tortoise sculpture, Phoenix Island

Serving the city's large population of Christians, **My Tho Church** functions both as a diocese and a Catholic school. Originally established in the 19th century, the current massive yellow building, with a high-vaulted ceiling and a red-tile roof, sits on sprawling grounds that are covered with trees and shrubs.

A short distance northwest of My Tho is the small but historically significant hamlet of **Ap Bac**. This was the site of the battle which resulted in the first major victory of the Vietcong against the US-backed South Vietnamese army in 1963.

🏯 **Vinh Trang Pagoda**
60 Nguyen Trung Truc St. **Tel** (073) 387 3427. **Open** 9–11:30am, 1:30–5pm daily.

⛪ **My Tho Church**
32 Hung Vuong St. **Tel** (073) 388 0075. **Open** 7am–6pm daily. ♿

Coconut Monk

The given name of the Coconut Monk was Nguyen Thanh Nam (1909–90). A student of chemistry, he eventually discarded the trappings of comfort and dedicated himself to meditation and abstinence. Subsisting on a diet of coconuts and water, he even started a religion, Tinh Do Cu Si, a whimsical blend of Buddhism and Christianity. He challenged the authorities on how to reunify the nation and restore peace after its partition in 1954, and often ended up in jail because of his views. His bizarre headquarters on Phoenix Island remain his most enduring legacy.

❷ Phoenix Island

Road Map B6. 2 miles (3 km) from My Tho. 🛥 🛥 Sanctuary: **Open** 8:30–11am, 1:30–6pm daily. 🚣

Midway between My Tho and Ben Tre are numerous small islands, the best known among them being Con Phung or Phoenix Island. This was the lonely bastion of the Coconut Monk. On this small spot of dry land, he built his odd little temple complex. On a circular base, about 75 ft (25 m) in diameter, are several free-standing blue-and-gold dragon columns, supporting nothing but the air above them. Nearby is a lattice-work structure that rather resembles a roller coaster. This is flanked by minarets and the monk's impression of a moon rocket. On the upriver side, a huge funerary urn lies on the back of a giant tortoise

The handsome mosaic-embellished façade of Vinh Trang Pagoda, My Tho

Blue-and-gold dragon columns on the Coconut Monk's Phoenix Island

sculpture. A small coconut candy factory operates on the perimeter of the island.

Neighboring Phoenix Island are several little islands, which make good venues for picnics. These include Con Tan Long or Dragon Island, home to beekeepers and boatwrights *(see p94)*; Thoi Son or Unicorn Island, full of narrow canals that irrigate lush longan orchards; and Con Qui or Tortoise Island, known for its coconut candy and potent banana liquor. Pineapples, jackfruit, and mangoes are also grown here in abundance. Each of these islands is served by a scheduled ferry.

Carved pillar, Phoenix Island

❸ Ben Tre

Road Map B6. 53 miles (86 km) SW of HCMC; 9 miles (14 km) S of My Tho. 🚌 116,000. 🚍 from HCMC. 🚤 from My Tho. 🛈 Ben Tre Tourist, 65 Dong Khoi St, (075) 382 9618.

Being off the tourist trail, Ben Tre does not get as many visitors as other delta cities, thus providing a rare glimpse into an ancient river town still living by its traditional ways.

The capital of Ben Tre Province, this town is famous in Vietnam for its coconut candy, and is lush with vast plantations yielding huge amounts of coconuts. To make the candy, the fruit's milk and flesh are boiled down to a sticky mass that is allowed to harden, then

cut into small pieces and wrapped in edible rice paper. The process is fascinating to watch and the results delicious to taste.

A "country" market in every sense of the word, the central market offers little finery, with preference given to hardware, lengths of cloth, and food. However, the most interesting stalls belong to the fishmongers, who sell a variety of fresh and dried fish.

A notable religious site in Ben Tre is **Vien Minh Pagoda**. Established around 1900, it is now the head office of the provincial Buddhist association. The sparse interior is enlivened by colorful wall hangings and images sporting neon halos.

📷 Vien Minh Pagoda

156 Nguyen Dinh Chieu St. **Tel** (075) 381 3931. **Open** sunrise–sunset daily.

❹ Tra Vinh

Road Map B6. 62 miles (100 km) W of Can Tho. 🚌 122,000. 🚍 from Vinh Long and Can Tho. 🛈 Tra Vinh Tourist Office, 64–66 Le Loi St, (074) 385 8556.

With its large Khmer, Christian, and Chinese population, Tra Vinh is distinguished by the diversity of its places of worship. Of the many Khmer-style religious buildings, **Ong Met Pagoda** is distinctive for its portico posts surmounted by four-faced images of the Buddha. The 10-ft (3-m) tall gilded *stupas*, mound-shaped reliquary monuments, are dedicated to deceased monks. One of the most vibrant Chinese pagodas in town is

Ong Pagoda, which was consecrated in 1556 and dedicated to the deified Chinese general Quan Cong of the 3rd century. The pagoda is known for its wildly colorful rear courtyard, one wall of which is engraved with red dragons disporting themselves between a range of blue mountains and a green sea. An interesting highlight is a fish pond where richly painted sculpted carp are shown in mid-leap as they break through the surface. These are all the works of Le Van Chot, who has a sculpture studio on the grounds.

However, it is the **Tra Vinh Church** that captures the spirit of the town's religious eclecticism best. Although the exterior of the building has a colonial-style design, a close examination of the eaves reveals "dragon flames," typically seen on Khmer-style temples.

Environs

About 3 miles (6 km) south of town, **Hang Pagoda** is a simple structure. Its main attraction is the hundreds of storks that nest here. The **Khmer Minority People's Museum** has some interesting exhibits but there is no English signage. While household items, costumes, and jewelry are self-explanatory, religious items might need a guide. The museum is located beside the tree-ringed **Ba Om Pond**, about 4 miles (7 km) southwest of Tra Vinh, which is ideal for picnics. The **Ang Pagoda** also lies close by. The age of the present building is uncertain, but it has been a religious site since the 11th century. A pride of sculpted lions guard the entry, flanked by murals depicting the Buddha's life.

Detail of statue, Ong Met Pagoda

🏛 Khmer Minority People's Museum

4 miles (7 km) SW of town on 3 SEB Luong Hoa St. **Tel** (074) 384 2188. **Open** 7.30–11.30am, 1:30–4:30pm daily.

Vendors in sampans at the early morning Cai Be Floating Market

❺ Vinh Long

Road Map B6. 84 miles (136 km) SW of HCMC; 46 miles (74 km) SW of My Tho. 🚋 145,000. 🚌 🚆 ℹ️ Cuu Long Tourist, 1 Thang 5 St, (070) 382 3616.

A small town on the bank of the Co Chien River, Vinh Long is mostly used by tourists as a base for exploring the islets dotting the waters around it. However, the town itself is also worth visiting. Vinh Long's large, French-Colonial Catholic church draws attention to the fact that the area was once an important target for Christian missionaries. On the outskirts of town, **Van Thanh Mieu Temple** is a simple yet elegant structure, which was dedicated to Confucius in 1866. In 1930, a new building was added to it in honor of Phan Thanh Gian, who led a rebellion against the French.

Boat tours are a popular way to take in the dramatic sweep of the river and the charm of the offshore islands, most of which boast lovely flower gardens. **An Binh** and **Binh Hoa Phuoc** are popular amongst visitors as idyllic picnic spots. Just north of the ferry landing at An Binh, is the outwardly unassuming **Tien Chau Pagoda**. Inside, however, are startlingly lurid murals depicting the horrors of Buddhist Hell. In this scary vision, perdition for the lapsed includes being trampled by horses, devoured by serpents, and decomposing eternally.

Surrounded by orchards, sampans, and monkey bridges, the boatwrights, candymakers, beekeepers, and artisans ply their trades. The rhythm of life on the delta is fascinating, and Vinh Long is an ideal place to experience it. Homestays (see p234), where visitors can eat, sleep, and work with a local family, are highly recommended.

Environs

Floating markets are common throughout the delta. **Cai Be Floating Market**, about an hour from Vinh Long by boat, is the easiest to reach. Open in the early morning, it is both a wholesale and a retail market, with large boats selling to merchants and small boats serving householders. Traders maneuver their boats agilely, loading fruit, coffee, and even hot noodles from one boat to another.

🏯 **Van Thanh Mieu Temple**
2 miles (3 km) S of town on Tran Phu Rd. **Tel** (070) 383 0174. **Open** 8am–sunset daily.

❻ Cao Lanh

Road Map B6. 100 miles (162 km) from HCMC. 🚋 170,000. 🚌 ℹ️ Dong Thap Tourist, 2 Doc Binh Kieu St, (067) 385 5637.

Although the town itself is not remarkable, the drive to Chau Doc (see p104) via Cao Lanh is pleasant. The **Dong Thap Museum**, which displays many of the traditional implements used by delta farmers and fishermen, including a large model of a boat and fish traps (see p103), is a worthwhile stop. The Soviet-style **War Memorial** is a big clam-shell structure, festooned with hammers, sickles, and flags. The cemetery at the memorial is filled with the graves of Vietcong soldiers. A mile southwest of town is **Nguyen Sinh Sac Tomb**, a memorial to Ho Chi Minh's father, surrounded by plaques stating his revolutionary credentials.

Statue in Dong Thap Museum

Environs

Stretching to the north of Cao Lanh, the rich swamplands of Dong Thap Muoi, or Plain of Reeds, are home to many birds. The **Tram Chim National Park**, 28 miles (45 km) northwest of town, once drew legions of birdwatchers who braved the long boat ride to see the red-headed cranes here. The red-headed crane can be spotted from December to May only and is becoming increasingly rare to sight. **Vuon Co Thap Muoi**, about 27 miles (44 km) northeast of Cao Lanh, is home to many white storks.

Southeast of Cao Lanh, the Rung Tram Forest once housed a hidden Vietcong base of resistance, **Xeo Quyt**. This restricted site can be reached by a 30-minute boat ride after seeking permission from the tourist office.

🏛️ **Dong Thap Museum**
162 Nguyen Thai Hoc St. **Tel** (067) 385 1342. **Open** 7–11am, 1–4pm daily.

🏛️ **War Memorial**
Off Hwy 30 at the eastern edge of town. **Open** daily.

Boatwrights of the Mekong Delta

Boats awaiting completion at a dock

The boatwright's craft is perhaps the oldest in the delta. Without it, there could be no transport, trade, and indeed, no homes for many. This skill is mastered by learning from family members who pass on age-old instructions, a few rules of thumb, and a few specialized tools. Often, when prized boats become decrepit, boatwrights dismantle them piece by piece to create exact replicas. Thus, any boat seen on the delta could be the descendant of one that looked identical nearly 500 years ago.

For hotels and restaurants see pp236–41 and pp246–53

Vinh Long Boat Tour

Possibly the best way of experiencing the timeless, bucolic character of the Mekong Delta is by taking a boat ride along the dense network of narrow canals around Vinh Long. Making its way through the small islands of An Binh and Binh Hoa Phuoc, the tour offers a close look at life on the river. Thatched houses sit amid luxuriant orchards and gardens interlaced with the sights and sounds of a colorful and bustling floating market.

Church looming over the shore near Cai Be Floating Market

① **Vinh Long** Surrounded by a complex patchwork of canals and several islets, Vinh Long is almost an island itself. Situated on the banks of the Co Chien River, it is an ideal base for exploring the region.

② **Cai Be Floating Market**
This lively market is packed with vendors selling a range of goods on boats. The best time to visit is in the early morning as the market disappears by noon. A small church on the nearby shore forms a scenic backdrop.

③ **Dong Phu**
A tiny village of farmers, orchardists, and boatmen, Dong Phu has barely changed over the centuries.

④ **Hoa Ninh** Reachable only by boat and a footbridge, Hoa Ninh is known for its flower gardens filled with jasmine plants, as well as apricot, mango, and longan trees.

⑤ **Binh Hoa Phuoc Village**
Located on an island by the same name, this small village is known for its bonsai orchards, and offers cozy homestay facilities as well.

0 kilometers 3
0 miles 3

⑥ **Fruit Orchards at An Binh**
The thriving orchards on this island nurture an impressive variety of fruits, including longan, jackfruit, rose apple, and uglifruit, a citrus that tastes far better than it looks.

Tips for Tourists

Length: 3 to 6 hours.
Boat rentals: Visitors can easily rent boats via Cuu Long Tourist, or book a tour through agents in Ho Chi Minh City. Private boats may be hired at the risk of incurring a fine.
Stopping-off points: Binh Hoa Phuoc Village is an ideal place to stop for a quick and tasty meal.

Tourist enjoying a boatride in the Mekong delta region ▶

❼ Can Tho

The largest city on the delta, Can Tho is one of the most delightful destinations in the south. Bordering six provinces, it serves as a transportation hub for the region, as well as a major agricultural center, with rice milling as its main industry. The city is also an ideal base for day trips, especially to the floating markets – the highlight of a visit here. Within Can Tho, the Central Market, known for its fresh produce and river fish; the Can Tho Museum; and the Khmer Munirangsyaram Temple are all worth seeing.

VISITORS' CHECKLIST

Practical Information
Road Map B6. 105 miles (169 km) SW of HCMC. 🚉 1,300,000. ⛴
🎪 Binh Thuy Temple Festival (Jan, May).

Transport
✈ 10 km S. 🚌 ⛴ ℹ Can Tho Tourist, 50 Hai Ba Trung St, (0710) 382 4221.

🏛 Ong Pagoda
32 Hai Ba Trung St. **Tel** (0710) 382 3862.
Devotees come to this small pagoda to pray before Than Tai, God of Fortune, and Quan Am, Goddess of Mercy. To ensure their prayers are heard, they often pay the temple calligrapher to pen their prayers onto scrolls and hang them on the wall. Several richly decorated urns burn constantly.

🏛 Can Tho Museum
1 Hoa Binh St. **Tel** (0710) 382 0955.
Open 8–11am, 2–5pm Tue–Thu; 8–11am, 6:30–9pm Sat–Sun.
This excellent museum illustrates life in Vietnam. Exhibits in this museum include a traditional teahouse, a life-like tableau of a herbalist tending to a patient, and various artifacts.

🏛 Munirangsyaram Temple
36 Hoa Binh St. **Tel** (0710) 381 6022.
Open 8am–5pm daily.
An Angkor-like tower rises over this Khmer Theravada Buddhist temple. Inside, Doric columns blend beautifully with Asian features, such as seated Buddhas and ceramic lotuses.

Floating Markets
Can Tho is central to at least two floating markets, all providing a glimpse into a unique commercial culture. Traders paddle from boat to boat, selling a variety of goods amid a traffic jam of sampans.

The morning market of **Cai Rang** is the closest and largest, located just 4 miles (7 km) southwest of the city. A bridge nearby offers great views, but nothing compares to exploring the market by boat. A farther 9 miles (14 km) west, **Phong Dien** market possesses an endearing simplicity. Sampans can be rented for both these markets from the riverfront off Hai Ba Trung Street or from local tour operators. About 32 miles (52 km) north of Can Tho is located the **Bang Lang Stork Garden**, a sanctuary for storks. The trees here attract thousands of storks each evening; a wonderful sight as they settle down to roost.

Fresh vegetables for sale at the Cai Rang morning market

Can Tho

① Central Market
② Ho Chi Minh Statue
③ Ong Pagoda
④ Can Tho Museum
⑤ Munirangsyaram Temple

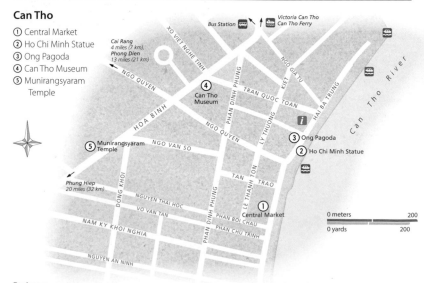

Bus Station 🚌

Victoria Can Tho / Can Tho Ferry

Cai Rang 4 miles (7 km), Phong Dien 13 miles (21 km)

XO VIET NGHE TINH

NGO QUYEN

HOA BINH

NGO GIA TU

TRAN QUOC TOAN

KIET

PHAN DINH PHUNG

NGO QUYEN

LY THUONG

HAI BA TRUNG

④ Can Tho Museum

⑤ Munirangsyaram Temple

NGO VAN SO

③ Ong Pagoda
② Ho Chi Minh Statue

Can Tho River

Phung Hiep 20 miles (32 km)

DONG KHOI

NGUYEN THAI HOC

VO VAN TAN

TAN THANH TON

TRAO

PHAN DINH PHUNG

LE THANH TON

① Central Market

PHAN BOI CHAU

PHAN CHU TRINH

NAM KY KHOI NGHIA

NGUYEN AN NINH

0 meters   200
0 yards   200

Rice Cultivation

Rice is Vietnam's primary food staple and the country's most vital cash crop. The rice industry employs almost 80 percent of the country's population in one way or another. The majority of rice production in Vietnam takes place in the Mekong Delta, the fertile soil of which has contributed significantly to making Vietnam the world's second-largest exporter of rice. A significant portion of this enormous productivity is the result of hard manual and animal labor. Fields are usually ploughed not by tractors but by water buffaloes, and irrigation is managed not by pumps, but by teams of people wielding two-handed buckets or watertight woven baskets.

Paddy farming is always a cooperative enterprise, facilitated by several members of the family

Irrigation canals are also used to mark property lines.

Rich delta soil is critical to the abundance of the harvest.

Transplantation

The seeds for paddy rice are germinated and allowed to shoot outside the fields, often in trays or pots. When the shoots are a few inches high, they are brought to the paddy field for final planting.

Baskets carry seedlings for transplantation.

Seedlings ready to be transplanted.

Harvesting is done by stoop labor, usually by men and women using hand sickles.

After threshing, winnowing, and separating the grain from the sheaves and chaff, the rice is laid out on mats to dry in the sun

Although some rice is transported by ox-cart and truck, water remains the most traditional as well as the most efficient means in the Mekong of getting the rice to market.

Woman preparing rice paper at a factory

Mixture of water and rice powder

Cloth stretched over a boiler

Rice paper drying on bamboo mats

The Rice Wrapper Factory

Rice wrappers *(banh trang)* are ubiquitous in Vietnamese cuisine. Almost any food can be wrapped in one and eaten like a sandwich or burrito. The wrappers are prepared in various kitchens and factories throughout the country. A thin batter of rice flour and water is poured over a cloth stretched over a pot of simmering water. The rising steam cooks the mixture in a matter of seconds; the wrapper is then laid on a woven bamboo mat or tray to dry, giving *banh trang* its distinctive crisscross pattern.

Wildly colorful collection of painted clay animals at Chua Dat Set, Soc Trang

❽ Soc Trang

Road Map B6. 39 miles (63 km) SE of Can Tho. 🚲 165,000. 🚌 ⓘ Soc Trang Tourist, 131 Nguyen Chi Thanh St, (079) 382 2024. 🎏 Oc Om Boc Festival (mid-Nov).

This lively town is famous for its festivals and religious sites. Once part of the Angkor Empire, the entire province is home to 90 Khmer, 47 Chinese, and 30 Vietnamese pagodas, many of which are in Soc Trang itself. Of the ten annual festivals held here, the largest is the carniva-lesque Khmer festival, Oc Om Boc *(see p37)*, with its famous boat racing.
Set in beautiful grounds, **Khleang Pagoda** is the best-known Khmer temple in town. The mandarin-orange building is topped by a peaked roof with gables, and festooned with colorful gargoyels. The sanctuary is lit by lotus-motif chandeliers, and a gilt Buddha dominates the altar.
About 356 ft (200m) east of the Khleang Pagoda, is **Chua Dat Set**, or Clay Pagoda, populated by fantastic clay figures sculpted by Ngo Kim Tong, also known as the Clay Monk, between 1930 and 1970. Standing guard at the door is an almost life-size statue of an elephant, while a golden lion, giant phoenix, and numerous other beasts contribute to the menagerie of imagery inside the pagoda.

The **Khmer Museum** doubles as a cultural center at times, hosting traditional dance and music recitals. The exhibits at the museum include ethnic cloth-ing, crockery, statues, and even a couple of boats. The building itself is a peculiar blend of Khmer and French-Colonial architecture.

Environs
Earning its nickname from the legions of fruit bats living in its dense groves, **Chua Doi** or Bat Pagoda is 2 miles (4 km) west of town on Le Hong Phong Street. At sunset, the bats take flight, filling the sky like a great screeching cloud. The pagoda's other highlights are its friendly monks, the graves of the five-toed pigs, and the vibrant murals inside showing scenes from the Buddha's life. Farther west, 9 miles (14 km) from town, **Xa Lon Pagoda** began about 200 years ago as a thatched Khmer structure, though it was almost

Altar statue, Khleang Pagoda

destroyed in 1968 by the intense combat of that year *(see pp48–9)*. Today a stout building, with exquisite exterior tilework, it serves as a pagoda as well as a Sanskrit school. Also worth a stop is the handsome, Khmer-style **Im Som Rong Pagoda**, located about one mile (1.6 km) east of Soc Trang.

🏛 **Khmer Museum**
23 Nguyen Chi Thanh St. **Tel** (078) 382 2983. **Open** 7:30–11am, 1:30–5pm Mon–Fri. **Closed** Sat–Sun.

❾ Bac Lieu

Road Map B6. 174 miles (280 km) from HCMC; 31 miles (50 km) SW of Soc Trang. 🚲 148,000. 🚌 ⓘ Bac Lieu Tourist, 2 Hoang Van Thu St, (781) 382 4272.

This small town is primarily an agricultural center, with a major part of its revenue coming from the shrimp and salt farms located along the coast. Most visitors use the place as a base to explore the region, including the nearby sanctuary. The town features some fine French-Colonial buildings, such as the impressive **Cong Tu Bac Lieu**, once the palace of the prince of Bac Lieu Province. Now a hotel, the building has been restored to its 1930s splendor, taking visitors on a journey back in time.

Environs
The **Bac Lieu Bird Sanctuary** is about 3 miles (5 km) south of town. Its mangrove forests are home to a splendid variety of species. More than 50 types of birds either reside here or use it as a way station in their annual migrations. There are large flocks of white herons, which are the main attraction for most visitors. Unfortunately, other than some primitive toilets and an observation tower, the sanctuary lacks facilities. The best time to visit this sanctuary is between July and December, as there is little to see for the rest of the year.

Entrance to the French-provincial style Cong Tu Bac Lieu

Flora, Fauna, and Birds of the Mekong Delta

The rich soil and lush green habitat of the Mekong Delta is home to a wide variety of plant and animal species, with new ones still being discovered. Dense mangrove swamps and tropical forests cover a large portion of the delta, while a range of fruits, such as mangoes, papayas, and bananas, grow in abundance. Several types of orchids, both wild and cultivated, are common as well. The region is also part of the East Asia Flyover and lies along the path of many migratory birds, including species of storks and cranes, especially the rare red-headed crane, also known as the Sarus crane. The delta's fauna includes wild boar, monkeys, and deer, as well as numerous snake and other reptile species.

Coconut Trees Lining Delta Waters

Among the most common and bountiful trees in the delta, coconut palms are an integral part of the region's economy. The fruit and its oil is used extensively in Vietnamese food, while the trees' long and strong leaves and branches are ideal for making roofs that often last for years.

Several colorful orchids are abundant in the delta. So many species exist that new ones are always being found. Botanists struggle to catalog them all.

Coconuts are eaten both green and ripe. The flesh is soft when green, and crunchy when ripe.

Delta waters carry rich alluvia from as far as Tibet, and support a diverse aquatic life.

Green bee-eaters, brightly colored birds with black beaks, nest in tunnels that they dig in the soft soil of the riverbank. They eat mostly bees and remove the sting by hitting the insect on hard ground.

The painted stork, a graceful and slender bird, is one of several rare varieties of stork that find safe refuge in the Mekong Delta's many bird sanctuaries.

Many species of snake reside in the Mekong Delta, but the best known are the king cobra and giant python. They are sometimes raised on farms but often taken from the wild for consumption.

The crab-eating macaque, or *Macaca fascicularis*, eats fruits and plants in addition to crabs and insects. These monkeys have black fur at birth, which eventually changes to grey or reddish brown.

Crocodiles can be seen in the wild but, like snakes, they are farmed abundantly. This practice saves them from being hunted to extinction.

⓿ Con Dao Islands

Road Map B6. 62 miles (100 km) off the southern tip of Vietnam. ⬛ 6,000. ✈ from HCMC. ⛴ from Vung Tao. ℹ Con Dao Transport, 430 Truong Cong Dinh St, (064) 385 9089.

A cluster of 16 islands, Con Dao may be remote but, with its remarkable forests, wildlife, and beaches, it is one of the most astounding destinations in Vietnam.

Declared a nature preserve in 1993, **Con Dao National Park** covers a massive portion of the archipelago, stretching across 154 sq miles (400 sq km). About two-thirds of it is on land, while the rest, including the beautiful coral reefs, is water. These seas are home to more than 1,300 aquatic species, such as sea turtles, dolphins, and dugongs, a manatee-like mammal *(see p194)*. Visits to the nesting sites of the endangered green turtle can also be arranged. On land are 135 species of fauna and 882 types of flora, including orchids unique to the island. The only home of the pied imperial pigeon, this park is a bird-watcher's dream.

The largest and only permanently inhabited island in the group is **Con Son**, often referred to as "Bear Island" because of its shape. About 6 miles (10 km) in length, and with well-marked trails, the entire island can be walked in a day. These idyllic surroundings, however, hold the remnants of a sad past. Con Son became a devil's island of sorts after the French built the **Phu Hai Prison** here in 1862. Political dissidents and revolutionaries were imprisoned under cruel conditions, often kept shackled to the floor. A re-creation of this is displayed in one of the cell blocks. In 1954, Phu Hai was handed over to the South Vietnamese, who carried on the tradition. The most inhumane cells were "tiger cages". These were tiny holes in the ground with steel bars for roofs. Vietcong operatives were routinely

A freshwater turtle

brought here. The **Revolutionary Museum** offers a tour of the complex, and also has displays on the treatment of political prisoners by the French and the South Vietnamese government.

For more cheerful outings, the islands boast many spectacular beaches. Diving is also possible offshore. **Dat Doc** on Con Son is the most popular beach, and dugong sightings have been reported here in recent years. Also on Con Dao is the isolated **Nho Beach**. To see the brown booby, a rare bird, visit **Hon Trung**, an hour's boat ride from Con Son. The beach on **Tre Nho Island** is a great picnic spot. The best time to visit Con Dao is between March and June; diving season runs June–September.

🏛 Revolutionary Museum

Near Saigon Con Dao Hotel, 18 Ton Duc Thang St, Con Son. **Open** 7–11am, 1:30–5pm Mon–Sat. 📷

⓫ Rach Gia

Road Map B6. 72 miles (116 km) from Can Tho. ⬛ 228,000. ✈ from HCMC. 🚌 ⛴ ⛴ ℹ Kien Giang Tourist, 190 Tran Phu St, (077) 386 2231.

A prosperous port town, Rach Gia boasts many religious buildings such as the charming **Pho Minh Pagoda**, which houses an order of mendicant nuns. Its Twin Buddhas, one in Thai style and the other Vietnamese, sit

Children playing on a beach at sunset, Con Dao Islands

companionably in the sanctuary. The sprawling 200-year-old **Phat Lon Pagoda** has a unique sanctuary, surrounded by many small altars. The main altar holds images of the Buddha in Khmer regalia. The pagoda has its own crematoria for the disposal of its monks' bodies, and tombs for those chosen for veneration.

The colorful **Nguyen Trung Truc Temple** is dedicated to a revered national hero who sacrificed his life in the struggle against the French in the mid-19th century. He was executed in Rach Gia's market square on October 27, 1868. In addition to the pagodas, the town also hosts the **Rach Gia Museum**, featuring an interesting collection of Oc Eo artifacts and pottery.

Environs

The ancient city of **Oc Eo** was a major trading center of the Indianized Funan Empire *(see p43)*, which once extended from southern Vietnam to as far as Malaysia. Artifacts recovered from an archaeological site located 6 miles (10 km) outside Rach Gia indicate that Funan's traders had contact with many nations of the region from the 1st to the 5th century AD. A Roman coin has also been unearthed in this area. There is not much to see at the excavation site, apart from a few foundations under a shelter.

🏛 Rach Gia Museum

27 Nguyen Van Troi St. **Tel** (077) 386 3727. **Open** 7–11am, 1:30–5pm Mon–Fri.

Houses in the Mekong Delta

Home to thousands of people who live not only beside the river, but on it, the Mekong Delta is known for two of Vietnam's most distinct forms of houses – stilt and floating. While stilt houses line the steep banks, villages of floating homes occupy the river, completely independent of land. Resting on tall bamboo poles, the stilt houses are firmly anchored to the ground. Floating houses, in contrast, sail adrift on pontoons or empty oil drums. Both types of houses are often connected to the shore by a monkey bridge – a crossing made of wooden poles tightly tied together, with the barest of footholds.

Stilt Houses

Built to accommodate the annual Mekong River floods, stilt houses were traditionally made of wood, but are now increasingly built of corrugated iron. They usually comprise one or two spacious rooms, and open out onto a deck. At low tide, the house is accessed via a ladder from the floor to the bank, while at high tide, boats sail right up to the door.

Monkey bridges, arched wooden structures, rarely feature any kind of safety railing. They are rickety, but delta people have used them for centuries.

Family sampan tied beside a stilt home.

Bamboo stilts can be up to 20 ft (6 m) tall. Remarkably sturdy and flexible, they can withstand the swiftest currents.

Thatched roofs were the norm in the delta, but corrugated metal is preferred now. In addition to being cooling, it lasts much longer

Floating villages, complete with homes, shops, and even industrial buildings, can cover several acres of the Mekong's waters. Without permanent anchors, it is easy to move house when opportunities are better downstream.

Fish Traps

Feeding fish in fish trap

A unique feature in many floating houses is the fish trap – a covered hole in the floor, under which is suspended a large net made of woven strips of bamboo or steel mesh. People of the delta have used this method to trap fish for generations, and today, utilizing scientific techniques, have begun using these traps as incubators for fertilized fish eggs. Fish caught in traps are kept until they are full grown and ready to eat.

Daily activities on the floating houses include everything from fishing and shopping to growing herbs and raising hens. Residents live their entire lives on the water, rarely setting foot on land.

⑫ Chau Doc

Road Map B6. 152 miles (245 km) SW of HCMC; 74 miles (119 km) NW of Can Tho. 🚍 158,000. 🚌 from HCMC, Can Tho, and Ha Tien. 🚢 from Phnom Penh, Cambodia. 🚢

Life and commerce in Chau Doc, a bustling border town, centers on the water. Many people live not only by the river in stilt houses, but on it in floating houses *(see p103)*. The town's exceptionally busy market is also located along the riverfront. During a period of several centuries, control over Chau Doc has passed between the Funanese, Cham, Khmer, and Vietnamese. It is no surprise that this is one of the most ethnically and religiously diverse towns in the region. It is also home to the Hoa Hao sect, an indigenous Buddhist order founded in the 1930s, and based on the rejection of religious practice and the intercession of priests. The small community of Cham Muslims residing in Chau Doc worship at the green **Mubarak Mosque** across the Hau Giang River and the larger **Chau Giang Mosque**. Neither has a proper address, but boatmen know how to reach them.

In the town center, the **Bo De Dao Trang Plaza** is dominated by a statue of Quan Am, Goddess of Mercy, standing in a gazebo. Behind the deity, a statue of the Buddha sits under a tree facing a small pagoda.

Bronze statue, Phat Thay Tay An Temple, Chau Doc

Close by, **Chau Phu Temple** is dedicated to a Nguyen lord, and also serves as a tribute to the dead, with many memorial tablets amid colorful artworks.

Environs

A sacred site for hundreds of years, **Sam Mountain** lies 4 miles (6 km) southwest of town. Its slopes are covered with shrines, grottos, pagodas, and ancient tombs. At the northern base, lies the **Phat Thay Tay An Temple**, packed with statues of elephants and monsters – all painted in lurid colors. Many women sell birds for release at the entrance. A statue of a monk guards the inner sanctum. Close by is **Chua Xu**, dedicated to a Vietnamese heroine, Lady Xu. Her statue is bathed and clad in finery every May. The view from the summit is most stunning, with the rice fields of Vietnam to the east and the plains of Cambodia on its west side.

⑬ Ha Tien

Road Map B6. 190 miles (306 km) W of HCMC; 57 miles (92 km) NW of Rach Gia. 🚍 120,000. 🚌 from HCMC and Chau Doc. 🚢 from Phu Quoc Island.

Overlooking the idyllic shores of the Gulf of Thailand, and surrounded by limestone promontories, Ha Tien is one of the more attractive towns in the delta. With its riverfront having undergone a major clean-up and a vast new suburb growing to the west

Statue of Quan Am at the entrance of Thach Dong Temple, Ha Tien

of the town center, it is also one of the fastest developing areas. It became part of Vietnam after a battle with the Thai in 1708. The hero of the war, Mac Cuu, was laid to rest with his family in the **Mac Tombs**, which are located on a hillside, Nui Lang, just west of town. On the northern side of Nui Lang, the **Phu Dung Pagoda** contains elegant 18th-century tombs. Its sanctuary features exquisite high-relief panels.

Environs

Sitting snugly in a system of caves, halfway up a karst formation *(see p186)* about 2 miles (4 km) west of town, **Thach Dong Temple** goes all the way through the limestone. There are altars everywhere, but the religious focus is on the stone pagoda in the largest cave. A statue of Quan Am stands near its entrance, and at a short distance is the **Stele of Hatred**. This monument is dedicated to the 130 people killed here by the Khmer Rouge in 1978.

About 18 miles (30 km) to the southeast of Ha Tien lies the secluded beach resort of **Hon Chong**. At the southern end of the beach is the Hang Pagoda, a grotto with stalactites that resonate like organ pipes when struck. Offshore, Nghe Island has many caves and shrines. About an hour by boat, it is ideal for a day trip.

Floating houses lining the riverfront in Chau Doc

⓫ Phu Quoc Island

Road Map A6. 28 miles (45 km) W of Ha Tien. 🚶 91,000. ✈ from HCMC. 🚢 from Rach Gia and Ha Tien.

Claimed by Cambodia, this kite-shaped island played a key role in Vietnam's history as the base for French missionary Pigneau de Behaine, who sheltered the future emperor, Gia Long, during the Tay Son Rebellion *(see p45)*. Around 31 miles (50 km) long and just 12 miles (20 km) wide, Phu Quoc Island is still relatively undeveloped, with most tourist facilities in its main town, **Duong Dong**. More like a big village, it features a lighthouse, central market, and fish sauce factory, which also offers tours.

Almost 70 percent of the main island is occupied by the **Phu Quoc National Park**. Established in 2001, it is covered with tropical forest. At present, there are few hiking trails, but the pools at the park's southern end are scenic and good for swimming.

Halfway between Duong Dong town and the park is the **Khu Tuong** black pepper plantation. The Vietnamese staple, *nuoc mam* (fish sauce) is also produced here, and connoisseurs can attest to its quality.

Phu Quoc is also blessed with many unspoiled beaches, known in Vietnamese as *bai*.

Bai Truong, along the southwest shore, is the best known. Lined by many hotels, it offers wonderful sunset views. To its north is the rugged **Bai Ong Lang**, with tiny resorts nestled in its coves. Just offshore is **Hon Doi Moi** with a coral reef teeming with marine life. It is also great for snorkeling and diving. The **An Thoi** island group at the southern tip also has a coral reef. The southeastern shore hosts the barely developed but stunning white-sand stretches of **Bai Sao** and **Bai Dam**. Scuba gear, island trips, and fishing equipment can be arranged in Duong Dong. Phu Quoc is also home to a fascinating cultured pearl farm and gallery on its southwest coast.

0 kilometers 5
0 miles 5

Chua 376 m
Tieu Khu
Bai Thom
Ganh Dau Cape
Ganh Dau
Chua 552 m
Bai Dai
Phu Quoc National Park
Hon Doi Moi
Khu Tuong
Bai Ong Lang
Da Bac 435 m
Bai Truong
Duong Dong
Bai Truong
Ham Ninh
Hon Doi Moi
Bai Vong
Pearl Farm
Bai Dam
Bai Sao
Bai Khem
An Thoi
Den Cape
Rach Gia
An Thoi Islands
GULF OF THAILAND

Key
━━ Main road
═══ Minor road
--- Ferry route

For keys to symbols *see back flap*

The beautiful Truong Beach, with its swaying palms and wooden boats

SOUTH CENTRAL VIETNAM

Covering much of the ancient Kingdom of Champa, South Central Vietnam possesses a densely populated coast scattered with fishing towns and quiet beaches, as well as a substantial hinterland inhabited by indigenous minorities. The resort towns of Nha Trang and Phan Thiet and the honeymoon hill station of Dalat are firmly on the tourist itinerary, but much of this region is relatively unexplored.

Under the steady influence of seaborne trade, Champa emerged during the 4th century AD as a powerful kingdom. At its peak, Champa extended from the Ngang Pass in the north to present-day Ho Chi Minh City and the Mekong River Delta in the south. From AD 1000, its power dwindled and one principality after another was annexed by the Vietnamese. By the late 18th century, only tiny Panduranga, extending from Phan Rang to Phan Thiet, held out, but it too fell in 1832. Today, Champa's remains, in the form of towers and temple complexes, cluster in the hills of the South Central region. People of the Cham minority still live in the old region of Panduranga, where the Kate Festival is celebrated with great ceremony in early fall.

The beaches of lower South Central Vietnam are some of the finest in the country. At Phan Thiet, an 11-mile (18-km) white-sand beach extends to the small fishing village of Mui Ne, Vietnam's fastest-growing resort. Up the coast, the seaside city of Nha Trang is justly celebrated for its seafood and its archipelago of offshore islands, which offer all manner of watersports. More beaches are a day-trip away and for those heading unhurriedly up the coast, tiny fishing towns and lovely, often deserted, stretches of sand beckon.

Inland, the main resort town is Dalat, a French-built hill station and a cool delight to visit. Deeper into the highlands, the towns of Buon Ma Thuot and Kontum are surrounded by villages populated by the Bahnar, Ede, and Jarai minorities. Some of these hamlets still feature traditional architecture, such as the extraordinary longhouses of the Bahnar, *nha rong*.

The region was badly scarred by the Vietnam War, and at Son My a moving memorial stands in remembrance of one of the worst atrocities of the time, the My Lai Massacre *(see p123)*.

Stepped vegetable fields on the fertile slopes around Dalat

◀ Datanla waterfall in the Dalat region

Exploring South Central Vietnam

With its numerous beaches and easy accessibility, the long coastal strip of South Central Vietnam sees many more visitors than the interior, and the resorts of Mui Ne and Nha Trang make good bases from which to explore much of the southern coast. Travelers tend to hurry past the fishing towns in the north of the region on their way to Central Vietnam, although attractive beaches and ancient Cham temples make them worthwhile stopovers.

Dalat is the most pleasant place to stay in the Central Highlands. Up on the plateau, Buon Ma Thuot makes a decent base for visiting the country's largest wildlife preserve, Yok Don National Park, as well as outlying minority communities. Heading north, toward friendly Kontum, roads are less traveled, and access, due to unrest among some minority groups, is still limited.

Dambri Falls, the region's most beautiful waterfall

The notably well-preserved Cham temple-towers of Po Klong Garai, Phan Rang–Thap Cham

Sights at a Glance

Towns and Cities

2 Phan Thiet
4 Phan Rang–Thap Cham
5 Nha Trang
6 Dalat
8 Buon Ma Thuot
10 Kontum
11 Quy Nhon
12 Sa Huynh
13 Quang Ngai

Beaches

3 Mui Ne Beach

Areas of Natural Beauty

1 Ta Cu Mountain
7 Lak Lake

National Parks

9 Yok Don National Park

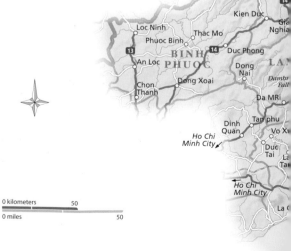

0 kilometers 50
0 miles 50

For hotels and restaurants see pp236–41 and pp246–53

Getting Around

Traveling through the region along coastal Highway 1 or via the Ho Chi Minh City–Hanoi rail link is straightforward. Bus services ply the coast, as do a plethora of minibuses organized by hotels and travel agents. Dalat is also easy to access, and Route 27 from the coast is spectacular. Exploring the Central Highlands takes more effort, and although minibuses do exist, a car and driver (or motorcycle) might serve better. Route 14 from Ho Chi Minh City has seen upgrades, although north of Buon Ma Thuot the road is winding and steep.

Key
- Major road
- Minor road
- Railroad
- International border
- Provincial border

Coracle on the white-sand beach of Doc Let, north of Nha Trang on the Hon Heo Peninsula

For keys to symbols *see back flap*

The serene Reclining Buddha near the peak of Ta Cu Mountain

❶ Ta Cu Mountain

Road Map C6. 18 miles (30 km) S of Phan Thiet. Pagodas & park **i** (062) 386 7484. 🛐 🚻 💻 🏠

The scenery around Ta Cu is flat and arid, and the mountain, although only 2,100 ft (650 m), affords spectacular views of the coast on clear days. **Linh Son Truong Tho Pagoda** and **Linh Son Long Doan Pagoda**, both established in the mid-19th century, are important sites for the many Buddhist pilgrims who come to this holy mountain. However, the main attraction for most visitors – nearly all of whom are Vietnamese – is a white Reclining Buddha, 160-ft (49-m) long and claimed by the Ta Cu custodians to be the largest in Vietnam. It was sculpted in 1962.

A cable car, located near Highway 1, is available to carry visitors up the mountain to the Reclining Buddha. Alternatively, it takes two hours to reach the site on foot.

❷ Phan Thiet

Road Map C6. 125 miles (200 km) E of Ho Chi Minh City. 🚍 216,000. 🚉 🚌 🚤 **i** Fish Egg Tree Tours, (090) 443 4895. 🎎 Nghinh Ong Festival (Aug–Sep), once every two years.

This pleasant seaside town features an active fishing fleet and a port extending along both banks of the Ca Ty river. For visitors staying at nearby Mui Ne Beach, the town is convenient for both shopping and exploration.

Phan Thiet was once at the heart of Panduranga, the last semi-independent Cham principality, which was finally absorbed by the Nguyen Emperor Minh Mang in 1832. The town's Cham name is Malithit, and there is still an appreciable Cham element among the local population. Locally, it is chiefly celebrated for its *nuoc mam* (fish sauce), and aficionados dispute whether the best sauce in the country comes from here or Phu Quoc Island *(see p105)*.

Environs

Just 4 miles (7 km) from the center of Phan Thiet, on a hill overlooking the town, stands **Thap Poshanu**, the southernmost collection of Cham religious buildings within the former Kingdom of Champa. The group consists of three *kalan*, or sanctuary towers, with supplementary structures dating back as far as the 8th century AD, making them some of the oldest Cham archaeological remnants in the country.

❸ Mui Ne Beach

Road Map C6. E of Phan Thiet. 📷 **i** (090) 443 4895. **w** muinebeach.net

A 12-mile (20-km) strip of palm-shaded white sand, Mui Ne Beach (Ham Tien) curves from just east of Phan Thiet to the small fishing village of Mui Ne. The coast is backed by two excellent roads that run parallel to the beach along its entire length.

By the end of the 1990s, the beach had developed a reputation among budget travelers as a relaxed hideaway within easy reach of Ho Chi Minh City, but, as one of the best beaches south of Nha Trang, its growing reputation has inevitably led to constant and ever-increasing development. Almost the entire length of beach is now overrun with resorts and upmarket bars and restaurants; the first high-rise hotel was erected in 2009. Today the area has become an enclave for Russian tourism. A number of resorts, bars, and restaurants are Russian-owned

Mui Ne Beach's gargantuan rolling sand dunes

and street signs appear in Vietnamese, Russian, and English. Above the beach, at Sealinks, is a golf course and there are plans to construct several other courses here.

Activities at Mui Ne include swimming, sunbathing, and, between November and March, kitesurfing and windsurfing. The sea here is not suitable for diving, and there are no stunning offshore coral reefs.

About halfway along the road to Mui Ne Village, **Suoi Tien** or Fairy Stream flows through the sand dunes to the sea. Still farther east, where the road leaves the beach and curves inland, a track to the north leads to Mui Ne's celebrated sand dunes, where children rent out tray-like bobsleighs for "sand sledding."

At **Mui Ne Village**, maturing vats of quality *nuoc mam* (fish sauce) fill backyards and gardens. The fishing fleet land their catch in the early mornings, and it is fascinating to wander along the beach by the village, watching the fish merchants from Phan Thiet and farther afield park their pickups on the sand and bargain with the fishermen for the freshly landed catch. Unsurprisingly, the whole area has great seafood.

Well-preserved tower at Po Klong Garai temple complex

Mukha lingam, Po Klong Garai

❹ Phan Rang–Thap Cham

Road Map C5. 65 miles (105 km) S of Nha Tranq. 161,000 🚉 🚌 🛈 45 Bac Ai St, (091) 917 4987. 🎭 Kate Festival (Sep or Oct).

A twin city located on an arid coastal strip known for its grape and Cham textile production, Phan Rang–Thap Cham is an important road junction linking the coastal provinces with Dalat and the Central Highlands. Thap Cham means Cham Towers, and three of the country's best-preserved Cham religious complexes are situated here.

Po Klong Garai is a group of three brick temple-towers in remarkably good preservation. Located on a hilltop, the temple was built in the 13th century by King Jaya Simhavarman III, and inscriptions in Cham script are clearly engraved on the entranceway. The temple has a *mukha lingam* with the face of King Jaya Simhavarman III in the main *kalan* or sanctuary. A statue of the bull Nandi, Shiva's mount, receives regular offerings. During the Kate Festival each autumn, traditional Cham musical ensembles play here, and folk dancers perform in the temple precincts.

Po Ro Me was built in the 17th century when the Cham principality of Panduranga was in decline. It too sits on a hilltop, but is more difficult to access than Po Klong Garai and a motorbike is recommended to reach the temple. The tower is dedicated to King Po Ro Me, and there is an image of him on a *mukha lingam* inside. A third temple complex, Hoa Lai, which is located a few miles north of Phan Rang.

Pleasant **Ninh Chu Beach**, shaded by casuarina trees, is located 4 miles (6 km) east of Phan Rang. During his regime (1967–75), it was reserved for President Nguyen Van Thieu and his cronies.

🏛 **Po Klong Garai**
Route 27, 4 miles (6 km) W of Thap Cham. **Tel** (091) 917 4987. **Open** sunrise–sunset daily. 🌀

🏛 **Po Ro Me**
9 miles (14 km) S of Thap Cham. **Open** sunrise–sunset daily.

Ancient Cham inscriptions on the entrance pillars at Po Klong Garai

❺ Nha Trang

A bustling city and major fishing port, Nha Trang is also Vietnam's primary beach resort, with numerous comfortable hotels and a wide range of restaurants specializing in seafood. An elegant promenade by the seafront overlooks the Municipal Beach, which is usually packed with travelers sunbathing and vendors selling their wares. The busy Central Market, Cho Dam, is at the city's heart, while most tourist facilities, and many hotels and bars, are farther south. Outside town are the hot springs of Thap Ba and Ba Ho. Catch a ferry from Cau Da to one of the islands in the bay, where the waters are ideal for snorkeling.

Coracles pulled up on Nha Trang's Municipal Beach

🏯 Long Son Pagoda

No 18, 23 Thang 10 St.
Tel (058) 381 6919. **Open** 7:30–11:30am, 1:30–5:30pm daily.

The most revered pagoda in Nha Trang, Long Son is located on the summit of Trai Thuy Hill to the south of the city. It was destroyed by a typhoon at the beginning of the 20th century and restored several times, most recently in 1940. It is now dedicated to the memory of the numerous Buddhist monks who were killed during or died protesting against the repressive regime of South Vietnam's President Ngo Dinh Diem (1955–63). Today, it remains a functioning pagoda, with monks in residence.

The pagoda is distinctly Sino-Vietnamese in style and is decorated with elaborate dragons and ceramic tiles. The main sanctuary building is dominated by a giant white sculpture of the Buddha, dating

Giant Buddha, Long Son Pagoda

from the 1960s and a full 46 ft (14 m) tall. Seated behind the temple at the top of the hill, the sculpture is reached via 150 steep steps. From here, there are panoramic views over Nha Trang and the neighboring countryside. Another large white Buddha, this time reclining, is located halfway up the steps on the right. It was sculpted by an artisan from Thailand in 2003.

✝ Nha Trang Cathedral

31 Thai Nguyen St.
Tel (058) 382 3335. Services held daily.

The seat of the Catholic Diocese of Nha Trang, this church was constructed in provincial French Gothic style in the 1930s. The building is dominated by a tall, square clock tower surmounted by a large crucifix. Stained-glass windows look onto colonnaded cloisters running the length of each side of the building. The three cathedral bells, cast in France in 1786, are still in fine

working order. The former cemetery of the cathedral has been leveled and the land used to extend the city's train station.

🏖 Municipal Beach

Nha Trang has a fine beach, almost 4 miles (7 km) long and sheltered by headlands to its north and south. Tran Phu Street follows the beach for its entire length, providing a fine promenade with great views across the bay. The entire esplanade area is undergoing rapid development, with new hotels and restaurants on the inland side, and numerous cafés and small food stalls between the road and the sea.

🏛 Alexandre Yersin Museum

10D Tran Phu St. **Tel** (058) 382 2355. **Open** 8–11am, 2–4:30pm Mon–Fri.

The Swiss physician Alexandre Yersin (1863–1943) moved to Vietnam in 1891 after studying in Paris under the renowned microbiologist Louis Pasteur. He quickly became fluent in Vietnamese and was involved in the founding of Dalat as a hill station in 1893. Yersin introduced cinchona trees to Vietnam for the production of the anti-malarial drug quinine. His most significant achievement came in 1894, when he identified the microbe that causes bubonic plague.

The cement-brick belfry of Nha Trang Cathedral

The North Tower (Thap Chinh) and Central Tower (Thap Nam), Po Nagar

VISITORS' CHECKLIST

Practical Information
Road Map C5. 280 miles
(450 km) N of Ho Chi Minh City.
392,000. Khanh Hoa
Tourist Company, 1 Tran Hung
Dao St, (058) 352 6753. Po
Nagar Festival (mid-Apr).

Transport
21 miles (34 km) S at Cam
Ranh.

The museum, located in Yersin's personal office within the Pasteur Institute, displays his lab equipment, desk, and books. Still operational, the institute produces vaccines and conducts medical research.

Cai River Estuary

Nha Trang's fishing fleet moors on the Cai River just north of downtown. A stroll over the bridge allows a vantage point for watching the blue boats at anchor, their red and yellow flags flapping in the breeze. The harbor is alive with activity and fishermen propel themselves from boat to boat in rotund, pitch-sealed coracles.

Po Nagar Cham Towers

North bank of Cai River. **Tel** (058) 383 1569 **Open** 6am–6pm daily.
Dedicated to the goddess Po Yan Inu Nagar and one of the most important Cham sites in Vietnam, Po Nagar dates back to the 8th century, when it was constructed by the kings of the Cham principality Kauthara. Although a Cham goddess, Yang Ino Po Nagar is now very much a patron goddess of Nha Trang, venerated by ethnic Viet and Chinese Buddhists, as well as by local Cham Hindus.

Of the original eight towers, four remain standing. Built in 817, Thap Chinh, the North Tower, is the most impressive and houses an image of the Hindu goddess Uma in her incarnation as Po Nagar. At the entrance, her consort, the Hindu god Shiva, dances on the back of his holy mount, the sacred bull Nandi. The columns of a ruined *mandapa* or meditation hall also still stand. A small museum displays Cham artifacts.

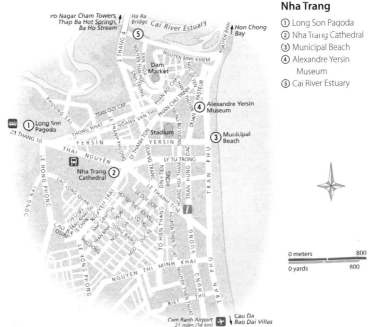

Nha Trang

① Long Son Pagoda
② Nha Trang Cathedral
③ Municipal Beach
④ Alexandre Yersin Museum
⑤ Cai River Estuary

0 meters   800
0 yards   800

For keys to symbols *see back flap*

Pleasure boats for trips to the islands around Nha Trang at Cau Da

🚩 Hon Chong

2.5 miles (4 km) N of Nha Trang.
Tel (058) 383 2189. **Open**
6.30am–6.30pm daily. 🐾

Just north of Nha Trang, a stack
of boulders named Hon Chong
thrusts into the sea, creating
a headland that shelters the
beach. One of the rocks bears
five indentations, said to be the
handprint of a giant. The bay is
picturesque but unsuitable for
swimming because of several
fishing villages in the area.
However, it is a great place for
reasonably priced seafood.
There are views of Nha Trang
Bay to the south, while Nui
Co Tien, or Heavenly Woman
Mountain, said to resemble the
female physiognomy, is visible
to the west.

Thap Ba Hot Springs

6 miles (10 km) NW of Nha Trang.
Tel (058) 383 5345. **Open** 7am–7:30pm
daily. 🐾 🅆 thapbahotsprings.com.vn

Locals and visitors alike gather
to wallow in the hot, muddy
waters of Thap Ba. The mud is
full of sodium silicate chloride
and is thought to be beneficial
in the treatment of arthritis and

Bathers soaking in tubs of warm mud at
Thap Ba Hot Springs

rheumatism. It is also said to
promote general relaxation.
Bathers make a point of rubbing
the curative mud all over their
bodies, and sit in the sun until
it dries and cracks. They then
wash the mud off with clean,
hot mineral water. Various types
of water massage are also on
offer, and a cool swimming
pool is available for a post-
mudbath dunk.

Ba Ho Stream plunging over boulders into a
pool

🏕 Ba Ho Stream

15 miles (25 km) N of Nha Trang.

A terrific spot for a picnic, Ba Ho
Stream or Suoi Ba Ho rises on
the flanks of Hon Long
Mountain (4,400 ft/1,342 m) and
then runs east to the South
China Sea. The river widens into
three adjoining pools, which
make for excellent but cold
swimming, and each pool is
linked to the next by a tumbling
cascade of water. There are very
few facilities, so take along food
and drink. On weekends, the
lakeside setting can be overrun
as it is very popular with locals.

Cau Da

2 miles (3 km) S of downtown Nha
Trang. **Oceanographic Institute:
Tel** (058) 359 0037. **Open** 6am–6pm
daily. 🐾 **Bao Dai Villas: Tel** (058)
359 0147. 🐾 for non-residents.

Sheltered in the lee of Chut
Mountain or Nui Chut, Cau Da
is a suburb of Nha Trang and
the main pier for ferries and
boat trips to the islands.

The **Oceanographic Institute**,
housed in a colonial mansion
near the pier, displays marine
specimens in glass bottles and
cases. Live creatures are kept
in a series of tanks, as well as
three outside ponds.

North of the docks, **Bao Dai
Villas** command fine views
across the South China Sea.
During the 1920s, the last
Nguyen emperor, Bao Dai,
ordered five houses to be built
in a hybrid Franco-Vietnamese
style with Art Nouveau
influences. After his abdication
in 1945, the villas became
the holiday residence of
senior officials of the South
Vietnamese government and,
from 1975, they were used by
high-ranking Commuist
officials. Today, the villas
function as a hotel, which
is sadly rather rundown
despite having been restored
and furnished with pieces
reminiscent of Bao Dai's
time and taste.

Regular ferries link Cau Da
with the fishing village of Tri
Nguyen on **Hon Mieu**, the
closest of the islands in the
archipelago. The local aquarium
is more of a fish farm, with a café
serving seafood overlooking
the concrete pools. A gravel
beach is nearby at Bai Soi.

Beaches Around Nha Trang

The numerous beaches scattered along the sandy shoreline to the north of Nha Trang, together with the small archipelago of pretty islands that lies just out to sea, add significantly to this seaside resort's appeal. Several tour companies organize day tours and usually offer a seafood lunch and plenty of iced beer. At the quieter and less developed northern destinations such as Dai Lanh and Hon Lao – the latter populated by monkeys – activities include swimming, snorkeling, and sunbathing. More organized, and often raucous, entertainment, such as waterskiing, parasailing, and drinking at a floating bar, is to be expected at the islands of the archipelago.

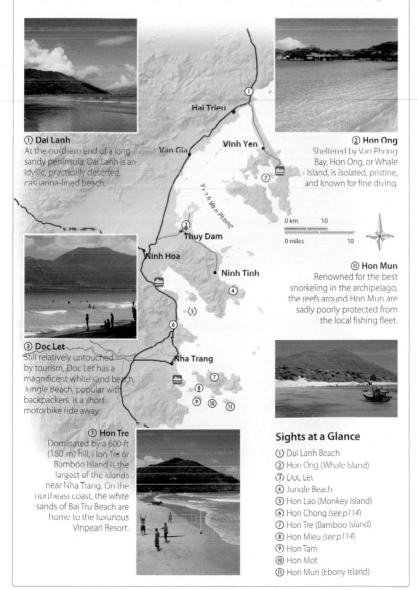

Hai Trieu

Van Gia **Vinh Yen**

Thuy Dam

Ninh Hoa

Ninh Tinh

Nha Trang

① **Dai Lanh**
At the northern end of a long sandy peninsula, Dai Lanh is an idyllic, practically deserted, casuarina-lined beach.

② **Hon Ong**
Sheltered by Van Phong Bay, Hon Ong, or Whale Island, is isolated, pristine, and known for fine diving.

⑪ **Hon Mun**
Renowned for the best snorkeling in the archipelago, the reefs around Hon Mun are sadly poorly protected from the local fishing fleet.

0 km   10
0 miles   10

③ **Doc Let**
Still relatively untouched by tourism, Doc Let has a magnificent white sand beach. Jungle Beach, popular with backpackers, is a short motorbike ride away.

⑦ **Hon Tre**
Dominated by a 600-ft (180 m) hill, Hon Tre or Bamboo Island is the largest of the islands near Nha Trang. On the northeast coast, the white sands of Bai Tru Beach are home to the luxurious Vinpearl Resort.

Sights at a Glance
① Dai Lanh Beach
② Hon Ong (Whale Island)
③ Doc Let
④ Jungle Beach
⑤ Hon Lao (Monkey Island)
⑥ Hon Chong (see p114)
⑦ Hon Tre (Bamboo Island)
⑧ Hon Mieu (see p114)
⑨ Hon Tam
⑩ Hon Mot
⑪ Hon Mun (Ebony Island)

The pristine waters of the picturesque Ebony Island, Vietnam ▶

❻ Dalat

In the mid-1890s, the physician Alexandre Yersin *(see p112)* visited Dalat and recommended it as a suitable location for a hill station and sanatorium. By 1910, the town had become a popular summer retreat for French colonists seeking a cool escape from the heat of the plains. Today, Dalat draws tens of thousands of Vietnamese honeymooners and holidaymakers, many of whom come to see the Valley of Love and Lake of Sighs, although such kitsch sights are of little interest to foreign visitors. Besides the fresh air and beautiful scenery, Dalat appeals to many for its fresh produce, wine, great food, and ethnic crafts. A short drive from Dalat are the Dambri, Elephant, Tiger, Datanla, and Pongour falls.

The exterior of Nga's Crazy House, built to resemble gnarled treetrunks

Swan-shaped pedal-boats on Xuan Huong Lake

🔵 Xuan Huong Lake

This crescent-shaped lake located right in the center of town was created by a dam in 1919 and rapidly became the central promenade for the Dalat bourgeoisie. Once called Le Grand Lac by the French, it was later renamed in honor of Ho Xuan Huong *(see p19)*, the celebrated 18th-century Vietnamese female poet whose name means Essence of Spring. Paddling around the waters in a swan-shaped pedal-boat or a more traditional kayak is the most popular activity on the lake. A pleasant walk or cycle along the 4-mile (7-km) shore passes the town's **Flower Gardens** on the north shore.

🔴 Dalat Cathedral

Tran Phu and Le Dai Hanh sts. **Tel** (063) 382 1421. **Open** daily. Mass at least twice a day.

Dedicated to St Nicholas and adding yet another French touch to this Gallic-inspired hill station, Dalat's Catholic cathedral was established to meet the spiritual needs of the colonists and the many local converts. Construction began in 1931 and was not complete until the Japanese invasion of the 1940s, an event which signaled the beginning of the end of French Indochina. The church boasts a 155-ft (47-m) spire and vivid stained-glass windows that were manufactured in 1930s France.

The bright interior of Dalat Cathedral

🏯 Hang Nga (Nga's Crazy House)

3 Huynh Thuc Khang St. **Tel** (063) 382 2070. **Open** 8:30am–7pm daily. 📷

The "Crazy House," as this guesthouse is called by locals, epitomizes everything visitors to Dalat either love or hate. This flight of fancy is constructed of wood and wire, then covered with concrete to form a treehouse. With giant toadstools, oversized cobwebs, tunnels, and ladders, it is a monstrosity to some and a charming miniature Disneyland to others, particularly kids. For a small fee, visitors can poke around unoccupied rooms, including one in the belly of a concrete giraffe.

Dr Dang Viet Nga, the owner and architect, is the daughter of the former senior Communist Party hardliner Truong Chinh, who was also briefly the General Secretary of the party in 1986.

🏯 Lam Ty Ni Pagoda

2 Thien My St. **Tel** (063) 382 1775. **Open** 8:30am–6:30pm daily.

This pagoda is very much suited to the atmosphere of eccentricity and questionable taste that surrounds many of Dalat's attractions. The building itself is unremarkable in the traditional sense, but has been extended and transformed by the pagoda's solitary inhabitant, the charming Buddhist monk Thay Vien Thuc. He has lived here since 1964, long accompanied by a pack of amiable dogs who bark loudly at new arrivals. When not reading or writing Zen poetry, he casts concrete busts, usually of himself. This industrious monk is also a prolific painter and creates dream-like landscapes and strange interpretations of the Buddhist religion and the cosmos. It is said that he makes a healthy profit from the sale of his work.

🏛 Bao Dai's Summer Palace

1 Trieu Viet Vuong St. **Tel** (063) 382 6858. **Open** 7am–5pm daily.

The last Nguyen Emperor, Bao Dai (*see p47*), regarded as a powerless puppet of the French, lived in Dalat from 1938 until 1945 with his wife, Empress Nam Phuong, and various members of his family and immediate entourage. He spent much of his time hunting and womanizing.

The Summer Palace was constructed in 1933–8 in a curious, semi-nautical Art Nouveau style, and, with just 25 rooms, it is far from palatial. Although little sense of grandeur is in evidence here, the palace remains popular with tourists who browse the memorabilia on display, which include Bao Dai's desk and an etched-glass map of Vietnam.

🚃 Dalat Train Station

1 Quang Trung St, off Nguyen Trai St. **Tel** (063) 383 4409. Departures 8am, 9:30am, 11am, 2pm, 3:30pm daily. 🚻

Built in 1932 in imitation of the station at Deauville in France, the Dalat Train Station retains its original Art Deco design. Bombing during the Vietnam War (*see pp48–9*) closed the line to Phan Rang, but a Russian engine travels a picturesque 5-mile (8-km) route to the village of Trai Mat.

🏛 Lam Dong Museum

4 Hung Vuong St. **Tel** (063) 382 2339. **Open** 7:30–11:30am, 1:30–4:30pm Mon–Sat. 🚻

The wide range of artifacts on display traces the rich history of Dalat and its surroundings. Exhibits include pottery from the Funan and Champa kingdoms, musical instruments, costumes of local ethnic minorities, and photographs. The museum is located in front of an elegant French-style villa, which was built for Bao Dai's father-in-law, Nguyen Huu Hao, in 1935,

VISITORS' CHECKLIST

Practical Information
Road Map C5.191 miles (308 km) N of Ho Chi Minh City. 🏙 207,000. ℹ Dalat Travel Service, 7, 3 Thang 2 St, (063) 382 2125.

Transport
✈ 🚌

and later became the home of Bao Dai's wife, Empress Nam Phuong.

🛕 Thien Vuong Pagoda

2.5 miles (4 km) from the center of Dalat on Khe Sanh St.

A more orthodox pagoda than Lam Ty Ni, Thien Vuong was built by the local Chinese community in 1958. This hilltop pagoda, which has monks in residence, comprises three low, wooden buildings set attractively amid pine trees. In the main sanctuary stand three big sandalwood statues, with Thich Ca, the Historical Buddha, forming the centerpiece. Stalls selling local jams, dried fruits, and artichoke tea line the path leading up to the pagoda.

Bronze Buddha, Thien Vuong Pagoda

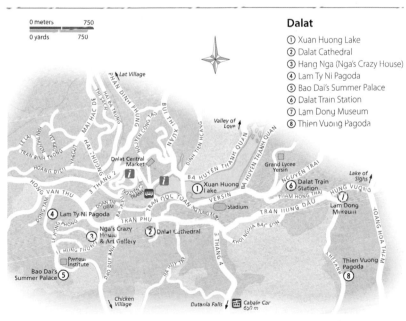

Dalat

1. Xuan Huong Lake
2. Dalat Cathedral
3. Hang Nga (Nga's Crazy House)
4. Lam Ty Ni Pagoda
5. Bao Dai's Summer Palace
6. Dalat Train Station
7. Lam Dong Museum
8. Thien Vuong Pagoda

0 meters 750
0 yards 750

Lat Village

Valley of Love

Dalat Central Market

Grand Lycee Yersin

Lake of Sighs

① Xuan Huong Lake

⑥ Dalat Train Station

⑦ Lam Dong Museum

④ Lam Ty Ni Pagoda

Stadium

③ Nga's Crazy House & Art Gallery

② Dalat Cathedral

Pasteur Institute

Thien Vuong Pagoda ⑧

Bao Dai's Summer Palace ⑤

Chicken Village

Datanla Falls | Cable Car 650 m

For keys to symbols see back flap

⚑ Dalat Central Market

Town center. **Open** daily. 🖥 🎨 🏛

Nestled in the lee of a tall hillside and surrounded by rows of cafés, Dalat Central Market is among the largest in the country. The stairs and ramps leading to the market are flanked with food vendors selling grilled corn, meat on skewers, sweet potatoes, hot soy milk, and sweet waffles stuffed with pork and cheese. The second floor of the central building is also devoted to food stalls.

The enormous concrete cockerel that gave Chicken Village its name

🏘 Chicken Village

11 miles (18 km) S of Dalat just off Hwy 20. 🏛

Renowned for the large and rather bizarre statue of a cockerel that stands at its center, Chicken Village, known locally as Lang Ga, draws a large number of sightseers. It is inhabited by the K'ho people, who eke out a living growing fruit and coffee, and making textiles. The village lies just off the highway between Dalat and the coast, and tour buses stop regularly to allow visitors to watch the K'ho women weave and to buy their wares. As a result of their regular dealings with foreign tourists, the women of the village speak remarkably good English.

🏘 Lat Village

6 miles (10 km) N of Dalat.

Made up of a number of small hamlets, Lat Village is inhabited mainly by members of the Lat ethnic minority, part of the K'ho tribe, but also by other local minority peoples, including the Ma and Chill. The villagers, once impoverished, are now better off as a result of tourism. The attraction here is the local weaving and embroidery. Visitors are offered cups of hot green tea to drink while they watch the village women at work on their looms. There are some fine bargains and the people are friendly, but be prepared to haggle.

🎋 Dalat Cable Car and Thien Vien Truc Lam

2 miles (3 km) S of Dalat, off 3 Thang 4 St/Hwy 20. **Open** 7:30–11:30am, 1:30–5pm daily. 🎨

The Dalat Cable Car hangs across 1.5 miles (2.4 km) of picturesque villages, farmland, and mountain forests all the way to Thien Vien Truc Lam, or

A typical house in one of the hamlets at Lat Village

The Dalat Cable Car, overlooking the Langbiang Plateau

Bamboo Forest Meditation Center. This Zen monastery was built in 1993 and houses about 180 monks and nuns. The temple overlooks Paradise Lake, which offers an abundance of free picnic tables and chairs.

🎋 Datanla Falls

3 miles (5 km) S of Dalat, Hwy 20. **Tel** (063) 383 2238. **Open** daily. 🎨

Set in the pine-forested hills to the southwest of Dalat, Datanla Falls are only a short distance from town, and a pleasant 15-minute walk from Highway 20. The falls, which tumble down a ravine in two cascades, are a popular destination for Vietnamese tourists, especially on weekends. It is not worth making the visit during the dry season.

🎋 Dambri and Bo Bla Falls

Dambri: 52 miles (85 km) SW of Dalat, off Hwy 20; Bo Bla: 50 miles (80 km) SW of Dalat on Hwy 28. **Open** 7am–5pm daily. 🎨

The most spectacular and easily accessible falls in South Central Vietnam are at Dambri, where the water cascades down a 295-ft (90-m) drop. It is a steep climb down but there is an elevator to carry the less energetic up and down in a few minutes. Above the falls, there is a small lake where boat rides are available.

A visit to Dambri Falls can easily be combined with a stop en route at Bo Bla Falls, another beauty spot, which lies just south of Di Linh.

⑦ Lak Lake

Road Map C5. 20 miles (32 km) S of Buon Ma Thuot on Hwy 27. **Tel** (0500) 384 2246. 🖉 🖵

Lying in the center of the picturesque Dak Lak Plateau, this large, serene freshwater lake was once a favorite retreat of former Emperor Bao Dai, who built one of his hunting lodges on its banks. Although the surrounding hills have been largely stripped of forest, there are still spectacular views across the lake. The area is an excellent place to stop for refreshments when traveling on the mountain highway between Buon Ma Thuot and Dalat, and an increasing number of visitors, mostly on Easy Rider motorbike tours, come here. The people living around Lak Lake are mainly from the Central Highland's Mnong minority.

Farmers working in the fields beside picturesque Lak Lake

⑧ Buon Ma Thuot

Road Map C5. 118 miles (194 km) NE of Nha Trang. 🚁 300,000 🚌 🚺 Dak Lak Tourist, 3 Phan Chu Trinh, (0500) 384 2246.

The capital of the Central Highlands province of Dak Lak, Buon Ma Thuot makes a great base for exploring the remote lakes, rainforests, waterfalls, and hilltribe villages of the surrounding areas.

The government claims that ethnic Vietnamese, or Kinh, now make up the majority of the local population, but the indigenous minority peoples, the Ede and Mnong, still live in villages throughout the province. The Ede call the capital Buon Ma Thuot and the Mnong call it Ban Me Thuot; both names translate as "Village of the Father of Thuot."

The town is Vietnam's coffee capital, and its high production levels boost the country's position as a coffee exporter, ranking it second only to Brazil. The coffee plantations here are interesting to visit. Buon Ma Thuot is also significant for being the site of the last major battle of the Vietnam War on March 10, 1975. The

Victory Monument in the center of town features a replica of the first North Vietnamese Army tank to enter the city during the invasion. It is perched high on a plinth to commemorate the town's liberation.

In addition, there is the interesting **Museum of Ethnography** on Nguyen Du. After an extensive renovation and expansion, the museum is now housed in a large concrete building which has been designed like a traditional tribal home. It is a good place to gain an insight into the culture, traditions, and handicrafts of the local Ede and Mnong peoples and the various other hill tribes that live in the region. There is also a section on tree species in the area and stuffed animals.

🏛 Museum of Ethnography
182 Nguyen Du St. **Tel** (0500) 385 0426. **Open** 7am–5pm daily. 🌐

Environs
Tur, a small village lying 9 miles (14 km) southwest of Buon Ma Thuot, is inhabited by members of the Ede minority. Their society is matrilineal so property is always owned by the women. After marriage, men move into their wives' homes and the houses are extended. The longhouses are built on stilts, providing a space beneath the living quarters to

store firewood and house a variety of domesticated animals, such as goats, pigs, and fowl. Because of its proximity to Buon Ma Thuot and Highway 14, Tur is easily accessible and is a good place to see Ede long houses. The village is located near the mighty Dak Krong, or Serepok River, which flows into Cambodia. A visit to Tur can easily be combined with a trip to the impressive Trinh Nu rapids nearby. Farther upstream, Dray Nur, Dray Sap, and Gia Long falls lead the visitor into wilder territory.

Ako Dong Village, situated just a mile (1.5 km) north of the city center also has a number of impressive Ede longhouses.

A thriving coffee plantation at Buon Ma Thuot

Steep-roofed *nha rong* or communal house in Kontum

❾ Yok Don National Park

Road Map C5. 26 miles (40 km) NW of Buon Ma Thuot. **Tel** (0500) 384 2246. minibus from Buon Ma Thuot.

The largest of Vietnam's national parks, Yok Don covers almost 470 sq miles (1,200 sq km), extending along the Cambodian frontier and cut through by the mighty Dak Krong or Serepok River. The park is home to leopards, tigers, and wild elephants, but of the 67 species of mammal, no fewer than 38 are endangered, and the chances of seeing any of the larger mammals are slight. The once large herds of wild elephants have diminished to less than 20 animals, and the number is dropping rapidly. Half-day treks include a visit to a Mnong village, which is the main attraction for most visitors to the park. Several shops selling handicrafts and sealed pots of a local rice liquor known as *ruou can*, complete with bamboo drinking straws, are clustered around the park's entrance. Accommodation is also available here.

Just beyond the northern limits of the park, and difficult to access without a private vehicle and government guide, **Thap Yang Prong** is the most remote of all Vietnam's Cham towers, and an indication of where the outposts and settlements of the former Kingdom of Champa during the 13th and 14th centuries were.

❿ Kontum

Road Map C4. 125 miles (200 km) NE of Quy Nhon. 150,000. Kontum Travel Service, 2 Phan Dinh Phung St, (060) 386 1626.

This remote, laid-back town receives relatively few visitors, yet rewards are plentiful for anyone prepared to wander this far. Despite being heavily bombed during the Vietnam War, Kontum has retained a couple of beautiful French-colonial wooden churches and a few French-style shopfronts. As the town has few attractions of its own, most visitors come here to explore the surrounding countryside and the many minority villages, remarkable for their trademark *nha rong* or communal houses. At the east side of town, the **Seminary Museum**, within an old French Catholic seminary, displays minority handicrafts and clothing.

Ethnic groups, including Jarai, Sedang, Rongao, and Bahnar (*see p24*), inhabit villages in the region, many of which can be easily accessed from Kontum. Within walking distance, the Bahnar village of **Kon Kotu** is about 3 miles (5 km) east of town. This community's *nha rong* is made entirely of bamboo

and wood, and boasts an immensely tall thatched roof typical of Bahnar design. **Kon Hongo** is 2.5 miles (4 km) to the west of Kontum and is peopled by the Rongao minority. Both journeys take visitors through pleasant countryside of sugarcane and cassava fields.

Seminary Museum

56 Tran Hung Dao St. **Open** 7:30–10:30am, 2–4pm Mon–Fri.

⓫ Quy Nhon

Road Map C5. 137 miles (220 km) N of Nha Trang. 285,000. Binh Dinh Tourist, 10 Nguyen Hue St, (098) 924 3394.

A substantial fishing port with reasonable beaches, Quy Nhon sees few visitors barring those who overnight here to break the trip between Nha Trang and Hoi An. **Long Khan Pagoda**, Quy Nhon's most revered Buddhist temple, is located right in the center of town on Tran Cao Van Street. Dating back to the early 18th century, it is dedicated to Thich Ca, the Historical Buddha. The temple receives much less interest than the many ancient Cham temples surrounding Quy Nhon. There is a busy beach in town,

Grand Thap Doi Cham surrounded by a manicured garden, Quy Nhon

Buddha statues and offerings, Long Khan Pagoda, Quy Nhon

but better stretches of sand are located about 3 miles (5 km) to the south, including **Quy Hoa Beach**, at the leper hospital of the same name. The **Thap Doi Cham** or Double Cham Towers, thought to date from the second half of the 12th century, are just 1 mile (1.6 km) west of the town center.

Environs

One of the major surviving works of Cham architecture and in a remarkably good state, **Banh It**, or Silver Tower, stands on a hilltop near Highway 1, about 12 miles (20 km) north of Quy Nhon. Farther north along Highway 1 are the few remains of **Cha Ban**, once called Vijaya and capital of the Cham principality of the same name. Founded in AD 1000, the city was razed to the ground in 1470 by the Dai Viets, signalling the end of Champa as a kingdom. Only the walls of the citadel and the Can Tien Cham Towers still stand

Roof detail, Long Khan Pagoda, Quy Nhon

⑫ Sa Huynh

Road Map C4. 37 miles (60 km) S of Quang Ngai. 50,000. Seafood Catching Festival (early May).

Known for its palm-fringed beach and salt pans, this attractive little fishing port is most celebrated as the site of the pre-Champa culture of Sa Huynh, which flourished

around 2,000 years ago. In 1909, 200 burial jars were unearthed, the first of many more finds in the area. Unfortunately, no artifacts of this bronze-age society are accessible to the public here, but the remains can be viewed in the National Museum of Vietnamese History in Hanoi (*see pp166–7*), and at the Museum of Sa Huynh Culture in Hoi An (*see p129*). The town's laid-back atmosphere is what really attracts visitors. The beach is relatively deserted, and the waves are sufficiently powerful for surfing. Sa Huynh is also a great place for seafood.

⑬ Quang Ngai

Road Map C4. 110 miles (177 km) N of Quy Nhon. 122,000. Quang Ngai Tourist, 310 Quang Trung St, (055) 382 5292.

A sleepy provincial capital, Quang Ngai is a hidden gem with ancient archaeological finds within short driving distance.

Environs

Son My was the site of the appalling My Lai Massacre of 1968 and a chilling **Memorial Park** has been set up in the sub-hamlet of Tu Cung. A dark, granite museum documents the events in horrific detail. On display are the photographs of the atrocity that shocked the world and contributed substantially to American disillusionment with the war. Motorbike taxis in Quang Ngai make the 9-mile (15-km) trip east to Son My.

Five miles (8 km) northeast of Quang Ngai, the 1,200-year-old **Chau Sa** citadel is evidence that the Cham once controlled the area. Closer to the western mountains, an ancient wall stretches some 79 miles (127 km). It was apparently built in 1819 by the Vietnamese for security and trade regulation between the Hre minority and the Viets.

My Lai massacre

During the Vietnam War, the area around Quang Ngai was considered sympathetic to the Vietcong. On March 16, 1968, a strong force of US infantry moved into the area seeking revenge for the deaths of several colleagues in the district. Over the next 4 hours, in the worst documented US war crime of the Vietnam War, about 500 Vietnamese civilians were systematically murdered, half of them women and children as the US soldiers ran out of control. Lieutenant William Calley, who organized the massacre, was convicted of murder but was released a few years later pending appeal on the orders of President Nixon. No others were ever convicted.

The moving My Lai Massacre Memorial at Son My near Quang Ngai

CENTRAL VIETNAM

Bound by the forested peaks of the Truong Son Range to the west, with the white shores of the South China Sea to its east, Central Vietnam is a study in contrasts. It offers several fine beaches as well as a rare assortment of historical treasures, including four of Vietnam's UNESCO World Heritage Sites, namely the awe-inspiring Phong Nha Cave, My Son, Hue Citadel, and the Old Quarter of Hoi An.

Flecked with rice paddies and home to a burgeoning fishing industry, the inhabited regions of Central Vietnam are largely limited to its narrow coastal strip. The unspoiled hinterland gives way to the dramatic peaks of the Truong Son Range, which divide Vietnam from Laos. The region is home to hill people, as well as to the Hai Van Pass, one of the most scenic vantage points in the country. In the foothills near Dong Hoi is the mysterious Phong Nha Cave.

Some of the country's most outstanding architectural legacies are located in Central Vietnam. Among them, Hoi An still houses exquisite structures built by Chinese, Japanese, and French traders, dating as far back as the 16th century, while Hue, with its grand Citadel and Royal Tombs, stands as an abiding memory of

the Nguyen Dynasty (1802–1945). In ruins, but just as evocative, is the Cham temple complex at My Son, which was constructed between the 4th and 12th centuries AD. Most of these sites still bear traces of the damage they suffered during the Vietnam War.

Of more current historical interest are the villages – and now national shrines – of Hoang Tru and Kim Lien where Ho Chi Minh spent part of his childhood, as well as the former Demilitarized Zone (DMZ). Not far north of Hue, the DMZ witnessed some of the bloodiest battles of the Vietnam War and stands as a grim reminder of the vicious struggle of that era. Battle sites such as Khe Sanh and Vinh Moc have become poignant places of pilgrimage and mourning for both the Vietnamese and Americans.

Four of the Nine Dynastic Urns, each of which commemorates an emperor, Hue Citadel

◀ Ruins of ancient Hindu temples at My Son, near Hoi An

Exploring Central Vietnam

Home to some of the most spellbinding historic sites in the country, Central Vietnam's natural beauty is no less compelling. On the drive between Hue and Danang, the Hai Van Pass, surrounded by rolling hills and green valleys, offers the most spectacular views. As a base for exploring north of the pass, the old imperial city of Hue is elegant and the most convenient; nearby the small town of Lang Co has one of the best beaches in the region. North of Hue, the Demilitarized Zone evokes a tumultuous past, while the magnificent Phong Nha Cave stands among the most tranquil and scenic surroundings. South of the Hai Van Pass, both Hoi An and My Son are steeped in history and filled with centuries-old architectural marvels.

The ornate interior of the House of Phung Hung (see p128), Hoi An

Sights at a Glance

Towns and Cities
① Hoi An pp128–33
④ Ba Na Hill Station
⑤ Danang
⑩ Hue pp142–9
⑭ Dong Hoi
⑯ Kim Lien

Historic and Military Sites
② My Son pp134–6
⑪ Khe Sanh Combat Base
⑫ Demilitarized Zone (DMZ)

Beaches
③ China Beach
⑧ Lang Co Beach
⑨ Thuan An Beach

Areas of Natural Beauty
⑦ Suoi Voi
⑮ Phong Nha Cave

National Parks
⑥ Bach Ma National Park

Tunnels
⑬ Vinh Moc Tunnels

Key
— Major road
═ Minor road
— Railroad
▬ International border
▬ Provincial border

0 km   25
0 miles   25

For hotels and restaurants see pp236–41 and pp246–53

Vibrantly colored dragon boats along the banks of the Perfume River (see p152), Hue

Getting Around

The best way to travel around Central Vietnam is to rent a car but if this is not feasible, the minibus services are the next best option. These ferry travelers from one destination to the other and are useful for day-trips such as to the DMZ, out of Hue, or the Hai Van Pass on the way to Hue. Visitors can also get around by train, using the Reunification Express between Ho Chi Minh City and Hanoi. At Hoi An and Hue, visitors can explore by renting a bike or walking. Even better is a breathtaking boat trip down the Perfume River from the wharf by Le Loi Street. Hotels and tour operators organize these tours.

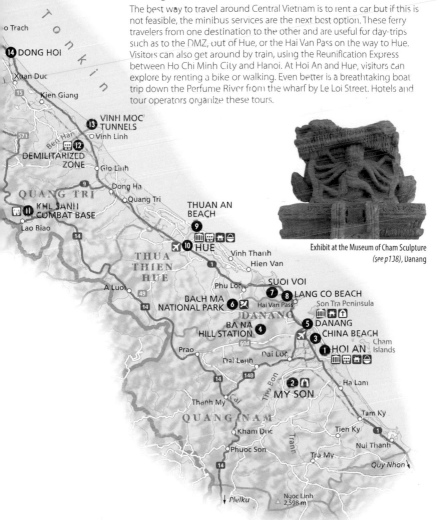

Exhibit at the Museum of Cham Sculpture (see p138), Danang

❶ Hoi An

Located on the north bank of the Thu Bon River, the historic town of Hoi An was an important trading port from the 16th to the 18th century. Attracting traders from China, Japan, and even Europe, the town acquired a rich cultural heritage, rivaled by few other cities in Vietnam. Designated a UNESCO World Heritage Site in 1999, Hoi An features long, narrow tube houses *(see p31)*, Chinese pagodas and ornate community halls, family shrines, and the Japanese Covered Bridge. There is also a recently restored small French-Colonial quarter southeast of Hoi An.

A shrine to the Tao god, Bac De, Japanese Covered Bridge

🏛 House of Phung Hung
4 Nguyen Thi Minh Khai St. **Tel** (0510) 386 2235. **Open** 8am–7pm daily.
📷 🏛

Built in 1780, this house has been home to the same family for eight generations. The clan

Colorful images of Chinese deities, House of Phung Hung

made its fortune in perfumed woods and spices, and maintain the same by selling souvenirs to tourists. Supported by 80 hardwood columns, the house shows a distinct Chinese influence in the galleries and window shutters. Japanese influence is evident in the glass skylights, while the general layout and design of the house is very much Vietnamese in style.

🏛 Japanese Covered Bridge
Intersection of Tran Phu and Nguyen Thi Minh Khai Sts. **Open** sunrise–sunset daily.

One of the town's most prominent landmarks, this rust-colored bridge *(see p130)* was constructed in 1593 by the

prosperous Japanese trading community, who were based on the west side of the town, in order to link it with the Chinese quarter farther to the east. However, in 1663, the Tokugawa Shogun Iemitsu issued edicts forbidding the Japanese from trading abroad, thus bringing the community to an abrupt end. In 1719, a Vietnamese temple was built into the northern section of the structure. Although a new name for the bridge, Lai Vien Kieu or Bridge from Afar, was carved over the temple door, locals continue to call it the Japanese Bridge. An effigy of Bac De, a reincarnation of the Taoist deity, the Jade Emperor, dominates the altar. The bridge,

Hoi An

① House of Phung Hung
② Japanese Covered Bridge
③ Cantonese (Quang Dong) Assembly Hall
④ Museum of Sa Huynh Culture
⑤ House of Tan Ky
⑥ House of Quan Thang
⑦ Tran Family Chapel
⑧ Museum of Trading Ceramics
⑨ Phuc Kien Assembly Hall
⑩ Quan Cong Pagoda
⑪ Hainan Chinese Assembly Hall
⑫ Central Market
⑬ Hoi An Artcraft Manufacturing Workshop

Key

◾ Street-by-Street area:
See pp130–31

↑ DANANG

PHAN DINH PHUNG · TRAN HUNG DAO · TRAN HUNG DAO

MY SON

Cua Dai Beach

LE LOI · NGUYEN HUE · HOANG DIEU · NGUYEN DUY HIEU · PHAN BOI CHAU

PHAN CHU TRINH

NGUYEN THI MINH KHAI

House of Phung Hung ①

⑦ Tran Family Chapel

Phuc Kien Assembly Hall

⑩ ⑪ Hainan Chinese Assembly Hall

Museum of Trade Ceramics ⑧ ⑨ Quan Cong Pagoda

② ③ Quang Dong Assembly Hall

④ Museum of Sa Huynh Culture

⑥ House of Quang Tang

⑫ Central Market

Japanese Covered Bridge

An Hoi Footbridge

⑤ House of Tan Ky

⑬ Hoi An Artcraft Manufacturing Workshop

BACH DANG

Cam Nam Bridge

Thu Bon River

AN HOI ISLAND

0 meters · 400
0 yards · 400

which is roofed in grey tiles, combines grace and strength in its short span across a tiny tributary of the Thu Bon River. It is a convenient pedestrian link between the art galleries of Tran Phu Street to those in the western part of town. Despite undergoing many renovations, the bridge's Japanese characteristics are intact.

🀄 Cantonese (Quang Dong) Assembly Hall

176 Tran Phu St. **Open** 7:30am–5pm daily. 🖼

Quang Dong is the Vietnamese name for the Chinese province of Guangdong, which was formerly known as Canton by Western countries. Built by seafaring merchants in 1786, this building is enlivened by bas-reliefs and colorful hangings. The main altar is dedicated to the great warrior Quan Cong (see p71), identifiable by his red face – emblematic of loyalty in Chinese society. Thien Hau, Goddess of the Sea, is also revered here.

🀄 Museum of Sa Huynh Culture

149 Tran Phu St. **Tel** (0510) 386 1535. **Open** 8am–5pm daily. 🖼

The small port of Sa Huynh (see p123), some 99 miles (160 km) south of the historic town of Hoi An, was the site of an eponymous prehistoric culture (1000 BC–AD 200). In 1909, more than 200 burial jars, filled with bronze tools, ornaments, and the remains of the dead, were unearthed from here. These fascinating artifacts, characterized by a very distinctive style of bronze work can now be admired in the small museum, which is housed in a fine Franco-Vietnamese building.

🀄 House of Tan Ky

101 Nguyen Thai Hoc St. **Tel** (0510) 386 1474. **Open** 8am–noon, 2–4:30pm daily. 🖼

Perhaps the most celebrated of Hoi An's many traditional abodes, the House of Tan Ky is an excellent representation of an authentic 18th-century Sino-Vietnamese shophouse style of construction. Built around a small courtyard, this structure, as is often the case in Hoi An, is an architectural hybrid. It carries fine Chinese crab-shell motifs on the ceiling, while its roof is supported by typically Japanese triple-beam joists. The floor is made with bricks imported from Bat Trang in the Red River Delta. Exquisite mother-of-pearl inlay Chinese poetry hangs from the columns that support the roof.

🀄 House of Quan Thang

77 Tran Phu St. **Open** 7:30am–5pm daily. 🖼

This one-story shophouse is a fine example of craftsmanship typical of Hoi An's traditional dwellings. Dating from the 18th century, this house was built by a sea-faring trader from Fujian in China, whose family have lived and prospered here for the last six generations. The house has a dark teak façade, and is roofed in curved Chinese style tiles. It can be accessed via the shop front, which leads into an interior courtyard. The walls of this enclosure are adorned with stucco bas-reliefs of flowers and trees. Beyond this beautiful courtyard is a narrow terrace used for cooking purposes. The wooden windows and shutters are finely carved.

Woodwork detail, Cantonese Assembly Hall

VISITORS' CHECKLIST

Practical Information
Road Map C4. 493 miles (793 km) S of Hanoi. 🚐 120,000. 🎎 Lantern Festival (every month). Ticketing System: Admission tickets for sights in the Old Quarter can be bought at the Tourist Office.
w hoian-tourism.com

Transport
🚌 from Danang. 🚉 🛈 Hoi An Tourist Office, 12 Phan Chu Trinh.

🀄 Tran Family Chapel

21D Le Loi St. **Tel** (0510) 386 1723. **Open** 7:30am–5pm daily. 🖼

This ancestral shrine was established more than two centuries ago to honor the forefathers of the Tran family. These venerable ancestors moved to Vietnam from China in the early 18th century, and eventually settled in Hoi An. The current descendants claim that they are the 13th generation since the migration from China. Over time, members of the family intermarried with local Vietnamese natives, and the chapel is appropriately hybrid (see p133). Artifacts belonging to the ancestors and memorial tablets decorate the main altar. A forefather who achieved the rank of mandarin is honored in a portrait in the reception hall of the chapel.

Carved wooden brackets in a courtyard, House of Tan Ky

Street-by-Street: Hoi An Old Quarter

Possessing an impressive historical and cultural legacy, Hoi An is a mosaic of various cultures. Its Old Quarter is redolent of an ancient period, along with a sense of timelessness. Its historic buildings, attractive tube houses, and decorated Chinese community halls have earned it the status of a UNESCO World Heritage Site. In efforts to protect the Old Quarter's character, stringent conservation laws prohibit alterations to buildings, as well as the presence of cars on its streets. In addition to its many monuments, the town has a wide array of delightful shops, offering almost everything Vietnam is famous for, as well as excellent roadside cafés. Combined with Hoi An's laid-back ambience, this creates an ideal setting where visitors can relax and unwind.

Sino-Japanese interiors of the ancient Tran Family Chapel

★ Cantonese Assembly Hall
Dating from 1885, this decorated community center is also known as the Quang Dong Assembly Hall *(see p129)*. Traditional Chinese paintings, with images of divine storks and the Goddess of Mercy, are showcased here.

To Tran Family Chapel

★ Japanese Covered Bridge
Symbolic of Hoi An and its rich mercantile past, this covered bridge was built in 1593 by the Japanese trading community to link them with the Chinese quarter in the eastern section of the town.

TRAN PHU

Key

— Suggested route

0 meters   50
0 yards   50

The Museum of Sa Huynh Culture is set in a French-Colonial house, and displays funerary urns, jewelry, and ceramics belonging to a 2,000-year-old society that flourished around Hoi An.

Chinese Assembly Hall was built in 1740 to serve the local Chinese community.

Phuc Kien Assembly Hall

Tran Phu 48

LE LOI STREET

To Central Market

NGUYEN THAI HOC

BACH DANG

Bach Dang Street overlooking Hoi An's Thu Bon River

Museum of Trading Ceramics
The ceramic ware displayed here dates from between the 16th and 18th centuries, including pieces from China, Japan, and Southeast Asia.

Tran Phu 77, a typical Hoi An tube house, has belonged to the same Fujian Chinese family for six generations.

★ **House of Tan Ky**
This unique 18th-century, two-story shophouse incorporates elements of Vietnamese, Chinese, and Japanese architectural design.

Roadside Cafés
The town's numerous cafés and restaurants offer visitors inviting places to relax and enjoy a selection of appetizing dishes and great drinks.

🏛 Museum of Trading Ceramics
80 Tran Phu St. **Tel** (0510) 386 2944.
Open 7:30am–5pm daily. 🖼

Housed in a traditional timber shophouse, with balconies and wood paneling, this museum is dedicated to Hoi An's historic ceramic trade, which flourished from the 16th to 18th centuries. Many pieces on display were recovered from shipwrecks, some near Cham Island off the mouth of Thu Bon River.

The riotously colorful façade of Phuc Kien Assembly Hall

🏯 Phuc Kien Assembly Hall
46 Tran Phu St. **Tel** (0510) 386 1252.
Open 7:30am–5pm daily. 🖼

A flamboyant building, this assembly hall was founded by merchants who had fled from the Chinese province of Fujian after the downfall of the Ming Dynasty in 1644. The temple complex is dedicated to Thien Hau, Goddess of the Sea, who is regarded as the savior of sailors. She presides over the main altar in the first chamber, and is flanked by attendants who are said to alert her whenever there is a shipwreck. To the right of the altar is a detailed model of a sailing junk, while in a chamber at the back, an altar honors the founding fathers who are represented by six seated figures.

🏯 Quan Cong Pagoda
24 Tran Phu St. **Tel** (0510) 386 2945.
Open 7am–6pm daily. 🖼

Also known as Chua Ong, this pagoda was founded in 1653, and is dedicated to the 3rd-century Chinese general, Quan Cong, a member of the Taoist

pantheon. An impressive gilded statue of him presides over the main altar, accompanied by two fierce-looking guardians, and a white horse, Quan Cong's traditional mount.

🏯 Hainan Chinese Assembly Hall
10 Tran Phu St. **Tel** (0510) 394 0529.
Open 8am–5pm daily.

This assembly hall was built in 1875 by Hoi An's immigrant community from Hainan Island in China. It is dedicated to the memory of 108 Hainanese seafarers killed by a renegade Vietnamese pirate-general in 1851. A lacquered board in the entry hall recounts their story in Chinese characters.

🛒 Central Market
Between Tran Phu and Bach Dang Sts.
Open sunrise–sunset daily.

Best visited in the morning, when the pace is not frantic, this lively market occupies two narrow streets that run south from Tran Phu to the banks of the Thu Bon River. There are stalls selling all kinds of fresh produce, kitchen utensils, and other equipment. To the east of the wharf is the market specializing in fresh seafood and meat. The main draws, though, are Hoi An's popular fabric and clothing stores *(see p256)*, which specialize in exquisite and inexpensive silks. Custom-made outfits can be ordered in less than a day.

🏛 Hoi An Artcraft Manufacturing Workshop
9 Nguyen Thai Hoc St. **Tel** (0510) 391 0216. **Open** 7am–6pm daily. 🖼 Tue–Sun.

Making lanterns at the Hoi An Artcraft Manufacturing Workshop

This handicrafts workshop specializes in the production of elegant lanterns, a specialty of Hoi An. These lanterns are handmade, using silk mounted on bamboo frames. Visitors can watch artisans at work, or make their own lanterns under expert supervision.

Traditional recitals featuring the *dan bau (see p28)*, a Vietnamese stringed musical instrument, are also staged in the workshop (10:15am and 3:15pm daily), and refreshments are available for visitors in the courtyard.

🏖 Cua Dai Beach
2.5 miles (4 km) E of Hoi An.

Cua Dai Beach is most easily reached by cycling down Cua Dai Road. The white sands look out onto the islands of the Cham archipelago making it a popular destination. Some of Vietnam's most attractive hotels such as the Victoria Hoi An Beach Resort and Spa *(see p239)*, and Ancient House *(see p239)* line the route and front the beach.

One of the finest beaches of Vietnam, Cua Dai Beach

Architectural Styles of Hoi An

Hoi An developed most of its uniquely eclectic townscape between the 16th and 19th centuries. During most of this time, it was a major port open to several foreign influences. The Japanese established a community west of the Covered Bridge during the 16th century, while the Chinese founded many communities in the center and east of town in the 18th century. Japanese and Chinese influence can be seen on the town's buildings. Later, the French left a distinct colonial stamp on the southeastern part of town. Over the years, many elements of these diverse architectural styles blended harmoniously with indigenous Vietnamese features. Hoi An was relatively untouched by the Vietnam War, and so the old world charm is still in place.

European-style balcony   Chinese roof

Vietnamese eyes, also known as *mat cua* or watchful eyes, are intended to protect the building and its inhabitants from malevolent influences.

French louvered shutters

Cultural and Architectural Mix

Hoi An's is a unique architectural amalgamation, not seen elsewhere in the country. In particular, Japanese, Chinese, and French influences are evident in Vietnamese tube houses, which feature Chinese tiled roofs, Japanese support joists, and French louvered shutters and lampposts. The town is a mosaic of cultures and yet a synthesis of all the influences.

French-Colonial architecture is reflected in the town's colonnaded houses. Most are painted warm yellow, with blue or green woodwork, and have verandas, balconies, and wooden shutters.

Vietnamese tube houses have two courtyards, an outer one to separate business from private quarters, and an inner one for the household's women. Most of them are elaborately decorated with carved wood, stucco, or ceramic designs.

The Chinese dragon is a mythical creature most closely associated with Sino-Vietnamese tradition, signifying continuity, power, stability, and prosperity. It is ubiquitous in Hoi An's buildings.

The Tran family chapel, which dates back more than two centuries, exhibits various Chinese and Vietnamese architectural elements, but is chiefly distinguished by its Japanese-style, triple-beam roof joists.

❷ My Son

A religious center between the 4th and 13th centuries, the Cham site of My Son became known to the world when French archaeologists rediscovered it in the late 1890s. Traces of around 70 temples may still be found at My Son, though only about 20 are still in good condition. The monuments are divided into 11 groups, the most important of which are Groups B, C, and D *(see p136)*. Group A was almost completely destroyed by US bombing during the Vietnam War. The most striking edifices are the famous Cham towers, which are divided into three parts: the base represents the earth, the center is the spiritual world, and the top is the realm between earth and heaven.

C1 Tower
This *kalan* or sanctuary was dedicated to Shiva, depicted as a standing sculpture in human form. The image is displayed at the Museum of Cham Sculpture *(see p138)*.

Ruins at B4
Built in the architectural style of structures at Dong Duong, another Cham city, the ruins here feature religious images carved on stone pilasters and elaborately embellished false doors.

★ **Shiva Lingam in B1**
A phallic symbol associated with Shiva, the *lingam* is shown within or above the *yoni*, a symbol of the goddess. Water was poured over the *lingam* and flowed through a spout on the *yoni* to symbolize creation.

★ **B5 Tower**
This 10th-century tower at B5 was used as a repository for temple treasures. It shows traces of the architectural marvel it was, with a boat-shaped roof, carved pilasters, and fine reliefs of Gajalakshmi, Goddess of Prosperity.

KEY

① **Finely carved stone pillars** belonging to the 8th century distinguish the ruins of B5.

② **The low walls** separating Groups B and C are of fine brickwork secured with limestone.

★ Deities on C1
The 8th-century celestial figures on C1 show distinct Javanese influence. The low wide belts worn by the figures are thought to be of Indian origin, and it is believed that the style came to Cham via Indonesia.

0 meters 30
0 yards 30

Central Causeway
A low, raised causeway extends between the two long halls of Group D that were once used as meditation chambers, as well as to receive guests and prepare offerings for the main shrines at Groups B and C.

Cham Statues
The exquisite statues (see p139) at My Son have been artistically carved out of brick and sandstone

Plan of My Son

Group A   Group F
Group A'   Group G
Group B   Group H
Group C
Group D
Group E

0 meters 500
0 yards 500

Key

▨ Area illustrated

★ Gallery at D2
The long hall of D2 has been transformed into a small museum showcasing sculptures saved from ruins of looted and bomb-damaged shrines. It is sheltered by the addition of a modern roof.

Exploring My Son

Designated a UNESCO World Heritage Site, My Son is best visited in the early or late hours of the day to avoid the stream of visitors. Although centuries of pillage and more recent bombings have taken their toll, the ruins provide a glimpse into a fascinating Indianized culture. Evocative as the complex is, the groups of monuments are rather unimaginatively named after letters of the alphabet. The most important edifices at Group B are reached first, while Group C is less well preserved. To the east, the halls of Group D house displays of Cham sculpture, while Groups E, F, G, and H require some imagination to truly appreciate.

Sculpture of an *apsara* in D2 gallery

Group C in a state of ruin at My Son

Groups A and A1
Said to be among My Son's most impressive edifices, Groups A and A1 were almost completely destroyed by USAF bombing in 1969. Little remains beyond rubble, but there are plans for restoration.

Records show that Group A once featured a striking tower, A1, said to have been the most important *kalan* (sanctuary) here. Unlike most Cham temples that only face east, A1 also had a door to the west, usually associated with death. This may have served as a link with Cham kings said to be interred in Groups B, C, and D. Also noteworthy is A9, with its winding patterns.

Groups B, C, and D
Situated at the center of the complex, Group B is remarkable for exhibiting elements of both Indian and Javanese art. The main sanctuary, built in the 11th century, was dedicated to King Bhadravarman, who built the first temple at My Son in the 4th

century, and to Shiva. One of the most unique structures in this group of monuments is B6, whose roof is decorated with an image of the Hindu god Vishnu being sheltered by a 13-headed *naga*. Group C forms a contiguous complex with Group B, separated only by a brick wall. Its central tower, C1, combines many elements from the older structures, including the tympanum and lintel. Built in the late 8th century, C7 is a squat tower with a stone altar, and is an architectural link between the styles of the Cham cities of Hoa Lai and Dong Duong. Toward the east of Groups B and C, the *mandapa* or meditation halls of Group D are now galleries for sculpture. Shiva *lingam*, as well as statues of Shiva and Nandi are

housed in D1, while D2 contains a stone Garuda, a Dancing Shiva, and *apsaras*.

Groups E, F, G, and H
Although the monuments in the northernmost reaches of the complex are the most damaged, they still offer fragments of beautiful craftsmanship. Built between the 8th and 11th centuries, Group E differs from the usual design of Cham temples. The main *kalan* has no vestibule, and only one temple faces eastwards. Adjoining it, Group F is badly damaged, but a finely carved *lingam* survives in the altar.

The 11th-century Group G has been restored over the last decade. Its tower's base features bas-reliefs of Kala, God of Time. Group H is badly damaged, and a carved stone tympanum of a Dancing Shiva that once adorned the temple is now in the Museum of Cham Sculpture *(see p138).*

Detail of *gopuram* or temple tower

Façade carvings made of brick

Carving of deity on the entrance

Stone pillars

Reconstruction of the once-spectacular Group A1 temple

Holiday resort set against the misted mountain tops of the Truong Son Range, Ba Na Hill Station

❾ China Beach

Road Map C4. 3 miles (2 km) SE of Danang.

The long stretch of beaches between Danang and the Marble Mountains is known to the Vietnamese as the My Khe, My An, and Non Nuoc beaches. However, these white sandy shores were known to US servicemen as China Beach and were later highlighted by an eponymous popular TV series. Though banned by the government, a number of developers have taken to using the designation China Beach in an attempt to encourage foreign visitors.

During the Vietnam War, the Americans – for whom Danang was among the most important and secure bases in South Vietnam – developed My Khe and My An beaches as a rest-and-recreation center for US forces taking a few days

leave from the war. Today, nothing remains of the former R&R facilities, although several souvenir stalls and seafood restaurants have sprung up here. A number of upscale resorts have opened towards the south end of the beach. The beach is fast becoming a popular destination for surfing and swimming (see p264). Summer months are the safest as the sea can be quite choppy.

❿ Ba Na Hill Station

Road Map C4. 25 miles (40 km) W of Danang.

A conveniently close getaway from Danang, this old French hill station is set at an altitude of 4,593 ft (1,400 m), and is

often shrouded in clouds or mist. In its French heyday, during the early 20th century, it is said to have been home to more than 200 villas, as well as restaurants and clubs. Sadly, Ba Na's glory days did not last long. Effectively abandoned during the Indochina Wars, it soon fell into disrepair.

However, the hill station has witnessed a resurgence of interest from the tourism authorities, and is being redeveloped into a vacation destination. Attractions include cliff-side resorts, karaoke bars, a cable-car ride, hikes to cascading waterfalls, views over Danang and the South China Sea, and the Linh Ung pagoda.

Saving My Son

Some of the greatest non-human casualties of the Vietnam War were the archaeological sites at My Son and Dong Duong. The situation in the area was particularly grave during and after the Tet Offensive in 1968 (see p49), when massive bombing raids by the US resulted in widespread

Warning sign at My Son

destruction. Previously, French archaeologists had listed around 70 structures at My Son. Only 20 escaped irreparable damage. Following this devastation, Philippe Stern, a leading authority on Cham history and art, complained bitterly to the US authorities, including President Richard Nixon. His attempts eventually bore fruit. In January 1971, the US ambassador was instructed by the US State Department to take all possible measures to preserve the historic site at My Son.

Today, with aid from UNESCO, archaeologists are still struggling to piece together what remains of My Son. Fortunately, the French left detailed architectural drawings, but the task remains all but impossible, and much of My Son has disappeared forever.

Street vendor selling snacks to visitors on China Beach

Altar to Quan Am, Goddess of Mercy, Pho
Da Pagoda

❺ Danang

Road Map C4. 67 miles (108 km)
S of Hue; 599 miles (964 km) N of
HCMC. 1,000,000. from
Hanoi, HCMC, and Nha Trang.
Reunification Express from Hanoi
and HCMC. from Hanoi, Hue,
HCMC, and Nha Trang.
ℹ Danang Tourism, 32A Phan
Dinh Phung, (0511) 386
3595. danang.gov.vn

Situated almost
halfway along the
country's coastline,
on the western bank
of the Han River,
Danang is one of the
fastest-changing
places in Vietnam. It
is the fifth largest
but third most
important city.

Stained-glass window,
Danang Cathedral

Though not a major destination
in its own right, Danang is an
excellent hub for exploring
several nearby attractions, and
is very well connected, with an
organized air, road, and rail
infrastructure linking it to points
north and south. Three of
Vietnam's world heritage sites –
Hoi An (see pp128–33), My Son
(see pp134–6), and Hue Citadel
(see pp144–7) – as well as scenic
beaches are main points of
interest here.

The city became prominent
during the 19th century. After
being captured by the French
in 1859, it rapidly developed,
replacing Hoi An as the main
port for Central Vietnam.
Further expansion took place
during the Vietnam War

(see pp48–9), when Danang
became an important military
base for the Americans. Vestiges
of all three eras can still be seen
in and around the city.

The **Museum of Cham
Sculpture**, or Bao Tang Dieu
Khac Cham, is one of the city's
highlights. Founded in 1915 by
École Française d'Extrême
Orient, the museum showcases
the world's best collection of
Cham sculpture, including
altars, sandstone pieces, busts
of Hindu gods such as Vishnu,
Shiva, and Brahma, and carvings
of scenes from the epic
Ramayana. All the sculptures
were recovered from nearby
Cham sites, including Tra Kieu,
the first Champa capital, My Son,
and Dong Duong among
others, and date from the 7th
to the 13th century.

The pink-colored **Danang
Cathedral** was constructed in
1923 and has five tiers rising
to a steeple crowned with
a cockerel. Another
interesting sight is the
Cao Dai Temple, the
largest after its main
counterpart, Cao Dai
Holy See (see pp78–9)
in Tay Ninh. Also worth
visiting are **Phap Lam
Pagoda**, honoring the
Thich Ca Buddha, and
Pho Do Pagoda,
which is pale cream,
with orange tiles and
green trimming. The
central temple building, which
houses the main altar, is flanked
by two triple-roofed towers
with flaring eaves. This lovely
pagoda is also used as a

Buddhist college for training
monks and nuns.

Danang's newest attraction
is the spectacular **Dragon
Bridge**, which spans the Han
River. Not only is it illuminated
with LED lighting at night,
it also breathes fire and
spouts water at intervals.

Environs
Some of Vietnam's most
breathtaking vistas can be seen
at **Hai Van Pass** on Truong Son
Range, about 18 miles (30 km)
north of Danang. The summit
of the pass offers splendid views
of mountains covered in thick
clouds, with the blue waters
of Danang Bay below. A short
distance southeast of the city
are the **Marble Mountains**. As
the name suggests, these rocky
formations are made of marble,
and comprise several caverns that
have long sheltered a series of
shrines dedicated to the Buddha
or to Confucius. Just northeast of
Danang is **Monkey Mountain** or
Nui Son Tra, named after its
primate population. To the west
of this are the **Tombs of Spanish
and French Soldiers**, killed in the
1858 French attack on Danang.

🏛 **Museum of Cham Sculpture**
Corner of Bach Dang and Trung Nu
Vuong Sts. **Tel** (0511) 347 0114.
Open 8am–5pm daily.
chammuseum.danang.vn

🏯 **Cao Dai Temple**
63 Hai Phong St. **Tel** (0511) 369 8710.
Open 6am–6pm daily.

🏯 **Pho Da Pagoda**
340 Phan Chu Trinh St. **Tel** (0511) 382
6094. **Open** 5am–9pm daily.

Limestone promontories, Marble Mountains, Danang

Cham Art and Sculpture

The Cham Empire existed in Vietnam for around 1,600 years, from the 2nd century AD to its downfall in 1832. Today, a thriving Cham community survives, but all that remains of their ancient kingdom is its artistic legacy, which reached its zenith in the 8th to 10th centuries. Part of this heritage is architectural, visible in the red brick temples found scattered across Central Vietnam. Other elements are sculptural, carved chiefly in sandstone and marble or, more rarely, cast in bronze, and discovered at sites such as Tra Kieu, My Son, and Dong Duong. Religious in inspiration, Cham art derives from the Indic tradition and represents Hindu deities with their celestial mounts, dancing girls, and demons. This tradition is expressive and exudes a unique sensuality.

The makara is a mythical sea creature from the Hindu pantheon. Cham art was inspired by Hinduism and many such Hindu sculptures decorate their temples.

Dancing girl of Tra Kieu

The early 10th-century dancing apsara, *or celestial nymph, from an altar pediment at Tra Kieu, outside Danang, is celebrated for her sensuality and grace. Close attention was paid to hairstyle, costume, and jewelry in Cham art.*

The headgear of the dancer is an elongated and elaborately decorated hair retainer.

Exquisite ornaments on the *apsara's* dress, both emphasize and conceal her femininity.

This altar pediment is embellished with a circular arrangement of sculpted breasts. The breast is a common motif in Cham art. It is thought to represent the Hindu mother goddess, Uma.

Garuda is the eagle mount of the Hindu god, Vishnu. Cham sculptors used stone or terracotta to carve various Hindu mythical gods and animals.

This altar frieze, dating back to the late 12th century, depicts a rider on horseback drawing a chariot. The fine detailing is clearly visible despite the sandstone's weathering.

Recovered from an altar in My Son, this well-preserved example of 7th- to 8th-century Cham art shows a flautist playing within an elaborate marble niche.

Five Lake Cascade Trail, Bach Ma National Park

🌀 Bach Ma National Park

Road Map C4. 28 miles (45 km) SE of Hue. **Tel** (054) 389 7360. 🚌 from Hue and Danang to Cau Hai. From Danang, Hue, Hoi An, and Cau Hai. **Open** daily. 🐾 🗐 🗐 🖥 📷 W bachmapark.com.vn

Located in the Hue-Danang provincial frontier, at an elevation of 4,757 ft (1,450 m), Bach Ma National Park was originally established as a hill station in the 1930s by the French. The Viet Minh did not take kindly to this imperialist occupation, and the area was subjected to many attacks during the First Indochina War *(see p47)*. By the time the war came to its close, most of the French had abandoned their beautiful villas. Later, in the 1960s, the Americans fortified Bach Ma and there were many bitter confrontations with the members of the Vietcong in the hilly forests. After the communist victory in 1975, however, the hill station lay forgotten for many years.

Fortunately for Bach Ma, in the early 1990s it underwent a revival. In 1991, the authorities granted national park status to this vast 85 sq miles (220 sq km) of forested land. Although sprayed with defoliants during the Vietnam War, the forest is showing encouraging signs of recovery due to dedicated conservation efforts. The park is

home to a wide variety of flora and fauna, which includes more than 2,140 plant species. Many of these are said to have medicinal properties. Almost 130 species of mammals have been identified in the park area. Among them are the rare *saola*, the giant muntjac, as well as the recently discovered Truong Son muntjac *(see p205)*. Primates living here include langurs, lorises, macaques, and the white-cheeked gibbon. It is possible that leopards and tigers inhabit remote corners of the park, but this has not been confirmed. Bach Ma National Park is also a bird-watcher's paradise, with an astounding 358 species listed by the park authorities, among them the endangered Edward's

Edward's pheasant, Bach Ma National Park

pheasant. While little remains of the former French hill station, a few ruins can be seen amid the foliage, lending the jungle an eerie atmosphere. A narrow path leads to an observation post at the park's highest point which, weather permitting, affords glorious views across the rugged Truong Son Range.

Bach Ma National Park can only be reached by private transport. Those who enjoy walking may like to wander along the **Pheasant Trail** where the calls of gibbons are often heard, or the **Rhododendron Trail** which leads to the 300-metre tall Do Queyen waterfall. Check that the park is open before visiting as road repairs can affect accessibility.

🌀 Suoi Voi

Road Map C3. 40 miles (65 km) S of Hue; 9 miles (15 km) N of Lang Co on Hwy 1. 🚌 from Hue. **Open** 6:30am–9:30pm daily. 🐾 🖥

A popular weekend destination for the inhabitants of Hue or Danang, Suoi Voi, also known as Elephant Springs, is named after a huge rock that resembles the animal. This is a wonderful bathing spot, not usually frequented by visitors.

On the way from Hue, in order not to miss its tucked away location, look out for a large sign that indicates a track leading off to the right toward the springs. About 1.5 miles (2.5 km) from here, passing the old Thua Lau Church on the way, is the entrance gate and car park for Suoi Voi. From here, the walk to the main springs is about 1 mile (1.6 km). Once there, the effects of the long, dusty walk can be washed away in its refreshing waters. Several large boulders surround the tree-filled area. All this is set scenically against the thickly jungled peaks

Macaque monkey, Bach Ma National Park

Visitors enjoying a relaxed lunch at a seaside restaurant, Lang Co Beach

of the Truong Son Range. Excellent for a break on the way to or from Hue, Suoi Voi is a perfect picnic spot. Facilities are minimal but there are usually food stands near the springs.

❽ Lang Co Beach

Road Map C3. 47 miles (75 km) S of Hue; 22 miles (35 km) N of Danang on Hwy 1. 🚌 from Hue and Danang. 🚆 from Hue or Danang.

To appreciate the full beauty of the Lang Co Peninsula, it is best to first catch a glimpse of it from the summit of the Hai Van Pass or from the wonderful, atmospheric train ride between Hue and Danang. Looking north from here, an idyllic picture in shimmering blue, white, and green appears. A narrow spit of pristine white sand runs south from the Loc Vinh commune, dividing a gleaming saltwater lagoon to its west from the choppy South China Sea to its east. It is an idyllic location, with miles of palm fringed, soft white sand contrasting beautifully with the aquamarine waters of the lagoon and the changing shades of the wave-flecked sea.

The beach is ideal for a leisurely swim, especially in the summer months before July, after which the area can get rather wet and dreary. Fortunately, an excellent seafood lunch can be enjoyed here in any season. There are also several resorts in the area for those wishing to make a longer stay. The sleepy Lang Co village provides a glimpse into Vietnam's simple coastal way of living.

Just south of Lang Co, a bridge vaults across the lagoon, leading to the road tunnel that carries Highway 1 beneath the Hai Van Pass. This sheltered area around the bridge provides a convenient harbor for local fishermen. A stroll along this inland part of the spit reveals brightly-painted fishing boats as well as coracles, which are tiny circular boats that look a little like wicker baskets.

❾ Thuan An Beach

Road Map C3. 9 miles (15 km) NE of Hue on Hwy 49.

One of the best beaches in the Hue region, Thuan An is located at the northern end of a long, slender island that runs all the way south from the mouth of the Perfume River (see p152), almost up to the little town of Phu Loc.

The beach is in many ways comparable to the one at Lang Co, some 56 miles (90 km) farther south. Like it, Thuan An features a pleasing strip of white sand flanked by tall, swaying coconut palms. It is washed by the calm blue waters of the Thanh Lam Lagoon to the southwest, while the rather stormy waves of the South China Sea lap its northeast shores.

Still relatively undeveloped, the village of Thuan An is sparsely settled by fishermen, whose boats are pulled up along the sandy shores. The manufacture of *nuoc mam* or fish sauce is an important industry here. Its pungent – some may say putrid – odor permeates the air in certain areas. The vats used for fermenting the liquid are obvious not only from the smell but also because of their vast size.

Thuan An is a convenient and enjoyable destination for a cycling day trip from Hue. Getting to the beach is half the fun, as it entails a ride through numerous tranquil villages and rural scenery, dotted with several quaint pagodas along the way. The island and beach can be accessed via a small bridge over the Thanh Lam Lagoon. A narrow road runs along the length of the island, hugging the lagoon side, as far as Thanh Duyen Pagoda on its southernmost tip.

Lagoon near Lang Co Beach, with a clear view of the summit of the Hai Van Pass

⑩ Hue

One of the most significant cultural and historic centers of Vietnam, the former imperial city of Hue is celebrated for its tradition of intellectual thought, Buddhist piety, and the sophistication of its cuisine. Despite the damage it suffered during the Indochina Wars, it remains a place of great beauty, with the Perfume River (see p152) flowing through it. To the north is the Citadel (see pp144–7), containing the Forbidden City and the royal palaces, while to the south are many ancient pagodas and tombs, and the town's French Quarter. Excellent hotels and restaurants along with its palpably French atmosphere add to the city's many attractions.

Business as usual in the constantly busy Dong Ba Market

🕮 Imperial City
See pp144–7.

🏛 Royal Antiquities Museum
3 Le Truc St. **Tel** (054) 352 4429.
Open 7am–5pm Tue–Sat. 🖼 🎫

Following extensive renovations, this museum has been relocated from the former private residence of Emperor Khai Dinh and his adopted son Bao Dai to its original location in Long An Palace in the Citadel. Originally built in 1845, the palace is supported by 128 ironwood columns and features a multi-tiered roof.

The exhibits, which are all from the Nguyen Dynasty (1802–1945) include silver crafts, fine porcelain, antique furniture, and items from the royal wardrobe, Khai Dinh's bed as well as Bao Dai's shoes. Unfortunately, there is little explanation or information offered on this grand collection.

🛕 Dieu De Pagoda
102 Bach Dang St. **Tel** (054) 381 5161.
Open sunrise–sunset daily.

Built during the reign of Thieu Tri (r.1841–7), the third Nguyen Emperor, Dieu De fell into disrepair over the years, but was restored in 1889 by Emperor Than Tha. Renovated many times since, it dates from 1953 in its present form.

The pagoda is distinguished by drum and bell towers, and a sanctuary dedicated to the Thich Ca Buddha, or the Historical Buddha. As with other Buddhist pagodas in Hue, it is closely associated with the politics of nationalism and opposition to the oppressive Diem regime (1955–63). In May 1963, Buddhist monk Nun Nu Thanh Quang immolated himself here in protest.

🏪 Dong Ba Market
Northeast of Tran Hung Dao St.
Open daily.

Hue's bustling Dong Ba Market is located to the north of the Perfume River, near the southeast corner of the Citadel. A popular local shopping center, it attracts huge crowds daily. Stalls here overflow with an astonishing variety of goods, from fresh produce and fish to clothing, toys, shoes, and cosmetics. The market is at its busiest and most fascinating in the early hours of the morning, even though it is open throughout the day.

✝ Notre Dame Cathedral
80 Nguyen Hue St. **Tel** (054) 382 8690.
Open during mass.

Built between 1937 and 1942 in a hybrid Franco-Vietnamese style, this large and somewhat unappealing church serves around 1,500 local believers. Two masses are held daily at 5am and 5pm, with a third mass at 7am on Sunday. At other times, the main gates are generally locked.

🛕 Bao Quoc Pagoda
Bao Quoc St. **Tel** (054) 383 3382.
Open sunrise–sunset daily.

Giac Phong, a Buddhist monk from China, founded this historic pagoda on Ham Long Hill in 1670. It was later granted royal status by the Nguyen lord, Phuc Khoat (r.1738–65). In the late 18th century, the powerful Tay Son (see p45) rebel, Quang Trung, used this house of worship for storing armaments. The temple was also given royal support by Emperor Minh Mang (r.1820–41). In 1940, it became a school for training Buddhist monks, a function it fulfills to this day. Though it was renovated in the

The colonnaded entryway of Bao Quoc Pagoda

mid-20th century, the pagoda retains its charm and aura of antiquity even today.

🏛 Tu Dam Pagoda

Lieu Quan St. **Open** sunrise–sunset daily.

Founded in the 17th century, this temple's chief importance is as a center for supporting Buddhism, a cause that has been at the heart of Central Vietnam's political culture for a long time. The Vietnamese Buddhist Association established its headquarters here in 1951, and the temple was a major hub of activity during the Buddhist agitation against President Diem's unpopular Catholic regime during the mid-20th century. As was the disturbing trend at the time, in 1963 a monk burned himself to death in the pagoda's courtyard in protest against the oppressive administration.

An exquisite urn in the courtyard of Tu Dam Pagoda

The central altar is presided over by the Thich Ca Buddha, and a tree in the temple grounds is said to have been grown from a cutting of the original *bodhi* tree in India.

🏛 Thanh Toan Covered Bridge

Thanh Thuy Chan Village, 4 miles (7 km) E of Hue.

VISITORS' CHECKLIST

Practical Information
Road Map C3. Capital of Thua Thien Hue Province, 62 miles (110 km) N of Danang.
🏛 360,000. 🛈 Hue Tourist, 120 Le Loi St, (054) 381 6263.

Transport
🚆 Reunification Express Hanoi and Ho Chi Minh City.
🚌 from Hanoi, Vinh, Danang, Nha Trang, and Ho Chi Minh City. 🚌

The little known but delightful covered bridge in Thuy Thanh Commune is architecturally similar to the famous Japanese Covered Bridge *(see p128)* at Hoi An, as well as the covered bridge across the canal at Phat Diem. Getting to it is half the fun, and provides a great trip through scenic villages.

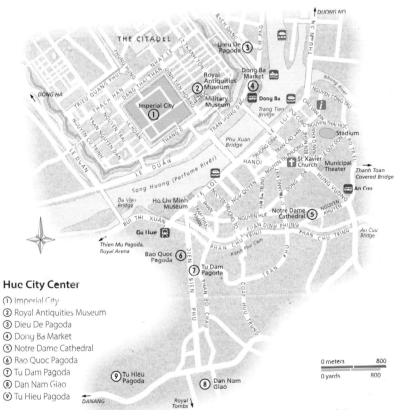

Hue City Center

0 meters 800
0 yards 800

For keys to symbols *see back flap*

Hue Citadel: Imperial City

Designated a World Heritage Site in 1993, the Citadel was established by Emperor Gia Long (r.1802–20) in 1805. The huge fortress comprises three concentric enclosures – the Civic, Imperial, and Forbidden Purple Cities. The Citadel was designed using the rules of Chinese geomancy, along with the military principles favored by French architect Sebastien de Vauban. The result is an unusual yet elegant complex, where beautiful palaces and temples coexist with massive ramparts, bastions, and moats. Despite the horrific damage caused by the Indochina Wars, recent restoration work has re-imagined some of the Citadel's lost architectural grandeur.

Richly decorated gilt and lacquer altar to a Nguyen king, The Mieu

Hung Mieu
Dedicated to the veneration of Emperor Gia Long's mother and father, this 19th-century temple is known for the glazed carvings on its tiled roof. Particularly noteworthy are the large gargoyle-like stone dragons keeping vigil over the spacious paved courtyard.

★ Nine Dynastic Urns
Cast between 1835 and 1837, these massive bronze funerary urns stand in the courtyard facing The Mieu. They represent the might of nine Nguyen Emperors, and are richly embellished with bas-reliefs of a host of powerful symbols.

KEY

① **The Mieu** honors ten Nguyen Emperors, and has been restored to its original splendor.

② **Royal Library**, an elegant two-story structure, heavily decorated with ceramic mosaics, is now on the brink of collapse.

Hien Lam Pavilion
Built by Emperor Minh Mang in 1824, Hien Lam Pavilion is a three-storied galleried portico, with a wooden façade, decorated with engraved wooden beams and panels in floral designs.

VISITORS' CHECKLIST

Practical Information
Road Map C3. 23 Thang 8 St,
Hue. ℹ Hue Tourist, 120 Le Loi
St, (054) 381 6263.
Open 7am–5pm daily.

Transport
✈ 🚂 HCMC and Hanoi.
🚌 Danang.

Royal Theater
Completed in 1826, the beautifully
constructed Royal Theater has
a pagoda-style curved roof, and
a colorful interior, featuring
lacquered columns,
etched with the
ubiquitous golden
dragon motif.

★ **Thai Hoa Palace**
The grand throne palace of the Nguyen Emperors,
Thai Hoa Palace is dominated by 80 red lacquered
wooden columns. These massive structures are
ornately decorated with golden dragons, the
emblem of the Nguyen Dynasty.

★ **Ngo Mon Gate**
The majestic main entrance to
the Citadel, Ngo Mon is a superb
example of Nguyen architecture.
Massive stone slabs form the
foundation, upon which rests
an elaborate watchtower, where
the emperor sat enthroned on
state occasions.

Exploring Hue Citadel: Imperial City

At the very heart of the vast Hue Citadel lies the Imperial City, also known as Dai Noi or the Great Enclosure. Over the past few years, this historic and unusually evocative part of the Citadel has undergone extensive restoration work, which has allowed more than just a glimmer of its former glory and grandeur to shine through. Entrance to this royal city is via the imposing Ngo Mon Gate, beyond which a bridge leads between lotus-filled ponds to the splendid Thai Hoa Palace. Behind this is an open courtyard that overlooks a stretch of land, once home to the Forbidden Purple City.

🎏 Cot Co or Flag Tower

Looming over the Citadel at a height of 120 ft (37 m), the Flag Tower or Cot Co has dominated Hue's skyline since 1809, when Emperor Gia Long (r.1802–20) erected it over a big 59-ft (18-m) brick redoubt.

On January 31, 1968, during the Tet Offensive (see p49), Cot Co achieved international recognition when the commu-nist forces seized the Citadel, hoisting the National Liberation Front's yellow-starred banner on the Flag Tower's mast.

Nine Deities' Cannons

Cast by Emperor Gia Long in 1803 as symbolic protection for his new capital, these colossal cannons were made out of bronze. Each weapon is said to represent one of the four seasons and five elements – earth, metal, wood, water, and fire. The cannons can be seen flanking the Ngan and Quang Duc Gates on either side of Cot Co.

🏛 Five Phoenix Watchtower

Located above the huge stone slabs of the Ngo Mon Gate, this elaborate pavilion was where the emperor sat enthroned on state occasions. Viewed from above, it is said to resemble a group of five phoenixes. The middle section of the roof is covered with yellow glazed tiles, and decorated with dragons, banyan leaves, and bats, while the panels along the eaves are embellished with ceramic orchid, chrysanthemum, and bamboo mosaics. Above the pavilion, a concealed staircase leads up to a room from where women of the court could see through finely carved grills.

🏛 Thai Hoa Palace

🎫 in the throne room.

Originally built by Emperor Gia Long in 1805, Thai Hoa or Hall of Supreme Harmony housed the throne room of the Nguyen Emperors. The most impressive of Hue's remaining palaces, it has been beautifully restored. It is easy to envisage the hall as the venue for coronations, royal anni-versaries, and the reception of ambassadors. On these occasions, the emperor would sit on the resplendent throne, wearing a crown with nine dragons, a gold robe, jade belt, and other attire. Only the most senior mandarins were allowed to stand in the hall, while others waited outside.

🏛 Halls of the Mandarins

On either side of a paved courtyard, just behind Thai Hoa, are the Halls of the Mandarins. One hall was for the military, and the other for civil mandarins. In keeping with their ranks, they would gather at their pavilions to dress in ceremonial robes for imperial functions. Some of these gorgeous vestments are now kept on display here.

Ancient bronze cauldron in the courtyard, Halls of the Mandarins

🏯 Forbidden Purple City

No man except the emperor was permitted to set foot in the 25-acre (10-ha) city-within-a-city known as Tu Cam Thanh or Forbidden Purple City – any male who crossed its threshold was condemned to death. Only the queen, nine separate ranks of concubines, female servants, and court eunuchs were allowed to enter.

Built during 1802 and 1833, the Forbidden City once comprised more than 60 buildings arranged around numerous courtyards, but unfortunately, it was damaged extensively by heavy bombing during the 1968 Tet Offensive.

🎭 Royal Theater

Originally built in 1825, the Duyet Thi Duong or the Royal Theater is once again a leading venue for traditional entertain-ment, offering performances of nha nhac (see p29) or court music. Declared a Masterpiece of the Oral and Intangible Heritage of Humanity by UNESCO, nha nhac features bamboo lutes, zithers, and fiddles, accompanied by drums.

Four of the Nine Deities' Cannons, one for each season and element

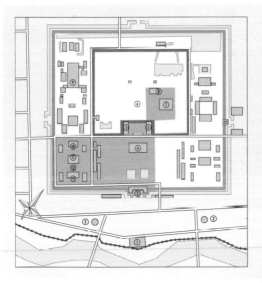

Plan of Imperial City

① Cot Co
② Nine Deities' Cannons
③ Five Phoenix Watchtower
④ Thai Hoa Palace
⑤ Halls of the Mandarins
⑥ Forbidden Purple City
⑦ Royal Theater
⑧ Royal Library
⑨ Dien Tho Palace
⑩ Hung Mieu
⑪ The Mieu
⑫ Nine Dynastic Urns
⑬ Hien Lam Pavilion

Key

▬▬ Imperial City
▬▬ Forbidden Purple City
▮ Area illustrated (see pp144–5)
•→•→ Wall of The Citadel

📖 Royal Library

In the northeastern quarter of the Forbidden City, the Royal Library was constructed by Emperor Minh Mang in 1821, as a retreat where he read in solitude. The decrepit building stands before an artificial pond, with a rock garden to its west. Small bridges, crossing other lakes and ponds, connect various galleries, creating a tranquil atmosphere. The library has been used to stage performances of Hue music, as well as various theatrical events.

Antique furnishings and wood paneling, Dien Tho Palace

🏛 Dien Tho Palace

Once the exclusive preserve of the Queen Mothers, Cung Dien Tho or the Residence of Everlasting Longevity was built

in 1803 during the reign of Emperor Gia Long. Open to the public, the elegant building is surrounded by a wall that is pierced on the south by Cua Tho Chi or the Gate of Everlasting Happiness. Inside the building, the crafted furniture is carefully inlaid with delicate mother-of-pearl, and carved lanterns hang from the ceiling, which is ornamented with fans made from feathers. To the east of the entrance to the palace is the Truong Du Pavilion, with a small artificial lake and a graceful rock garden.

🏛 Hung Mieu

Emperor Minh Mang built Hung Mieu in 1821 to honor his grandparents. The temple was seriously damaged by fire in 1947 at the beginning of the First Indochina War, but has now been restored. It is renowned for its refined design and fine roof carvings.

🏛 The Mieu

Located in the southwest area of Imperial City, The Mieu or the Temple of Generations is dedicated to the Nguyen Dynasty, and contains altars

Miniature funerary urn, The Mieu

honoring emperors, from Gia Long to Khai Dinh. The building has a roof of yellow glazed tiles, the ridge of which is decorated in the shape of a wine gourd. The altars were once stacked high with gold ingots, but today these have been replaced with gilt and lacquer ornamentation.

Nine Dynastic Urns

Cast on the orders of Emperor Minh Mang, Cuu Dinh or Dynastic Urns of the Nguyen Dynasty weigh up to 2.75 tons each. Decorated with traditional patterns, and rich in symbolic detail, they play a big role in the cult of imperial ancestor veneration.

📖 Hien Lam Pavilion

Located in the center of the The Mieu court, Hien Lam was built in 1824 by Emperor Minh Mang to honor those who gave the great Nguyen Dynasty its formidable status. As a mark of respect, it was declared that no other building in the Citadel could rise higher than Hien Lam, which is distinguished by its pyramid shape, as well as its finely crafted wooden façade and brick paving.

🛈 Dan Nam Giao

2 miles (3 km) S of city center, southern end of Dien Bien Phu St. **Open** 8am–5pm daily. 📷

Built by Emperor Gia Long in 1802, Dan Nam Giao or the Altar of Heaven stands beyond the former French Quarter on the east side of the Perfume River *(see p152)*. For more than a century, this was the most important ceremonial site in the country. Approximately every three years, between 1806 and 1945, the Nguyen Emperors reaffirmed the legitimacy of their rule through a series of elaborate sacrifices to the Emperor of Heaven. The ritual was consciously modeled on the rites practiced in Beijing by the Chinese emperors at the 15th-century Tian Tan or Temple of Heaven.

Today, not much remains of this ceremonial site other than a series of three raised terraces. The first two are square-shaped and are said to represent humanity and earth. The circular terrace at the top symbolizes the heavens. Though there isn't much of the building left, the site has plenty of atmosphere. In this setting, it is easy to conjure up images of the emperors as the rightful Sons of Heaven, interceding with the gods on behalf of their subjects.

🏛 Tu Hieu Pagoda

Thon Thuong 2, Thuy Xuan Village, 3 miles (5 km) SW of Hue. **Tel** (054) 383 6389. **Open** 6am–6pm daily.

Set amid the attractive pine woods to the north of Tu Duc's tomb, Tu Hieu Pagoda is surrounded by a delightful crescent-shaped lotus pond.

The crumbling but fairly intact remains of the Royal Arena

One of the most serene pagodas in the Hue region, it was established in 1848 by imperial eunuchs. Since they could not have children, the eunuchs financially secured the temple, thus guaranteeing that future generations of monks would always be on hand to perform the necessary ceremonies for their lives in the hereafter. Indeed, several monks still inhabit Tu Hieu and hold prayer services daily. The main shrine is dedicated to Sakyamuni Buddha, also known as the Thich Ca Buddha. Lesser altars carry images and tablets honoring various deities and some prominent eunuchs of the past.

🏛 Thien Mu Pagoda

3 miles (5 km) SW of Hue Citadel. **Open** sunrise–sunset daily.

Rising on a bluff above the northwest bank of the Perfume River, Thien Mu or Heavenly Lady Pagoda is an iconic symbol of Hue. Founded in 1601 by Lord Nguyen Hoang, the pagoda is dominated by a seven-story octagonal tower, Thap Phuoc Duyen, which translates as Source of Happiness Tower. A pavilion close by shelters a huge bronze bell cast in 1710. Weighing more than 4,409 lb (2,000 kg), it can purportedly be heard at least 6 miles (10 km) away. A second pavilion houses a stone stele erected in 1715, which eulogises the history of

Thich Quang Duc's blue Austin, Thien Mu Pagoda

Buddhism in Hue. Inside, the main shrine is presided over by a laughing bronze Buddha and statues of the ten kings of hell and 18 arhat or holy disciples of the Buddha. Close by is a striking image of the Thich Ca Buddha. The monks' quarters and gardens are at the back of the temple. In an open garage to the west is the car that drove monk Thich Quang Duc *(see p48)* to Saigon in June 1963, where he immolated himself in protest against the Diem regime. Images of this horrific event were shown all over the world, provoking widespread shock and outrage.

🏛 Royal Arena

Phuong Duc Village, 3 miles (4 km) SW of Hue. **Open** sunrise–sunset daily.

Built for the entertainment of the Nguyen Emperors and the mandarins, this amphitheater is also known as Ho Quyen or the Tiger Arena. It was used to stage combats between elephants, symbolizing royalty, and tigers, signifying the former Champa Kingdom. As a result, these contests were rigged so that the elephant would win. To achieve this, the tiger was declawed and had its mouth sewn shut. Fortunately, no fights have been held since 1904, but the place remains in fairly good condition. The viewing platforms are intact, as are the five doors opposite leading to the tigers' cages.

Lotus pond in front of the small and serene Tu Hieu Pagoda

Exploring the Royal Tombs

Scattered across the scenic countryside to the south of Hue, the tombs of the Nguyen Emperors *(see p45)* are among the area's most compelling attractions. Although 13 rulers sat on the imperial throne between 1802 and 1945, only seven were given the honor of their own mausoleum, or *lang*, as the others died during exile or in disgrace. All seven tombs have features of outstanding architectural merit, and can be reached by bicycle, motorbike, taxi, and by boat. The tomb of Duc Duc is most modest of the lot.

Concrete exterior of the least traditional royal tomb, Khai Dinh

🏛 Tomb of Tu Duc

4 miles (6 km) SW of Hue. **Tel** (054) 383 6428. **Open** 7am–5pm daily. 🖼

Considered by many to be the most elegant tomb in Vietnam, the mausoleum of Tu Duc (r.1848–83) was designed by the king himself. Set on a pine-forested hill, it is flanked by beautiful lotus ponds and aromatic frangipani trees. Tu Duc was known to have preferred the quiet comforts of his future tomb to his own palace. It is said that when Tu Duc died, he was buried secretly along with a great treasure. All those involved in his burial were later executed to keep his final resting place safe from desecration.

🏛 Tomb of Dong Khanh

0.3 miles (0.5 km) SE of Lang Tu Duc. **Tel** (054) 383 6427. **Open** 7am–6pm daily. 🖼

The smallest of all Nguyen tombs is the mausoleum of Dong Khanh (r.1885–88). The French influence is quite prominent in its interior, where images of Napoleon Bonaparte hang from the red-lacquered ironwood pillars. The tomb benefitted from a restoration project completed in 2009.

🏛 Tomb of Thieu Tri

1 mile (1.5 km) S of Lang Tu Duc. **Open** 7am–5pm daily. 🖼

The small tomb of Thieu Tri (r.1841–47) features several artificial ponds, although it lacks the usual extensive walled gardens. The complex is divided into two parts. To the east, a delicate temple salutes the deceased, while to the west is the tomb itself.

🏛 Tomb of Khai Dinh

6 miles (10 km) S of Hue. **Tel** (054) 386 5875. **Open** 6am–5.30pm daily. 🖼

Khai Dinh (r.1916–25), the penultimate Nguyen Emperor, was the last to be buried in a royal tomb at Hue. His tomb makes use of concrete, combining European and Vietnamese architectural styles in a unique but not entirely successful fusion. Built into the side of a hill, the tomb rises steeply through three levels. In the temple at the summit is a bronze bust of the emperor, cast at Marseilles in 1922.

🏛 Tomb of Minh Mang

7 miles (12 km) S of Hue. **Tel** (054) 356 0277. **Open** 7:30am–5:30pm daily. 🖼

Located on the west side of the Perfume River, the mausoleum of Emperor Minh Mang, who died in 1841, is one of the most impressive royal tombs. The complex comprises picturesque lakes and gardens, as well as numerous buildings.

🏛 Tomb of Gia Long

10 miles (16 km) SE of Hue. 🖼

The mausoleum of the first Nguyen Emperor, Gia Long, is best reached by boat, either from Hue or from the tiny village of Tuan, opposite Lang Minh Mang. The most remote of all, it suffered extensive damage during the Vietnam War and sadly is still in a state of disrepair.

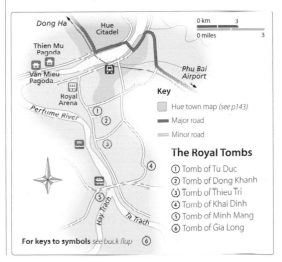

The Royal Tombs

① Tomb of Tu Duc
② Tomb of Dong Khanh
③ Tomb of Thieu Tri
④ Tomb of Khai Dinh
⑤ Tomb of Minh Mang
⑥ Tomb of Gia Long

Key

◻ Hue town map *(see p143)*
━ Major road
═ Minor road

For keys to symbols see back flap

Perfume River Boat Tour

One of the main highlights of a visit to Hue is a boat ride along Song Huong or the Perfume River. Though not very long, the slow-winding river is extraordinarily beautiful. The effect is enhanced by the reflection of the Citadel, pagodas, towers, and the scenic countryside. Added to this spectacular view is the picturesque river traffic – women sculling tiny, single-oared vessels, larger boats piled high with fish and fresh vegetables, and fishermen in narrow crafts, casting their nets or retrieving fish traps.

A fishing boat on the calm blue waters of Perfume River

② Thien Mu Pagoda

Set amidst verdant greenery, this is the oldest pagoda in Hue. Built in 1601, the 69-ft (21-m) high tower is an official symbol of the city of Hue (see p148).

③ Temple of Literature

This tiny temple was built by Emperor Gia Long in 1808 to replace the venerable Temple of Literature in Hanoi.

Phu bai Airport

① Citadel

Once the royal seat of the Nguyen Emperors, this imposing structure is a UNESCO World Heritage Site (see pp144–7).

④ Royal Arena

This royal amphitheater, used for entertaining the Nguyen Emperors, is a unique kind of architectural work that is rarely found in Southeast Asia (see p148).

⑤ Hon Chen Temple

Full of altars, spirit houses, and stelae, this attractive temple dates back more than a thousand years, to the ancient Champa. It can be approached only by boat.

0 kilometers 2
0 miles 1

Key

▬▬ Major road

══ Minor road

⑥ Tomb of Minh Mang

This is possibly the best preserved royal tomb in Hue. Graceful statuary, ponds, and beautifully landscaped gardens add to the mausoleum's grandeur (see p149).

Tips for the Trip

Tour boats: Hire boats from the wharf by Le Loi Street. Try to haggle the price quoted. Or take a well-organized tour.
Time taken: Half a day.
Stopping-off points: Snacks available at Thien Mu and Minh Mang. Most boatmen arrange a lunch on request.

⓫ Khe Sanh Combat Base

Road Map B3. 90 miles (145 km) NW of Hue on Hwy 9. **Tel** (053) 388 0840. 🚌 minibus from Hue. Museum: 1 mile N of Khe Sanh town. **Open** 7am–5pm daily. 🅿 🚻 🖵

Situated close to the Laos border, the Khe Sanh Combat Base lies about 2 miles (3 km) away from Khe Sanh village, now known as Hoang Ho. It was initially developed as an airstrip by the Americans in 1962, and later enlarged and developed into a US Special Forces base charged with intercepting traffic on the Ho Chi Minh Trail (*see p155*).

However, Khe Sanh is best known as the site of one of the most ferocious battles of the Vietnam War, and as the beginning of the end for the Americans in Vietnam. In 1968, the famous US General William Westmoreland started a massive build up at the base with a view to forcing the North Vietnamese Army into direct confrontation. Vietnam's General Vo Nguyen Giap took the bait, but in a masterful doubleplay, used the siege, which lasted from January to April 1968, to distract attention from the Tet Offensive (*see p49*). Diversionary tactic or not, the heavy deployment of bombs and relentless gunfire resulted in a number of casualties. An estimated 207 American and 9,000 Vietnamese soldiers died, and several thousand civilians lost their lives.

Although this battle was not, as President Johnson feared, another Dien Bien Phu (*see p199*), the Americans, though undefeated, were forced to withdraw from Khe Sanh. They took great pains to bury, remove, or destroy, rather

Military memorabilia from the Vietnam War, DMZ

The historic Hien Luong Bridge over the Ben Hai River, DMZ

than abandon their military equipment where it could be used as propagandist evidence of their "defeat."

Today, Khe Sanh is on the tourist map, with guided tours available. The drive along Highway 9, past statues and plaques, is part of the Central Vietnam experience. Though nothing had been left behind, American weaponry and vehicles were brought in from elsewhere in the south to fill the small **Museum** here.

⓬ Demilitarized Zone

Road Map B3. 55 miles (90 km) NE of Khe Sanh on Hwy 9. **Tel** (053) 385 2927. 🚌 minibus and taxi from Hue. **Open** 7am–5pm daily.

Though it lost all strategic and political importance after reunification in 1975, the Demilitarized Zone (DMZ) has

become a major tourist attraction and can be visited on a day trip from Hue or Dong Ha. Most tours start with the **Hien Luong Bridge** over the Ben Hai River, which once formed the frontier, and a visit to the well-constructed Vinh Moc Tunnels (*see p154*). The Truong Son National Cemetery, based to the west of Highway 9, honors the many thousands of North Vietnamese soldiers and Vietcong fighters killed in the area.

From here, it is convenient to head inland from Dong Ha along Highway 9, passing former US bases en route. Camp Carroll, Khe Sanh, and Hamburger Hill (*see p49*) have entered popular consciousness through Hollywood movies. While there is not very much in the way of "sights," the DMZ provides an often saddening tour. It is especially popular with military historians and American visitors.

History of the DMZ

During the 1954 Geneva Conference, a decision was taken to establish the DMZ at the 17th Parallel as a "provisional demarcation line" between North and South Vietnam (*see pp48–9*). The boundary stretched 3 miles (2 km) on either side of Ben Hai River, continuing to the Lao border. From the beginning, however, the North Vietnamese Army (NVA) managed to penetrate the DMZ with their tunnels, trails, and guerilla tactics. In response, the Americans and South Vietnamese planted mines and built extensive electrified fences along Highway 1 in what became known as the McNamara Line after Robert McNamara, the then US Secretary of Defense. Ironically, the DMZ saw some of the heaviest fighting of the Vietnam War, particularly during the siege of Khe Sanh and the 1972 Easter Offensive, when the NVA seized the entire area, leading to a massive American retaliation.

Canon displayed at Khe Sanh near DMZ

The cavernous depths of a tunnel at the Vinh Moc complex

⑬ Vinh Moc Tunnels

Road Map C3. 8 miles (13 km) E of Ho Xa on Hwy 1; 12 miles (20 km) NE of the DMZ. **Tel** (053) 382 3184. 🚌 minibus from Hue and Dong Ha. **Open** 7:30am–5pm daily. 🎒 📷

Some of the most resilient tunnels built in Vietnam were at Vinh Moc, a village along the South China Sea shore. Occupied by hundreds of people between 1968 and 1972, these tunnels were intended for long-term inhabitation. They are different from the better-known ones at Cu Chi (see p76), which was more of a frontline fighting base.

Vinh Moc's troubles began because of its location. After the nation's partition in 1954, villages along the north of the Demilitarized Zone (see p153), including Vinh Moc, found themselves under almost constant attack. Moreover, Vinh Moc faces Con Co Island, a North Vietnamese base used for transporting weapons and supplies to the south, making it a key target for strikes by the South Vietnamese Army. The United States Air Force (USAF) also contributed to the huge barrage of bombs, and Vinh Moc was nearly razed to the ground. While some inhabitants fled, others decided to stay, even if they had to go underground. The villagers, aided by the Vietcong, worked with nothing but spades, baskets, and their bare hands to excavate the complex tunnel network.

Created in about 18 months, the network stretches for 2 miles (3 km), with 13 entrance points. Family rooms, a hospital, and a meeting hall fill its three levels. The villagers and the North Vietnamese soldiers lived here for more than four years – 17 children were born here. From these tunnels, almost 12,000 tons of military supplies and equipment were sent to Con Co.

Today, the marvel created by the villagers of Vinh Moc can be seen almost exactly as they were in 1972. Unlike Cu Chi, it is possible to negotiate these tunnels standing up straight, though taller visitors do have to stoop. The museum here makes for a fascinating browse. An added advantage are the sunny beaches nearby.

Bombed church in Dong Hoi

⑭ Dong Hoi

Road Map B3. 101 miles (162 km) N of Hue on Hwy 1. 🚍 115,000. 🏠 🚌 from Vinh, Dong Ha, and Hue. 🛈 Quang Binh Tourism, 1 Me Suot St, (052) 382 2018. 🌐 **quangbinh tourism.vn**

The capital of Quang Binh Province, Dong Hoi was once a charming little fishing village. However, mirroring Vietnam's changing economic policies, it has evolved into a leading transit town. Though there are no major sights here, it is remarkable to see how the town has recovered from the ravages of war. What was rubble a few decades ago has now changed to wide avenues and well-maintained buildings.

It is also interesting to note that for the best part of 150 years, Dong Hoi marked the de facto frontier between the Trinh and Nguyen lords (see p45). Two major ramparts were constructed to keep the enemies separated, but all that remains of them is a crumbling gateway.

Though often only used as a stopover on the way to the Phong Nha Cave, there are some fine beaches nearby. Nhat Le, 2 miles (3 km) north of town, has one of the best.

⑮ Phong Nha Cave

Road Map B3. Son Trach Village, 34 miles (55 km) NW of Dong Hoi. **Tel** (052) 367 5323. 🚌 from Dong Hoi. 🚤 from Son Trach. **Open** 7am–4pm. 🎒 📷 🚤 🖥 📷

Phong Nha dates back at least 20 million years and well deserves its designation as a UNESCO World Heritage Site. Its name translates somewhat alarmingly as Wind's Fangs, but this is only an allusion to its stalagmites. Packed with underground grottos, stalactites, stalagmites, and river systems, it extends back into the hills for many miles. The main cavern is some 5 miles (8 km) deep, with several smaller yet stunning caves clustered near it. Although speleologists have penetrated 22 miles

(35 km) into the cave system, there are further mysteries of Phong Nha still to be revealed

Not surprisingly, this is a very popular destination, and fleets of sampans wait at the visitors' center to ferry passengers upstream for about 3 miles (5 km), and then into the huge cavern. About a mile (1.6 km) into the cave is an area once held sacred by the Cham. The cave wall still bears an inscription carved by them many centuries ago.

Nearby are two recently-discovered caves - **Thien Duong** (Paradise Cave) and **Son Doong** (Mountain River Cave). Both the caves are now open to the public. Son Doong, also believed to be the biggest cave in the world, is the object of many scientific researches as well. Only a handful of tourists are permitted entry in a year and at the cost of thousands of dollars each.

⑯ Kim Lien

Road Map B2. 9 miles (14 km) NW of Vinh. 🚌 minibus from Vinh.

A pilgrimage site of sorts, Kim Lien is celebrated as the birth-place and childhood home of Ho Chi Minh *(see p173)*, who was born in nearby **Hoang Tru** village in 1890. He stayed there until he was five years old, and then moved to Hue with his father. In 1901, however, he returned and stayed here for another five years.

A bamboo loom in the model of Ho Chi Minh's childhood home, Kim Lien

A sampan dwarfed by the magnificence of Phong Nha Cave

A man who always shunned the trappings of power, Ho Chi Minh vetoed the construction of a museum to his life at Kim Lien, arguing that the funds could be better used. Since his death in 1969, museums and shrines have proliferated here. About 1 mile (1.6 km) away at Hoang Tru, is a reconstruction of the house where he was born. A small museum nearby displays pictures and other personal memorabilia related to the leader's life. Also in this area is a reconstruction of the house where he lived from 1901 to 1906. In keeping with the great man's high principles, entry to all these sites is absolutely free of charge.

Ho Chi Minh Trail

A complex network of hidden tracks and paths, the Ho Chi Minh Trail, or Duong Truong Son, was used as a strategic connection between North and South Vietnam during the Vietnam War (1957–75). Built on simple tracks that had existed for centuries, the trail provided logistical support to communist forces in the south, supplying them with weapons, food, and legions of North Vietnamese troops (NVA).

Section of the trail running through bomb craters

It is assumed that the labyrinthine trail started in the north near the port of Vinh. From there, it wound its way west through the Truong Suong Range, before snaking along the Vietnamese-Lao border and crossing into Laos and Cambodia. It finally entered South Vietnam at various obscure points. It is estimated that the total length of tracks and roads forming the trail was around 12,427 miles (20,000 km).

In 1972, South Vietnamese forces mounted a large scale incursion into Laos to cut the trail, but withdrew after sustaining heavy losses. Other failures followed despite massive bombing and defoliation by the South Vietnamese and Americans. In the meantime, NVA activity continued along the trail, playing a decisive role in the victory of the North.

HANOI

The oldest and one of the most attractive capital cities in Southeast Asia, Hanoi exudes a rare sense of gracious charm and timelessness. At its core exists a 600-year-old ancient quarter, augmented by a century-old colonial city. Today, the rich cultural heritage of both blends in perfect harmony with growing modernization, as Hanoi claims its position as the heart of Vietnam.

Hanoi, the "City within the River's Bend," was founded by Emperor Ly Thai To in AD 1010, near Co Loa, the ancient capital of the first Viet state dating back to the 3rd century BC. Ly Thai To structured this city, then known as Thang Long, around a massive citadel. To the east of this, a settlement of guilds was established to serve the needs of the royal court. By the 16th century, this area had developed into Hanoi's celebrated Old Quarter (see pp160–61).

The arrival of the French in the 19th century marked a period of reconstruction, as they tore down parts of the citadel and some ancient temples to make way for the new European quarter. However, this cultural vandalism was compensated for, to a large extent, by the magnificent colonial architecture they bequeathed the city. During the First Indochina War (see p47), the city's central districts escaped largely unharmed, and subsequently, in 1954,

Hanoi was proclaimed the capital of independent Vietnam. Sadly, this was not the end of its violent history as it was then plunged into the conflict-ridden years against the US. Hanoi entered the 21st century a little run down yet structurally sound despite the years of warfare. The Opera House is still grand, as is the Sofitel Legend Metropole Hotel.

Today, Hanoi is emerging as an elegant, cultured, and affluent city, where museums and galleries coexist with chic shops and fashionable restaurants. One can wander, in a few minutes, from the narrow streets of the Old Quarter to the imposing mansions and buildings lining the leafy boulevards of the former French Quarter. Hanoi's past has also ensured a superb culinary legacy, where French and Chinese cuisines blend marvelously with Viet traditions. The same is true of Hanoi's lively arts scene, which is among the most sophisticated in Southeast Asia.

Well-maintained French-Colonial building in the old French Quarter of Hanoi

◀ St Joseph's Cathedral in Hanoi, Vietnam

Exploring Hanoi

Hanoi's most significant sights and districts are marked on this map. Hoan Kiem Lake is popular for romantic strolls, morning exercise, and evening entertainment. The natural focus of the city center is to the north of the lovely lake. Known as the Old Quarter or 36 Streets, this area is packed with every imaginable merchandise, from shoes and silk to bamboo and lacquer products. To the south, which constitutes the downtown area, are the boulevards and architectural marvels of the former French Quarter. To the west is the tranquil Temple of Literature, and Ho Chi Minh Mausoleum, notable for its grandeur.

Sights at a Glance

Churches, Temples, and Pagodas
2. Bach Ma Temple
5. St. Joseph's Cathedral
7. Ambassador's Pagoda
11. Hai Ba Trung Temple
12. Lien Phai Pagoda
13. *Temple of Literature pp170–71*
17. One Pillar Pagoda
22. Kim Lien Pagoda
25. Thay Pagoda
26. Tay Phuong Pagoda
27. Hung Kings' Temples

Historic Buildings
19. Ho Chi Minh's Stilt House
20. Hanoi Citadel
23. Co Loa Citadel

Markets
1. Dong Xuan Market

Museums and Theaters
3. Thang Long Water Puppet Theater
6. Hoa Lo Prison Museum
9. Opera House
10. National Museum of Vietnamese History
14. Vietnam Fine Arts Museum
15. Vietnam Military History Museum
16. Ho Chi Minh Museum
18. Ho Chi Minh Mausoleum
24. Museum of Ethnology

Lakes
4. Hoan Kiem Lake
21. Ho Tay

Hotels
8. Sofitel Legend Metropole Hotel

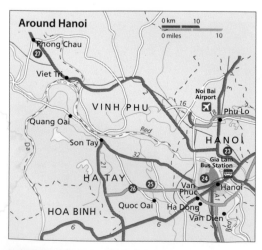

Getting Around

Hanoi's Old Quarter is small and fascinating enough to explore on foot, as is the area around Hoan Kiem Lake. Self-driven cars are not yet an option, though the brave, or reckless, may rent a bicycle or motorbike. Farther afield, It is better to take a taxi, since the city bus service is still in its infancy. Most hotels and travel agencies can arrange taxis or minibuses to visit sights within the city as well as to the outskirts, on full or half-day tours.

Street-by-Street: Old Quarter

Buzzing with noise and activity, the Old Quarter is the oldest and most lively commercial district in Hanoi. During the 13th century, several artisans settled along the Red River to cater to the needs of the palace. Later, the crafts became concentrated in this area, with each street specializing in a particular product. Over the years, 36 distinct crafts guilds came into existence, and the area earned its nickname of 36 Streets. Today, with narrow alleys packed with hundreds of small shops, restaurants, and ancient tube houses *(see p31)*, the Old Quarter retains its historic charm.

View of the centuries old, narrow, and long tube houses in the Old Quarter

❶ ★ Dong Xuan Market
Occupying a three-storied building, Dong Xuan is the oldest market in town, selling a variety of goods, including clothes, foods, household items, and more.

Hang Ma Street
Overflowing with sparkling paper products, Hang Ma or Votive Paper Street sells bright and colorful lanterns, "gold" ingots, tinsel, paper money, paper houses, and other paper replicas of material possessions to be burned as votive offerings to deceased ancestors.

LÃ VỌNG

0 meters 100
0 yards 100

Cha Ca La Vong
One of Hanoi's oldest eateries, Cha Ca La Vong has been serving a single dish – monkfish in a marinade of galangal, saffron, fermented rice, and fish sauce – for more than a century.

Key

━ Suggested route

For hotels and restaurants see pp236–41 and pp246–53

Hang Buom Street
Formerly the Sailmakers Street, Hang Buom now sells a remarkable selection of locally made sweetmeats and candies, many different varieties of fresh ground coffee, and imported alcohol, chiefly whiskies, brandies, and even wines.

Locator Map

Quan Chuong or the Gate of the Commander of the Regiment is the only remaining gateway to the Old Quarter out of the original 36.

Hang Mam Street or Pickled Fish Street is now lined with shops selling marble headstones, often engraved with an image of the deceased.

❷ ★ **Bach Ma Temple**
The oldest religious building in the Old Quarter, this small temple is dedicated to the city's guardian spirit, represented by a magical white horse.

To Den
Ngoc Son

Street Names in the Old Quarter

Most of the streets in the Old Quarter are named after the trade guilds that they once represented. The street names generally begin with the word *hang*, which means merchandise, while the second word describes the type of product. Streets here include Hang Gai (Silk Street), Hang Tre (Bamboo Street), Hang Bac (Silver Street), Hang Huong (Incense Street), and so on. Today, most of the streets in the Old Quarter offer products other than just what their name suggests. Even so, the survival of this system of guild streets is probably unique in East Asia.

Musical instruments, Hang Non Street

Memorial House Museum
Once the home of an affluent Chinese family, this beautifully restored tube house provides an excellent insight into the lives of merchants who lived in the Old Quarter centuries ago.

Memorial altar to General Ma Vien set amid flowers, Bach Ma Temple

The temple was restored in the 19th century, with contributions from the Hoa Chinese community settled on Hang Buom Street. Although a statue of the white horse still features prominently, the Hoa also introduced the veneration of Ma Vien, the Chinese general who re-established Chinese control over Vietnam in AD 43. An antique, carved palanquin is also on display.

❸ Thang Long Water Puppet Theater

57 B Dinh Tien Hoang St, Hoan Kiem District. **Map** 2 E3. **Tel** (04) 3825 5450. **Open** performances at 1:45pm, 3pm, 4:10pm, 5:20pm, 6:30pm, 8pm and 9:15pm daily; also 9:30pm Sun. 🎥 extra for still and video cameras. 🖥 🎦 Ⓦ thanglongwaterpuppet.org

This is possibly the best place, not just in Hanoi, but in the entire country, to see performances of the traditional art of *roi nuoc* or water puppetry. The showmanship is excellent as master puppeteers make extensive use of dramatic music from the traditional orchestra and startling special effects, such as smoke, firecrackers, and water-spraying dragon puppets to create a lively performance. At the end of the show, the bamboo curtain behind the watery stage rises to show the puppeteers, standing waist deep in water. Seats closest to the stage provide superb opportunities for photography.

❶ Dong Xuan Market

Intersection of Dong Xuan and Hang Chieu sts, Old Quarter. **Map** 2 E2. **Tel** (04) 3829 5006. **Open** 6am–6pm daily. 🖥 🎦

As the oldest and largest covered market in Hanoi, Cho Dong Xuan holds a dominant position in the city. Near the end of the 19th century, the French tore down the old East Bridge Market that stood at this site, and replaced it with a covered building with five large halls. Dong Xuan is named after a hamlet that once stood on this site and is now a commercial center. However, in 1994, the market suffered a major setback when a massive fire burnt down much of the building. Although it was rebuilt in 1996, all that remains of the original structure is the restored 1889 façade.

Today, this bustling three-story structure is packed with a wide range of clothing and household goods, fresh vegetables, meat and fish, and varieties of rice. Apart from local items, some low-cost, foreign goods are sold too. Located nearby is the historic

Long Bien Bridge. Its strategic importance as the only bridge across Hanoi's Red River made it a prime target of the US Air Force during the Vietnam War*(see pp48–9)*. It survived the heavy bombing and is now used by crowds of hawkers and pedestrians.

❷ Bach Ma Temple

76 Hang Buom St, Old Quarter. **Map** 2 E2. **Open** sunrise–sunset daily.

This small yet elegant temple is the oldest building in the Old Quarter *(see pp160–61)*, dating in its original form from the founding of the capital city of Thang Long *(see p164)*, which became known as Hanoi in the 19th century. According to legend, when King Ly Thai To established the capital in 1010, the city walls kept falling down until a magical white horse appeared and indicated where the new fortifications should be built. In an expression of his gratitude, Ly Thai To built the Bach Ma or White Horse Temple, and Bach Ma became the guardian spirit of the city.

Puppets at the popular Thang Long Puppet Theater

Water Puppet Theater

Originating in the Red River Delta, and believed to date back almost a thousand years, *roi nuoc* or water puppetry is one of the most authentic expressions of Vietnamese culture. In times past, performances were held in villages, using rivers, lakes, or rice fields. Today, they are staged in large water-filled tanks at theaters. Hiding behind the stage, the puppeteers stand waist deep in water and maneuver their wooden charges to the music of a traditional orchestra. Special effects, including fire-breathing dragons, smoke, and fireworks add excitement to the show. The tales are told from the age-old perspective of a peasant culture and feature traditional protagonists and villains such as warrior heroes, corrupt landlords, and cruel rulers.

Ty ba, a popular plucking stringed instrument, used by musicians in many traditional orchestras. Made of light wood, it has four strings on its long neck.

Live singers and instrumentalists enhance the puppeteers' performance. The music rises to a crescendo at key moments in the story and accompanies the show at all times.

Popular Themes

The themes of *roi nuoc* are usually traditional and pertain to rural life. Mythical beasts in Viet culture such as dragons, phoenixes, and unicorns, feature prominently, as do water buffalos and other domestic animals.

A palanquin is being carried by servants.

An elaborate parasol symbolizes rank and authority.

Puppets are carved from water-resistant wood, generally that of the fig tree or *sung*, and painted with bright colors.

A fake palm tree adds a rural touch to the set.

Village folk surround a dragon, a much-loved and auspicious mythical creature that is one of the most prominent characters.

Puppeteers emerge from behind the curtain at the end of the show. Their skill is acknowledged by claps and rousing cheers.

Scenic setting of The Huc or the Sunbeam Bridge, Hoan Kiem Lake

❹ Hoan Kiem Lake

Hoan Kiem District. **Map** 2 E3.
Open 24 hours daily. 🖉 🖵 🏛 Den
Ngoc Son Hoan Kiem Lake.
Open 7am–7pm daily.

Situated in the heart of Hanoi, this delightful body of water also lies close to the hearts of the Vietnamese people. Legend has it that in the early 15th century, during the Ming Chinese occupation (see p44), General Le Loi was presented with a magical sword by a divine, golden turtle, which lived in the lake's waters. With the help of this sword, Le Loi expelled the Chinese from Thang Long, present-day Hanoi, and established himself as Emperor Le Thai To. Some time later, when the emperor was sailing on the lake, the divine turtle once again rose to the surface and reclaimed the sword. Since then, the lake has been known as Ho Hoan Kiem, or the Lake of the Restored Sword.

In the mid-19th century, a small pagoda called **Thap Rua** or Turtle Tower was built to commemorate this supernatural event. Located on an islet in the center of the lake, the structure has since become a prominent city icon.

On an island at the northern end of Hoan Kiem Lake stands **Den Ngoc Son** or Jade Mountain Temple, one of the most beautiful and revered religious buildings in the capital. The temple can be accessed by an attractive red-painted, arched wooden bridge. This is the celebrated **The Huc** or Sunbeam Bridge. Dating from the Nguyen Dynasty in the early 1800s, the temple's building is exquisitely preserved. Decorated with upswept eaves and elaborate carved dragons, the predominant colors are red, gold, yellow, and black. The temple was established by a mandarin named Nguyen Van Sieu. A stylized stone ink slab rests atop the temple's gate, while nearby, a tapering stone pillar represents a traditional writing brush. The ideograms on the stele translate as "writing on a clear sky." A giant turtle that died in the lake in 1968 is preserved in a room at the back. Den Ngoc Son is dedicated to the spirits of the soil, medicine, and literature, as well as to Tran Hung Dao, the general who defeated the Mongols in the 13th century (see p44).

To the east of the lake is the large, bronze **Statue of Ly Thai To**, honoring the great founder of Thang Long. The statue, which has already become quite popular with pious Vietnamese, is venerated with incense and flowers.

Today, Hoan Kiem Lake is one of the city's most popular venues, generally packed with couples taking a stroll, people practicing Tai Chi, and old men playing chess. The lake also plays a major role during the city's Tet celebrations (see pp32–3), with stages for live music and a huge fireworks display.

The Thap Rua, or Turtle Tower reflected in Hoan Kiem Lake

The Founding of Thang Long

In AD 968, Tien Hoang De, the first ruler of the Dinh Dynasty, moved his capital from Dai La, situated in the immediate vicinity of modern-day Hanoi, to Hoa Lu, 50 miles (80 km) to the south in Ninh Binh Province. With this move, Tien Hoang intended to relocate to a region that would be as far removed as possible from the Chinese frontier. However, this shift would not last for long. Just 42 years later, Ly Thai To, founder of the Ly Dynasty, grew dissatisfied with the physical isolation of Hoa Lu and determined to move the capital back to Dai La. In 1010, he returned to the former capital, defeated the Chinese in a violent battle, and established his kingdom here. According to legend, as he entered the city, a golden dragon took off from the top of the citadel and soared into the heavens. This event was taken by the emperor as an auspicious sign, and he renamed the city Thang Long or Ascending Dragon.

Puppets of golden dragons, an auspicious mythical creature

Neo-Gothic façade and imposing spires of St Joseph's Cathedral

❺ St Joseph's Cathedral

Nha Tho St, Hoan Kiem District. **Map** 2 E3. **Tel** (04) 3828 5967. **Open** 5am–7pm daily. **Chua Ba Da** 3 Nha Tho St, Hoan Kiem District. **Open** sunrise-sunset daily.

Hanoi's most important church, St Joseph's Cathedral, also known as Nha Tho Lon, was inaugurated in 1886, and provides a focal point for the city's Catholics. Built in the late Neo-Gothic style, the building, with its majestic spires, is architecturally similar to a cathedral that might be found in any French provincial town. The interiors, which are more noteworthy, feature an ornate altar, French stained-glass windows, and a recent bas-relief painting of the Three Kings, complete with camels, on the cathedral's rear wall. St. Joseph's is usually packed to capacity on Sundays and on major holidays such as Easter and Christmas. However, on most days, its main doors are generally closed except during mass, but it is possible to gain entry via the side door.

Located to the east of the cathedral is **Chua Ba Da** or Stone Lady's Pagoda. Dating back to the 15th century, the pagoda was once known as Linh Quang or Holy Light. However, according to legend, the discovery of a woman's stone statue when the pagoda was being constructed led to its more common local name.

Entered by a narrow alley, Chua Ba Da is an oasis of tranquility in the heart of old Hanoi. The pagoda features several statues of the Thich Ca or Sakyamuni Buddha, and also contains two large, antique bronze bells.

❻ Hoa Lo Prison Museum

1 Hoa Lo St, Hoan Kiem District. **Map** 2 D4. **Tel** (04) 3824 6358. **Open** 8am–5pm daily.

Located in downtown Hanoi, the infamous Hoa Lo Prison was built by the French administration in 1896. Originally intended to hold around 450 prisoners, by the 1930s the number of detainees had soared to almost 2,000, the majority of them being political prisoners. During the Vietnam War, Hoa Lo Prison achieved notoriety as a place of incarceration for downed US pilots, who ironi-

Mural showcasing colonial torture, Hoa Lo Prison Museum

cally nicknamed it the Hanoi Hilton. Named Maison Centrale during the French rule – the original sign still hangs over the entrance – most of the prison complex was demolished in 1997 in order to make way for the Hanoi Towers buildings. However, the architects preserved enough of the old prison to create the Hoa Lo Prison Museum.

The majority of the exhibits here include a horrifying array of shackles, whips, and other instruments of torture, as well as tiny solitary confinement cells, which date from the French-colonial period. Also on display is part of the old, narrow sewer system through which more

than 100 prisoners escaped in August 1945. A small section of the museum is devoted to the American period, contriving to show how well US prisoners (including US senator John McCain) supposedly fared in contrast to the brutality shown to the Vietnamese by the French. At the back of the museum is a guillotine, a surprisingly simple yet terrifyingly efficient killing machine.

❼ Ambassador's Pagoda

73 Quan Su St, Hoan Kiem District. **Map** 2 D4. **Tel** (04) 3825 2427. **Open** 8–11am, 1–4pm daily.

Established as a stopping point for visiting Buddhist dignitaries, Chua Quan Su or Ambassador's Pagoda is named after a guesthouse that once stood here in the 15th century. The official center of Mahayana Buddhism in Hanoi, it is one of the most popular pagodas in the city, attracting hundreds of followers, especially during important Buddhist holidays.

The present-day pagoda dates from 1942 and houses images of the past, present, and future incarnations of the Buddha – the A Di Da or Amitabha, Thich Ca or Sakyamuni, and Di Lac or Maitreya Buddhas. Many nuns and monks are in attendance. A small shop by the entrance sells Buddhist paraphernalia and ritualistic items.

Ornate altar with multi-armed Buddha, Ambassador's Pagoda

❽ Sofitel Legend Metropole Hotel

15 Ngo Quyen St, Hoan Kiem District.
Map 2 F4. **Tel** (04) 3826 6919.
Open 24 hours daily. 🅰️ 🖊️ 💻 📷
🅦 **sofitel-legend.com** Government
Guest House: 10 Ngo Quyen St, Hoan
Kiem District. **Closed** to public.

Hanoi's most prestigious and oldest hotel, the Metropole was built in French-Colonial style, with plenty of wrought iron and Art Nouveau decorations. Originally opened in 1901, it was for many years the most favored accommodation in all of French Indochina. Notable guests, both past and present, include actors, writers, heads of state, and many other well-known public figures, such as W. Somerset Maugham (1874–1965), Charlie Chaplin (1889–1977), Graham Greene (1904–91), Noël Coward (1899–1973), Michael Caine, and Vladimir Putin.

Although the hotel became deplorably rundown during the austere years of state socialism between 1954 and 1986, it has since been magnificently restored to its former glory and luxurious grandeur.

The striking **Government Guest House**, just to the north of the Metropole, was built in 1919 as the palace of a French governor. Its colonial façade and multi-tiered portico in cast iron are attractive and well worth a second look.

❾ Opera House

1 Trang Tien St, Hoan Kiem District.
Map 2 F4. **Tel** (04) 3933 0133.
Open during performances. 🅰️ 🅰️
💻 🅦 **hanoioperahouse.org.vn**

Modeled on the Paris Opera designed by Charles Garnier, the Hanoi Opera House, also known as Nha Hat Lon or Big Song House, opened in 1911. It formed the centerpiece of French-Colonial architecture, not just in Hanoi, but in all of French Indochina.

Before World War II, the Opera House was at the center of the city's cultural life. At the end of the French rule, however, it gradually fell into disrepair. During the years prior to the nation's economic and

Courtyard garden and restaurant of the Sofitel Legend Metropole Hotel

cultural liberalization in the late 1980s, visiting Chinese or Russian artistes would appear. Performances such as the militant ballet *Red Detachment of Women* or a musical recital by an ensemble from Kiev, now in the Ukraine, were held here. By the mid-1980s, even these limited cultural exchanges had ceased, and the Opera House was all but abandoned. Then, in 1994, the authorities decided to restore and reopen the Opera in a three-year project costing US$14 million. Today, the colonnaded building, with refurbished gilt mirrors and grand stairways, is a magnificent sight. The 600-seat theater, boasting state-of-the-art audio facilities, stages Vietnamese operetta, ballets, and piano recitals. Home to the Hanoi Symphony Orchestra, it also hosts shows by visiting companies such as the Philadelphia Symphony Orchestra.

❿ National Museum of Vietnamese History

1 Pham Ngu Lao St, Hoan Kiem
District. **Map** 2 F4. **Tel** (04) 824 1384.
Open 8am–noon, 1:30–5pm daily.
Closed first Mon of each month. 📷
🅲 by prior arrangement. 📷
🅦 **nmvnh.com.vn**

Originally known as the École Française d'Extrême-Orient, this museum was built in 1925. Designed by Ernest Hébrard, it heralded a new hybrid style of architecture – Indochinoise – incorporating several elements of French, Khmer, and Vietnamese styles. Anchored by an octagonal pagoda, the building is painted ochre-yellow, and offset by dark green shutters. And although it is ornamented with fanciful colonnades, brackets, and balustrades, the overall effect is Oriental.

Known in Vietnamese as Bao Tang Lich Su, the museum is one of the best in Vietnam. It is spread over two floors and features a fine collection of artifacts from the prehistoric Dong Son culture of the Red River Delta, as well as the ancient Sa Huynh and Oc Eo civilizations of southern Vietnam. The museum also has sculptures dating from the Champa Empire. Some of the exhibits include wooden stakes from the 13th-century Battle of Bach Dang (*see p44*). The park behind the museum has a

Sculpture, Vietnamese History Museum

Grand colonnaded façade of the Opera House

Indochinoise architecture of the National Museum of Vietnamese History

⓫ Lien Phai Pagoda

Ngo Chua Lien Phai St, Hai Ba
Trung District. **Tel** (04) 3863 2562.
Open 7–11am, 1:30–5:30pm daily.

Lien Phai Pagoda or the Pagoda of the Lotus Sect, is one of the few surviving relics of the Trinh lords *(see p45)* in Hanoi. According to the inscription on the central stele, Lord Trinh Thap had a palace in this area, and one day his workers dug up a huge rock shaped like a lotus root in the palace gardens. Trinh Thap took this as an indication from the Buddha that he should abandon his privileged life and become a monk. He ordered a temple to be built at the palace where the stone was discovered. The pagoda was built in 1726, and Trinh Thap spent the remainder of his life here as a monk. When he died, his ashes were interred in the pagoda, and some of his calligraphy hangs by the main altar. The most impressive structure here is the Dieu Quang or Miraculous Light Tower, which rises through ten levels. The Lotus Sect, founded by Trinh Thap, honors the A Di Da or Amitabha Buddha, and believes that by chanting his name and ridding oneself of desire, one can be reborn in the Western Paradise of Sukhavati or Pure Land. This sect is very popular in China and Japan.

garden with statues of Cham goddesses and Khmer lions, and Vietnamese-style dragons.

⓫ Hai Ba Trung Temple

Dong Nhan St, Hai Ba Trung District.
Open only during festivals. ✴ Hai Ba Trung Festival (early Mar).

One of the most important temple complexes in the country, the Hai Ba Trung Temple is dedicated to the popular cult of deified heroes. It honors the heroic Trung Sisters, who were successful in expelling the Chinese for a brief period in the first century AD. Founded by Emperor Ly Anh Ton in 1142, the temple enshrines the supposedly petrified mortal remains of the sisters.

The temple stands on the west bank of a small artificial lake called Huong Vien, and is entered through a broad gateway flanked by tall white columns bearing auspicious Chinese symbols and characters for longevity, and surmounted by stylized lotus flowers. The temple is generally not open to the public. However, during the annual festival *(see p34)*, it attracts hundreds of devotees. During this grand event, both the statues are bathed in water from the nearby Red River and dressed in new red robes.

Guardian, Hai Ba Trung Temple

Trung Sisters

The first century AD was a period of resentment against Chinese rule. In AD 40, Trung Trac and her sister, Trung Nhi, set up an army with the aid of the Vietnamese lords. Fighting fearlessly, they expelled the Chinese, and established their own kingdom at Me Linh in the Red River Delta. In AD 43, however, the Chinese quelled the rebellion. To avoid capture, the sisters committed suicide by jumping into the Hat River. Centuries later, stone figures of two women washed up on a sandbank in the Red River. Believed to be the earthly remains of the Trung Sisters, petrified and turned into statues, they were taken to Dong Nhan village, now Hai Ba Trung District, and installed in a temple there. Today, the sisters are honored as heroes of national independence.

Ornate altar venerating the Trung Sisters

⑬ Temple of Literature

See pp170–71.

A many-armed statue of the Buddha, Vietnam Fine Arts Museum

⑭ Vietnam Fine Arts Museum

66 Nguyen Thai Hoc St, Ba Dinh District. **Map** 1 B3. **Tel** (04) 3823 3084. **Open** 8:30am–5pm daily. 🖼 📷 **W** vnfam.vn

Housed in a fine old colonial building, the Bao Tang My Thuat or Fine Arts Museum boasts a varied and interesting selection of Vietnam's artifacts, architecture, paintings, sculpture, and many other works of art. The exhibits are displayed chronologically, starting with a fine collection of Stone and Bronze Age relics on the first floor. Several wood, stone, and lacquer sculptures feature as well, illustrating the versatile nature of Vietnamese art. One of the highlights here is an extraordinary Bodhisattva or Enlightened Being that supposedly has 1,000 eyes and arms.

The exhibition rooms on the second floor contain some of the country's best lacquer paintings, and the third floor hosts many watercolor and oil works by Vietnamese artists. Other exhibits include carvings from the Central Highlands, wood-block paintings from the Dong Ho culture, and ethnic clothing. Replicas of antique pieces are for sale in the museum shop.

⑮ Vietnam Military History Museum

28A Dien Bien Phu St, Ba Dinh District. **Map** 1 C3. **Tel** (04) 3823 4264. **Open** 8–11:30am, 1–4:30pm Tue–Thu & Sat–Sun. 🖼 📷.

Located at the southern end of the historic Hanoi Citadel and adjacent to the Flag Tower, the Vietnam Military History Museum is set in former French barracks, comprising a complex of 30 galleries. Tracing the development and history of Vietnam's armed forces over the centuries, this museum is one of the most important war museums of the country. It features a varied collection of displays relating to the country's early battles against the Chinese and the Mongols. Precedence is, however, given to the nation's more recent wars against France, Cambodia's Khmer Rouge, China, and the US. The exhibits include films, black-and-white photographs, and other archival footage. The diorama of the Battle of Dien Bien Phu *(see p199)* is definitely worth seeing.

The courtyard outside the museum is filled with several reminders of war, including wrecked French, Soviet, and American military equipment, weaponry, and fighter planes, as well as a carefully preserved Soviet MIG-21, a must-see.

Next to the museum is the hexagonal Flag Tower or **Cot Co**. Like the Turtle Tower on Hoan Kiem Lake *(see p164)*, the tower is an important symbol, not just of Hanoi, but of Vietnamese armed forces.

Opposite the museum, situated in a small park is a commanding statue of Lenin.

Stern, whitewashed façade of the Ho Chi Minh Museum

⑯ Ho Chi Minh Museum

19 Ngoc Ha St, Ba Dinh District. **Map** 1 B2. **Tel** (04) 3845 5435. **Open** 8am–4:30pm Tue–Thu & Sat–Sun; 8am–12pm Mon, Fri. 🖼 📷 **W** baotanghochiminh.vn

Established in 1990 – one century after Ho Chi Minh's birth *(see p173)* – this museum chronicles and celebrates the revolutionary leader's life and achievements in an often bizarre series of displays. These include an eclectic mix of his personal memorabilia, as well as black-and-white photographs from his youth and the long period he spent abroad in Europe and China. Other displays include art installations that represent abstract concepts such as freedom and social progress. Unapologetically partisan, the museum is nevertheless informative, unusual, and well presented.

Tank of the National Liberation Front in the Vietnam Military History Museum

⑰ One Pillar Pagoda

8 Chua Mot St, Ba Dinh District. **Map** 1 B2. **Open** 8:30–11:30am, 1–4pm daily.

Rivaling Cot Co as one of Hanoi's most prominent icons, the Chua Mot Cot or the One Pillar Pagoda was constructed by Emperor Ly Thai Tong in AD 1049. Situated within the tiny Dien Huu Pagoda, also dating from the 11th century, this wooden pagoda is built, as the name suggests, on a single stone pillar, standing in an elegant lotus pond. According to legend, the king, who had no son, had a dream in which he was visited by Quan Am, Goddess of Mercy. She was sitting on a lotus flower and presented him with a baby boy. Soon after, Ly Thai Tong married a new young queen who bore him a son. To show his gratitude, the emperor ordered the construction of a single-pillared pagoda representing a lotus flower. It represents purity, like a lotus blossoming in a muddy pond. The pillar is built of stone and is 4 ft (1.25 m) in diameter. Over the centuries, One Pillar Pagoda has been damaged and reconstructed on numerous occasions. However, none of these acts of destruction is harder to fathom than its burning by the French in 1954.

Steps leading up to the small and charming One Pillar Pagoda

⑱ Ho Chi Minh Mausoleum

Ba Dinh Sq, Ba Dinh District. **Map** 1 B2. **Open** 8–11am Tue–Thu & Sat–Sun. **Closed** closed for about two months a year, usually in Oct & Nov, for embalming maintenance.

On the west side of Ba Dinh Square, a heavy grey structure, built of stone quarried from Marble Mountain near Danang (see p138), is Ho Chi Minh's last resting place.

An unassuming man, who prided himself on an austere, almost ascetic public image, Ho Chi Minh had allegedly requested that he be cremated and his ashes scattered in Northern, Central, and Southern Vietnam, symbolizing the national unity to which he had devoted his life. In keeping with these beliefs, it is said that he also vetoed the construction of a small museum on his life at his home village near Kim Lien (see p155), arguing that the funds could be better employed in building a school. However, after Ho Chi Minh's death in 1969, the leading members of the Vietnamese politburo reportedly altered his final testament by deleting his request to be cremated. Instead, with the help of Soviet specialists, the leader was embalmed and installed at the Ho Chi Minh Mausoleum in 1975

The building's exterior is considered by many as both ponderous and unappealing. Astonishingly, the architects supposedly intended the structure to represent a lotus flower, though it is difficult to understand how.

Inside, the mood is somber and decidedly respectful. Ho Chi Minh, dressed in simple clothing favored by Chinese nationalist leader Sun Yat Sen, lies in a chilled, dim room, his crossed hands resting on dark cloth covers.

The mausoleum is an important pilgrimage site for many Vietnamese, especially from the north, and should be approached with respect and reverence. Any kind of noisy behavior, loitering, and inappropriate clothing is strictly forbidden.

The somber exterior of Ho Chi Minh Mausoleum

⑲ Ho Chi Minh's Stilt House

1 Bach Thao St, Presidential Palace, Ba Dinh District. **Map** 1 B2. **Open** 7:30–11:30am, 2–4pm Tue–Thu & Sat–Sun. Botanical Gardens. Hoang Hoa Tham St. **Open** 7:30am–10pm daily.

Believing that the Presidential Palace was too grand for him, Ho Chi Minh, on becoming president of the Democratic Republic of Vietnam in 1954, arranged for a modest wooden structure to be built in a corner of the palace's extensive grounds. Modeled on an ethnic minority stilt house, this unassuming two story structure is known as Nha Bac Ho or Uncle Ho's House. Next to the stilts and surrounded by plants are the tables and chairs that were used by members of the politburo during meetings with Ho Chi Minh.

Wooden stairs at the back of the house lead to two rooms: a study and a bedroom, both kept just as they were when the great man was alive. The study has an antique typewriter and a book-case. The bedroom is even more spartan, with a bed, electric clock, an old-fashioned tele-phone, and radio as the only concessions to comfort. Surrounding the modest house are carefully tended gardens with weeping willows, mango trees, and fragrant frangipani and jasmine. Ho Chi Minh lived here from 1958 to 1969.

Close to the presidential stilt house, the **Botanical Gardens** boast two lakes and abundant greenery, as well as a perma-nent sculpture exhibition.

⓭ Temple of Literature

The oldest and possibly the finest architectural complex in Hanoi, Van Mieu or the Temple of Literature, was established in 1070, during the Ly Dynasty (1009–1225). Founded in honor of the Chinese philosopher Confucius, it served as a center for higher learning, educating future mandarins for more than seven centuries. The temple was modeled on the original Temple of Confucius in the Chinese city of Qufu, and consists of five courtyards, the first two of which feature well-tended gardens. Each courtyard is separated by walls and ornamental gateways, and a central pathway through the complex divides it into two symmetrical halves.

Van Mieu Gate, the elegant entrance to the Temple of Literature

Well of Heavenly Clarity
A square pool known as Thien Quang Tinh or the Well of Heavenly Clarity dominates the third courtyard. On either side of the pond are covered buildings that house 82 stone stelae, the most prized relics of the temple.

Human Chess
During Tet, the fourth courtyard is the venue for human chess. Dressed in colorful costumes, the participants, each representing a chess piece, move according to directions given by players.

★ **Khue Van Cac**
Also known as the Constellation of Literature, this ornate gate was built in 1805 to reflect the brilliance of Van Mieu's literary legacy. Its upper story features four radiating suns facing the cardinal points.

KEY

① **A magnificent bell tower** was added to the fifth courtyard during recent restoration.

② **The Thai Hoc Hall** shelters an altar dedicated to Chu Van An, former director of the Imperial Academy, as well as images of three Ly Dynasty emperors.

Buddhist monks strolling through the gardens of the first courtyard

The Music Room
A small orchestra of traditional musicians and singers stage regular performances next to the Altar of Confucius, using traditional Vietnamese stringed instruments (see pp28–9).

VISITORS' CHECKLIST

Practical Information
Quoc Tu Giam St.
Map 1 B4, **Tel** (04) 3845 2917.
Open 7:30am–5:30pm Apr–Sep, 8am–5pm Oct–Mar.

Great Drum
The counterpart of the bell tower to the west of Thai Hoc Hall is a giant drum standing to the east. These two towers appear together in traditional Sinitic architecture.

★ Temple of Confucius
Located just behind Bai Duong, is the long, red-lacquered and gilt temple to Confucius. Inside are statues of the great philosopher and four of his main disciples, all dressed in rich robes of red and gold.

★ Tortoise Stele
Mounted on giant tortoise pedestals, these stone stelae are inscribed with the names and brief personal details of scholars who passed Van Mieu's examinations. Dating from the 15th to the 18th centuries, only 82 out of the original 112 stelae survive today.

★ Altar of Confucius
Bai Duong or the House of Ceremonies hosts the elaborately decorated altar of Confucius, flanked by statues of cranes standing on top of tortoises – an auspicious symbol. The king and his mandarins would make offerings and sacrifices here.

Colorful swan-necked leisure boats docked on the shores of Ho Tay

⑳ Hanoi Citadel

9 Hoang Dieu, Ba Dinh District.
Map 1 C2. **Open** 8–11:30am, 1:30–5pm Tue–Sun. 🖼

For centuries, Hanoi Citadel was only accessible to the country's rulers, but in 2010, it was recognized by UNESCO as a World Heritage Site and is now open to the public. Unfortunately, much of the site was destroyed by the French in the late 19th century, however, the surviving buildings are worth a visit.

At the south end of this mammoth complex, adjacent to the Military History Museum is the Cat Co, or the Flag Tower. North of here, the Doan Mon Gate is probably the most impressive structure of the Citadel still remaining. The imposing walls containing five archways and supporting a double-roofed pavilion can be seen once the main entrance to the forbidden realm is entered. Beyond the gate are the excavations showing a sophisticated waterway, probably once used for irrigation. Nothing remains of the Kinh Tien Palace, which once functioned as the imperial residence, apart from its beautifully sculpted dragon balustrades.

In the heart of the complex is a squat colonial building named D67, which was a command center for northern forces during the Vietnam War. The conference table still has the reserved seats of luminaries such as General Giap (1911–2013), who was the mastermind behind many

Vietnamese victories. There is also a bomb shelter deep below the ground.

North of the D67 building are two more structures of interest– Hau Lau and Cua Bac, the northern gate. However, on the west side of Hoang Dieu Street is a massive archaeological dig, consisting mostly of foundations of former palaces, that gives an idea of the enormous scale of the Citadel.

㉑ Ho Tay

Map 1 A1. 🚗 🚲 🖥 🖼 Tran Quoc Pagoda: Kim Ngu Island, Thanh Nien Causeway. **Open** sunrise–sunset daily. Quan Thanh Temple: Intersection of Thanh Nien Causeway and Quan Thanh Sts. **Open** sunrise–sunset daily. 🖼

To the west of Hanoi are two beautiful lakes, separated from the Red River by the great dyke to the north. The larger of the two is Ho Tay or West Lake, which is home to Hanoi's sailing club. It is separated from Truc Bach or White Silk Lake to the east by an artificial causeway. In times past, Ho Tay was

The brick-built exterior of Tran Quoc Pagoda

associated with the Trinh lords, who built palaces and pavilions along its shores, as well as many Buddhist temples. The palaces are gone, but many temples remain, including the city's oldest, **Tran Quoc Pagoda**. According to legend, it was established by the banks of the Red River during the reign of Trinh lord, Ly Nam De (r.544–8), but was moved to its current location during the 17th century. Also worth a visit is **Quan Thanh Temple**, reputed to have been patronized by Emperor Ly Thai To, founder of the Ly Dynasty (see p44). Rebuilt in 1893, it is dedicated to Tran Vo or Guardian of the North. An image of this Taoist divinity dominates the altar.

Today, the area around Ho Tay is becoming increasingly upscale, with lots of luxury hotels along its shore. It is also home to several high-end restaurants and bars.

㉒ Kim Lien Pagoda

Ho Tay, Tu Liem District.
Open sunrise–sunset daily.

Situated on the northern shore of Ho Tay, the very attractive Kiem Lien Pagoda is somewhat out of the way, but well deserving of a visit. Legend has it that Princess Tu Hoa, daughter of 12th-century Emperor Ly Than Tong, brought her ladies-in-waiting to the area so they could cultivate silkworms for cloth. In 1771, a pagoda was built on the foundations of her palace and named Kim Lien, which means Golden Lotus, in memory of the princess.

Now entered through a triple-arched gate, it comprises three pavilions, that are laid out in three lines, supposedly representing the Chinese character *san* or three. They each have sweeping eaves and stacked roofs.

Ho Chi Minh

Acclaimed as the leader and primary force behind Vietnam's struggle for independence, Ho Chi Minh was born in 1890 at Hoang Tru Village, near Vinh. After studying in Hue, Ho Chi Minh, then known as Nguyen Tat Thanh, left Vietnam in 1911 to travel the world. Influenced by socialist ideologies during his stay in Europe, he founded communist organizations in Paris, Moscow, and China. He returned to Vietnam in 1941, where he took the name Ho Chi Minh (Bringer of Enlightenment) and formed the Vietnamese Independence League, or Viet Minh. In 1955, he became president of the Democratic Republic of Vietnam, leading long and bitter wars against France and the United States. Though he died six years before reunification, Vietnam's independence is considered his greatest achievement.

The prestigious Quoc Hoc School in Hue is where Ho Chi Minh studied, along with future general Vo Nguyen Giap and Pham Van Dong, the future prime minister of Vietnam.

Nguyen Ai Quoc or Nguyen the Patriot is a pseudonym that Ho Chi Minh adopted during the 1920s. Greatly taken with socialist beliefs, he was a founding member of the French Communist Party in Paris, part of the Soviet Union Communist Party, and founder of the Indochinese Communist Party in China

A photograph dated 1945 shows Ho Chi Minh preparing for a military campaign against the French. Full-scale war broke out in 1946, and the Viet Minh, led by Ho Chi Minh, waged a bloody battle that would last eight long years.

Camped in secret tunnels and caverns, Ho Chi Minh spent hours perfecting military strategies, which included employing underground resistance and guerilla tactics to expel the French forces, who were finally defeated in 1954.

Personally a gentle and unassuming man, Ho was much loved by children and adults alike. He could also speak several languages fluently, including Chinese, Russian, French, and English.

Revered and loved as the father of modern Vietnam, Ho Chi Minh is featured in the form of statues and portraits throughout the country, honoring his commitment to the unity of the nation. Kim Lien (see p155), his childhood village, is now a national shrine.

Reconstruction of a Central Highland ethnic home, Museum of Ethnology

❷ Co Loa Citadel

10 miles (16 km) N of Hanoi, Dong Anh District. **Open** 8am–5pm daily. 🏞 🏠 🏛 Co Loa Festival (Feb).

The first known capital of an independent Vietnamese kingdom, this ancient fortress dates from a time when mythological history was slowly evolving into historical fact. The stories surrounding its creation and subsequent fall rest on oral tradition long since written down but impossible to verify.

Believed to have been built by King An Duong Vuong *(see p41)* in the 3rd century BC, the citadel was invaded soon after by the Chinese. According to legend, the son of the Chinese general tricked An Duong's daughter, My Chau, into giving him her father's magic crossbow, which was used by the Chinese to defeat the king. Fact or fiction, the remains of this great citadel and the huge quantity of bronze arrowheads found buried around the fortress indicate that fierce battles once took place here. At present, only vestiges of the

citadel remain. In the center of the complex are temples dedicated to An Duong and My Chau. Both these structures are well preserved. However, it seems evident that they were built long after the citadel's destruction in 208 BC.

Stylized stone lions sitting guard outside distinguish the temple dedicated to King An Duong. A major festival takes place at the temple each year in honor of the legendary king, and a statue of him is carried in a palanquin from the temple to the local *dinh* or communal house. In efforts to promote both tourism and a revival of

traditional culture, the festivities include elaborate games of human chess, cockfighting, singing, and dancing. On the final day, An Duong is carried in state from the *dinh* back to his temple.

The Hanoi Architecture and Planning Department is currently working on restoring the vast area originally covered by the citadel.

❷ Museum of Ethnology

60 Nguyen Van Huyen St, Cau Giay District. **Tel** (04) 3756 2193. **Open** 8:30am–5:30pm Tue–Sun. 🏞 🗋 🖥 🏛 🗂 **vme.org.vn**

Located west of the city center, the Bao Tang Dan Toc Hoc or the Museum of Ethnology offers informative and well-documented displays on the country's many ethnic groups *(see pp24–5)*. These range from the dominant Kinh to the smallest minorities in the highlands of the north and center.

Exhibits in the main building include elaborate and colorful hill-tribe costumes, weaving designs, musical instruments, fishing implements, work tools, and other functional objects. The displays continue on to the extensive grounds outside, with fascinating examples of minority housing from the Central Highlands, such as communal houses, steep pitched roofs, and elaborately carved tombs. A highlight here is the re-creation of a Black Thai house.

The museum also serves as a research center for Vietnam's 54 recognized ethnic groups.

Mural depicting people from the Dong Son culture, Co Loa Citadel

Massive clay image of a warrior behind the altar at Thay Pagoda

㉕ Thay Pagoda

20 miles (32 km) W of Hanoi, Ha Tay Province. **Open** sunrise–sunset daily. Thay Pagoda Festival (early Apr).

Dedicated to the Thich Ca or the Sakyamuni Buddha, Chua Thay or Master's Pagoda is named for Tu Dao Hanh – a 12th-century monk and master water puppeteer. The temple is mainly renowned for being home to more than 100 religious statues, including the two largest in Vietnam. Made of clay and papier-mâché, these giants weigh more than 2,200 lb (1,000 kg) each.

Inside, to the left of the main altar stands a statue of the master, and to the right is a statue of Emperor Ly Nhan Tong (r.1072–1127), believed to be a reincarnation of Tu Dao Hanh, and under whose reign this attractive house of worship was established. The pagoda also hosts a variety of water puppet shows (see p163) during its much-anticipated annual festival.

㉖ Tay Phuong Pagoda

24 miles (38 km) W of Hanoi, Ha Tay Province. **Open** sunrise–sunset daily.

This small temple is perched on top of a hill said to resemble a buffalo, and lies a short distance west of Thay Pagoda, hence its name, which means Western Pagoda. Originally dating from the 8th century, it is best known for its impressive collection of more than 70 finely carved, jackfruit-wood statues representing incarnations of the Buddha, Confucian disciples, and various *arhats* (Buddhist saints) in meditative poses. The Tay Phuong Pagoda is also distinguished by particularly fine wood carvings of flowers and mythical animals, such as the phoenix and dragons. Other striking features of the temple include a large bell cast in 1796, and the double-tiered roof, which has elegant, upward-sweeping eaves, beautifully decorated with symbols of the sun, moon, and stars.

Jackfruit-wood statue, Tay Phuong Pagoda

㉗ Hung Kings' Temples

62 miles (100 km) NW of Hanoi, Phong Chau District, Phu Tho Province. **Museum Tel** (021) 386 0026. **Open** 8–11:30am, 1–4pm daily. in museum. Hung Kings' Temple Festival (Apr).

Believed by the Vietnamese to be the very earliest relics of their civilization, the temples of the Hung kings are located on Mount Nghia Linh. Built by rulers of the Vang Lang Kingdom, between the 7th and 3rd centuries BC, they are objects of great veneration. Flights of stone stairs climb sharply upwards through the trees to the lowest temple, **Den Ha**, the middle temple, **Den Hung**, and ultimately the superior temple near the top of the hill, **Den Thuong**. The entire area is filled with a plethora of pagodas, lotus ponds, and small shrines. The most important of these is **Lang Hung** – a tiny shrine, with candle and incense holders, located a few meters lower down the slope from Den Thuong. This is, supposedly, the main tomb of the Hung kings, though it is evident that it has undergone some extensive reconstructions.

The views from Mount Nghia Linh's summit sweep across the surrounding rural Phu Tho landscape, and are absolutely spectacular. At the foot of the mountain there is a small **Museum**. A varied selection of displays such as frog drums, pottery, arrowheads, and other historic relics are shown here. The annual Hung Kings Festival in April is now a national holiday and attracts huge crowds.

One of the pleasing Hung kings' temples, set amid lush greenery

HANOI STREET FINDER

The stately city of Hanoi is divided into four principal districts. Named after the lovely lake at the center of town, Hoan Kiem District includes the bustling alleys of the Old Quarter, while the city's former French Quarter is in Hai Ba Trung district. The other two districts are Ba Dinh, and Dong Da. Note that the street names can be preceded by the word *pho*, which is a central city street; *duong*, which is a more common road; or *dai lo*, which is a large avenue or boulevard. Some common words used in street names have been abbreviated on the Street Finder. For example, Nguyen is Ng and Hang is H. The symbols used for sights and other features on the Street Finder are listed in the key below.

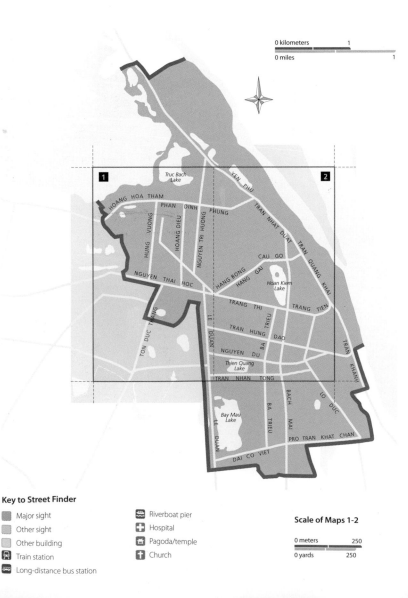

0 kilometers 1
0 miles 1

Key to Street Finder

- Major sight
- Other sight
- Other building
- 🚉 Train station
- 🚌 Long-distance bus station
- 🛥 Riverboat pier
- ➕ Hospital
- Pagoda/temple
- ✝ Church

Scale of Maps 1-2

0 meters 250
0 yards 250

Street Finder Index

NORTHERN VIETNAM

Northern Vietnam is a rich repository of history and tradition, with many of the country's oldest temples and fortresses. It is also blessed with great natural grandeur, ranging from the high mountains and craggy canyons of the west, to the magical karst islands rising from Halong Bay in the east. In addition, the northwest mountains are inhabited by several diverse and culturally unique ethnic minorities.

Crowned by the serrated peaks of the Hoang Lien Mountains, Northern Vietnam boasts a remarkably unspoiled topography, as well as a diverse cultural landscape. The pristine forests and plunging valleys in the mountainous reaches of the north and northwest are inhabited by dozens of minorities such as the Hmong, Thai, Dao, and Nung. Their villages in Son La, Bac Ha, and Sapa are extremely picturesque, with wooden stilt houses punctuating jade-green terraced rice fields. Also in the far west, the valley of Dien Bien Phu is of great historical importance. It is famous as the site of the Viet Minh victory over the French in 1954 – a triumphant chapter in Vietnam's history.

The northeast, on the other hand, is known for the hundreds of enchanting karst outcrops that loom over the Gulf of Tonkin's Halong and Bai Tu Long Bays.

Similar formations soar above the tropical forests of Cat Ba Island, also home to golden beaches and spectacular coral reefs. In sharp contrast, the nearby port city of Haiphong, in the northernmost province of the Red River Delta, bustles with commerce and industry. Just south of here are the region's fertile flatlands, home to the ethnic Viet or Kinh people, and marked by extensive paddy fields.

Northern Vietnam also has its share of national parks such as Ba Be and Cuc Phuong, celebrated for flora and fauna endemic to the region. It also boasts the spectacular Dong Van Karst Plateau Geopark. The area is renowned for the festivals and events that enliven its religious sites, including especially the Perfume Pagoda, which is thronged by hundreds of Buddhist pilgrims for three months every year.

Rural hamlet set amid the lush terraced fields surrounding Sapa

◀ H'Mong tribal women in traditional clothing as they shop at the Sunday market in Bac Ha town, Lao Cai

Exploring Northern Vietnam

The oldest settled part of the country, Northern Vietnam is unusually rich in culture and history. The fertile plains of the Red River Delta are full of ancient temples, clan houses, and pagodas, including the very scenic and highly venerated Perfume Pagoda. Farther north, neatly cultivated fields and urban settlements give way to the magnificent Hoang Lien Mountains. The most popular destination here is the hill resort of Sapa, from where it is easy to visit nearby Bac Ha, and explore the surrounding remote areas that are home to several minority peoples. In the east, Halong Bay is Vietnam's most celebrated natural beauty spot, while to the south are the dense green forests of Cuc Phuong National Park.

The crystal clear waters of Thac Bac or Silver Waterfalls near Sapa *(see pp200–201)*

Sights at a Glance

Towns and Cities
2 Halong City
5 Haiphong
7 Ninh Binh
10 Hoa Binh
12 Moc Chau
13 Son La
14 Dien Bien Phu
15 Sapa
16 Bac Ha
18 Cao Bang

Areas of Natural Beauty
1 Halong Bay *pp186–8*
4 Bai Tu Long Bay
11 Mai Chau Valley
19 Dong Van Karst
Plateau Geopark

National Parks
9 Cuc Phuong National Park
17 Ba Be National Park

Islands
6 Cat Ba Island

Religious Sites
3 Yen Tu Pilgrimage Sites
8 Perfume Pagoda *pp196–7*

Group of Flower Hmong girls dressed in traditional outfits, Bac Ha Market *(see p201)*

0 kilometers 50

0 miles 50

Magnificent limestone karst formations at Halong Bay *(see pp186–8)*

Key

═══ Highway

▬▬ Major road

═══ Minor road

--- Railroad

▬▬ International border

▬▬ Provincial border

Getting Around

Traveling around Northern Vietnam, especially in the northeast, is getting easier with the construction of new roads to Haiphong, Halong City, and the Chinese frontier. The northwest is another matter, and it is better to take the night train to Lao Cai or a flight to Dien Bien Phu rather than endure the arduous road trip. The best way to get around and take in the stunning scenery is by hiring a car and driver. Plenty of buses ply the roads too, and can be arranged by hotels and tour agencies in Hanoi, Ninh Binh, and Sapa. Halong Bay can be explored by boat. It is possible to hire a boat for a reasonable price from the pier at Bai Chay in Halong City or in Hanoi. Hydrofoil services connect Haiphong with Cat Ba Island.

For keys to symbols *see back flap*

❶ Halong Bay

Designated a UNESCO World Heritage Site, the magnificent Halong Bay is spread across a 580 sq mile (1,500 sq km) area, with more than 2,000 pinnacle-shaped limestone and dolomite outcrops scattered across it. According to legend, the bay was formed when a gigantic dragon – *ha long* means descending dragon – plunged into the Gulf of Tonkin, and created the myriad islets by lashing its tail. Geologists have explained that the karst topography is the product of selective erosion over the millennia. The result is a labyrinthine seascape of bizarrely shaped outcrops, isolated caves, and sandy coves *(see p188)*.

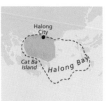

Locator Map

▨ Area illustrated

--- World Heritage Site area

★ Hang Dau Go
Named Grotte des Merveilles or Cave of Marvels by the French in the 19th century, Hang Dau Go is full of strangely formed stalactites and stalagmites, enchantingly lit with green and blue colored floodlights.

Tuan Chan

①

② Dau Go

Cat Ba

KEY

① **Dao Tuan Chau**, a large island to the southwest of Bai Chay, is the site of Ho Chi Minh's former residence. It is now a sprawling recreation complex.

② **Hang Thien Cung**, or Celestial Palace Grotto features sparkling stalactites and stalagmites. Like Hang Dau Go, it is softly illuminated with colored lights.

③ **Ferries at Halong City**, constantly shuttle back and forth from Bai Chay in the west to Hong Gai in the east to the islands.

④ **Dong Tam Cung** which was discovered only in the mid-1990s, is one of the most impressive caves in the bay.

⑤ **Hang Trong**, or Drum Cave is filled with stalactites and stalagmites that produce a sound like distant drumming when wind blows through the cave.

⑥ **Dao Titop** is home to a tiny, isolated beach. It is also possible to hike to the top of the islet.

Formation of Karst

Across much of the Gulf of Tonkin, both offshore in Halong Bay and on land at Tam Coc, weathered limestone pinnacles rise almost vertically from the surrounding plain, creating truly breathtaking scenery. These karst outcrops are made of sediment that settled on the seafloor in prehistoric times, which subsequently rose to the surface through geological upheaval and erosion. On exposure to warm, acidic rainfall, these striking alkaline limestone formations are worn into strange, almost spectacular shapes providing a remarkable sight.

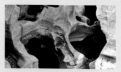

Limestone rock eroded due to acidic action

Floating Villages
Located near Hong Gai's harbor, these villages include not only houseboats, but also floating fuel stations, herb gardens, kennels, and even pigpens.

VISITORS' CHECKLIST

Practical Information
Road Map C1. 102 miles (164 km) E of Hanoi; 37 miles (60 km) NE of Haiphong. 🚤 for some islets and caves. 🛥 can be hired from Hanoi, Halong City, and Haiphong. 🚢 Halong City.
Caution: Some boats have had safety problems. Inquire about life jackets and safe practices before booking boat trips.

Transport
🚌 from Hanoi, 🚌 from Haiphong. 🚢 from Bai Chay Jetty. (taxi from Hanoi and Haiphong.)

Hong Gai

Halong City
③

Dragon Boats
These brightly painted boats represent the legendary beast that created Halong Bay. Dragons are also held to be symbols of royalty and good luck in Vietnam.

④

★ Hang Bo Nau
A favorite among photographers, Hang Bo Nau, also known as Pelican Cave, is famous for the framed views it offers of ships sailing in the bay.

⑥

Bo Hon

⑤

★ Hang Sung Sot
Hang Sung Sot or Cave of Awe is best known for its phallus-shaped rock, a fertility symbol. The formations in the inner chamber are said to resemble a group of sentries conversing.

0 kilometers 2
0 miles 2

Exploring Halong Bay

Sailing past the evocatively shaped islets and dramatic caves of Halong Bay can be a magical experience. At least an entire day can be spent exploring the islands and grottos, many of which house religious shrines. Most of the best-known sites lie in the western part of the bay and these are often overcrowded. It generally makes for a more relaxing trip to charter a private boat, hire a knowledgeable guide, and sail around the less visited areas of the shimmering bay.

Hang Dau Go

One of the most famous caves in Halong Bay, Hang Dau Go or Hidden Timber Cave is on Dau Go Island, on the way to Cat Ba Island *(see p193)*. The cave's name dates from the 13th century when General Tran Hung Dao *(see p44)* used it to hide his lethally sharpened metal stakes. The weapons were later planted in the shallow waters near the shore to destroy enemy Mongol fleets.
Hang Dau Go is filled with many bizarre-shaped stalactites and stalagmites.

Hang Thien Cung

Also on Dau Go Island, Hang Thien Cung or the Celestial Palace Grotto can be reached by a steep flight of steps. It was discovered only in the mid-1990s. Floodlights in pink, green, and blue illuminate the sparkling stalactites that hang from the high ceiling.

Hang Sung Sot

Aptly known as the Cave of Awe, Hang Sung Sot is located on Bo

Pink-lit, phallus-shaped rock, revered by locals, in Hang Sung Sot

Hon Island, which the French knew as the Isle de la Surprise. The first cavern in the three-chambered Sung Sot features a large, phallus-shaped rock, lit in lurid pink, and worshipped as a fertility symbol by the locals.
The formations in the inner chamber, named the Serene Castle, on the other hand, are fascinating, seeming to come alive when the reflections of the water outside play upon them. Nearby, **Hang Bo Nau** or Pelican Cave draws visitors for the fantastic views it offers across the bay.

Dong Tam Cung

A massive karst fissure, Dong Tam Cung or Three Palaces consists of three chambers, each of which is packed with stalactites and stalagmites. All three grottos are illuminated by strategically placed spotlights, which emphasize the strange, massed, carrot-shaped array of stalactites. Opinion is divided, but some consider Dong Tam Cung to be even more impressive than Hang Dau Go.

Hang Trong

A short distance southeast of Hang Bo Nau, the small Hang Trong or Drum Cave echoes faintly with an eerie percussive sound when a strong wind blows past its stalactites and stalagmites.

Dao Tuan Chau

A large island to the south of Bai Chay, Tuan Chau has been developed as a recreation complex, with a few restored French-Colonial villas and a resort holding unimpressive whale, dolphin, and sea lion shows. Better reasons to visit are the seafood restaurants and small sandy beaches.

Dao Titop

The main attraction of this island is its isolated beach, which is very popular with swimmers. It is possible to hike to the top of the islet where there is the most spectacular view of Halong Bay. Visitors can enjoy the few watersports facilities available at the small beach, including swimming and parasailing.

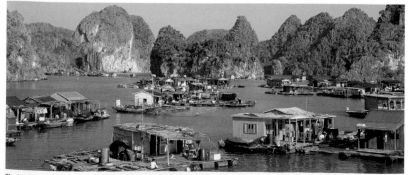

The brightly painted houses of a floating village in Halong Bay

Ferries docked at Hon Gai, Halong City

❷ Halong City

Road Map C1. 102 miles (164 km) E of Hanoi on Hwy 18, 37 miles (60 km) NE of Haiphong on Hwy 10. 🏠 200,000. 🚌 from Haiphong and Hanoi. 🚢 from Haiphong. 🚆 ℹ️ Halong Tourism, (033) 362 8862. 🎫 Long Tien Pagoda Festival (late Apr).

Formed in 1994 with the official amalgamation of the towns of **Bai Chay** and **Hon Gai**, Halong City is bisected by the narrow Cua Luc straits, which is straddled by a new suspension bridge.

Located to the west of the straits, Bai Chay is an affluent tourist town, home to a number of tour operators, hotels, and restaurants. It is also popular with the Vietnamese for its nightlife, which centers on karaoke bars and massage parlors of questionable repute.

However, for most visitors, there is little of appeal in Bai Chay itself, which is simply a convenient place to stay and eat. Local authorities have tried to improve the situation by laying two artificial stretches of beach on the seafront, but not much has changed. The waters remain muddy, and the sand is polluted.

East of the new bridge, the town of Hon Gai is the older, more historic part of Halong City. Although this town has its share of hotels and restaurants, it does not revolve around tourism. In fact, most of its wealth comes from industry, particularly the huge opencast coal mines that dominate the coast east of Cua Luc.

Beyond the coal dust of the docks is **Nui Bai Tho** or Poem Mountain, one of the few attractions of Halong City. The limestone mountain has earned its name from the weathered inscriptions on its sides, written in praise of the beauty of Halong Bay. The earliest of these is said to have been composed by King Le Thanh Tong in 1468. On the northern lee of the mountain stands Long Tien Pagoda, Halong City's most colorful and interesting religious site.

❸ Yen Tu Pilgrimage Sites

Road Map B1. 81 miles (130 km) NE of Hanoi; 9 miles (14 km) N of Uong Bi. 🚌 from Hanoi, Halong City, and Haiphong to Uong Bi. 🚰 🛏️ 🍴 🎫 Yen Tu Pagoda Fest (mid-Feb–end Apr).

The holy mountain, Yen Tu, at 3,477 ft (1,060 m) is the highest peak in the range of the same name. It is named for Yen Ky Sinh, a monk who attained nirvana at the peak, about 2,000 years ago. Yen Tu became further renowned during the 13th century, when Emperor Tran Nhan Tong (r.1278–93) retired there to become a monk. Some of the 800 religious structures claimed to have been built by the emperor and his successors are still present here. For centuries, thousands of pilgrims have made the arduous ascent to the summit of Yen Tu by foot, although now a cable car whisks sightseers to Hoa Yen Pagoda, just over halfway up the mountain. From here, it is still necessary to make the climb on foot to the most important structure at the summit, **Chua Dong** or Bronze Pagoda. This is the spiritual home of the Truc Lam or Bamboo Forest sect of Mahayana Buddhism, and was built during the 15th century. It has been beautifully refurbished, with 70 tons (64 tonnes) of bronze used to form a 215 sq ft (20 sq m) temple intended to symbolize a lotus.

Environs
Situated on the western slopes of the Yen Tu range, about 3 miles (5 km) north of Sao Dao on Highway 18, are two of the country's most important pilgrimage sites. **Chua Con Son**, one of the attractive pagodas in the north, is dedicated to Nguyen Van Trai, the poet-warrior who aided Emperor Le Loi *(see p44)* in expelling the Chinese from Vietnam in the 15th century. The popular pagoda is always active, with monks and nuns chanting prayers almost constantly.

Located nearby is the small temple, **Den Kiep Bac**, which is dedicated to Tran Hung Dao, a general of the Tran Dynasty *(see p44)* during the late 13th century and a deified national hero. An annual festival is held in his honor during the 8th lunar month.

Stairway to the revered Chua Con Son, Yen Tu

Floating fishing village in Halong Bay ▶

Tiny floating village near the town of Cai Rong, Bai Tu Long Bay

④ Bai Tu Long Bay

Road Map C1. 37 miles (60 km) E of Halong City. 🚌 from Halong City. 🚢 from Halong City and Cai Rong.

An island-peppered stretch of shallow coastal waters, Bai Tu Long Bay may not be quite as celebrated as Halong Bay, but it is just as spectacular. With hundreds of karst outcrops, tiny islets, as well as a few large islands and lovely beaches, it is less crowded and more pristine than Halong Bay.

The largest, most developed island in the area is **Van Don**, accessible by both road and sea from the industrial port of Cua Ong. Gorgeous beaches and dense mangrove swamps line the southeast coast of the island, making it a popular destination. Most of the accommodation in the Bai Tu Long area is concentrated in Van Don's main town, the colorful fishing port-town of Cai Rong. This makes it an excellent base for excursions

Silhouette of karst formations near Van Don Island, Bai Tu Long Bay

to neighboring islands. Unfortunately, Bai Tu Long Bay offers few tourist facilities. This is partly due to its isolated location, lying beyond the grimy coastal coal belt that stretches from Hon Gai District in Halong City to the small town of Cam Pha. As a result, most visitors prefer to join a tour from Hanoi, spending the night on board a boat and exploring the bay. Another option is to drive from Hon Gai to Bai Tu Long Bay, passing through Cam Pha and Cua Ong. The huge, open-cast coal mines on the way are quite a sight. From here, boats may be chartered to explore the outlying reaches of the bay.

Environs

The outermost of the three islands south of Van Don is **Quan Lan**. The main attraction on this destination is Bai Bien, a splendid white-sand beach. This is one of the few places beyond Cai Rong with facilities for an overnight stay.

Co To, well into the South China Sea, is the most distant island lying off Cai Rong. The ferry journey takes about five hours each way. With a small beach and simple accommodation at Co To village, it makes for a quiet getaway.

About 12 miles (20 km) from Cai Rong is **Bai Tu Long National Park**. Spread over Ba Mun Island and its surrounds, this park, established in 2001, is slowly gaining popularity as an ecotourism destination.

⑤ Haiphong

Road Map B1. 62 miles (100) km E of Hanoi on Hwy 5. 👥 1,837,000. ✈ from HCMC and Danang. 🚉 from Hanoi. 🚌 from Hanoi and Halong City. 🚢 from Cat Ba Island. ℹ Haiphong Tourism, 18 Minh Khai St, (031) 382 2616. 🌐 **haiphong tourism.gov.vn**

The third-largest city in the country after Ho Chi Minh City and Hanoi, Haiphong is the north's most important port. Its strategic location made it the target of foreign invaders over the years. It also faced heavy bombing during the First Indo-china War (*see p47*), and later, in the war against the US. Having survived its violent past, Haiphong today is a leading industrial metropolis, specializing in cement manufacture, oil refining, and coal transportation.

Haiphong draws few tourists, even though the atmosphere is relaxed, and the food and accommodation good. The most attractive and noteworthy sights of this city are the beautiful French-Colonial buildings. These include a 19th-century cathedral by Tam Bac River, the **Opera House** on Quang Trung Street, and the **Haiphong Museum**, the Gothic façade of which is more remarkable than the exhibits inside. Situated some distance away from the town center, the 17th-century **Du Hang Pagoda**, on Chua Hang Street, is known for its elaborate architecture, while **Dinh Hang Kenh**, on Nguyen Cong Tru Street, is a fine old communal house.

🏛 Haiphong Museum

11 Dien Tien Hoang St. **Open** 8–11:30am Tue & Thu, 7:30–9:30pm Wed & Sun. 🚫

The colorful, embellished entrance to Du Hang Pagoda, Haiphong

⑥ Cat Ba Island

Road Map C1. 28 miles (45 km) E of Haiphong; 14 miles (22 km) S of Halong City. 22,000. 🛥 Hydrofoil from Haiphong, charter boats from Halong City and Bai Chay.
🅦 asiaoutdoors.com.vn

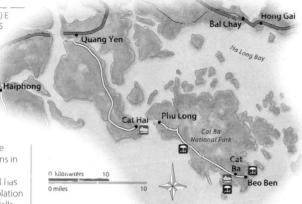

The largest island in a scenic sprawling archipelago of more than 350 islets and islands, Cat Ba is one of the most delightful destinations in Northern Vietnam.

The island's main appeal has always been its relative isolation and bucolic charm. Waterfalls, freshwater lakes, hills, mangrove swamps, and coral reefs are just some of the features of Cat Ba's amazingly diverse ecosystems. Although these characteristics are evident in the island's forests, idyllic beaches, and sparse sprinkling of tiny villages, **Cat Ba Town** is now becoming increasingly polluted and crowded. Nevertheless most boats dock here as it is the only settlement in the area where it is possible to stay overnight and eat in some comfort. With its shabby little karaoke bars, a few small restaurants serving fresh seafood, some seedy massage parlors, and a couple of noisy discotheques, there is little to recommend it except as a gateway to the beautiful **Cat Ba National Park**, the main attraction of the island.

In 1986, to help safeguard the island's varied habitats, almost half of Cat Ba was given the status of a national park. Famous for its rugged landscape, with craggy limestone outcrops, lakes, caves, grottoes, and thick mangroves, the park offers visitors much to explore and experience. The astonishing range of flora found here is also impressive, with more than 800 species cataloged to date. The forests also sustain a variety of fauna, including wild boars, deer, macaques, as well as a large number of bird and reptile species. The park is especially renowned for its community of endangered Cat Ba langurs, found only here on Cat Ba Island.

Today, their number is estimated at a dismal count of 50 animals.

Apart from sightseeing, the park also offers activities such as trekking (see p265) and camping for the adventurous. However, facilities are very limited, and currently visitors need to bring along their own equipment and supplies. The shortest and most popular trek climbs to the 656-ft (200-m) summit of Ngu Lam peak, where a watchtower offers superb views across the park. A longer hike, which can take between four to six hours, leads through the park's tree-canopied interior, past the vast Frog or Ech Lake, to the small hamlet of Viet Hai. From here, boats can be chartered back to Cat Ba Town.

Boats may also be chartered from Cat Ba to explore the Halong Bay (see pp186–8), a short distance to its north, or the smaller but picturesque Lan

A bright Musella bloom in the Cat Ba National Park

Ha Bay, which is located to its northeast, and has tiny but exclusive beaches that can be enjoyed for a small fee.

🏞 Cat Ba National Park
12 miles (20 km) NW of Cat Ba Town. **Open** sunrise–sunset daily. 🐾 📷 for a small fee.

Small hotels and guesthouses overlooking the waterfront, Cat Ba Town

Coral Reefs and Sea Life in Vietnam

Set amid the warm waters of the tropics, Vietnam's 2,037-mile (3,260-km) long coastline, with its numerous offshore islands, is home to many resplendent coral reefs. These extend from the cool waters of Halong Bay in the north, through the warmer seas off Nha Trang and Phu Quoc, to the remote Con Dao Islands in the south. They also provide an immensely diverse habitat for a variety of sea life. The World Wild Fund for Nature (WWF) has identified nearly 280 species of coral living in Vietnamese waters – almost 20 percent of the world's coral species. Though most of the reefs here are endangered by dynamite fishing and cyanide poisoning, various organizations are working actively toward the preservation of Vietnam's magnificent coral heritage.

Hard coral   Soft coral

Schools of colorful fish.

The rare green turtle grows to 5 ft (1.5 m) in length and can weigh up to 440 lb (200 kg), making it the largest hard-shelled sea turtle.

Moray eels frequent coral reefs to a depth of 656 ft (200 m). On average 5-ft (1.5-m) long, they are voracious predators that hide in crevices in the coral.

Reef Ecosystem

Coral reefs are composed of the skeletons of millions of algae and coral polyps, accumulated over millennia. They flourish best in clear tropical waters, and form an immensely diverse habitat for a range of life forms, including mollusks, turtles, and a countless variety of brightly colored fish.

The cuttlefish, a small relative of the squid, has an internal shell, eight arms, and two tentacles covered with suckers for catching prey.

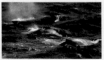

Dugongs or sea cows are gentle mammals that grow up to 10 ft (3 m) in length, and inhabit the shallow reef waters where they graze on sea grass.

Stingrays are armed with a razor-sharp tail that is covered with toxic venom. Propelled by their large pectoral fins, these fish appear to fly through the water.

Marine Mammals of Vietnam

Bottlenose dolphins frolicking in water

Vietnam's seas are home to many species of marine mammals, such as dolphins, porpoises, and even whales. The endangered Irrawaddy dolphin once lived in the Mekong Delta, but there have been no sightings for several years. The agile bottlenose dolphin, the humpback, and the southern right whale are among some of the rare marine mammal species seen in the waters off Vietnam.

Humpback whale

Southern right whale

Farmers at Kenh Ga using buckets to irrigate a field, a common practice

❼ Ninh Binh

Road Map B2. 59 miles (95 km)
S of Hanoi on Hwy 1. 🚗 133,000.
🚉 Reunification Express between
Hanoi and HCMC. 🚌 Hanoi. ℹ️ Ninh
Binh Tourism, Dinh Tien Hoang Rd,
(030) 388 4101.

An ideal base from which to
explore the southern part of
the Red River Delta, Ninh Binh
is becoming a popular tourist
destination. While the town
itself is not remarkable, it does
feature several interesting
attractions in its vicinity.

The historic site of **Hoa Lu**,
7 miles (12 km) northwest of Ninh
Binh, was established as a royal
capital in AD 968 by Emperor
Tien Hoang De, the founder of
the Dinh Dynasty (r.968–980). A
massive palace and citadel constructed by him, though now
mostly in ruins, is still impressive.

A second royal temple in the
vicinity is dedicated to Le Dai
Hanh, founder of the Early Le
Dynasty (r.980–1009), which
succeeded the Dinh Dynasty.
They are credited with replacing
Chinese currency with
Vietnamese coinage.

Just 7 miles (12 km) northwest
of Hoa Lu, is the country's

biggest temple complex, **Bai
Dinh Temple**. It opened in 2010
and features statues of 500
arhats (enlightened Buddha)
and a 100-ton (91 tonnes)
bronze Buddha image. To the
southwest of Hoa Lu in the
Thanh Hoa Province is the
Ho Citadel, Vietnam's newest
World Heritage Site, recognized
by UNESCO in 2011. Established
by the Ho Dynasty in the early
15th century, all that remains of
the citadel are the four massive
stone gateways facing the
cardinal points.

Tam Coc or Three Caves at
6 miles (10 km) southwest of
Ninh Binh town is often
promoted as Vietnam's "Halong
Bay on Land." It also features
karst outcrops, but while those
at Halong Bay thrust upwards
from the waves, at Tam Coc
they rise majestically from a sea
of green rice fields. It takes
about three hours to visit Tam
Coc, punted in metal boats
along the watery landscape
and through three long caves.
In places, these are so low that
it is necessary to duck, while
boatwomen propel the craft by
pushing on the cave roof with
their hands. Nearby, **Bich Dong**

or Jade Cavern is just 2 miles
(3 km) north of Tam Coc. This
unique pagoda is cut into the
side of a karst outcrop.

Not far from here, the idyllic
fishing village of **Kenh Ga** is
worth a visit. Centered on a small
island and surrounded by stark
karst formations, it largely
comprises of gently floating
houseboats. The pier is at Tran
Me, just 4 miles (7 km) south of
Ninh Binh. It takes three hours
or so to tour Kenh Ga, and it is
wonderfully relaxing to chug
slowly along to Van Trinh Grotto
observing tranquil rural scenery
en route. About a mile (1.6 km)
east of Tran Me are the reed-
filled marshes of **Van Long
Nature Reserve**, where a
small community of the rare
Delacour's langur live, secure
among the inaccessible limestone outcrops.

Around 19 miles (30 km)
southeast of Ninh Binh, Phat
Diem town is home to **Phat
Diem Cathedral**, one of the
most well-known churches in
Vietnam. Alexandre de Rhodes,
a French Jesuit priest who
developed the nation's
Romanized writing system,
preached here in 1627, but it
was Tran Luc, a Vietnamese
priest, who organized the
construction of this unique
cathedral. It was completed
in 1898, and combines
European Gothic church architecture with Sino-Vietnamese
temple tradition.

🏞️ **Van Long Nature Reserve**
Gia Vien Dist, Ninh Binh Province
Tel (030) 388 4141. **Open** daily. 📷
🎫 by arrangement.

⛪ **Phat Diem Cathedral**
Tel (030) 386 2058. **Open** daily. ♿

Boats approaching one of the many low, long cave passages found at Tam Coc

❽ Perfume Pagoda

Nestled in forested limestone cliffs, and overlooking the Suoi Yen River, Perfume Pagoda is arguably one of Vietnam's most spectacular sights. Located on Nui Huong Tich or Fragrant Vestige Mountain, the pagoda is actually a complex of around 30 Buddhist shrines. The most fascinating of these is the Huong Tich Pagoda, which is set in a deep cavern in the mountainside, and is dedicated to Quan Am, the Goddess of Mercy. Each year, during the Perfume Pagoda Festival (*see p34*), thousands of Buddhists embark on a pilgrimage up the mountain, praying for absolution, good health, and, in the case of childless couples, a baby.

Thien Tru Pagoda nestled amid the lush green peaks of Nui Huong Tich

★ Huong Tich Pagoda
This revered grotto is filled with incense smoke and several gilded figurines of the Buddha and Quan Am. The phrase "Most Beautiful Cavern under the Southern Sky" is carved near its entrance, where 120 steps lead into the cave.

Cua Vong

②

①

★ Thien Tru Pagoda
Also known as the Heavenly Kitchen Pagoda, this 18th-century shrine rises through three levels on the mountainside. An elegant triple-roofed bell pavilion stands in front of the temple and a statue of Quan Am dominates the main altar inside.

Thanh Son

Huong Dai

KEY

① **Giai Oan Pagoda**, or the Undoing Injustice Pagoda is popular with pilgrims seeking purification and justice.

② **Tien Son Pagoda**, is set in a cave and is one of the holiest shrines here. It is dedicated to Quan Am and contains four ruby statues.

③ **Den Trinh Pagoda**, is the first stop on the mountain as all pilgrims are required to "register" or pray and ask for acceptance of their journey up to Huong Tich.

Steps leading to Huong Tich
The steep walk up to Huong Tich takes at least an hour. During the Perfume Pagoda Festival, thousands of pilgrims throng the steps, greeting everyone with a pious *nam mo A Di Da phat*, or "praise to the Amitabha Buddha."

★ Suoi Yen River
A fleet of boats, all rowed by women, ferries tourists up this breathtaking river on their way to the Perfume Pagoda. The hour-and-a-half journey is a tranquil glide through verdant paddies, the profound silence broken only by the slap of the oars.

VISITORS' CHECKLIST

Practical Information
Road Map B1 40 miles (65 km) SW of Hanoi along Hwy 21, My Duc township. **Open** daily. 🚫 📷 📖 📷 A cable car carries passengers from Thien Tru Pagoda to Huong Tich Pagoda. The cost of this ticket is not included in the admission price.

Transport
🚌 from downtown Hanoi and Ninh Binh. 🚌

Rare Cervus nippon deer in Cuc Phuong National Park

❾ Cuc Phuong National Park

Road Map B2. Nho Quan District, 28 miles (45 km) W of Ninh Binh; 87 miles (140 km) SW of Hanoi. **Tel** (030) 384 8006. 🚌 minibus from Ninh Binh. **Open** 8am–5:30pm daily. 🚫 📷 by arrangement with park authorities. 📷 📖 📷
🌐 cucphuongtourism.com

Established as Vietnam's first national park in 1962, Cuc Phuong covers 86 sq miles (223 sq km) of largely primary tropical forest, and is home to an impressive variety of fauna, including almost 100 species each of mammals and reptiles, and more than 300 types of birds. The park is also famous for its range of flora, which includes soaring 1,000-year-old trees and medicinal plants.

One of the main highlights at the park is the **Endangered Primate Rescue Center**. Set up in 1993, the sanctuary cares for animals rescued from hunters, promotes breeding and conservation programs, and also rehabilitates endangered primates for release into the wild. Home to many species of langur, gibbon, loris, and other primates, the center is a great place to see these animals at close range.

Cuc Phuong has excellent trekking opportunities (see p265) and many attractions such as waterfalls, prehistoric caves, and nearby Muong villages that offer overnight stays.

📷 **Endangered Primate Rescue Center**
Tel (030) 384 8002. **Open** daily.
🌐 primatecenter.org

Suoi Yen River

⊞ ③

Trip to Perfume Pagoda
Rowboats made of metal await passengers for the trip to the magnificent Perfume Pagoda from the township of My Duc.

⑩ Hoa Binh

Road Map B3. 46 miles (74 km) SW of Hanoi. ⚁ 115,000. ⛟ Hanoi. ℹ Hoa Binh Tourist, 395 An Duong Vuong St, (018) 385 4374.

A pleasant little town, Hoa Binh means "peace." Ironically, its strategic location next to the Song Da or Black River Valley made it the site of many battles during the First Indochina War *(see p47)*. Relics from these turbulent times are displayed in the **Hoa Binh Museum**. A French landing craft and a destroyed French tank can be seen on its grounds.

Traditionally home to the Muong community, the town has shaded avenues and some decent eateries, which makes it a convenient stop on a tour from Hanoi to neighboring places such as Moc Chau and around Mai Chau Valley.

A few miles northwest of Hoa Binh is **Song Da Reservoir**. Boat trips to the minority villages and the reservoir can be arranged through local tour operators.

🏛 **Hoa Binh Museum**
6 An Duong Vuong St. **Tel** (018) 385 2177. **Open** 7–11am, 1:30–4:30pm daily. 📷

French tank captured in the First Indochina War, Hoa Binh Museum

⑪ Mai Chau Valley

Road Map B2. 87 miles (140 km) SW of Hanoi; 43 miles (70 km) SE of Moc Chau on Hwy 6. ⚁ 50,000. ⛟ from Hanoi and Son La.

Surrounded by the foothills of the Truong Son Range, this charming and fertile valley is dotted with green rice paddies and small, quaint stilt-house villages. Most of the inhabitants here are White Thai. Well known

for their hospitality, families here offer homestay *(see p234)* facilities in stilt huts. As the standards of hygiene and cuisine are good, this is an authentic yet comfortable way of experiencing life on the hills. Some of the larger homestays even put on displays of traditional Thai music and dancing. At night, visitors can enjoy the local alcohol *ruou can*, which is drunk communally from large jars through long bamboo straws.

One of the main highlights here is the excellent trekking opportunities provided by the valley's delightful trails, fields, and villages.

⑫ Moc Chau

Road Map B1. 124 miles (200 km) SW of Hanoi; 75 miles (121 km) SE of Son La on Hwy 6. ⚁ 152,000. ⛟ from Hanoi and Son La.

The semi-rural, market town of Moc Chau, surrounded by a plateau of the same name, is renowned for its tea plantations and its burgeoning dairy industry. The generous yield of fresh cow's milk, as well as the creamy yogurt and rich sweets made here are transported to Hanoi daily.

Since Moc Chau is not as convenient as Mai Chau for longer stays, most people stop here only for refreshments on the drive from Hanoi to Son La. Ethnic minorities such as the Hmong *(see pp202–3)* and Thai occupy the neighboring hamlets, which are definitely worth a visit.

White Thai girls in traditional costume perform a folk dance, Mai Chau

⑬ Son La

Road Map A1. 199 miles (320 km) NW of Hanoi on Hwy 6; 93 miles (150 km) E of Dien Bien Phu on Hwy 6. ⚁ 92,000. ✈ Hanoi. ⛟ from Hanoi and Dien Bien Phu.

Bisected by the narrow Nam La River, the busy little town of Son La was once known as "Vietnam's Siberia." The infamous French-era prison, **Son La Prison**, which earned it this label, stands menacingly on a wooded hill. Son La's isolation and cold weather were considered ideal conditions for the incarceration of Vietnamese nationalists and revolutionaries. Recalcitrant prisoners were shackled and confined in windowless cells, and the prison guillotine saw regular use. However, as is often the case, the prison also served as a revolutionary academy of sorts. Some of the political prisoners held here included luminaries

Black Thai women selling their wares in makeshift stalls, Son La

such as Truong Chinh and Le Duan, both of whom later became General Secretaries of the Vietnamese Communist Party. The prison complex also includes a museum displaying remnants of French brutality and torture such as cramped underground cells and leg irons. Somewhat incongruously, exhibits such as hill tribe artifacts and clothing are also displayed here.

A major attraction in town is the market on the east bank of the Nam La. Fresh fruit and vegetables, as well as handicrafts and cloth hand-woven by the White and Black Thai are on sale here. Chickens, ducks, and pot-bellied pigs are for sale, while small food stalls serve Son La's specialty, goat meat or *thit de*. The more adventurous can sample *tiet canh*, congealed goat's blood served with chopped peanuts and shallots.

Located 3 miles (5 km) south of town are the warm water springs known as Suoi Nuoc Nong. It is possible to bathe here for a small fee. The scenery around Son La is very attractive and the drive to Dien Bien Phu leads past picturesque fields, hills, and interesting minority villages

Wooden stilt huts amid the flooded paddy fields around Son La

Son La Prison

Dai Khao Ca. **Tel** (022) 385 2859. **Open** 7:30–11am, 1:30–4.30pm daily.

⑭ Dien Bien Phu

Road Map A1. 292 miles (470 km) NW of Hanoi; 93 miles (150 km) W of Son La. 48,000. Hanoi. from Hanoi, Son La, and Lai Chau.

Situated in a fertile valley near the Lao border, this historic town's main claim to fame is the decisive battle of Dien Bien Phu *(see p47)*. In 1954, following French infiltration of the area, Viet Minh troops systematically broke down the French position. In the end, General de Castries, commander of the French army, and his troops were captured. Today, the town has moved past its violent history and is developing at a rapid pace. Dien Bien Phu was once part of the Lai Chau

Province, a section of which has now been submerged by the waters of the rising Son La Dam. As a result, the new province of Dien Bien Phu was created, leading to a boom in construction work, both for administrative buildings and for resettlement purposes.

Rapidly being encroached on by new buildings, the main battlefield on the east bank of the Nam La River has a few old, rusty French tanks lying around even today. Nearby stands a poignant memorial to the

Marble headstone of a hero, Dien Bien Phu Martyrs' Cemetery

French dead. Chronicling the great battle, **Dien Bien Phu Museum** is full of weapons, pictures, maps, dioramas of the battlefield, and personal possessions of soldiers. Just opposite is the **Dien Bien Phu Martyrs' Cemetery**, where the Viet Minh fallen are buried. To the north is the famous **Hill A1**, named Eliane by the French, after one of General de Castries' mistresses. The most interesting relic here is the French general's subterranean bunker, covered with a rusting, corrugated-iron roof and reinforced with concrete.

On the hilltop is a monument to martyred Vietnamese heroes, and a tunnel entrance used by the Viet Minh to reach a French camp, which they blew up with a mine. Farther north is the 120-ton (109-tonne) victory monument in bronze, which commemorates the battle's 50th anniversary. This is the largest monument in the entire country.

Dien Bien Phu Museum

1 Muong Thanh. **Tel** (023) 383 1341 **Open** 7:30–11am, 1:30–5pm daily.

View of the spectacular Tram Ton Pass, north side of Mount Fansipan, Sapa

⓯ Sapa

Road Map A1. 236 miles (380 km) NW of Hanoi. 🚠 41,000. 🚉 from Hanoi to Lao Cai. 🚌 Lao Cai. 🛈 Sapa Tourism, 2 Fansipan St, (020) 387 1975. 🚋 Sat & Sun. 🌐 **sapa-tourism.com**

With cascading rice terraces and lush vegetation, Sapa is perched on the eastern slopes of the Hoang Lien Mountains, also known as the Tonkinese Alps. Jesuit priests first arrived here in 1918 and sent word of the idyllic views and pleasant climate back to Hanoi. By 1922, Sapa was established as a hill station where the French built villas, hotels, and tennis courts, transforming the place into a summer retreat.

In this scenic setting, French colonists or *colons* would flirt, gossip, eat strawberries, and drink lots of wine. These idyllic conditions lasted until World War II and the Japanese invasion of 1941. Many villas and hotels were destroyed or abandoned in the next four decades during wars with the French and the US *(see pp47–9)*. Still more destructive was the Sino-Vietnamese War of 1979, when the town itself was damaged.

Fortunately, following the introduction of Vietnam's economic reforms or *doi moi* in the 1990s and the subsequent gradual opening of the country to tourism, Sapa gained a fresh lease on life. Revived by local entrepreneurs and rediscovered by foreign visitors, the town slowly regained the distinction it enjoyed in colonial times.

Set on several levels joined by small sloping streets and steep flights of steps, Sapa is home to diverse hill peoples, as well as ethnic Kinh and a growing army of visitors who come for the stunning views and fresh mountain air. Trekking has become a popular activity, and walks to nearby villages are open to all. Visitors often time their stay to coincide with the weekend market, though it is now open on weekdays too. A major section of hill people are the Black Hmong, who generally wear indigo, followed by the Red Dao. Young women turn up for this colorful bazaar wearing exquisitely embroidered skirts and jackets, elaborate headdresses, and heavy silver jewelry. The small and simple Sapa church, which was built in 1930 and set in a square, forms the center of town where the locals collect on feast days.

Southeast of the town is Ham Rong or Dragon Jaw's Hill. A gentle climb leads up through rockeries and grottos to a summit. From here, there are magnificent views of the tree-filled valleys below, dotted with the colorful villas. Dance

Black Dao woman in traditional garb, and a child

Hotels with balcony views in Sapa

For hotels and restaurants see pp236–41 and pp246–53

performances by the ethnic minorities are staged at the top of the hill.

Environs

The "Gateway to Sapa," **Lao Cai** lies at a distance of about 25 miles (40 km) northeast of Sapa. A rather unappealing border town, it is not really a place to linger in. However, if crossing to China or passing through to visit Sapa and Bac Ha, it is comfortable enough, with adequate hotel facilities and some good restaurants.

About 5 miles (8 km) from Sapa, **Mount Fansipan** is the country's highest peak. Around 10,300-ft (3,140-m) tall, it is covered in lush subtropical vegetation to a height of about 660 ft (200 m), and then by temperate forest.

Although the terrain can be difficult and the weather bad, the peak attracts trekkers *(see p265)*. Warm clothes, sturdy boots, camping gear, and a guide are essential for the five-day round trip. There is no sign of humanity for most of the climb, with only lush green forests and spectacular mountains for company. The silence is broken only by the sounds of birds, monkeys, and the gentle rustling of trees.

The lovely Black Hmong *(see p203)* village of **Cat Cat** is just 2 miles (3 km) south of Sapa. Visitors normally walk down the steep trail, but take a motorcycle taxi for the uphill ride back to town. The Hmong live in houses of mud, wattle, bamboo, and thatch, surrounded by vats of indigo-colored liquid, which is used to dye their clothing. Just 2.5 miles (4 km) beyond Cat Cat is the less commercialized Hmong village of **Sin Chai**, while the Red Dao *(see p25)* village of **Ta Phin** is only about 6 miles (10 km) from Sapa. The route to Ta Phin passes through a low-slung valley that is carved with curved rice terracing, which glints very brightly in the sun. Just before

Ta Phin is an abandoned, semi-destroyed French seminary, which was built in 1942.

Just around 9 miles (15 km) northwest of Sapa, on the road to the Tram Ton Pass is the **Thac Bac** or Silver Waterfall. This powerful 330-ft (100-m) high cascade is a magnificent sight, attracting many visitors. Here, women – Kinh, Black Dao, and Red Hmong – set up stalls selling delicious fruit.

🟢 Bac Ha

Road Map A1. 205 miles (330 km) NW Hanoi, 43 miles (69 km) E of Lao Cai. 🗺 54,000. 🚌 from Lao Cai and Sapa. 🗓 Sun. ℹ (020) 378 0661. 🌐 bachatourist.com

A small town at 2,950 ft (900 m) above sea level in the Chay River massif, Bac Ha has a deserted air for much of the week. However, on Sunday mornings, it attracts hill peoples, such as the Dao, Tay, Thai, Nung, and the colorful Flower Hmong among many others from all over the surrounding mountains. All of them head for Bac Ha's dusty town center and market, leading ponies stacked high with firewood, and carrying baskets loaded with merchandise.

Items sold and exchanged include bush meat, vegetables, fruits, spices, and exquisitely embroidered goods. Most hill people also use this occasion to stock up on necessities as well

Colorful embroidered accessories by the Red Dao

Brightly dressed Flower Hmong women gathered at Bac Ha market

as luxuries that are not available in the hills. Toiletries, religious paraphernalia, and incense sticks, as well as needles, thread, and cloth for embroidery are just some of the products in demand here.

Environs

Many visitors to Bac Ha also head farther north in order to combine a visit to the Sunday market with a trip to the small settlement of **Can Cau**. Located about 12 miles (20 km) from Bac Ha town, this charming village hosts a Saturday market, which is very popular with locals and visitors alike, especially for being delightfully vibrant and extremely colorful.

Bac Ha district is also known for its potent maize alcohol, distilled most especially at the small village of **Ban Pho**, a Flower Hmong settlement just 2.5 miles (4 km) to the west of Bac Ha town.

Local hill people completing their weekly shopping, Bac Ha market

Hmong of Northern Vietnam

One of the largest ethnic minority groups in Vietnam, the Hmong or Meo were a nomadic group who emigrated from China to Vietnam in the early 19th century, and settled in the northern highlands. Known for their independent spirit – *hmong* means free in their language – the group has remained fiercely loyal to its indigenous customs, resisting assimilation with the Viet majority. Today, the Hmong have largely abandoned slash-and-burn agriculture, and lead a settled, often impoverished life, farming and raising livestock. These people are categorized under five main subgroups – Flower, Black, Green, Red, and White – based on the dress of the women.

Vietnamese is taught in schools to encourage assimilation

Hmong villages, known as *giao*, are small communities featuring wooden huts with thatched roofs. Unlike other hill communities, their homes are not built on stilts. They are usually constructed according to ancient customs, stipulating that houses must be built on land blessed by ancestors.

The ritualistic sacrifice of buffalos is common during festivals. The Hmong are traditionally animists, who believe that the meat will appease the region's guardian spirits. A number of special musical instruments are used for such ceremonies, including large drums, water buffalo horns, and the *queej*, a kind of mouth harp.

Bright strips of cloth, embroidered in vibrant patterns of flowers, birds, and geometric designs decorate the blouses of the women.

The Black Hmong are distinguished by their black-dyed clothing. The men dress in baggy trousers, short tunics, and skullcaps, while women wear trousers or skirts and leggings, often piling their hair into an open hat. Most Black Hmong villages are found around Sapa.

Dry rice cultivation, which is based on traditional slash-and-burn agriculture, has been adopted by the Hmong on the uplands. Maize, corn, and rye are other staples, while hemp and cotton are grown for cloth. In some remote areas, poppies are illegally harvested for opium.

Indigo is used by the Black and Green Hmong to dye trousers, skirts, and sashes, which are hand-woven out of hemp. Batik is often utilized to further embellish these richly colored outfits.

Hmong textile stalls are a staple of the weekly markets of the northern highlands. The Hmong have been relatively successful in selling their handicrafts to visitors. Their appliqué work and embroidered fabrics are now very popular.

Gui, or woven baskets, into which babies are tucked, are strapped to the backs of Hmong mothers, which helps keep their hands free for daily tasks.

Flower Hmong flock to Bac Ha Market once a week to sell fresh produce, honey, bamboo, and herbs. They also stock up on necessities such as matches, cloth, needles, and kitchenware.

Appliqué bags and aprons are indicators of marital status and social position

Colorful Flower Hmong

Admired for their extravagant and elaborate clothing, the Flower Hmong are the largest subdivision of the Hmong in the country. The vividly patterned costumes worn by the women include brightly colored head scarves, and full pleated skirts, as well as flamboyant silver or tin jewelry. The women are also successful in business, and often sell clothes and accessories featuring their exquisite embroidery, batik, and appliqué work.

Red Hmong women are known for their giant, bouffant hairdos. They painstakingly collect all the hair they shed naturally, and then weave it around a headpiece, along with their living tresses. Occasionally, the hair of dead relatives is also woven in.

Heavy silver jewelry is worn by Hmong women both as adornment and as a mark of status. The intricately crafted earrings, necklaces, and bracelets often feature the snake motif – a talisman against evil forces. Men and children also wear jewelry, as it is believed to bind the body and soul together.

Dawn breaking above the shimmering expanse of Ba Be National Park's lake

ⓘ Ba Be National Park

Road Map B1. 149 miles (240 km) N of Hanoi; 37 miles (60 km) N of Bac Kan Town. **Tel** (0281) 389 4721. 🚗 by arrangement with park authorities. 🏞️

Located in a remote upland region, this lush park is centered on three linked lakes – Ba Be means Three Bays. Together they form the country's largest freshwater lake area. Covering about 40 sq miles (100 sq km), the park is dominated by dramatic limestone peaks, waterfalls, and grottos. The region's tropical forests are also home to an abundance of wild life, including the François langur and the endangered Tonkin snub-nosed monkey.

Some of the main attractions in Ba Be National Park include the **Dau Dang Falls**, a spectacular series of cascades, found at the northwest end of the lake. Also worth seeing is the **Hang Puong**, a fascinating grotto that tunnels its way all through the mountains. Situated around 7 miles (12 km) up the Nang River, this narrow cave can be navigated in a small boat, though the trip takes the better part of a day. To the south of the lake lies **Pac Ngoi**, a charming village, which is inhabited by the Tay minority. The surrounding hills are home to other ethnic peoples.

ⓘ Cao Bang

Road Map B1. 168 miles (270 km) N of Hanoi on Hwy 3. 🚗 45,000. 🚌 Hanoi and Lang Son.

Well off the beaten track in the high mountains along the Chinese frontier, the thickly forested area around the small town of Cao Bang is home to several ethnic minorities, including the Tay, Dao, and Nung. While the town itself is not particularly distinctive, its surroundings are spectacular, and many visitors are drawn to its abundant trekking opportunities. The Vietnamese regard it as a place of historical significance. The scions of the 16th-century Mac Dynasty ruled here, and years later, Ho Chi Minh *(see p173)* made it his first base on returning to Vietnam after nearly three decades.

Nung girl in rural Cao Bang

Environs
Around 37 miles (60 km) northwest of town, **Hang Pac Bo** or Water Wheel Cave is where Ho Chi Minh stayed on his return in 1941 from self-imposed exile. The cave has great historical importance as the birthplace of the Viet Minh struggle. A small museum here makes for an interesting stop.

About 56 miles (90 km) northeast of Cao Bang, **Thac Ban Gioc** is the largest waterfall in Vietnam. It straddles the Sino-Vietnamese border and it is necessary to get a pass at Cao Bang's police station to visit the area.

ⓘ Dong Van Karst Plateau Geopark

Road Map B1. 212 miles (342 km) N of Hanoi. 🚌 Ha Giang 🛈 For permit: Immigration Office, 5 Tran Quoc Toan, Ha Giang. **Tel** (026) 385 2245. **Open** 7–11:30am, 1:30–4:30pm Mon–Fri.

Vietnam's northernmost province of Ha Giang contains unforgettable landscapes in the Dong Van Karst Plateau Geopark, recognized by UNESCO as the first global geopark in Vietnam.

Covering over 900 sq miles (2,500 sq km), this wonderland of limestone peaks rise to an average of 4,920 ft (1,500 m). Visitors need to acquire a permit in Ha Giang and a 4WD or a motorbike is necessary to navigate the rough mountain roads.

The spectacular views begin at Heaven's Gate, just above the town of Tam Son, where a lush valley is bordered by rugged karst outcrops. From here the route passes through Yen Minh to Dong Van, the northernmost town of Vietnam passing villages of minority groups like the White Hmong. Sights of interest near Dong Van include the Vuong Palace, and Lung Cu Flag Tower, which marks the northernmost point in the country. From Dong Van, the route continues to Meo Vac via the Ma Phi Leng Pass, which offers breathtaking views of the Nho Que River in the canyon below. From Meo Vac, it is possible to head south to Cao Bang or Ba Be Lake via the small town of Bao Loc.

A generous growth of weed amongst rocks in the Dong Van Karst Plateau Geopark

For hotels and restaurants see pp236–41 and pp246–53

Flora, Fauna, and Birds of Northern Vietnam

Under a thick, rich canopy of evergreen forests, the rugged mountainous hinterland of Northern Vietnam protects an amazingly diverse biosphere. Thousands of types of flora flourish here, as do a plethora of bird, mammal, and reptile species. However, a vast number of animals, many endemic to Vietnam, are currently under threat. Critically endangered species include the kouprey and the Tonkin snub-nosed monkey. The Asian elephant and the white-rumped black lemur are also facing serious threat. Fortunately, the authorities are beginning to take notice and have adopted a proactive stance against poaching. With sustained conservation and reforestation measures, it is hoped that the north will eventually reach an ecological balance.

Flora

The mountains and valleys of Northern Vietnam are covered with thick forests, sheltering a wealth of tropical and subtropical flora, ranging from towering rainforests, dwarf bamboos, and tiny ferns to creeping vines, exquisite orchids, and colorful rhododendrons.

Karst mountains covered with forests dominate the landscape, especially around Tam Coc, Cao Bang, and Halong Bay.

A dazzling variety of orchids bloom all over Vietnam. Of around 40 endemic species, 18 are found on Mount Fansipan (*see p201*).

Millions of cave swiftlets, tiny, fast-flying insect-catchers which live in the limestone caves of the north, leave their nests at dawn and return at dusk.

The Annamese silver pheasant lives on the slopes of the Truong Son and Hoang Lien Son Mountains. Its red legs, red face, and black crest set off its lovely silver plumage.

Fauna

The Truong Son Range has revealed more previously unknown large mammals than any other location during the late 20th century. These include the Vu Quang ox, the giant muntjac, and the Truong Son muntjac. Deer, wild boar, as well as many primate species inhabit the forests, especially in Cuc Phuong (see p197).

The red-shanked Douc langur has bright maroon hind legs and reddish patches around the eyes. Its long tail adds to its considerable agility

The Vu Quang ox, or *saola*, is a rare forest-dwelling bovine, first discovered in 1992 at Vu Quang Nature Reserve. Weighing around 200 lb (90 kg), it has a brown coat with a black stripe along the back. Both sexes have large, curving horns.

The Indochinese tiger once roamed the forests of Northern Vietnam freely. Mainly due to the use of tiger parts in traditional medicine, less than 50 of these majestic beasts survive in Vietnam today.

EXCURSION TO ANGKOR

INTRODUCING ANGKOR

The ancient capital of the great Khmer Empire, Angkor is, beyond doubt, one of the most magnificent wonders of the world and a site of immense archaeological significance. Located in dense jungle on the hot and torpid plains of western Cambodia, its awe-inspiring temples transport visitors into an enchanting and mysterious world of brooding grandeur and past glory.

Situated in southwestern Indochina, the flat, low-lying country of Cambodia covers an area of about 69,500 sq miles (180,000 sq km), bordering Laos to the north, Thailand to both the north and west, and Vietnam to the east. Although Cambodia's capital is now Phnom Penh, this title was once held by Angkor. For six centuries, between AD 802 and 1432, it was the political and religious center of the great Khmer Empire, which once extended from the South China Sea almost to the Bay of Bengal. The remains of the metropolis of Angkor now occupy 77 sq miles (200 sq km) of northwest Cambodia, and although its old wooden houses and palaces decayed centuries ago, the stunning array of stone temples erected by a succession of self-styled god-kings still stand. Set between two *baray* or reservoirs, Angkor today contains around 70 temples, tombs, and other ancient ruins. Among them is the stunning Angkor Wat, the world's single largest religious complex.

Classical dancer, Cambodian Royal Ballet

Religion

Ancient Cambodia was highly influenced by South Asia, and Hindu gods such as Vishnu and Shiva were revered. From the 10th century AD onward, Buddhism gradually began to spread throughout the Khmer Empire, receiving a significant boost during the reign of Angkor monarch Jayavarman VII (r.1181–1218). As the two religions flourished, Angkorian architecture incorporated elements from both Hinduism and Buddhism. Eventually, Theravada Buddhism or the Way of the Elders emerged as the predominant school, and replaced Hinduism as the national religion.

History

The Khmer Empire was founded in the beginning of the 9th century AD, when Jayavarman II (r.802–850) proclaimed himself *devaraja* or the divine king of the land. A follower of Shiva, he built a gigantic, pyramidal temple-mountain representing Mount Meru, the sacred mythical abode of the Hindu gods. This structure laid the foundation of Angkor's architecture *(see pp218–19)*. His successor, Indravarman I (r.877–89) expanded the empire, but it was Yasovarman I (r.889–910) who shifted the former capital at Roluos to Angkor. He established his new seat of power by

Meandering river near Siem Reap *(see p212)*, the gateway to the temples of Angkor

Buddhist monks walking past the grand Angkor Wat complex (see pp216–17)

constructing a magnificent temple on the hill of Phnom Bakheng and another one on the massive East Baray. Angkor's grandest structures, Angkor Wat was built by Suryavarman II (r.1113–50), and Angkor Thom by Jayavarman VII. Following Jayavarman VII's death, Angkor entered a long era of decline, lying forgotten as Thai invaders ravaged the land.

It was not until the 19th century that spellbound European explorers stumbled upon Angkor. Following their "discovery," the ancient city underwent a period of restoration until the mid-20th century, when it disappeared again behind a curtain of war. During the Vietnam War (see pp48–9), Vietnamese communists used Cambodia as a staging post, and the US responded with large-scale bombings, killing thousands of Cambodians, and giving rise to Pol Pot's Khmer Rouge. This extreme Maoist party seized power in 1975, and by the time it was overthrown by the Vietnamese in 1979, it had killed an estimated two million Cambodians in one of the worst acts of genocide In history.

Angkor Today

Since the collapse of the Khmer Rouge in the early 1990s, Angkor has gradually reopened to the world. Miraculously,

in a nation so devastated by war, the great temple complexes have survived remarkably unscathed. Today, after painstaking clearance of unexploded ordinance and dense vegetation, restoration and conservation are once again in full swing. One of the most important archaeological sites in the world, Angkor attracts millions of visitors each year, providing a substantial boost to Cambodia's economy.

Key Dates in History

AD 802 Khmer Empire established.

AD 900 Capital moved from Roluos to Angkor.

1113–1150 Suryavarman II builds Angkor Wat.

1181–1201 Jayavarman VII builds the Bayon and Angkor Thom.

1352–1431 Siam attacks Angkor on four separate occasions.

1863 Cambodia becomes a French protectorate.

1953 Cambodia gains full independence from France under King Sihanouk.

1970 US begins carpet bombing of northern and eastern Cambodia.

1975 Khmer Rouge seizes power

1979 Vietnamese forces overthrow Khmer Rouge.

1998 Khmer Rouge leader Pol Pot dies.

2005 UN approves tribunal for trying surviving Khmer Rouge leaders.

Exploring Angkor

Set among dense green forests and neat rice paddies, the massive monuments at Angkor are arguably the most remarkable and striking architectural masterpieces in Southeast Asia. Located north of Siem Reap, in the heart of Angkor, the vast Angkor Wat complex, with its imposing towers, and the great city of Angkor Thom, with its impressive causeway and gigantic smiling faces of the Bayon, are breathtaking sights, especially during sunrise or sunset. Farther north are the smaller yet unique temples of Preah Khan and Preah Neak Pean. To the east of Angkor Thom is the magical Ta Prohm, with large trees growing through the temple walls. Farther out, the pink sandstone structure of Banteay Srei lies to the northeast, while to the southeast are the ruins of the Roluos Group, the oldest in Angkor.

Exquisite carvings of dancing *apsaras* at Bayon, Angkor Thom

Sights at a Glance

Historic Monuments

② *Angkor Wat pp216–17*
③ Phnom Bakheng
④ *Angkor Thom pp220–23*
⑤ Preah Khan
⑥ Preah Neak Pean
⑦ Ta Prohm
⑧ Prasat Kravan
⑨ Banteay Srei
⑩ Roluos Group

City

① Siem Reap

```
0 kilometers        3
0 miles             3
```

Thick tree roots covering the stone walls and ceilings of Ta Prohm

Getting Around

The temples at Angkor require both time and motorized transport to visit. It is possible to visit the main sites by motorbike, but the most comfortable way to travel in this hot and dusty area is in an air-conditioned car with a driver. In colonial times, the French defined two circuits, both starting at Angkor Wat, which are still used today. The 11-mile (18-km) "small circuit" takes at least a day and covers the central temples of the complex, continuing to Ta Prohm, before returning to Angkor Wat by way of Banteay Kdei. The "great circuit," a 17-mile (27-km) route, takes in the small circuit as well as the outer temples, going past Preah Neak Pean to Ta Som before turning south to Pre Rup. It takes at least two full days.

Locator Map

Key

☐ Urban areas
⎯ Archaeological sites
⎯ Major road
⎯ Minor road

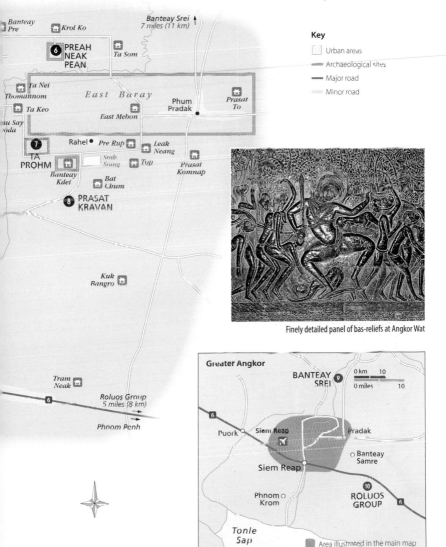

Finely detailed panel of bas-reliefs at Angkor Wat

For keys to symbols *see back flap*

❶ Siem Reap

Pronounced "See-em Reep," Siem Reap literally means Siam Defeated, celebrating the 17th-century Khmer victory over the Thai kingdom of Ayutthaya. The town is the capital of Siem Reap Province, located in northwest Cambodia, and has achieved prominence as the main base for people visiting the temples of Angkor and Roluos. As a burgeoning center of tourism with a new airport, Siem Reap features many new hotels and restaurants, and further development is ongoing.

Verdant lawns outside the Raffles Grand Hotel d'Angkor *(see p241)*, Siem Reap

Exploring the city

Siem Reap has managed to retain its calm, rural ambience despite becoming increasingly busy catering to millions of visitors every year. Its relaxed, well-equipped setting provides the ideal place to unwind after a day exploring Angkor.

The French-Colonial **Raffles Grand Hotel d'Angkor**, which stands out regally opposite the Royal Gardens in the northern part of town, has been splendidly restored. The small **Royal Palace**, which is rarely visited by the reigning King Sihamoni, is close by.

South of a statue of Vishnu marking the center of town, Pokambor Avenue runs down the right bank of the Siem Reap River to **Psar Chaa**. This old market is a great place to shop for souvenirs. Nearby, the renovated old French Quarter is home to some of the most atmospheric restaurants in the Angkor area. For those who wish to explore the area, the

banks of the Siem Reap River offer a pleasant stroll. Several blue-painted stilt houses and creaky bamboo waterwheels can be seen here.

Farther south, situated some 6 miles (10 km) away, is the ferry landing on the **Tonle Sap**. The largest freshwater lake in Southeast Asia, it is also a biosphere reserve. The **Krousar Thmey Tonle Sap Exhibition** in the northern outskirts of Siem Reap has displays on the lake, floating villages, and wildlife.

The main monuments at Angkor, the ticket office, and conservatory are all about 4 miles (6 km) north of town. About halfway, at **Wat Thmei**, is a *stupa* displaying the skulls of local Khmer Rouge victims.

🏛 Krousar Thmey Tonle Sap Exhibition

On the road to Angkor Wat. **Tel** (063) 964 694. **Open** 9–11:30am, 2–6pm daily.

VISITORS' CHECKLIST

Practical Information
155 miles (250 km) NW of Phnom Penh. 🛈 Khmer Angkor Tour Guide Association, (063) 964 347 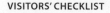 khmerangkortourguide.com

Transport
✈ 🚌 from Battambang and Phnom Penh.

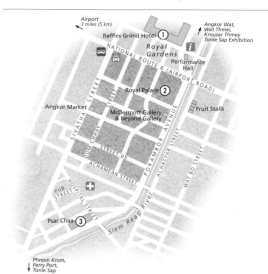

Airport
3 miles (5 km)

Raffles Grand Hotel ①
NATIONAL ROUTE 6 (AIRPORT ROAD)
Royal Gardens
Performance Hall
Angkor Wat, Wat Thmei, Krousar Thmey Tonle Sap Exhibition
SIVATHA STREET
OUM CHHAY STREET
Royal Palace ②
Angkor Market
McDermott Gallery & Beyond Gallery
Fruit Stalls
POKAMBOR AVENUE
ACHASVAR STREET
STREET 05
ACHAMEAN STREET
WAT BO STREET
PUB STREET
HOSPITAL STREET
Psar Chaa ③
Siem Reap River

Phnom Krom, Ferry Port, Tonle Sap

Siem Reap

① Raffles Grand Hotel d'Angkor
② Royal Palace
③ Psar Chaa

Key

 French Quarter

0 meters   500
0 yards   500

For keys to symbols *see back flap*

Visitors enjoying sunset views across Angkor, Phnom Bakheng

❷ Angkor Wat

See pp216–17.

❸ Phnom Bakheng

Just S of Angkor Thom.
Open sunrise–sunset daily. 🚫
general Angkor ticket.

The ancient temple complex of Phnom Bakheng sits on a steep hill that rises 220 ft (67 m) above the surrounding plain.

Built by King Yasovarman I (r.889–910) and honoring the Hindu god, Shiva, the Bakheng complex features one of the region's first temple-mountains (*see p210*) – a distinctive style of temple architecture that has become a mainstay of Khmer-style religious buildings. The complex was also surrounded by 109 towers, but most of them are now missing. However, the well-crafted statues of lions, flanking each of the five terraced tiers of the temple, can be seen even today. The central sanctuary, one of five in all, is adorned with several decorative posts and statues of *apsaras* or celestial dancing girls, and *makaras* or mythical sea creatures.

On the east side of the hill, a steep flight of broken stone stairs leads to the summit. The winding path on the south side is safer and is the usual path taken to carry tourists, on elephants, to the top. Here, there are spectacular views over Angkor and the Western Baray. At dusk, the setting sun illuminates the Tonle Sap and the spires of Angkor Wat with an ethereal glow.

❹ Angkor Thom

See pp220–23.

❺ Preah Khan

1 mile (1.6 km) NE of Angkor Thom.
Open sunrise–sunset daily. 🚫
general Angkor ticket.

Named for the sacred sword owned by the 9th-century king, Jayavarman II, Preah Khan temple complex was established by Jayavarman VII (r.1181–1218), and functioned as a monastery and religious college. It is also believed to have served as a temporary capital for Jayavarman VII during the restoration of Angkor Thom following the city's sacking by the Kingdom of Champa in 1177. An inscribed stone stele found here in 1939 indicates that the

temple, the largest such enclosure in Angkor, was based at the center of an ancient city, Nagarajayacri – *jayacri* means sacred sword in Siamese. The central sanctuary was originally dedicated to the Buddha, but the Hindu rulers succeeding Jayavarman VII vandalized many of the temple's Buddhist aspects, replacing several Buddha images on the walls with carvings of Hindu deities.

Today, the complex extends over a sprawling 141 acres (57 ha), and is surrounded by a 2-mile (3-km) long laterite wall. The premises also have a massive reservoir or *baray*. Access to the central sanctuary, built on a cross-shaped layout, is through four gates, set at the cardinal points of the compass. One of the main highlights at Preah Khan is the Hall of Dancers, so named for the exquisite *apsara* bas-reliefs that line the walls. The shrine of the White Lady, a wife of Jayavarman VII, is still venerated by locals who leave behind offerings of flowers and incense. The most notable temple on the grounds, however, is the Temple of Four Faces, named for the carvings on its central tower. Like Ta Prohm (*see p224*), Preah Khan is studded with great trees whose creeping roots cover and, in places, pierce the laterite and sandstone structures on which they grow. Yet, unlike Ta Prohm, the complex has undergone extensive restoration. Many of the giant trees here have been felled, and the walls are being painstakingly rebuilt.

Statue of a hermit in prayer, Preah Khan

Intricately detailed bas-relief of *apsaras* in the Hall of Dancers, Preah Khan

Young monks reading in Bayon Temple, Angkor Wat ▶

② Angkor Wat

The single largest religious monuments in the world, Angkor Wat literally means "the City which is a Temple." Built during the 12th century by King Suryavarman II (r.1113–50), this spectacular complex was originally dedicated to the Hindu god Vishnu, the Protector of Creation. The layout is based on a *mandala* or sacred design of the Hindu cosmos. A five-towered temple shaped like a lotus bud and representing Mount Meru, the mythical abode of the gods and the center of the universe, stands in the middle of the complex. The outer walls represent the edge of the world, and the moat is the cosmic ocean. Especially outstanding are the intricate carvings that adorn the walls, including a 1,970-ft (600-m) panel of bas-reliefs and around 2,000 engravings of *apsaras* or celestial dancing girls with enigmatic smiles. Angkor Wat, unusually among Khmer temples, faces west and toward the setting sun, a symbol of death.

Highly detailed carvings on the outer walls of the Central Sanctuary

★ Central Sanctuary
Towering over the complex, the Central Sanctuary can be a steep climb. Its four entrances feature images of the Buddha, reflecting the Buddhist influence that eventually displaced Hinduism in Cambodia.

★ Apsaras
The carvings of hundreds of sensual *apsaras* or celestial dancing girls line the walls of the temple. Holding alluring poses, they are shown wearing ornate jewelry and exquisite headgear.

For hotels and restaurants see pp236–41 and pp246–53

View of Towers
The five towers of Angkor Wat rise through three levels to a grand central shrine. The entire complex is surrounded by thick walls and a wide moat that represent the outer edge and the ocean of the universe. The view of the temple from the other side of the moat is stunning with its towers reflected in the still water.

★ **Gallery of Bas-Reliefs**
The southern section of the Western Gallery depicts several scenes from the Hindu epic Mahabharata. The bas-reliefs here detail images of hundreds of weapon bearing warriors engaged in furious combat during the Battle of Kurukshetra

The Causeway
The wide pathway leading to the temple's main entrance on the west side affords a spectacular view of Angkor Wat's grand exterior. Balustrades carved in the form of *nagas* or serpents line both sides of the avenue.

KEY

① **Bas-reliefs in the Southern Gallery** depict images of King Suryavarman II who initiated the construction of Angkor Wat.

Architecture

Angkor-period architecture generally dates from Jayavarman II's establishment of the Khmer capital near Roluos *(see p225)* in the early 9th century AD. From then until the 15th century, art historians identify five main architectural styles. The earliest, Preah Ko, is rooted in the pre-Angkorian traditions of Sambor Prei Kuk to Angkor's east and the 8th-century style of Kompong Preah, relics of which are found at Prasat Ak Yum by the West Baray. Khmer architecture reached its zenith during the construction of Angkor Wat, but began declining soon after.

Pink sandstone library building in the inner enclosure of Banteay Srei

Preah Ko (AD 875–890)

Characterized by a relatively simple temple layout, with one or more square brick towers rising from a single laterite base, the Preah Ko style saw the first use of concentric enclosures entered via the *gopura* or gateway tower.

Another innovation was the library annex, which may have been used to protect sacred fire.

This well-preserved guardian figure is carved from sandstone and set in the brick outer wall of a sanctuary tower at the 9th-century Lolei Temple of the Roluos Group.

The eastern causeway of Bakong runs straight from the main *gopura* to the high central tower. This structure is raised on a square-based pyramid, rising to a symbolic temple-mountain.

Bakheng to Pre Rup (AD 890–965)

The temple-mountain style, based on Mount Meru, evolved during the Bakheng period. Phnom Bakheng *(see p213)*, Phnom Krom, and Phnom Bok all feature the classic layout of five towers arranged in a quincunx – a tower at each side, with a fifth at the center. The Pre Rup style developed during the reign of Rajendra-varman II (r.944–68). It continues the Bakheng style, but the towers are higher and steeper with more tiers.

Phnom Bakheng impressively exemplifies the Bakheng style. It was the state temple of the first Khmer capital at Angkor, and dates from the late 9th century. It rises majestically through a pyramid of square terraces to the main group of five sanctuary towers.

Pre Rup is distinguished by its size and the abrupt rise of its temple-mountain through several levels to the main sanctuary. The carved sandstone lintels are more finely detailed than in earlier styles. Archaeologists speculate that the structure may have served as a royal crematorium – *pre rup* means turn the body.

Banteay Srei to Baphuon (AD 965–1080)

Represented by the delicate and refined Banteay Srei *(see p225)*, this eponymous style is characterized by ornate carvings of sensuous *apsaras* (celestial dancing girls) and *devadas* (dancers). By the mid-11th century, when Khmer architecture was reaching its majestic apogee, this style had evolved into the Baphuon style, which is distinguished by vast proportions and vaulted galleries. The sculpture of the period shows increasing realism and narrative sequence.

The five-tiered Baphuon was the state temple of King Udayadityavarman II (r.1050–66). The massive structure was described by 13th-century Chinese traveler Zhou Daguan as "a truly astonishing spectacle, with more than ten chambers at its base."

Banteay Srei, constructed between 967 and 1000, is known for its fine craftsmanship, evident in the exquisite detail of the bas-reliefs and carved stone lintels.

Angkor Wat (AD 1080–1175)

Art historians generally agree that the style of Angkor Wat *(see pp216–17)* represents the apex of Khmer architectural and sculptural genius. The greatest of all temple-mountains, it also boasts the finest bas-relief narratives. The art of lintel carving also reached its zenith during this period.

Bas-reliefs of Suryavarman II in the west section of the Southern Gallery portray the king seated on his throne, surrounded by courtiers with fans and parasols. Below him, princesses and women of the court are carried in palanquins. In another fine bas-relief, the king is shown riding a great war elephant.

An aerial view of Angkor Wat makes the vast scale and symbolic layout of the complex very clear. Every aspect of Angkor is rich with meaning, the most apparent being the central quincunx of towers rising to a peak, representing the five peaks of the sacred Mount Meru.

Bayon (AD 1175–1240)

Considered a synthesis of previous styles, Bayon – the last great Angkor architectural style – is still magnificent, but also characterized by a detectable decline in quality. There is more use of laterite and less of sandstone, as well as more Buddhist imagery and, correspondingly, fewer Hindu themes.

The bas-reliefs depicting scenes of battle at the temple of Bayon in Angkor Thom *(see pp220–23)* provide a remarkable record of contemporary wars between the Khmer Empire and the Kingdom of Champa. The war resulted in the victory of Khmer King Jayavarman VII in 1181

The south gate of Angkor Thom is surmounted by a large, four-faced carving of the god-king or *devaraja*, Jayavarman VII. He is depicted as the Bodhisattva Avalokitesvara, gazing somberly in the four cardinal directions for eternity.

❹ Angkor Thom

Remarkable in scale and architectural ingenuity, the ancient city of Angkor Thom, which means "Great City" in Khmer, was founded by King Jayavarman VII in the late 12th century. The largest city in the Khmer Empire at one time, it is protected by a 26-ft (8-m) high wall, about 8 miles (13 km) long, and surrounded by a wide moat. There are five gates to the city – four facing the cardinal directions and an extra one on the east side – all bearing four giant stone faces. Within the city are several ruins, the most celebrated of which is the Bayon, a particularly atmospheric temple at the center of this historic complex.

Rows of gods lining the path to Angkor Thom's South Gate

★ **Enigmatic Faces**
The temple's central towers are decorated with four huge, mysteriously smiling faces gazing out in the cardinal directions. These are believed to represent the all-seeing and all-knowing Bodhisattva Avalokitesvara as personified by Jayavarman VII himself.

The Western Gallery
A devotee burns incense sticks before a statue of Vishnu, a Hindu god. The idol is thought to date from the time of the founding of the temple, and is installed in the southern section of the Western Gallery, one of the many long galleries surrounding the Bayon.

South Entrance

★ **Bas-Reliefs on the Southern Gallery**
Carved deep into the walls, the bas-reliefs here feature images from everyday life in 12th-century Angkor. These include depictions of a cockfight, meals being cooked, festival celebrations, and market scenes.

0 meters		25
0 yards		25

KEY

① Outer Enclosure

② Central Tower

③ Bas-reliefs of a Khmer circus

④ Inner Enclosure

★ **Southern View of the Bayon**
From a distance, the Bayon appears to be a complicated, almost erratically
structured temple. On closer inspection, however, its 54 majestic towers
and 216 eerie stone sculptures take a more definite shape – their
architectural grandeur inspiring the visitor with a sense of awe.

Detail of Devada
The *devada* or dancer differs
from the sensual *apsara*
(*see p216*) and could be
either male or female. A
devada is portrayed in less
alluring postures.

East Entrance

The Bayon
Located in the heart of Angkor Thom, the Bayon is one of the city's
most extraordinary structures, epitomizing the "lost civilization" of
Angkor. This symbolic temple-mountain rises on three levels, and
features 54 towers bearing more than 200 huge, yet enigmatic
stone faces. It is entered through eight cruciform towers, linked by
galleries that were once covered and which are gradually being
restored. These galleries have some of the most striking bas-reliefs
at Angkor, showcasing everyday scenes as well as images of battles,
especially against the Cham.

Khmer Army in Procession
The bas-reliefs on the Eastern
Gallery provide scenes from
the struggle between the
Khmers and the Cham,
which has been recorded in
painstakingly fine detail. Here,
the Khmer king, seated on
an elephant, leads his
army into battle.

Exploring Angkor Thom

The fortified city of Angkor Thom is spread over an area of nearly 4 sq miles (10 sq km). At its peak, it had a population of around one million. Of the five gateways into the city, the most commonly used is the South Gate, from which a pathway leads straight to the Bayon temple. Beyond this lie the ruins of many other striking monuments, including Baphuon and Phimeanakas. Although most are in a state of disrepair, these colossal, beautifully sculpted structures, adorned with intricate carvings, still reflect the glory and power of the Khmer Empire.

Massive smiling faces gazing into the distance, South Gate

South Gate

The imposing South Gate is the best-preserved of the five gateways into Angkor Thom. Its approach is via an impressive causeway flanked by 154 stone statues, gods on the left side and demons on the right, each carrying a giant serpent.

The South Gate itself is a massive, 75-ft (23-m) high structure, surmounted by a triple tower with four gigantic stone faces facing the cardinal directions. On either side of the gate are statues of the three-headed elephant Erawan, the fabled mount of the Hindu god Indra.

Bayon

Representative of the period's artistic brilliance, the Bayon is the city's most unique temple. Shaped like a pyramid, its two most awe-inspiring features are the several huge calm, smiling faces that adorn its towers, and the fascinating bas-reliefs on its many galleries *(see pp220–221)*.

Baphuon

Believed to be one of the grandest of Angkor's temples, Baphuon was built by King Udayadityavarman II in the 11th century. A Hindu temple, its pyramidal mountain form represents Mount Meru, the mythical home of the gods. A central tower with four entrances once stood at its summit, but has long since collapsed.

The temple is approached via a 656-ft (200-m) long raised causeway and has four gateways decorated with elegant bas-relief scenes from Hindu epics such as the *Mahabharata* and *Ramayana* (*Reamker* in Khmer). Inside, spanning the western length of Baphuon, is a huge Reclining Buddha. As the temple was dedicated to Hinduism, this image was probably added later, in the 15th century. The temple has undergone intensive restoration, and is fully open to the public.

Phimeanakas

This royal temple-palace was built during the 10th century by King Rajendravarman II and added to later by Jayavarman VII. Dedicated to Hinduism, it is also known as the Celestial Palace, and is associated with the legend of a golden tower that once stood here, and where a nine-headed serpent resided. This magical serpent would appear to the king as a woman, and the king would couple with her before going to his other wives and concubines. It was believed that if the king failed to sleep with the serpent-woman, he would die, but by sleeping with her, the royal lineage was saved.

The pyramid-shaped palace is rectangular at the base, and surrounded by a 16-ft (5-m) high wall of laterite enclosing an area of around 37 acres (15 ha). It has five entranceways, and the stairs, which are flanked by guardian lions, rise up on all four sides. There are corresponding elephant figures at each of the four corners of the pyramid. The upper terrace offers great views of the Baphuon to the south.

Preah Palilay and Tep Pranam

Two of the lesser, yet still impressive structures at Angkor Thom, Preah Palilay and Tep Pranam are located a short distance to the northwest of the Terrace of the Leper King.

Preah Palilay dates from the 13th or 14th century and is a small Buddhist sanctuary set within a 164-ft (50-m) square laterite wall. The sanctuary, which is partially collapsed, is entered via a single gateway, and rises to a tapering stone tower. A 108-ft (33-m) long causeway leads to a terrace to the east of the sanctuary, which is distinguished by fine *naga* or serpent balustrades. Nearby, to the east, lies Tep Pranam, a Buddhist

Pyramidal exterior of Phimeanakas, Angkor Thom

Intricately carved and sculpted bas-reliefs and elephant figures adorning the Terrace of Elephants

sanctuary built in the 16th century. This was probably originally dedicated to the Mahayana school. Now used as a place of Theravada worship, it features a big sandstone Buddha image, seated in the "calling the earth to witness" *mudra* (posture).

Step-by-step restoration in progress at the Terrace of the Leper King

Terrace of the Leper King

Situated a short walk southeast of Tep Pranam, this small platform dates from the late 12th century. Standing on top of this structure is a headless statue, known as the Leper King. Once believed to be an image of King Jayavarman VII, who, according to legend, had the disease, it is in fact a representation of Yama, the Hindu God of the Underworld. This statue is, however, a replica, as the original was taken for safekeeping to Phnom Penh's National Museum.

The terrace is marked by two walls, both beautifully restored and decorated with exquisite bas-reliefs. Of the two, the inner one is more remarkable, and is covered with figures of underworld deities, kings, celestial females,

nagas with five, seven, or nine heads, *devadas*, *apsaras*, warriors with drawn swords, and strange marine creatures

The exact function of this terrace, which appears to be an extension of the Terrace of Elephants, is not clear. It was probably used either for royal receptions or cremations.

Terrace of Elephants

Built by King Jayavarman VII, this structure is over 950 ft (300 m) long, stretching from the Baphuon to the connecting Terrace of the Leper King. It has three main platforms and two smaller ones. The terrace was primarily used for royal reviews of military and other parades. The entire terrace is elaborately decorated with almost life-size images of sandstone elephants in a procession and accompanied

by mahouts. There are many images of tigers, lions, serpents, sacred geese, and Garuda, the eagle mount of Vishnu.

North and South Khleang

These two essentially similar buildings are located to the east of the main road running past the Terrace of Elephants. The North Khleang was built toward the end of the 10th century by King Jayaviravarman, and the South Khleang was constructed during the early 11th century by King Suryavarman I (r.1002–50). The main architectural feature of the Khleangs are their sandstone lintels and elegant balustered stone windows. Unfortunately, the original function of the buildings is not known. Khleang, which means storehouse, is a modern designation and is considered misleading.

Angkor Thom

List of sites

① South Gate
② Bayon
③ Baphuon
④ Phimeanakas
⑤ Preah Palilay and Tep Pranam
⑥ Terrace of the Leper King
⑦ Terrace of Elephants
⑧ North and South Khleang

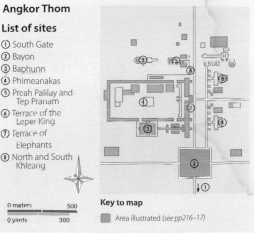

| 0 meters | 500 |
| 0 yards | 500 |

Key to map

Area illustrated (*see pp216–17*)

❻ Preah Neak Pean

2.5 miles (4 km) NE of Angkor Thom.
Open sunrise–sunset daily.
🖼 general Angkor ticket. 📷 💻 🖼

One of the most unusual temples at Angkor, Preah Neak Pean or Coiled Serpents is a unique structure dating from the late 12th century. Like much else at Angkor, it was founded by King Jayavarman VII. Dedicated to Buddhism, it is located in the middle of the now dry lake, North Baray.

The temple is built around an artificial pond surrounded by four smaller square ponds, usually dry except during the rainy season. In the center is a circular island with a shrine dedicated to Bodhisattva Avalokitesvara. A couple of intertwined serpents circle its base, thus giving the temple its name. To the east of the island is the sculpted figure of the horse Balaha, a manifestation of Avalokitesvara, who, according to Buddhist mythology, transformed himself into a horse to rescue shipwrecked sailors from a sea ogress.

The pond represents a mythical lake, Anavatapta, believed to be the source of the four great rivers of the world. They are symbolically reproduced by four gargoyle-like heads with spouts for mouths, from which water flows into four outer ponds. The east head is that of a man, the south a lion, the west a horse, and the north an elephant. When the temple was functioning, Buddhist devotees would seek the advice of resident monks, and then bathe

Human head-shaped fountainhead at Preah Neak Pean

in the holy waters flowing from the spout of whichever head had been prescribed by the monk.

❼ Ta Prohm

0.6 miles (1 km) E of Angkor Thom.
Open sunrise–sunset daily.
🖼 general Angkor ticket. 🎨 🖼

Perhaps the most evocative and mysterious of all the temple structures at Angkor, Ta Prohm, which means Ancestor of Brahma, was originally a Buddhist monastery, built during King Jayavarman VII's reign. A stone stele at the complex describes how powerful the monastery used to be. At its peak, it owned more than 3,000 villages, and was maintained by 80,000 attendants, including 18 high priests and over 600 temple dancers. The wealth of the temple, and of its founder, Jayavarman VII, is also listed, and included more than 35 diamonds and 40,000 pearls.

The French started their archaeological restoration during the colonial period, and a deliberate attempt was made to preserve Ta Prohm in its existing condition, limiting restoration, and cutting down as little of the dense jungle as possible. As a result, the temple buildings remain smothered with the roots of giant banyan trees, preserving the atmosphere that 19th-century explorers must have experienced.

The temple sits on the peak of a hill and has a complex of stone buildings, surrounded by a rectangular laterite wall. The narrow passageways of the structure, along with huge kapok trees, provide relief from the tropical sun, and link a series of musty, darkened galleries. The main entrance is decaying yet magnificent, and filled with images of the Buddha that were recovered from the ruins. Beyond the gate is the fascinating Hall of Dancers. This must-see sandstone building rests on square pillars, and is decorated with false doorways and rows of intricate *apsara* (celestial dancing girl) bas-reliefs. To the west is the main sanctuary, a simple stone structure distinguished by its jungle setting.

❾ Prasat Kravan

2 miles (3 km) E of Angkor Wat.
Open sunrise–sunset daily.
🖼 general Angkor ticket.

Dating from the early 10th century, Prasat Kravan was founded by Harshavarman I (r.915–23). Comprising five brick towers, it is one of the smaller temples in the complex, and was dedicated to the Hindu god, Vishnu.

The temple, whose name means Cardamom Sanctuary, is chiefly remarkable for its brickwork and bas-reliefs. These represent Vishnu, his consort Lakshmi, Garuda his eagle mount, *naga* the serpent, and a number of other divine attendants.

The doorways and lintels of all five towers are made of sandstone, and that of the southernmost tower has a fine

The Ta Prohm Temple covered by giant banyan trees

THE TEMPLES OF ANGKOR | 225

image of Vishnu riding his Garuda mount. In the middle of the central tower is a raised stone that was used to receive water for purification rites.

❾ Banteay Srei

19 miles (30 km) km NE of Siem Reap. **Open** sunrise–sunset daily. general Angkor ticket.

The remote temple complex of Banteay Srei or the Citadel of Women inspires through its exquisitely detailed carving. Executed in pink sandstone, the complex was founded in the second half of the 10th century by Hindu priests, and so, unlike most other monuments in Angkor, is not a royal temple.

Rectangular in shape, and enclosed by three walls and the remains of a moat, the central sanctuary contains ornate shrines dedicated to Shiva, the Hindu God of Destruction. The intricately carved lintels reproduce scenes from the great Hindu epic *Ramayana*. Representations of Shiva, his consort Parvati, the monkey-king Hanuman, the divine goatherd Krishna, and the demon-king Ravana are all beautifully etched. Also exceptional are the elaborate and finely detailed carved figures of gods and goddesses in the

Central sanctuary, Lolei Temple, Roluos Group

recessed niches of the towers in the central sanctuary. The male divinities carry lances and wear simple loincloths. By contrast, the goddesses, with their long hair tied in buns or plaits, are dressed in loosely-draped Indian-style skirts, and almost every inch of their bodies is laden with gorgeous heavy jewelry.

Ancient statue in Banteay Srei

❿ Roluos Group

7 miles (12 km) SE of Siem Reap. **Open** sunrise–sunset daily. general Angkor ticket.

These ancient temples have borrowed their name from the small town of Roluos. The oldest monuments in the Angkor area, the temples mark the site of Hariharalaya, the very first Khmer capital established by Indravarman I (r.877–89). Three main complexes can be found here. To the north of Highway 6, on the way to Phnom Penh from Siem Reap, is Lolei. Founded by Yasovarman I (r.889–910), this temple stands on an artificial mound in the middle of a small reservoir, and is based on a double platform, surrounded by a thick laterite wall. The four central brick towers have surprisingly well-preserved false doors and inscriptions.

To the south of Lolei stands **Preah Ko** or the Sacred Bull. Built by Indravarman I, this Hindu temple was dedicated to the worship of Shiva. It was built to honor the king's parents, as well as Jayavarman II, the founder of the Khmer Empire. The main sanctuary consists of six brick towers resting on a raised laterite platform. Close by are three statues of the sacred bull Nandi, for whom the temple was named, which are in a remarkably good condition. The motifs on the false doors, lintels, and columns are very well-preserved. They include *kala*, mythical creatures with a grinning mouth and large bulging eyes, *makara*, sea creatures with a trunk-like snout, and Garuda, the eagle mount of the god Vishnu. The temple sits resplendent in its serene rural setting, and has undergone large-scale restoration.

Beyond Preah Ko, the huge mass of **Bakong** cannot be missed. This temple is also dedicated to Shiva, and was founded by Indravarman I in the 9th century. By far the largest monument of the Roluos Group, it is approached by a pathway protected by a seven-headed *naga*, and flanked by guesthouses built for pilgrims. In the center of the complex is an artificial mound representing the mythical Mount Meru, said to be the center of the Hindu world and the abode of the gods. The mount rises in five stages, the first three of which are enhanced by stone elephants on their edges. At the summit rests the square central sanctuary, with four levels and a lotus-shaped tower rising from the middle. The mound is surrounded by eight massive brick towers which, like the rest of Roluos Group, feature finely carved sandstone decorations.

A goddess on the central shrine, inner enclosure, Banteay Srei

Angkor Travel Information

Most visitors to Angkor arrive by air as the large number of international and domestic carriers servicing the country make flying a comfortable and viable option. Local as well as long-distance buses from Vietnam and Thailand provide an affordable alternative. However, though the highway from Phnom Penh has improved, the poor condition of most roads can result in delays and much discomfort in reaching Siem Reap. A more scenic approach is by ferry or boat. Regular hydrofoil services link Siem Reap with Phnom Penh, as well as Siem Reap and Chau Doc *(see p104)* in Vietnam. Moving around within Angkor is easy, with several inexpensive modes of transport to choose from.

Boarding a Bangkok Airways flight, Siem Reap International Airport

When to Go

The best time to visit Angkor is during the country's cool season, between November and February, although it can still be rather warm for most tourists. Alternatively, during the rainy season between June and November, Angkor is green and relatively cool, if rather wet. At this time, the *barays* (reservoirs) and certain temples such as Preah Neak Pean *(see p224)* overflow with water. It is best to stay away during the hot season between March and May, when temperatures in Angkor can be stifling.

Getting There

There are two international airports in Cambodia – **Phnom Penh International Airport** and **Siem Reap International Airport**. With several national and international airlines offering flights to both Phnom Penh and Siem Reap, visitors will find getting to Angkor easy. Major international airlines include **Vietnam Airlines**, **Lao Airlines**, **Malaysia Airlines**, **SilkAir**, **Thai Airways**, **Bangkok Airways**, **Jetstar**, and **Air Asia**. Except for Thai Airways, all these airlines operate direct flights to Siem Reap from popular holiday destinations such as Hanoi, Ho Chi Minh City, Kuala Lumpur, Bangkok, and Singapore.

Domestic carrier **Cambodia Angkor Air**, flies from Phnom Penh to Siem Reap on a daily basis. Note that it is not uncommon for flight schedules to change suddenly or even for local airlines to shut down completely. For up-to-date information on

air fares, routes, and flight timings, check with your travel agent.

Traveling by bus or taxi across land borders from Thailand, Laos, and Vietnam is a feasible and cheap option. Visitors entering from Vietnam have the choice of up to eight different border crossings. The most popular are from Moc Bai to Bavet and from Chau Doc to Phnom Penh. Several scheduled buses run from Ho Chi Minh City to Phnom Penh. This six-hour journey costs about US$11. From Phnom Penh, you can take a shared taxi or minibus to Siem Reap on a five-hour trip.

Another mode of traveling to Angkor is by ferry or boat, though this is becoming less popular as air and road connections improve. River ferries from Phnom Penh to Siem Reap run daily and are easily available, but the journey can take up to six hours (US$25–US$35). Boat tours also operate from Ho Chi Minh City to Siem Reap. They take a week or so to get there and costs over US$35. One of the best known companies to offer boat tours is **Pandaw Cruises**.

Visas and Passports

A one-month visa for Cambodia is issued on arrival at international airports and land and river border crossings. Tourist visas cost US$20. A passport photograph is required. Visitors who wish to stay longer should apply for an extension in Phnom Penh. Those who overstay their visa are fined US$5 each day. E-visas can be purchased online at evisa.mfaic.gov.kh for US$25

One of the many tourist buses providing access to Siem Reap

payable by credit card. They are emailed to and printed by the applicant.

Tours from Vietnam

There are several reputed travel agencies in both Hanoi and Ho Chi Minh City that arrange tours from Vietnam to Angkor. Although packaged tours are pre-determined, visitors can also draw up personalized itineraries. The prices are usually inclusive of travel costs, sightseeing, and a guide. Visas, departure tax, and entry tickets to Angkor are generally not included.

Getting Around

Transport in Siem Reap and Angkor is readily available and comes in various forms, including bicycles, *motos* (motorbike taxis), minibuses, tuk-tuks, and elephants. A great way to explore Angkor is on a bicycle, available to rent from bike shops and

Motorcycle taxis are very common in Siem Reap

hotels. The most comfortable way to travel is by hiring a car, easily arranged through hotels in town. An air-conditioned car with driver costs between US$25 and US$50 per day depending on the distance and time.

Customs Information

Customs procedures tend to be lax, but penalties for violations are strict. The usual prohibitions on importing drugs and pornography apply. Signs warn against bringing explosives into the country, and

you need to declare if you carry above US$10,000. The most enforced custom regulation is the smuggling of antiquities dating from or before the Angkorian period.

Departure Tax

For international flights there is a departure tax of US$25 per person. This is payable in US dollars. The departure tax for domestic flights is US$6, but this is usually included in the cost of the ticket.

DIRECTORY

Embassies

Australia
16B National Assembly St, Phnom Penh. **Tel** (023) 213 470. W cambodia. embassy.gov.au

Canada
Canadian interests are managed and represented by the Australian Embassy (see above).

United Kingdom
27–29 St. 75, Phnom Penh. **Tel** (023) 427 124. W gov.uk/government/ world/organisations/ british-embassy-phnom-penh

United States
1 Christopher Howes, Phnom Penh. **Tel** (023) 728 000. W cambodia. usembassy.gov

Vietnam
436 Monivong Blvd, Phnom Penh. **Tel** (023) 726 274. W vietnamembassy-cambodia.org

Airports

Phnom Penh International Airport
Tel (023) 890 890. W cambodia-airports. aero

Siem Reap International Airport
Tel (063) 761 261. W cambodia-airports. aero

Airlines

Air Asia
179 Street Sisowath. **Tel** (023) 890 035. W AirAsia.com

Bangkok Airways
Siem Reap. **Tel** (063) 965 422/3. W bangkokair.com

Jetstar
Siem Reap. **Tel** (063) 761 261 W Jetstar.com

Lao Airlines
114, Hwy 6, Siem Reap. **Tel** (063) 963 169. W laoairlines.com

Malaysia Airlines
Siem Reap International Airport. **Tel** (063) 964 135. W malaysiaairlines. com

SilkAir
Siem Reap International Airport. **Tel** (063) 964 993. W silkair.com

Thai Airways
1F Unit 8A, Regency Complex-A Building, 298 Mao Tse Toung Blvd, Phnom Penh. **Tel** (023) 214 359. W thaiair.com

Vietnam Airlines
342, Hwy 6, Siem Reap. **Tel** (063) 964 488. W vietnamairlines. com

Boat Tours

Pandaw Cruises
Tel (090) 371 1239 (Ho Chi Minh City). W pandaw.com

Tour Companies

Diethelm Travel
65 St 240, Phnom Penh. **Tel** (023) 219 151. W diethelmtravel.com

Hanuman Tourism
310 St 12, Phnom Penh. **Tel** (023) 218 396. W hanuman.travel

Exotissimo Travel
B20-21, St 60m (Spean Neak), Siem Reap. **Tel** (063) 964 323 W exotissimo.com

Angkor Practical Information

After years of much unrest, Cambodia is presently undergoing a phase of economic growth and rapid development. An important part of this process is its tourism industry, which has experienced a major boom. The credit for this is largely due to the rich cultural heritage of Angkor, and the millions of visitors it attracts each year. As a result, the sleepy town of Siem Reap, serving as a gateway to Angkor, has transformed into a bustling tourist town, with lodgings and eateries to suit all pockets. The simple ticket system, easily arranged transport, and new communication facilities have made sightseeing in Angkor a straightforward affair.

Well decored and bright room in the Victoria Sapa Resort *(see p241)*

Admission Charges and Opening Hours

To gain access to the Angkor complex, visitors need to buy a pass from the booth at Angkor's main entrance (open 5am–6pm daily). The ticketing system in effect here might seem a bit expensive at first glance but offers good value for money, especially because part of the funds collected go toward the preservation of Angkor's many historic monuments.

Three types of passes are available, each allowing entry into all the monuments in the complex except Phnom Kulen, Koh Ker, and Beng Melea, for which extra charges apply. Choices range from a one-day pass for US$20, ideal for a quick walk through the main ruins; a three-day pass for US$40 to be used within one week and sufficient for exploring the prominent temples; and a seven-day pass for US$60 to be used within one month.

A passport-size photograph has to be provided along with the entry fee to create an identity pass. You can carry your own picture or have one taken at the admission booth. Passes must be shown at each site.

Tourist Information

The privately-owned **Tourism Information Office** in Siem Reap is housed in a white building on Pokambor Avenue, but is not particularly helpful except for making bookings. More useful, and in the same building, is the **Khmer Angkor**

Tour Guide Association, which offers cars for rent, along with licensed and well informed, English-speaking drivers.

The quarterly publication *Siem Reap Angkor Visitors Guide* provides up-to-date travel-related information to visitors. It includes shopping and transport listings, as well as a detailed list of restaurants and hotels in the area. It is available free of charge at many hotels all over town.

Where to Stay

At one time, accommodation in Siem Reap was scarce and unappealing, but today, new hotels and guesthouses open every month. The variety of lodgings available is wide, with options to suit every budget. From five-star luxury hotels such as Raffles Grand Hotel d'Angkor *(see p241)* to a range of family-run hotels with basic conveniences and a selection of well-equipped and reasonably priced guesthouses.

Visitors who have not opted for a pre-booked tour will find plenty of information regarding accommodation at the airport. Many touts also hover around

the airport, but it is wise to exercise caution when dealing with them – scam artists are not rare. Most establishments, even down to the humblest guesthouses, will send a car and driver to meet you at the airport. Another easier and often substantially cheaper option is to book online. Note that room rates usually fluctuate between expensive during peak season from November to March, to very cheap during the low season from May to November.

Where to Eat

The assortment and quality of cuisines available in Siem Reap is varied enough to suit all tastes, ranging from Thai, Cambodian, Vietnamese, and Chinese to French, Indian, American, and Italian.

The array of eateries to choose from is also impressive *(see p253)*. There are many reasonably priced restaurants, especially near Psar Chaa. This area is also full of street food vendors, serving local fare. Baguettes, pâté, and good coffee can be found throughout the area.

Guests enjoying a meal at the Red Piano *(see p253)*, Siem Reap

Most guesthouses have small cafés, while the larger hotels boast fine restaurants. Most can pack picnic baskets as well if requested.

Personal Health and Security

Cambodia is a poor country, and not particularly advanced in healthcare. In almost any serious situation, it makes sense to be evacuated for treatment to nearby Bangkok. However, with proper precautions most visitors have a safe and healthy stay. Drink only bottled water, eat well-cooked food, avoid ice, and be sure to wash your hands before eating. To avoid dehydration, heat exhaustion, and even heatstroke when visiting Angkor, carry bottled mineral water and wear a hat or headscarf. Avoid going out during the hottest part of the day.

Malaria is present in parts of Cambodia, including Angkor, and travelers can take a prophylactic. Other risks are dengue fever, hepatitis, and rabies. Ask your doctor about immunization requirements before you travel. STDs and AIDS are also prevalent in Cambodia.

Unexploded mines are a serious concern in Siem Reap. Tourists should steer clear of areas off the well-beaten path, and stay close to their guides.

Personal security in Angkor can be taken care of by applying common sense. Avoid dark and remote areas, do not wear too much jewelry or revealing clothes in the case of women, and leave valuable items in the hotel safe. Tourist police and guards are stationed at points throughout the complex.

Banking and Currency

The Cambodian currency is the *riel*, worth approximately 4,000 to the US dollar. *Riel* notes come in denominations from 50r to 100,000r, though even the latter is worth only around US$25. However, visitors to Angkor infrequently need to use the *riel* since, for many tourist transactions, the US dollar is the preferred currency. Failing this,

the Thai *bhat* is often acceptable in Siem Reap. Still, it is a good idea to keep some change in *riel* handy for giving small tips or buying very cheap items.

There are several banks in Siem Reap, offering facilities for exchanging currency and cashing traveler's checks. Banking hours are generally 9am–4pm Monday to Friday. Major credit cards are widely accepted, and can be used to obtain a cash advance from a bank. ATMs are another source of cash.

One of the many banks and money exchanges in Siem Reap

Communications

The communication network in Angkor is fairly well developed. Making international calls is simple, using either prepaid calling cards for public telephones, or Internet phone services, available in most cyber cafés. It is also possible to call from your hotel, but this is a more expensive option. The area code for Siem Reap is 063.

Internet cafés and Wi-Fi are plentiful and affordable, and there are no government restrictions on Internet access. For postal and courier services, visitors can head to the main post office in town, or agencies such as **DHL** and **EMS**.

Disabled Travelers

There are presently virtually no special facilities for disabled travelers anywhere in Angkor. Many of the new luxury hotels, however, are making an effort to become better equipped to meet the needs of those who require special assistance.

TRAVELERS' NEEDS

WHERE TO STAY

Accommodations in Vietnam run the gamut from historic boutique hotels and plush resorts to basic guesthouses. Luxury hotels are found in all large cities and beaches, while budget lodgings are available throughout the country. Major hotels offer amenities such as swimming pools, gyms, restaurants, and even nightclubs. Resorts, many of which are concentrated along the central coast, also offer ample opportunities for self-indulgence. While budget hotels and guesthouses lack the high-end frills, all but the very cheapest are air-conditioned and have Western-style toilets and hot water. Dormitories are rare and camping almost unheard of, but an alternative is the homestay, where travelers can lodge with a family from the village. Not only does this give you a close-up glimpse into daily life in rural Vietnam, but it often allows you to sample the most delicious and authentic local cuisine.

Hotel Grading

There is an official system for grading hotels in Vietnam, but the price remains the only indication of luxury or the lack thereof. Typically, establishments charging more than US$100 per night would fall into the four- or five-star category in Europe or the US. Keep in mind that overall prices notwithstanding, the same hotel may demonstrate varying standards across rooms, ranging from opulent suites to motel-style quarters.

Also note that there is a distinction between a hotel (*khach san*) and a guesthouse (*nha khach*). While the latter can resemble budget hotels, they have fewer amenities.

The stately façade of the Continental Hotel *(see p236)*, Ho Chi Minh City

Prices

Vietnam offers reasonably priced accommodation options for all. A room in the most upscale resort will not cost anywhere near what it would in most Western countries. In major cities, a room with basic amenities such as a TV and air-conditioning will be available for as little as US$15 a night, and in smaller towns US$8–US$10. Mid-range hotels average between US$40 to US$70, and all the luxury of a high-end hotel can be experienced for US$100 and up.

Note that most establishments charge different prices for Vietnamese and foreign tourists; this is especially true in government-owned hotels.

Booking

Advance booking is advisable for visitors traveling during the high season *(see p270)*, especially at major hotels and resorts. Both Ho Chi Minh City and Hanoi receive a steady stream of business travelers throughout the year, and hotels catering to them may be booked solid at any time of year.

While any travel agent can help make reservations, all high-end hotels have websites offering online booking services. A surprising number of budget hotels also provide this facility. Alternatively, contact one of the several reliable accommodation service outfits in operation, such as **Hotels in Vietnam**, **Vietnam Stay**, and **Vietnam Lodging**. All have websites on which they represent a range of hotels, resorts, apartments, and guesthouses. In addition to being efficient and quick, such groups also negotiate with hotels to ensure the best rates.

The plush and elegant interior of the luxurious Caravelle *(see p236)*

◀ Collection of colorful straw hats in the floating market

Checking in

When checking in, guests will normally be asked for their passport, which is then kept by the hotel for the duration of their stay. The hotel needs it to report a guest's presence to the local police. Large establishments in Ho Chi Minh City and Hanoi may simply copy the information and return the passport instead of retaining it for the duration of your stay. If your passport has been sent to an embassy for visa renewal, or if you are uncomfortable leaving it with the hotel, a photocopy is usually acceptable.

Pool table adjoining the lobby lounge at Miss Loi's Guesthouse *(see p236)*

Luxury Hotels

A selection of luxury hotels is available at every major tourist destination in Vietnam. As a result, the country is popular with more than just the backpacking set – it is also a getaway for the rich and famous. Places like Ho Chi Minh City, Hanoi, Nha Trang, and Mui Ne boast multinational chains such as Sheraton, Hilton, Novotel, Sofitel, and Six Senses. The Victoria Hotels and Resorts chain offers luxurious and chic accommodations in beautiful buildings and scenic locations.

Business travelers will find a wide array of facilities in most of these hotels, including meeting rooms, conference calls, and Internet services.

Virtually every four- and five-star hotel boasts a spectacular food service, employing skilled international chefs. Their superb restaurants serve gourmet foreign cuisine, including French, Chinese, Japanese, and Italian. Breakfast is an extremely lavish affair, featuring a spread of American, Continental, and Vietnamese fare.

In the evenings, a number of high-end hotels are transformed into glamorous venues for Western-style entertainment. Some boast discotheques, and several provide some kind of musical performance in their lounges every night.

Resort Hotels

Vietnam is no stranger to elegant resort hotels, which were first introduced to the country by leisure-loving French colonists. A few of these charming old quarters, now substantially upgraded and renovated, still remain. The Dalat Palace *(see p238)* in Dalat, for instance, has been converted into a beautiful holiday getaway.

The trend, however, is for the development of modernly outfitted resorts, mostly along the extensive coastline. A couple of the most luxurious are the Nam Hai *(see p239)* in Hoi An and the Six Senses Hideaway *(see p238)* in Ninh Van Bay. Some resorts do not look very different from any other high-rise hotel, but qualify as resorts on the technicality that they are somewhat isolated from the towns. Particularly affected by tourist-oriented development, both Nha Trang and Phan Thiet have earned reputations as resort towns. Their seaside establishments have all the usual amenities such as a swimming pool, fine restaurants, and, of course, a beautiful, white-sand beach. Most also offer a range of adventure activities, including diving and kiteboarding.

A large number of resorts also offer specialized tours and holiday packages. Treks to hill-tribe communities are arranged by Sapa's local tour guides and operators, while in Hue, the Saigon Morin arranges historic trips down the Perfume River. The Sun Spa Resort *(see p239)* in Dong Hoi offers free early morning yoga and tai chi classes on the beach.

Swimming pool of the Victoria Resort, Can Tho *(see p237)*

The Majestic hotel *(see p236)* on Dong Khoi Street, Ho Chi Minh City

Guesthouses and Budget Hotels

Vietnamese guesthouses generally offer comfortable and clean rooms, with Western toilets, hot water, cable TV, and frequently a refrigerator with a minibar. They are often family-owned and operated. Extra services usually include laundry, breakfast, booking facilities (tours, as well as bus, train, and airplane tickets), luggage storage, bicycle and motorcycle rental, and free Wi-Fi.

In cities that have long been on the tourist map, such as Ho Chi Minh City and Nha Trang, budget hotels are often clustered together (like in the Pham Ngu Lao neighborhood of Ho Chi Minh City).

A room in a guesthouse or a budget hotel ranges from as little as US$8 in cities like Dalat to US$25 in Ho Chi Minh City. Expect to pay an average of US$10–US$15. A plain room with a fan and no window can be rented for as little as US$6, and a bed and locker in a decent dormitory costs around $5.

Homestays

Homestays are growing in popularity and are most easily available in parts of the Mekong Delta, such as Vinh Long *(see p94)*, and in the Northern Highlands. This invaluable experience costs upwards of US$15 per night. It is fairly easy to arrange a homestay through a travel agency in Ho Chi Minh City or Hanoi. **Innoviet** for one,

specializes in customized and themed tours, including homestays. Alternatively, contact the local tourist office in the area of interest.

Rental Apartments

For those staying in one part of Vietnam for more than a few weeks, a serviced apartment or condo can be rented to cut back on costs but still live in luxury. There are not many such operations at present, but they are in demand and more companies may start offering the service. One of the best arrangements in the country is **Sedona Suites** in Hanoi and Ho Chi Minh City, which offers stylish, fully furnished individual suites.

A cheaper, if considerably more tiresome, procedure is to go out into the real estate market to rent an apartment. However, this requires a lot of paperwork, and you must register with the local police. It is much easier and cheaper to rent a room in a private home. This allows visitors to experience first-hand the day-to-day life of ordinary people of the country. The best place to find such opportunities are on the bulletin boards of backpacker cafés and restaurants. Registration with the local police is still required when renting a room.

Taxes

All high-end hotels levy a ten percent tax on the room tariff, plus a five percent service charge. Both amounts are displayed on the bill. In budget operations, the taxes are included in the basic charge, and are not reflected on the bill.

Bargaining

Every hostelry is open to some kind of bargaining if it is not packed to capacity. It is more difficult to lower the price if booking online or on the phone, but if you arrive in person, the published fare is negotiable. For those planning to stay longer

The lush poolside gardens of Ancient House *(see p239)*, Hoi An

than a week, or willing to take a less desirable room, the price can drop by as much as 30 percent in a major hotel. Budget hotels will usually oblige by taking a few dollars off, but they do not have as much room to maneuver.

Tipping

Although tipping was formerly not customary in Vietnam, with the advent of tourism, it is now becoming the norm. There is no need to tip in major hotels as there is already a service charge, but if a staff member proves to be extremely obliging and helpful, a gratuity of US$1 is considered generous.

Facilities for Children

Although there are virtually no special facilities for kids (see p272), except in top-end hotels, all establishments will welcome them. Most hotels allow children under 12 to share a bed with their parents free of charge. For a small fee, parents can rent an extra bed or cot in any decent hotel. Even the more basic establishments will receive children with open arms, and go all out to ensure that they have a comfortable stay. Virtually any hotel, big or small, grand or cheap, would be willing to arrange for an experienced babysitter to watch children for a reasonable fee.

Facilities for Disabled Travelers

Unfortunately, most hotels in Vietnam provide limited facilities for the disabled (see p272). While the major and newest luxury properties do have wheelchair ramps, elevators, and other special facilities, such considerations are almost non-existent in lesser establishments. Most hotels will be glad to help a guest hire an attendant, although he or she is unlikely to possess any particular qualifications.

Beautiful exterior of the Victoria Sapa

Recommended Hotels

The establishments listed on the following pages have been carefully selected as the best in the country in their respective categories: luxury, boutique, resort, budget, and hostel. These categories reflect the growing variety of accommodations available in Vietnam, a country that had no significant tourist industry only 20 years ago. These days the country is making up for lost time, and many international chains are opening up new properties in major tourist towns. The criteria for selection include not only major considerations such as range of facilities, value for money, convenience of location, and level of service, but also small but important points such as whether the staff has sufficient command of English to be able to help guests with any difficulties they face. Those places that excel in several aspects have been selected as 'DK Choice', and they have detailed descriptions to explain their particular merits.

DIRECTORY

Booking

Hotels in Vietnam
24–26 Bat Su St, Hoan Kiem Dist, Hanoi.
Map 2 E3.
Tel (04) 3923 2982
w hotels-in-vietnam.com

Vietnam Lodging
220 De Tham St, Dist. 1, HCMC.
Map 2 D5.
Tel (08) 3920 5847/4767.
w vietnamlodging.net

Vietnam Stay
Suite R10, IBC Building 1A, Me Linh Sq, Dist.1, HCMC.
Map 2 F4.
Tel (08) 3823 3771
91 Ly Nam De St, Hoan Kiem Dist, Hanoi.
Map 2 D2.
Tel (04) 3747 2597.
w vietnamstay.com

Homestays

Innoviet
158 Bui Vien St, Dist.1, HCMC.
Map 2 D5. **Tel** (08) 6291 5408.
w innoviet.com

Rental Apartments

Sedona Suites
65 Le Loi Blvd, Dist.1, HCMC. **Map** 2 E4.
Tel (08) 3822 9666.
96 To Ngoc Van St, Hanoi.
Tel (04) 3718 0888.
w sedonahotels.com.sg

Bright and elegant façade of the La Veranda Resort

Where to Stay

Ho Chi Minh City

Cholon

Hotel Equatorial   **$$$**
Luxury   **Map** 4 F3
242 Tran Binh Trong
Tel *(08) 3839 7777*
W equatorial.com/hcm
Exclusive high-rise hotel to
the west of the city center.
Has superb restaurants, including
The Orientica.

Windsor Plaza   **$$$**
Luxury   **Map** 4 F4
18 An Duong Vuong
Tel *(08) 3833 6688*
W windsorplazahotel.com
Rooms on the top floors of this
towering hotel have expansive
views. The buffet at Café Central
is not to be missed.

District 1

An An   **$**
Value   **Map** 2 D5
40 Bui Vien
Tel *(08) 3837 8088*
W anan.vn
Good-sized rooms equipped with
computers and free Wi-Fi. Well-
located at the heart of the action.

Dong Do   **$**
Value   **Map** 2 F4
35 Mac Thi Buoi
Tel *(08) 3827 3637*
W dungdohotel.com
One of the cheapest places
near Dong Khoi, with all the basic
amenities, including free Wi-Fi.

Lac Vien   **$**
Value   **Map** 2 D5
28/12–14 Bui Vien
Tel *(08) 3920 4899*
W lacvienhotel.com
Good option from the many such
hotels in District 1. Opt for the
superior or VIP rooms. Free Wi-Fi.

Linh Linh   **$**
Value   **Map** 2 D5
175/14 Pham Ngu Lao
Tel *(08) 3837 3004*
On a quiet lane with comfortable
rooms, wide, plant-strewn
balconies, and friendly service.
Free Wi-Fi.

DK Choice

Madam Cuc   **$**
Value   **Map** 2 D5
64 Bui Vien
Tel *(08) 3836 5073*
W madamcuchotels.com
Madam Cuc has a simple
formula – treat all guests like
family. It works so well that she
now has several branches in
the district, of which this is the
most conveniently located.
Rooms are simple but spotlessly
clean, and breakfast, tea, and
snacks are included. Free Wi-Fi.

Miss Loi's Guesthouse   **$**
Value   **Map** 2 E5
178/20 Co Giang
Tel *(08) 3837 9589*
Located on a narrow lane south
of District 1, with simple rooms
and friendly staff. Free Wi-Fi.

Spring   **$**
Value   **Map** 2 F3
44–46 Le Thanh Ton
Tel *(08) 3829 7362*
W springhotelvietnam.com
Comfortable, carpeted rooms at
reasonable prices make this one
of the best deals in town.

Lavender   **$$**
Boutique   **Map** 2 E4
208–210 Le Thanh Ton
Tel *(08) 2222 8888*
W lavenderhotel.com.vn
Provides smartly furnished rooms
and good service. Good location
near the Ben Thanh market.

DK Choice

Caravelle   **$$$**
Luxury   **Map** 2 F3
19–23 Lam Son Square
Tel *(08) 3823 4999*
W caravellehotel.com
Considered one of the best
hotels in Saigon, Caravelle offers
well-appointed deluxe rooms,
signature rooms, and suites. It is
ideally located near the shops
in Dong Khoi. The facilities are
superb, and service is top-
notch. There is free Wi-Fi.

Catina   **$$$**
Luxury   **Map** 2 F4
109 Dong Khoi
Tel *(08) 3829 6296*
W hotelcatina.com.vn
Near the Notre Dame Cathedral,
with small but stylish rooms.
Efficient staff.

Continental   **$$$**
Luxury   **Map** 2 F3
132–134 Dong Khoi
Tel *(08) 3829 9201*
W continentalvietnam.com
The grand old dame of Saigon
hotels, featuring high-ceilinged
rooms and a Colonial aura.

Grand   **$$$**
Luxury   **Map** 2 F4
8 Dong Khoi
Tel *(08) 3915 5555*
W grandhotel.vn
An expanded and refurbished
Colonial gem. The rooms are
quite plush and there are a lot
of peaceful corners.

Hotel Nikko Saigon   **$$$**
Luxury   **Map** 2 D5
235 Nguyen Van Cu
Tel *(08) 3925 7777*
W hotelnikkosaigon.com
Upmarket option featuring large
rooms with minimalist design
and a range of dining options.

Majestic   **$$$**
Luxury   **Map** 2 F4
1 Dong Khoi
Tel *(08) 3829 5517*
W majesticsaigon.com.vn
Glorious colonial hotel by the
river with Art-Deco interiors. Free
Wi-Fi. No smoking.

Brightly lit swimming pool of the elegant Caravelle hotel

Park Hyatt $$$
Luxury Map 2 E3
2 Lam Son Square
Tel *(08) 3824 1234*
🅦 saigon.park.hyatt.com
Excellent location by the Opera
House, with superb dining options
and one of the best spas in town.

Rex $$$
Luxury Map 2 E4
141 Nguyen Hue
Tel *(08) 3829 6536*
🅦 rexhotelvietnam.com
Famed for its rooftop bar, this
historic hotel offers plush rooms
and suites in three different wings.

Tan Binh District

Park Royal $$
Modern Map 1 A1
309B Nguyen Van Troi
Tel *(08) 3842 1111*
🅦 parkroyalhotels.com
Formerly the Novotel Garden
Plaza, well-equipped alternative,
a few minutes from the airport.

Around Ho Chi Minh City

**LONG HAI: Thuy
Duong Resort** $$
Resort Map C6
Phuoc Hai Town
Tel *(064) 388 6215*
🅦 thuyduongresort.com.vn
Affordable resort fronting a
soft-sand beach shaded by
casuarina trees. Has a number
of different types of rooms.

**LONG HAI: Anoasis
Beach Resort** $$$
Resort Map C6
Road 44, Long Hai, Ba Ria
Tel *(064) 386 8227*
🅦 anoasisresort.com.vn
Once a villa belonging to the
emperor, this award-winning
resort is a truly special getaway.

VUNG TAU: Son Thuy Resort $
Resort Map C6
165C Thuy Van
Tel *(064) 352 3460*
🅦 sonthuyresort.com.vn
A collection of A-frame
bungalows facing the long
Back Beach. An excellent
budget choice for families.

VUNG TAU: Palace Hotel $$
Modern Map C6
1 Nguyen Trai
Tel *(064) 385 6411*
🅦 palacehotel.com.vn
Reliable high-rise hotel featuring
good-sized carpeted rooms, with
flatscreen TVs and mood lighting.

A comfortable and well-lit room in the
Victoria Chau Doc Hotel

DK Choice

**VUNG TAU: Binh
An Village** $$$
Resort Map C6
1 Tran Phu
Tel *(064) 351 0016*
🅦 binhanvillage.com
This lovely resort has just ten
traditional villas built around
massive wood columns and
furnished in a blend of ancient
and modern styles. All suites
and some rooms have outdoor
living rooms looking out to a
garden. The superb restaurant
overlooks the ocean.

Mekong Delta and Southern Vietnam

BAC LIEU: Bac Lieu Hotel $
Value Map B6
4–6 Hoang Van Thu
Tel *(0781) 395 9697*
🅦 baclieuhotel.com
Looks great from the outside and
though the rooms are rather
basic, they are comfortable. Car
and motorbike rentals available.

BEN TRE: Hung Vuong $
Value Map B6
166 Hung Vuong
Tel *(075) 382 2408*
🅦 hungvuonghotelbentre.vn
Conveniently located near the
center of town, offers good
value for money. Ask for a
river-view room.

CAN THO: Tay Ho $
Value Map B6
42 Hai Ba Trung
Tel *(0710) 382 3392*
🅦 tayhohotel.com
Well-located establishment with
helpful owners. Ask for a room
with a view of the river.

CAN THO: Saigon Can Tho $$
Modern Map B6
55 Phan Dinh Phung
Tel *(0710) 382 5831*
🅦 saigoncantho.com.vn
Reliable business hotel with nice
rooms, a good range of facilities,
and attentive staff.

CAN THO: Victoria Can Tho $$$
Resort Map B6
Cai Khe Ward
Tel *(0710) 381 0111*
🅦 victoriahotels-asia.com
Colonial-style elegance at this
fancy hotel situated on its own
peninsula just north of town.

CHAU DOC: Song Sao $
Value Map B6
12 Nguyen Huu Canh
Tel *(076) 356 1777*
High-rise option with comfortable
rooms, welcoming staff, and a
central location. Free Wi-Fi.

CHAU DOC: Chau Pho $$
Modern Map B6
88 Trung Nu Vuong
Tel *(076) 356 4139*
🅦 chauphohotel.com
Probably one of Chau Doc's
classiest hotels, with bright, spacious rooms and efficient service.

**CHAU DOC: Victoria
Chau Doc** $$$
Resort Map B6
32 Le Loi
Tel *(076) 386 5010*
🅦 victoriahotels-asia.com
The town's only five-star resort
offers spacious rooms with great
balcony views of the river.

**CON DAO ISLAND: Saigon
Con Dao Resort** $$
Resort Map B6
18–24 Ton Duc Thang
Tel *(064) 383 0336*
🅦 saigoncondao.com
The next best bet on Con Dao
for those who do not want to
splurge on the Six Senses.

**CON DAO ISLAND: Six
Senses Hideaway** $$$
Resort Map B6
Dat Doc Beach
Tel *(064) 383 1222*
🅦 sixsenses.com
Super luxurious resort on its own
private beach. Offers stylish villas,
each with its own private butler.

MY THO: Chuong Duong $
Value Map B6
10, 30 Thang 4
Tel *(073) 387 0875*
Reasonably comfortable
rooms with river-view balconies.
Has one of the best restaurants
in town.

For more information on types of hotels *see page 233*

PHU QUOC ISLAND:
Beach Club $
Value **Map** A6
Long Beach
Tel *(077) 398 0998*
W beachclubvietnam.com
Beachfront bungalow with
simple rooms around a
restaurant. Free Wi-Fi.

DK Choice

PHU QUOC ISLAND:
La Veranda $$$
Resort **Map** A6
Long Beach
Tel *(077) 398 2988*
W laverandaresorts.com
Occupying a French Colonial-
style building in the middle of
Long Beach, this is one of the
most luxurious resorts on Phu
Quoc. Facilities include a spa, a
pool, and a restaurant, Pepper
Tree, on the upstairs terrace.

PHU QUOC ISLAND: Saigon
Phu Quoc Resort $$$
Resort **Map** A6
62 Tran Hung Dao
Tel *(077) 384 6999*
W sgphuquocresort.com.vn
At the north end of Long Beach,
this fancy resort has a spa, pool,
and lots of watersports.

SOC TRANG: Phong Lan I $
Value **Map** B6
124 Dong Khoi
Tel *(079) 382 1619*
Simple riverside hotel with basic
rooms in the center of Soc Trang.
Free Wi-Fi.

TRA VINH: Cuu Long $
Value **Map** B6
999 Nguyen Thi Minh Khai
Tel *(074) 386 2615*
Just outside the town center,
with well-equipped rooms and
friendly staff. Free Wi-Fi.

VINH LONG: Phuong Hoang $
Value **Map** B6
2H Hung Vuong
Tel *(070) 382 5185*
Well-maintained mini hotel.
Better bet than the government
hotels in Vinh Long. Free Wi-Fi.

South Central
Vietnam

BUON MA THUOT: Dam
San Hotel $
Value **Map** C5
212 Nguyen Cong Tru
Tel *(500) 385 1234*
W damsanhotel.com.vn
Comfortable, with spacious,
carpeted rooms and great views.

Well-laid tables at the open dining space of
La Veranda Resort, Phuc Quoc Island-

DK Choice

DALAT: Dreams $
Value **Map** C5
151 Phan Dinh Phung
Tel *(063) 383 3748*
W dreamshoteldalat.com
So popular that it is almost
always full; book ahead. The
hotel also provides generous
breakfasts, free Wi-Fi, and 24-
hour room service. The second
branch, just up the road,
features Jacuzzis in some rooms.

DALAT: Hotel du Parc $$
Boutique **Map** C5
7 Tran Phu
Tel *(063) 382 5777*
W dalatresorts.com
Refurbished Colonial building in
the center of town that offers all
facilities and a classy atmosphere.

DALAT: Dalat Palace $$$
Luxury **Map** C5
12 Tran Phu
Tel *(063) 382 5444*
W dalatresorts.com
Dalat's top hotel, featuring
sumptuously furnished rooms
and elegant common areas.

KONTUM: Indochine $
Value **Map** C4
30 Bach Dang
Tel *(060) 386 3335*
W indochinehotel.vn
Eight-story monolith, with well-
equipped rooms that enjoy great
river views.

MUI NE: Mui Ne Backpackers $
Value **Map** C6
88 Nguyen Dinh Chieu
Tel *(062) 384 7047*
W muinebackpackers.com
Popular spot with a mix of dorms
and private rooms. Free Wi-Fi.

MUI NE: Coco Beach $$$
Resort **Map** C6
58 Nguyen Dinh Chieu
Tel *(062) 384 7111*
W cocobeach.net
Mui Ne's original resort and one
of the best, with stylish, stilted
bungalows in a coconut grove.

MUI NE: Mia Resort $$$
Resort **Map** C6
24 Nguyen Dinh Chieu
Tel *(062) 384 7440*
W miamuine.com
Exclusive boutique resort with
luxurious thatched huts set in
a lush tropical garden.

NHA TRANG: La Suisse $
Value **Map** C5
34 Tran Quang Khai
Tel *(058) 352 4353*
W lasuissehotel.com
The best of many budget options
in Nha Trang, just a few steps
from the beach. Free Wi-Fi.

NHA TRANG: Nha
Trang Lodge $$
Modern **Map** C5
42 Tran Phu
Tel *(058) 352 1500*
W nhatranglodge.com
Decent option with good-sized
rooms. Located in the middle of
the beachfront promenade.

NHA TRANG: Sheraton $$$
Luxury **Map** C5
26 Tran Phu
Tel *(058) 388 0000*
W sheratonnhatrang.com
Right on Nha Trang's beachfront.
Has ten types of rooms and
extensive facilities.

NINH HOA: Six Senses
Hideaway $$$
Resort **Map** C5
Ninh Van Bay
Tel *(058) 352 4268*
W sixsenses.com
Set on its own private island, this
retreat offers an experience filled
with every imaginable luxury.

PHAN RANG: Ho Phong $
Value **Map** C5
363 Ngo Gia Tu
Tel *(068) 392 0333*
Few tourists stay overnight in Phan
Rang, but this is the best option
for those who do decide to.

PHAN THIET: Du Parc Ocean
Dunes & Golf Resort $$
Resort **Map** C6
1A Ton Duc Thang
Tel *(062) 382 5682*
W phanthiethotels.com
Formerly the Novotel Ocean
Dunes, this serene getaway is near
Mui Ne, yet away from the crowds.

QUANG NGAI: My Khe Resort $
Resort   Map C4
8 Nguyen I lue
Tel *(056) 389 2401*
Laid-back, friendly resort on
a long beach near Quang Ngai,
though it has limited facilities.

**QUY NHON: Avani Resort
& Spa** $$
Resort   Map C5
Ghenh Rang, Bai Dai Beach
Tel *(056) 384 0132*
W avanihotels.com
Beautifully designed resort on a
gorgeous beach. Offers compli-
mentary wellness classes.

Central Vietnam

**CHINA BEACH:
Furama Resort** $$$
Resort   Map C4
Truong Sa
Tel *(0511) 384 7333*
W furamavietnam.com
One of Vietnam's top resorts.
Completely self-contained and
offering a wide range of activities.

**CHINA BEACH:
Fusion Maia Da Nang** $$$
Resort   Map C4
Truong Sa St, Danang
Tel *(0511) 396 7999*
W fusionmaiadanang.com
An all-inclusive spa resort, where
all rooms have a private pool.

**DANANG: Grand
Mercure Danang** $$
Modern   Map C4
Hoa Cuong Bac, Danang
Tel *(0511) 379 7777*
W accorhotels.com
Located on its own island, this
hotel has smartly furnished rooms.

DANANG: Sun River $$
Modern   Map C4
132–136 Bach Dang
Tel *(0511) 384 9188*
W sunriverhoteldn.com.vn
Glass-fronted high-rise with great
river views, and efficient staff.

DONG HOI: Sun Spa Resort $$
Resort   Map B3
My Canh, Bao Ninh
Tel *(052) 384 2999*
W sunsparesortvietnam.com
Delightful setting with bright, airy
rooms and extensive facilities.

HOI AN: Cua Dai Hotel $
Resort   Map C4
54A Cua Dai
Tel *(0510) 386 2231*
W hotelcuadai-hoian.com
Located between the town and
Cua Dai Beach, this small, friendly
place is a convenient choice.

HOI AN: Ancient House $$
Resort   Map C4
377 Cua Dai
Tel *(0510) 392 3377*
W ancienthouseresort.com
This family-run resort is set in
extensive grounds, and includes
a 200-year-old house.

DK Choice

HOI AN: Nam Hai $$$
Resort   Map C4
Hamlet 1, Dien Duong Village
Tel *(0510) 394 0000*
W thenamhai.com
Prepare to be pampered at this
luxurious resort, offering one-
to five-bedroom villas, set in
beautiful grounds and facing an
idyllic strip of beach. Many also
have private pools.

HOI AN: Victoria Hoi An $$$
Resort   Map C4
Cua Dai Beach
Tel *(0510) 392 7040*
W victoriahotels.asia.com
A characterful resort designed like
a traditional fishing village.

HUE: Hue Nino $
Value   Map C3
14 Nguyen Cong Tru
Tel *(054) 625 2171*
W hueninohotel.com
Offers antique Vietnamese
furnishings in rooms and friendly
service at rock-bottom rates.

**HUE: La Residence Hotel
& Spa** $$$
Luxury   Map C3
5 Le Loi
Tel *(054) 383 7475*
W la-residence-hue.com
One of Hue's top hotels,
featuring stylish artwork on
the walls and tastefully
decorated rooms.

HUE: Saigon Morin $$$
Luxury   Map C3
30 Le Loi
Tel *(054) 382 3526*
W morinhotel.com.vn
For over a century, this landmark
lodging has been taking care of
travelers with its top facilities.

**LANG CO BEACH: Lang Co
Beach Resort** $$
Value   Map C3
Lang Co Town
Tel *(054) 387 3555*
W langcobeachresort.com.vn
A great place for a restful
escape on one of the country's
best beaches, with a number
of facilities.

VINH: Saigon Kim Lien $$
Modern   Map B2
25 Quang Trung
Tel *(038) 383 8099*
W saigonkimlien.com.vn
Reasonable, government-run
place in the center of Vinh,
boasting a small swimming pool
and a tourism information desk.

Hanoi

French Quarter

De Syloia $$
Boutique   Map 2 F5
17A Tran Hung Dao
Tel *(04) 3824 5346*
W desyloia.com
A good choice in the French
Quarter, with well-equipped
rooms, personal service, and
a convenient location.

Movenpick $$
Modern   Map 2 D4
83A Ly Thuong Kiet
Tel *(04) 3822 2800*
W movenpick-hotels.com
Business hotel with plush rooms
and plenty of facilities.

Hilton Hanoi Opera $$$
Luxury   Map 2 F5
1 Le Thanh Tong
Tel *(04) 3933 0500*
W hanoi.hilton.com
A cut above the average
Hilton, with Vietnamese
furnishings and decor, plus
excellent service.

The elegant dining area in the glass-fronted Sun River hotel, Danang

For more information on types of hotels *see page 233*

Melia $$$
Luxury Map 2 E4
44B Ly Thuong Kiet
Tel *(04) 3934 3343*
W meliahanoi.com
Stands out for its elegantly designed rooms, comprehensive facilities, and efficient service.

Sofitel Legend Metropole $$$
Luxury Map 2 F4
15 Ngo Quyen
Tel *(04) 3826 6919*
W sofitel.com
Set in a beautifully restored Colonial building, with sound-proof rooms and huge bathtubs.

Zephyr $$$
Luxury Map 2 E4
4 Ba Trieu
Tel *(04) 3934 1256*
W zephyrhotel.com.vn
Small luxury hotel near Hoan Kiem Lake with spacious rooms.

Old Quarter

Classic Street $
Value Map 2 E3
41 Hang Be
Tel *(04) 3825 2421*
W classicstreet-phocohotel.com
Surprisingly stylish rooms for budget prices, with friendly staff and a great location. Free Wi-Fi.

Hanoi Backpackers Hostel $
Hostel Map 2 E2
9 Ma May
Tel *(04) 3935 1891*
W vietnambackpackerhostels.com
The most convenient location of this growing empire. Smart dorms and doubles; plus regular parties.

Hong Ngoc Tonkin $
Value Map 2 E3
14 Luong Van Can
Tel *(04) 3826 7566*
W hongngochotels.com
Slightly higher prices than most budget places, but smarter furnishings and fittings too. Free Wi-Fi available.

Nam Hai 1 $
Value Map 2 E2
37 Ma May
Tel *(04) 3926 3632*
Formerly the Anh Dao, this mini hotel has good-value family rooms and a decent buffet breakfast. Free Wi-Fi.

Win $
Value Map 2 E3
34 Hang Hanh
Tel *(04) 3828 7371*
W win-hotel-hanoi.com
Excellent location on a quiet lane in the noisy Old Quarter, with well-equipped rooms and helpful staff.

Hanoi Moment $$
Modern Map 2 E2
15 Hang Can
Tel *(04) 3923 3988*
W hanoimomenthotel.com
Fashionable rooms in black and white with wood floors, double glazing, and mood lighting.

DK Choice

Queen Travel $$
Boutique Map 2 E3
65 Hang Bac
Tel *(04) 3826 0860*
W azqueentravel.com
Characterful place, lovingly designed by its owner. Offers atmospheric rooms equipped with traditional furnishings. All rooms have wooden floors and extras like DVD players and free Wi-Fi. This boutique property is also the base office for Queen Travel, a reputable tour operator.

Sunshine Suites $$
Modern Map 2 E2
52 Ma May
Tel *(04) 3926 4920*
W sunshinesuites.com.vn
Big, bright rooms equipped with computers and free Wi-Fi. Great location.

West of Hoan Kiem Lake

Church Boutique $$
Boutique Map 2 E3
9 Nha Tho
Tel *(04) 3928 8118*
W nhatho.churchhotel.com.vn
The original of three Church Boutique properties, with a great location in the shopping district. Offers classic comfort.

Bright room with a comfortable bed in the Nikko Hanoi hotel

Hanoi Spring II $$
Modern Map 2 D3
38 Pho Au Trieu
Tel *(04) 3826 8500*
W hanoispringhotel.com
Spacious rooms with wood floors, and balconies offering views of the cathedral.

Nikko Hanoi $$$
Luxury Map 1 C5
84 Tran Nhan Tong
Tel *(04) 3822 3535*
W hotelnikkohanoi.com.vn
A business hotel with luxurious rooms, a nice spa, and a great Japanese restaurant.

Sheraton Hanoi $$$
Luxury Map 1 A3
K5 Nghi Tam, 11 Xuan Dieu
Tel *(04) 3719 9000*
W sheraton.com/hanoi
Lovely location on the shores of West Lake, with the usual excellent Sheraton facilities.

Sofitel Plaza $$$
Luxury Map 1 B1
1 Thanh Nien
Tel *(04) 3823 8888*
W sofitel.com
Towering high-rise on the shores of West Lake, offering panoramic views and lots of dining options.

Northern Vietnam

BA BE NATIONAL PARK: Ba Be National Park Guesthouse $
Value Map B1
National Park Headquarters, Ba Be
Tel *(0281) 389 4126*
Great place to stay if visiting this national park. Smart rooms, a pool, and a restaurant.

BAC HA: Sao Mai $
Value Map A1
Ban Pho
Tel *(020) 388 0228*
W saomaibachahotel.com
Good bet for visitors to the Sunday market, with a range of rooms in three buildings.

CAO BANG: Hoang Anh $
Value Map B1
131 Kim Dong
Tel *(026) 385 8969*
The best of a poor bunch in this remote town. Spacious rooms with river views.

CAT BA ISLAND: Noble House $
Value Map C1
1 Thang 4 St
Tel *(031) 388 8363*
Large, well-equipped rooms at this conveniently located place, with good harbor views.

CAT BA ISLAND: Holiday View $$
Modern   **Map** C1
1 Thang 4 St
Tel *(031) 388 7200*
W holidayviewhotel-catba.com
Typical high-rise hotel with good views of the bay. Efficient staff.

**DIEN BIEN PHU: Muong
Thanh** $$
Modern   **Map** A1
514, 7 Thang 5
Tel *(0230) 381 0043*
W muongthanh.vn
This is the best spot in town, with a good restaurant, pool, and helpful service.

HAIPHONG: Harbour View $$$
Luxury   **Map** B1
4 Tran Phu
Tel *(031) 382 7827*
W avanihotels.com/haiphong
No real harbour views, although the rooms are classy. Excellent service and a good restaurant.

**HALONG CITY: Novotel
Halong Bay** $$
Modern   **Map** C1
Halong Road, Bai Chay
Tel *(033) 384 8108*
W novotelhalongbay.com
Reliable Novotel comforts such as well-equipped rooms, comfy common areas, and warm service.

**HALONG CITY: Indochina
Sails** $$$
Luxury   **Map** C1
27 An Duong Trieu, Hanoi
Tel *(04) 3984 2362*
W indochinasails.com
The best way to experience Halong Bay is from the deck of this luxurious junk.

**MAI CHAU VALLEY: Mai Chau
Lodge** $$$
Luxury   **Map** B2
Mai Chau Town
Tel *(0218) 386 8959*
W maichaulodge.com
Swimming, kayaking, cycling and rock-climbing are all offered at this pricey option in Mai Chau.

NINH BINH: Emeralda Resort $$$
Luxury   **Map** B2
Van Long Reserve, Gia Van Commune, Gia Vien District
Tel *(030) 365 8333*
W emeraldaresort.com
Huge rooms, comfortable beds, and mountain views at this lovely resort with free internet.

SAPA: Sapa Goldsea $
Value   **Map** A1
58 Fansipan Rd
Tel *(020) 387 1869*
Fantastic views, comfortable rooms with heaters, plus free Wi-Fi.

Well-decorated and comfortable sitting area of the Victoria Sapa

DK Choice

SAPA: Victoria Sapa $$$
Resort   **Map** A1
Hoang Dieu
Tel *(020) 387 1522*
W victoriahotels-asia.com
Sitting at the top end of town, this Alpine-looking resort is Sapa's best lodgings. It offers pleasant rooms, great views, and tours of the region. They even have their own luxury train - the Victoria Express – to help guests get there from Hanoi.

SON LA: Trade Union Hotel $
Value   **Map** A1
4, 26 Thang 8
Tel *(022) 385 2804*
Friendly, helpful staff at this basic but pleasant hotel. Free Wi-Fi

Angkor

SIEM REAP: Earthwalkers $
Hostel   **Map** A5
Sala Kanseng Village, Sangkat No. 2
Tel *(012) 967 901*
W earthwalkers.no
Great-value, Norwegian-run place for backpackers, with dorm beds, doubles, and family rooms.

SIEM REAP: Eight Rooms $
Value   **Map** A5
138–139 Streoung Thamey Village, Svydangkum Commune
Tel *(063) 969 788*
W ei8htrooms.com
Classic travelers' haunt near the town center. Rooms include air-con, cable TV, and free Wi-Fi.

SIEM REAP: Rosy's Guesthouse $
Value   **Map** A5
74 Phum Slor Kram
Tel *(063) 965 059*
W rosyguesthouse.com
Lovely old villa run by a Western couple, with well-equipped rooms and hammocks. Free Wi-Fi.

**SIEM REAP: Two
Dragons Guesthouse** $
Value   **Map** A5
110 Wat Bo Village
Tel *(063) 965 107*
W twodragons-asia.com
Spartan rooms, but a friendly vibe and excellent travel advice.

**SIEM REAP:
Mysteres d'Angkor** $$
Boutique   **Map** A5
235 Phum Slor Krum
Tel *(063) 963 639*
W mysteres-angkor.com
French run boutique hotel with colonial-style rooms and a pool set in a lush garden. Free Wi-Fi.

**SIEM REAP: La Residence
d'Angkor** $$$
Luxury   **Map** A5
River Rd
Tel *(063) 963 390*
W residencedangkor.com
Rooms and suites set in a large tropical garden, with a spa, pool, and fitness center.

DK Choice

**SIEM REAP: Raffles Grand
Hotel d'Angkor** $$$
Luxury   **Map** A5
1 Charles de Gaulle St, Khum Svay Dang tum
Tel *(063) 963 888*
W raffles.com
One of the best places to stay while visiting the Angkor Complex, this Colonial builiding exudes sophistication. Rooms are lavishly furnished and equipped with every facility. Frequent dance performances.

SIEM REAP: Shinta Mani $$$
Luxury   **Map** A5
Junction of Oum Khun and 14th sts
Tel *(063) 761 998*
W shintamani.com
Upscale hotel with a spa, cooking classes, a library, and free Wi-Fi

WHERE TO EAT AND DRINK

The Vietnamese are passionate about food, which means that fresh ingredients and experienced cooks are bountiful. Whether opting for a quick bite or a full meal, visitors to the country will find an amazing variety of eateries throughout the country, from pushcarts, roadside stalls, and sidewalk cafés to pizzerias and gourmet restaurants. Washing down tasty treats is easy as well, with hot tea or cold beer never too far away. The best news is that the prices are extremely reasonable, as the country's eclectic and innovative culinary repertoire offers a range of delicious options to suit every budget. Increasingly, this also includes Western-style fast food, and there are plenty of Italian, American, and Indian restaurants now located in big cities and towns. The most reliable places to find well-prepared international food are high-end restaurants catering to foreign tourists and expats, while roadside stalls serving tasty Vietnamese fare provide a memorable cultural experience.

Terrace overlooking the Hoan Kiem Lake at Thuy Ta café *(see p252)*, Hanoi

appeals. Meats, either grilled, braised, or stewed, and fish in some kind of sauce are common, as are braised bamboo shoots, grilled eggplant, fried greens, and tofu preparations.

Vietnam's national noodle-soup breakfast dish, *pho (see p244)* often features in small, family-run eateries. It is typically served with beef or chicken, and has an unmistakable star anise aroma. Fresh herbs and a variety of condiments are added according to taste.

Restaurants

Eateries with trained waiters, printed menus, and starched napkins are found mainly in the major cities, as well as in big hotels and resorts.

Sit-down restaurants that offer Vietnamese food often specialize in a particular type of dish. One of the most common is *bun thit nuong*, where grilled, marinated meat (most commonly beef or pork) is served on a bed of rice noodles, fresh herbs, and pickled vegetables, with a sweet and spicy fish-sauce broth. *Banh xeo* is a flavorful rice or cornflour pancake stuffed with pork, seafood, and beansprouts, and served with a sweet and sour fish-sauce broth. *Lau*, often translated as 'steamboat' or 'hotpot,' is a fragrant broth that is placed on a stove in the center of the table. It is eaten communally, and diners can add a selection of vegetables, herbs, noodles, and meat according to taste.

Chinese restaurants are also common, while Vietnam's surfeit of cafés ensures that freshly baked baguettes, hot coffees, and fruit juices are never far away. American-style diners, pizzerias, and fast-food chains such as KFC have emerged in Hanoi, Ho Chi Minh City, and major tourist destinations, and some major hotels and restaurants offer European haute cuisine.

Com and pho

A restaurant that serves an ample portion of rice along with meat and vegetables is called a *quan com* (com is the Vietnamese word for rice). It is usually a humble affair, often seating as few as half a dozen people. The food is displayed in a glass case at the front, and one need only point to what

Street Food

Vietnam has a long and rich tradition of street food. Vendors in all cities and towns patrol the streets with baskets of delicious snack foods such as tamarind pods, pastries, baguette sandwiches, sticky rice, or fresh fruits. Some cooks carry savory or sweet treats wrapped in banana leaves, which are then steamed or roasted. Pushcarts can carry entire kitchens, typically offering *pho*, fried noodles, tofu preparations, and *chao* – a rice porridge also known as *congee*. The best part is that the food is cooked in front of customers. Some vendors carry their food in a yoke slung across their shoulder. They may offer anything from dry snack foods to fresh fruits and vegetables, while some even carry a small stove with which to prepare a hot meal on the spot.

The brightly lit interior of the Bassac, Chau Doc

Beer Gardens and Bia Hoi Bars

Especially plentiful in the south, where the weather never turns cold, beer gardens are always promoting one beer or another, and the brand can change every week. They usually sell snacks to accompany the beer, such as make-your-own spring rolls, which are accompanied by piquant dipping sauces.

Fresh beer or *bia hoi* is a specialty of Hanoi. Although it can be found throughout the country, this refreshing drink is free of preservatives and costs only pennies per glass. Bars serving *bia hoi* are usually simple, hole-in-the-wall places, visited mostly by local men. Foreign visitors are welcome as long as they don't mind squatting on tiny stools. These joints can be an insightful way to experience the country's bar culture.

Vegetarian Options

There are very few exclusively vegetarian restaurants in the country, but those wishing to avoid red meat will find it easy to do so. A wide selection of fish, poultry, and vegetables is always available in every restaurant. However, vegans and strict vegetarians should be aware that *nuoc mam*, the much-beloved fermented fish sauce, finds its way into most meals. While most restaurateurs are aware of vegetarian practice, and willing to make accommodations, it is nevertheless

necessary for vegetarians to be vocal and specific about their dietary needs and requirements.

Prices

Food will probably be the least expensive item on the budget of any visitor to Vietnam. Even a full meal in a hotel can cost less than US$15 per head, though imported alcohol can easily quadruple the price. Taxes on wine can be ruinous, but imported spirits are more manageable, and local beer is quite reasonable. Budget travelers eschewing alcohol, and dining largely in smaller eateries or on street food can eat fairly lavishly for as little as US$6 a day.

Eating Customs

Unlike at the Western table, meals in Vietnam are not served in a succession of courses. Dishes are brought to the table as they are ready. The usual practice is to order one different dish per person, plus one for the table. Diners then proceed to sample the dishes liberally, relishing the sharing as much as the food. Table manners (see p273) are simple to follow. Feel free to slurp the noodles and throw the fish and meat bones on the floor. Enthusiastic dining and loud conversations are the norm.

Tipping

While tipping has not always been customary in Vietnam, it has become common in better restaurants and backpacker areas with the advent of modern

tourism. If the service is good, a 10 percent tip is appreciated. Do not tip if the service is poor. In upscale hotels and restaurants, a five percent charge is usually levied. However, patrons may wish to offer a small tip in addition to that small fee.

Recommended Restaurants

The restaurants on the following pages have been carefully selected to give a cross-section of options from across the country – not only is there lots of Vietnamese cuisine, with regional variations such as Hue Imperial cuisine, but also Japanese and Thai, as well as Chinese, Indian, French, Italian and Mexican dishes. In fact, in tourist areas these different cuisines are sometimes listed on a single menu. Some of the more innovative places serve fusion dishes that combine ingredients and techniques from various cuisines, such as Vietnamese and-French. Besides the quality of the food, these recommendations take into account the ambience and level of service. However, since taste is more important than presentation for most Vietnamese diners, many of the places listed here lack the kind of sophisticated ambience so sought after by restaurants in the West. Those places that are particularly worth seeking out either for their culinary excellence or their memorable atmosphere are described in more detail as a 'DK Choice.'

Chic exterior of a French style café in Ho Chi Minh City

Flavors of Vietnam

Over the course of history Vietnam has absorbed many culinary influences but has still managed to preserve its own distinct cuisine. The long period of Chinese domination left its mark on Vietnamese cooking, not least in the use of chopsticks, soy sauce, and bean curd. Western tastes were also imported during French colonial rule, notably coffee, bread, and dairy products. In the south, Indian, Khmer, and Thai influences are apparent in a cuisine that features coconut and aromatic curries.

Bunches of mint, basil, and coriander

Woman preparing food at a market stall in Hoi An

Vietnamese cuisine relies on herbs and spices – especially coriander, mint, ginger, lemongrass, and spring onions – and fish sauce. Rice *(see p99)*, however, is Vietnam's staple. Its significance is even reflected in the language; for example, the most common greeting *(Ban an com chua?)* literally translates as "Have you eaten rice yet?" There is a vast vocabulary referring to various types of rice, the

individual stages of the process of planting, growing and harvesting, as well as a plethora of expressions for meals prepared from rice. It accompanies every meal: for everyday consumption the Vietnamese use *gao te* (ordinary, non-sticky rice), while special occasions such as anniversaries, festivals, and votive offerings call for *gao nep* (glutinous sticky rice). Ground

The Cuisine

The fertile deltas of the Red River in the north and the Mekong River in the south guarantee Vietnam's supply of rice. The country's long coastline, rivers, ponds, and lakes provide a plentiful stock of fish and seafood, while the tropical climate means that fruit and vegetables grow in abundance.

Durian   Mangosteens   Pomelo

Limes   Bananas   Rambutans

A selection of tropical fruit found throughout southeast Asia

Local Dishes and Specialties

Garnish for *pho*

There are three main regions in Vietnamese cuisine. The north with its cooler climate has a simple cooking style. Exotic meats, including dog, are delicacies, and snake wine is widely available. Central Vietnam boasts a rich vegetarian tradition as well as the sophisticated imperial cuisine of the former royal capital Hue. The southern regions benefit from richer tropical produce.

Pho, a traditional noodle soup, captures the essence of Vietnamese cooking. This humble dish originated in the north but has become the nation's favorite dish. With slices of raw beef that cook in a bowl of hot broth, *pho* is a nutritious meal in itself. The quality of the soup can vary; connoisseurs prefer to come late to *pho* stalls to benefit from a stronger broth.

Pho This classic dish combines white noodles, slices of beef, and spring onions in a rich broth.

Fish drying in the sun for use in *nuoc mam*, Nha Trang

rice is the basis of a wide range of products including noodles, cakes, and rice paper, while distilled rice is used to make rice wine and liquors.

Vietnam's long Buddhist tradition has been responsible for the popularity of a vegetarian cuisine perfected over centuries. Especially renowned is the vegetarian cooking of Hue, which is the country's traditional center of Buddhism. Here, Vietnamese women are skilled in offering sumptuous feasts that include vegetarian versions of famous dishes with meat replaced by beancurd or mushrooms.

Among the more unusual aspects of Vietnamese cuisine is the consumption of exotic meats such as frogs, snakes, sparrows, snails, and turtles. Some restaurants even serve wild species, such as porcupine, despite these being officially banned.

Street Food

Com binh dan (popular food) or *com bui* (dusty food) refers to street food. Almost everywhere

Street vendor selling baguettes in Ho Chi Minh City

you go in Vietnam, you will be only a few paces away from a stall serving mouthwatering meals and snacks. Stalls that are packed with people sitting around on plastic seats are likely to serve the tastiest dishes. *Pho* (noodle soup), *banh xeo* (pancake), and filled baguettes are favorite snacks.

A typical sight on the streets of Vietnam is a woman carrying a long pole with a basket on each side. These are filled not only with ingredients, such as noodles, herbs, meat, and vegetables, but also with bowls, chopsticks, and a charcoal stove, making them portable kitchens that can produce remarkable feasts.

ON THE MENU

Nuoc mam A pungent sauce made of fermented salted fish.

Nuoc cham A fish sauce made with sugar, lemon, water, garlic, and chili.

Nem ran Fried spring rolls wrapped in rice paper usually dipped in *nuoc cham*.

Banh cuon Raw rice flour rolls stuffed with meat.

Chao tom Prawn paste served on a sugar-cane stick.

Canh chua ca Sour soup.

Lau Hotpot.

Chao Rice gruel.

Cahn Chua Ca A hot and sour soup usually made with pineapple, catfish, and plenty of chili.

Banh Xeo A pork and prawn pancake often wrapped in a lettuce leaf and served with a tangy lime and chili dip.

Cha Ca Originating from Hanoi, this dish features fried fish, noodles, dill, peanuts, and *nuoc cham*.

Where to Eat and Drink

Ho Chi Minh City

Cholon

Café Central An Dong $$
International   Map 4 F4
18 An Duong Vuong
Tel *(08) 3833 6688*
It is worth skipping a meal
before visiting this fantastic
buffet in order to sample as
many dishes as possible.
Vietnamese, Japanese, and
international cuisine is served for
breakfast, lunch, and dinner. An
à la carte menu is also available.

Orientica $$$
Vietnamese/Seafood   Map 4 F3
242 Tran Binh Trong
Tel *(08) 3839 7777*
Superb, award-winning restaurant
located in the Equatorial Hotel.
There is a "wet market" where
guests can choose their own
fresh seafood. Chefs prepare
meals in an open kitchen.

District 1

Asian Kitchen $
International   Map 2 D5
185/22 Pham Ngu Lao
Tel *(08) 3836 7397*
Tucked away in an alley, this
eatery has a huge menu of
Vietnamese, Japanese, and
vegetarian dishes in a relaxed
atmosphere. Try the pork
cooked in a clay pot.

Black Cat $
International   Map 2 F4
13 Phan Van Dat
Tel *(08) 3829 2055*
Serves comfort food such as
waffles and burgers. For the
ravenous, the 1-lb (500-gram)
cheeseburger is a great choice.
Also has some Vietnamese and
Italian dishes.

Bo Tung Xeo $
Vietnamese   Map 2 E3
31 Ly Tu Trong
Tel *(08) 3825 1330*
A large restaurant with a
sprawling garden, named after
its signature dish, *bo tung xeo* –
strips of beef that are grilled on
a brazier at the table by the
customers themselves.

Bun Cha Hanoi $
Vietnamese   Map 2 F3
26/1 Le Thanh Ton
Tel *(08) 3827 5843*
Bun Cha Hanoi is one of the most
popular places in the city to
sample grilled pork served with

vegetables (typically lettuce, bean
sprouts, and cucumber) and rice
vermicelli – a Hanoi specialty.

DK Choice

Nha Hang Ngon $
Vietnamese   Map 2 E3
160 Pasteur
Tel *(08) 3827 7131*
With simple cooking stations
producing delectable regional
specialties, this place is aptly
named 'Ngon,' which means
'delicious.' It is a must-visit for
an introduction to Vietnamese
cuisine, served in and around a
lovely Colonial villa at rock-
bottom prices. Popular with
locals and can get crowded at
peak hours.

Original Bodhi Tree $
Vegetarian   Map 2 D5
175/4 Pham Ngu Lao
Tel *(08) 3837 1910*
Serves a fantastic range of
vegetarian fare, including
Vietnamese, Italian, and Mexican
dishes, plus delicious shakes.
The 'original' in the name
distinguishes it from copies.

Pho 24 $
Vietnamese   Map 2 F4
71-73 Dong Khoi
Tel *(08) 3825 7505*
Branches of this popular
franchise can be found all over
the country, serving *pho* – the
national dish, consisting of a
noodle soup, usually served
with beef – in a hygienic, air-
conditioned environment.

Sozo $
International   Map 2 D5
176 Bui Vien
Tel *(08) 870 6580*
This lovely little café and bakery
located in District 1 is the perfect

place to sit back and unwind
over a leisurely meal. The
staff comprises of local street
children being trained to run
businesses themselves.

Wrap and Roll $
Vietnamese   Map 2 F3
62 Hai Ba Trung
Tel *(08) 3822 2166*
Foodies who really like to get
their hands dirty, will love this
place. Order up the ingredients,
roll them in rice paper, and then
dip them in tangy sauces.

Lemongrass $$
Vietnamese   Map 2 F4
4 Nguyen Thiep
Tel *(08) 3822 0496*
Spread over three floors, with
a menu that offers a range of
classic dishes such as prawns
on sugarcane and crab in a spicy
sauce. The set lunch is a good
deal. Reservations recommended
for dinner.

Ngoc Suong Marina $$
Vietnamese/Seafood   Map 2 D3
172 Nguyen Dinh Chieu
Tel *(08) 3930 2379*
Popular among locals for its
seafood, Ngoc Suong has
branches all over the country.
Try the crab in tamarind sauce
or the sugarcane prawns.

Tandoor $$
Indian   Map 2 F3
74/6 Hai Ba Trung
Tel *(08) 3930 4839*
Consistently good food at
this centrally located Indian

Chefs preparing meals in the open kitchen of Orientica

Elegant interior of the popular Thai restaurant, Spice

restaurant. The good-value set lunches are popular with office workers in the vicinity.

Temple Club $$
Vietnamese Map 2 E4
29–31 Ton That Thiep
Tel *(08) 3829 9244*
One of the city's most atmospheric restaurants, set in a former Chinese temple. Try the chicken curry or *cha ca* Hanoi, then relax in the retro lounge over dessert and coffee.

DK Choice

Vietnam House $$
Vietnamese Map 2 F4
93 95 Dong Khoi
Tel *(08) 3829 1623*
For those not familiar with Vietnamese cuisine, this is a great place to start discovering its wonderful range of flavors. Set in a lovely Colonial-style house, with waiters in traditional attire and live gentle music, it offers the choice of à la carte or fixed-price menus.

Zan Z Bar $$
International Map 2 F4
19 Dong Khoi
Tel *(08) 6291 3686*
Hugely popular restaurant and bar in the heart of the city, serving a variety of tapas as well as tempting main courses such as lamb and steak. The tables outside are ideal for people-watching.

Bonsai Cruises $$$
Vietnamese Map 2 F4
Bach Dang Pier at the foot of Nguyen Hue
Tel *(08) 3910 5560*
The dinner cruise run by Bonsai Cruises on the Saigon River can be great fun. It includes a

Vietnamese and international buffet spread and a live band on deck.

Camargue $$$
Mediterranean Map 2 F3
74/7D Hai Ba Trung
Tel *(08) 3520 4888*
Located among a clutch of restaurants and bars in the city center, Camargue serves top-notch Mediterranean cuisine in a stylish setting. Enjoy an aperitif at the bar, then head upstairs for a feast.

Maxim's Nam An $$$
Vietnamese Map 2 F4
13–17 Dong Khoi
Tel *(08) 3829 6676*
Journey back in time with ancient French-style architecture, warm, wood-carved restrooms, elegantly laid tables, and musical performances in the evening. The food is reassuringly traditional Vietnamese.

Xu Restaurant and Lounge $$$
Vietnamese Map 2 F3
71–75 Hai Ba Trung
Tel *(08) 3824 8468*
An ultra-chic venue that is part restaurant and part nightclub. Serves innovative Vietnamese dishes in an intimate setting, with plush seating and dim lighting.

District 3

Au Lac do Brazil $$
International Map 1 C2
238 Pasteur
Tel *(08) 3820 7157*
Serves excellent Brazilian fare in stylish surroundings. Go for the *churrasco*, a platter of grilled meats, guaranteed to satisfy even the most voracious carnivore.

Spice $$
Thai Map 2 D3
27 Le Quy Don
Tel *(08) 3930 7873*
Conveniently located near the War Remnants Museum, this is probably the best Thai restaurant in town, serving classics like *tom yam kung* and spicy curries.

Around Ho Chi Minh City

VUNG TAU: Binh An Village $
Vietnamese/International Map C6
1 Tran Phu
Tel *(064) 351 0016*
Set in a resort of the same name, Binh An Village is Vung Tau's most atmospheric

restaurant. Beautiful building with a tasteful decor, this restaurant has great sea views and excellent food.

VUNG TAU: Ganh Hao $
Vietnamese/Seafood Map C6
3 Tran Phu
Tel *(064) 355 0909*
Ganh Hao serves some of the best seafood in Vung Tau. Has tables on a terrace on a promontory above the sea as well as a snug dining room. Try the lobster, jumbo shrimp, or sea bass.

VUNG TAU: Bistro Nine $$
International Map C6
9 Truong Vinh Ky
Tel *(064) 351 1571*
Welcoming café, great for a Continental breakfast, a filling lunch, or a simple espresso. Also serves home-made French bread and ice cream.

Mekong Delta and Southern Vietnam

CAN THO: Nam Do $$
Vietnamese/International Map D6
1 Ngo Quyen
Tel *(0710) 381 9139*
A recently revamped Can Tho institution. Offers Vietnamese fusion and international fare, with a boat-shaped bar on the top floor.

CAN THO: Spices $$$
Vietnamese/International Map B6
Victoria Can Tho Resort, Cai Khe Ward
Tel *(0710) 381 0111*
A meal on the poolside terrace of Victoria Resort is worth heading out of town for. Order traditional Vietnamese cuisine or international favorites such as salmon and trout tartar

CAO LANH: A Chau $
Vietnamese Map B6
42 Ly Thuong Kiet
Tel *(067) 385 2202*
Situated just north of the town center, A Chau has an English menu and serves good *banh xeo* (fried pancakes) as well as several dishes with rice.

CHAU DOC: Bay Bong $
Vietnamese Map B6
22 Thuong Dang Le
This simple eatery with tiny stools and plastic tables serves excellent clay-pot dishes and sour fish soup.

For more information on types of restaurants *see page 242*

Open dining area of Bassac, overlooking the Bassac river

CHAU DOC: Bassac $$$
Vietnamese/International
Map B6
32 Le Loi, Victoria Chau Doc Hotel
Tel *(076) 386 5010*
The best spot in Chau
Doc for a romantic evening
meal on the terrace, with views
of the Bassac River. Order the
roasted duck or the local fish,
and wash it down with a fine
glass of wine.

CON DAO ISLAND:
Saigon Con Dao $$
Vietnamese **Map** B6
18–24 Ton Duc Thang
Tel *(064) 383 0336*
Among the best of the few
eating options in Con Son
Town. Serves fantastic seafood
that can be enjoyed in the
smart dining room or out on
the breezy terrace.

HA TIEN: Hai Van $
Vietnamese/International
Map B6
57 Sam Lon
Next to the hotel of the same
name, Vai Han has been
decorated in a simplistic way. It is
known for its consistently good
Vietnamese fare as well as
excellent Western breakfasts.

MY THO: Chuong Duong
Restaurant $$
Vietnamese **Map** B6
10, 30 Thang 4
Tel *(073) 387 0875*
Located on the banks of the
Tien Giang River, with a menu
that is slanted towards river fish
and seafood, but there are
plenty of alternatives. Also
has rooms that are popular
among foreign tourists.

Key to Price Guide *see page 246*

PHU QUOC ISLAND: Oasis $
Vietnamese/International **Map** A6
118/5 Tran Hung Dao
Located in the lane behind
La Veranda Resort, a find for
anyone craving comfort food
like mashed potatoes or pies.
Gets busy in the evening with
sports on TV and a pool table.

DK Choice

PHU QUOC ISLAND:
Palm Tree $
Vietnamese **Map** A6
Tran Hung Dao
The simple furnishings and
decor can be misleading,
as the kitchen turns out
consistently tasty, well-cooked
food. Try one of the clay-pot
dishes, or go for the seafood
barbecue in high season.
There are no sea views to
boast of, but the food makes
up for it.

PHU QUOC ISLAND:
Pepper Tree $$$
Vietnamese/International **Map** A6
La Veranda Resort, Long Beach
Tel *(077) 398 2988*
Phu Quoc's fanciest restaurant,
situated on a veranda overlooking
the beach at La Veranda Resort.
Excellent preparation and presen-
tation of a small range of dishes.

SOC TRANG: Quan Com Hung $
Vietnamese **Map** B6
6/24 Hung Vuong
Tel *(079) 382 2268*
As few tourists visit Soc Trang,
ordering can be difficult. Use
a phrase book or simply point to
a dish that appeals. Try the goat
curry or pickled shrimps.

VINH LONG: Thien Tan $
Vietnamese **Map** B6
56/1 Pham Thai Buong
Tel *(070) 382 4001*
It is worth heading south of
the town center to check out
this eatery that specializes in
barbecued dishes. The fish
baked in a bamboo tube is
particularly delicious.

South Central Vietnam

BUON MA THUOT: Black
& White $$
Vietnamese **Map** C5
171 Nguyen Cong Tru
Tel *(0500) 384 4960*
Smartly decorated restaurant
is located right opposite the
Dam San Hotel, a short walk
from the town center. Has
a wide range of well-prepared
dishes on the menu.

DALAT: An Lac $
Vegetarian **Map** C5
71 Phan Dinh Phung
Tel *(063) 382 2025*
A nice variety of vegetarian
options that make the most
of the bountiful fresh produce
that fills the markets of this town.
Also has some dishes that
include mock meat.

DALAT: Café V $
Vietnamese/International **Map** C5
1/1 Bui Xui Thuan
Tel *(063) 352 0215*
Homely place run by an
American-Vietnamese couple
that serves some well-prepared
Vietnamese dishes such as
barbecued pork, as well as
home-made cakes and pies.

DALAT: Long Hoa $
Vietnamese/International **Map** C5
6, 3 Thang 2
Tel *(063) 382 2914*
Bistro-style restaurant right in the
town center, with wonderful hot
pots and soups, as well as some
superb home-made yogurt.
There is a room out back if it is
busy in front.

DALAT: Café de la Poste $$
International **Map** C5
Tran Phu
Tel *(063) 382 5444*
Operated by the Du Parc Hotel
and located opposite the post
office, this classy French-style
café serves a filling buffet
breakfast as well as sandwiches,
steaks and pasta. Daily à la carte
menu includes Western and
Asian delicacies.

DALAT: Le Rabelais $$$
French **Map** C5
Dalat Palace Hotel, 12 Tran Phu
Tel *(063) 382 5444*
By far Dalat's most upscale eating option, both in quality and price. Top-notch French cuisine served in a majestic setting by wait staff who gladly help with suggestions.

KONTUM: Dakbla $
Vietnamese/International **Map** C4
168 Nguyen Hue
Tel *(060) 386 2584*
Small, quirky café that is a big favorite among travelers, not only for its tasty stir-fries, sandwiches, and coffee, but also for its display of hill-tribe paraphernalia, much of which is for sale.

MUI NE: Shree Ganesh $
Indian **Map** C6
57 Nguyen Dinh Chieu
Tel *(062) 374 1330*
A reliable choice for a hearty meal, featuring North Indian cuisine and tandoori dishes. There is a balcony upstairs and the music creates an intimate atmosphere.

MUI NE BEACH: Lam Tong $
Vietnamese/International **Map** C6
92 Nguyen Dinh Chieu
Tel *(062) 384 7598*
No-frills eatery located on the beach. Serves better and tastier food than most fancy restaurants in Mui Ne, at a fraction of the price.

MUI NE BEACH: Rung (Forest) $$
Vietnamese **Map** C6
67 Nguyen Dinh Chieu
Tel *(062) 384 7589*
Kids love Rung because it is like dining in the jungle, surrounded by vines and running streams. The food is great too, and traditional musicians perform in the evening.

DK Choice

MUI NE BEACH: Champa $$$
Mediterranean **Map** C6
Coco Beach Resort, 58 Nguyen dinh Chieu
Tel *(062) 384 7111* **Closed** *Mon*
Open for dinner only, Champa offers a romantic setting on a terrace overlooking the resort's swimming pool and a coconut grove. The menu includes tempting dishes such as roast lobster in whisky and veal tenderloin in black pepper-sesame crust. Save room for the heavenly chocolate fudge.

NHA TRANG: Da Fernando $$
Italian **Map** C5
96 Nguyen Thien Thuat
Tel *(058) 352 8034*
The place to go to for consistently good pizzas and pastas as well as delicious mains like steak with green peppercorns. Also has a good range of Italian wines.

NHA TRANG: Lanterns $$
Vietnamese **Map** C5
34/6 Nguyen Thien Thuat
Tel *(058) 247 1674*
Another restaurant that trains disadvantaged youth for a stable career in hospitality. They serve excellent seafood hotpot and fish in clay pot, and offer cooking classes too.

NHA TRANG: Louisiane Brewhouse $$
International **Map** C5
29 Tran Phu
Tel *(058) 352 1948*
Beachfront brewery that has an extensive menu of Vietnamese, Japanese, and other international dishes, as well as delicious home brewed beer.

NHA TRANG: Sandals $$
International **Map** C5
72–74 Tran Phu
Tel *(058) 352 4628*
Fancy restaurant, right on the beach, with a choice of indoor or outdoor seating and a wide range of dishes such as beef carpaccio and shellfish paella.

QUANG NGAI: Cung Dinh $$
Vietnamese **Map** C4
5 Ton Duc Thang
Tel *(055) 381 8555*
One of the best in town, in a riverside location; serves an excellent seafood salad as well as dishes like *don* (snail soup).

QUY NHON: Seafood 2000 $$
Vietnamese/Seafood **Map** C5
1 Tran Doc
Tel *(056) 381 2787*
Eating on the Vietnamese coast is all about seafood, and this place is often packed with regulars enjoying giant prawns, shark steaks, and seafood hotpot.

Central Vietnam

CHINA BEACH: My Hanh $$
Seafood **Map** C4
My Khe Beach
Tel *(0511) 383 1494*
One of many seafood spots on My Khe Beach. Very popular with locals, but keep an eye on the pricing of what is ordered.

DANANG: Bread of Life $
International **Map** C4
4 Dong Da
Tel *(0511) 356 5185* **Closed** *Sun*
This unusual café, run by an American family, serves comfort food like burgers and pizza. Staffed entirely by the deaf, it gives them a chance to lead an independent life.

DANANG: Waterfront $$
Vietnamese/International **Map** C4
150–152 Bach Dang
Tel *(0511) 384 3373*
A smart new spot occupying two levels – a bar downstairs and a restaurant with good river views upstairs. Try the fettuccini marinara or the barbecued pork ribs. Offers a wide range of drinks.

DANANG: Apsara $$$
Vietnamese **Map** C4
222 Tran Phu
Tel *(0511) 356 1409*
Danang's swankiest restaurant, with Cham-style decor and a replica Cham tower in the garden. The menu features classic Vietnamese cuisine, including lots of seafood.

DK Choice

HOI AN: Miss Ly $
Vietnamese **Map** C4
22 Nguyen Hue
Tel *(0510) 386 1603*
In a town awash with fancy restaurants serving beautifully presented food, when it comes to taste, this simple, family-run eatery tucked away on a quiet street, is hard to beat. Try the local white rose dumplings (stuffed with shrimp), *cao lau* (a delicious noodle soup with bean sprouts and pork), and fish grilled in banana leaves.

A usual day at Lanterns, serving their best seafood and fish in clay pot

For more information on types of restaurants *see page 242*

HOI AN: Morning Glory $
Vietnamese **Map** C4
106 Nguyen Thai Hoc
Tel *(0510) 324 1555*
One of several eating places
operated by local restaurateur
Trinh Diem Vy, Morning Glory
is set in a Colonial-style building
and serves tasty *banh xeo*
(pancakes stuffed with shrimp
and bean sprouts).

HOI AN: Nhu Y (Mermaid) $
Vietnamese **Map** C4
2 Tran Phu
Tel *(0510) 386 1527*
Simple eatery that is hugely
popular for its special fried
wontons, squid stuffed with
pork, and stuffed tomatoes.
They also offer cooking classes.

HOI AN: Red Bridge $
Vietnamese **Map** C4
Thon 4, Cam Thanh
Tel *(0510) 393 3222*
A stylish, out-of-town restaurant,
that is tempting enough to
spend a day at – attend
cookery classes, enjoy a
delicious lunch, or simply
lounge by the pool. Dinner
is by appointment only.

HOI AN: Tam Tam Café & Bar $
International **Map** C4
110 Nguyen Thai Hoc
Tel *(0510) 386 2212*
A hugely popular spot among
visitors. Serves good French,
Italian, and Mediterranean
cuisine, as well as some
Vietnamese dishes. It also
has one of the town's most
popular bars.

Food served at the out-of-town restaurant
Red Bridge

HOI AN: Mango Rooms $$
Fusion **Map** C4
111 Nguyen Thai Hoc
Tel *(0510) 391 0839*
The names of dishes on the
menu are as innovative as the
preparation itself. The exotic
dance is shrimp wrapped in slices
of beef and la cubana is beef
served with mango salsa.

HUE: La Boulangerie Francaise $
French **Map** C3
46 Nguyen Tri Phuong
Tel *(054) 383 7437*
Established to give disadvan-
taged kids a chance to learn a
profession, this French bakery
serves excellent baguettes and
pastries, and is an especially
good breakfast choice.

HUE: Lac Thien $
Vietnamese **Map** C3
6 Dinh Tien Hoang
Tel *(054) 352 7348*
One of a trio of places operated
by a mute family with a real flair
for cookery. They specialize in
Hue cuisine, with dishes such as
banh xeo (pancakes stuffed with
pork, shrimp, and bean sprouts).

HUE: Les Jardins de la
Carambole $$
Vietnamese/French **Map** C3
32 Dang Tran Con
Tel *(054) 354 8815*
Set in an attractive Colonial
villa in the old city, this eatery
serves wonderful French cuisine
as well as some Vietnamese
dishes. The friendly French
owner is often around to
make recommendations.

HUE: Ong Tao $$
Vietnamese **Map** C3
31 Chu Van An
Tel *(054) 352 2031*
A bit tricky to find, but worth
tracking down for its local
specialties like fried chicken
wings in fish sauce and stewed
duck with Chinese herbs.

HUE: Le Parfum $$$
Vietnamese/International **Map** C3
La Residence Hotel, 5 Le Loi
Tel *(054) 383 7475*
Located in La Residence Hotel, Le
Parfum serves some of the best
Western food in Hue. Go for the
lamb with rosemary or the
steamed fish of the day. The ambi-
ence is sophisticated and relaxing.

LANG CO BEACH: Thanh Tam $$
Vietnamese **Map** C3
Thanh Tam Resort, Lang Co Beach
Tel *(054) 387 4456*
It is worth stopping at this
resort's restaurant, so well-known

for its seasonal oyster specialties.
Breathe the sea air and sample
fresh seafood. Diners are allowed
to use the pool here.

Hanoi

French Quarter

Pho 24 $
Vietnamese **Map** 2 E4
31 Hang Khay
Tel *(04) 3976 2424*
Doing for the Vietnamese
national dish what McDonald's
did for burgers, Pho 24 outlets
serve *pho* in various forms and in
spotless, hygienic surroundings.

Quan An Ngon $
Vietnamese **Map** 2 D4
18 Phan Boi Chau
Tel *(04) 3942 8162*
Successful restaurant serving
a fantastic range of regional
specialties. Has pleasant indoor
and outdoor seating, but be
prepared for crowds at peak hours.

Al Fresco's $$
International **Map** 2 E4
23L Hai Ba Trung
Tel *(04) 3826 7782*
Just the place to indulge a
craving for generous portions of
comfort food, such as ribs, steaks,
or pizza. Has delicious desserts as
well as beer and coffee.

Cay Cau $$
Vietnamese **Map** 2 F5
De Syloia Hotel, 17A Tran Hung Dao
Tel *(04) 3933 1010*
Set in the refined surroundings
of the Colonial-style De Syloia
Hotel, this classy dining room
serves excellent Vietnamese
fare. There is live traditional
music from 7 to 9pm.

Indochine $$
Vietnamese **Map** 1 C4
38 Thi Sach
Tel *(04) 3942 4097*
Very much a tourist spot, but
worth visiting for the attractive
Colonial house in which it is set,
and the wide range of classic
Vietnamese dishes.

Pots 'n Pans $$
Vietnamese **Map** 2 E5
57 Bui Thi Xuan
Tel *(04) 3944 0205*
Staffed by graduates of the
KOTO Academy (Know One,
Teach One), service here is
impeccable and the ambience
sophisticated. The innovative
menu features dishes like slow-
cooked lamb shoulder in
aromatic spices.

San Ho $$
Vietnamese/Seafood   **Map** 2 D4
58 Ly Thuong Kiet
Tel *(04) 3934 9184*
Specializes in seafood dishes, and is often busy with big groups enjoying a feast and downing a few pitchers of beer. Live piano music in the evening. Attentive staff.

Le Beaulieu $$$
French   **Map** 2 F4
Sofitel Legend Metropole, 15 Ngo Quyen
Tel *(04) 3826 6919*
Set in Hanoi's top hotel, La Beaulieu serves French cuisine prepared using only the best ingredients. The Sunday brunch is the stuff of legends, but be prepared to pay for the experience.

Ly Club $$$
Vietnamese/International
Map 2 F4
4 Le Phung Hieu
Tel *(04) 3936 3069*
One of the city's most exclusive restaurants, Ly Club features a cocktail bar on the ground floor, and dining with performances of traditional music (7–9pm) on the first floor.

Hai Ba Trung District

Wild Rice $$
Vietnamese   **Map** 2 E5
6 Ngo Thi Nham
Tel *(04) 3943 8896*
A restored Colonial building provides a very classy ambience in which to enjoy traditional Vietnamese cuisine with a modern twist. Try the grilled chicken with chili and lemongrass or the braised eggplant with pork.

Old Quarter

Cha Ca La Vong $
Vietnamese   **Map** 2 E2
14 Cha Ca
Tel *(04) 3825 3929*
Serves *cha ca thang long* (a famous Hanoi fish dish served with dill, chives, and bean sprouts) in a no-frills setting. Quite touristy, but the food is authentic.

Little Hanoi $
International   **Map** 2 E3
21–23 Hang Gai
Tel *(04) 3928 5333*
A friendly and convenient little eatery located near the north end of Hoan Kiem Lake – a good spot to escape the bustling traffic outside. The

Elegant exterior of the exclusive restaurant, Ly Club

menu includes favorites like baguette sandwiches, fried chicken, burgers, and salads.

DK Choice

New Day $
Vietnamese   **Map** 2 E2
72 Ma May
Tel *(04) 3828 0315*
Sometimes the simplest things are best. That is certainly the case with New Day, a no-frills eatery in the heart of the Old Quarter, where the food is better than in many of the city's more expensive restaurants. Serves fantastic spring rolls and spare ribs at rock-bottom prices.

Tandoor $
Indian   **Map** 2 E3
24 Hang Be
Tel *(04) 3824 5359*
Unpretentious Indian restaurant with a convenient Old Quarter location. Serves a good range of dishes, including vegetarian and non-vegetarian *thalis*. Go up to the second floor to escape the street noise.

Highway 4 $$
Vietnamese   **Map** 2 F3
3 Hang Tre
Tel *(04) 3926 4200*
Probably the most convenient of this unusual restaurant and bar's several outlets, Highway 4 serves not only great Vietnamese cuisine but also locally brewed spirits.

Khazaana $$
Indian   **Map** 2 F3
11 Ly Thai To
Tel *(04) 3934 5657*
Head here for delicious Indian food served in a stylish setting. Presentation and service is excellent, and the set lunch is reasonably priced.

DK Choice

Green Tangerine $$$
Fusion   **Map** 2 E3
48 Hang Be
Tel *(04) 3825 1286*
One of Hanoi's most atmospheric restaurants, set in an old Colonial house and courtyard. The ever-changing menu that blends the best of French and Vietnamese cooking techniques is wonderfully inventive. Opting for the set lunch is a good way to taste two or three dishes without breaking the bank.

Tay Ho

Restaurant Bobby Chinn $$$
Fusion   **Map** 2 E4
77 Xuan Dieu
Tel *(04) 3934 8577*
Run by celebrity chef Bobby Chinn, this dimly lit place with wild artwork on the walls features a short menu of fusion dishes. Try the BBQ pork ribs with Asian slaw.

West of Hoan Kiem Lake

Hoa Sua $
International   **Map** 1 C1
34 Chau Long
Tel *(04) 3942 4448*
A training school for disadvantaged youth set in and around a lovely old Colonial villa. A great way to support a cause while enjoying a scrumptious meal.

Khai's Brothers $$
Vietnamese   **Map** 1 C3
26 Nguyen Thai Hoc
Tel *(04) 3733 3866*
Hosts a great buffet spread in a Colonial building. There are a range of delicious dishes for both lunch and dinner.

For more information on types of restaurants *see page 242*

Mediterraneo $$
Italian   Map 2 E3
23 Nha Tho
Tel *(04) 3826 6288*
Traditional Italian restaurant, with
a real trattoria vibe. Conveniently
located near St Joseph's Cathedral
and the trendy shops on Nha Tho.

Moca Café $$
Vietnamese/International
Map 2 E3
14–16 Nha Tho
Tel *(04) 3825 6334*
Serving both Western and
classic Vietnamese cuisine,
Moca is a great eating option
for shoppers on Nha Tho looking
for a relaxed meal.

Thuy Ta $$
International   Map 2 F3
1 Le Thai To
Tel *(04) 3828 6290*
Popular café ideally located on
the northwest shore of Hoan
Kiem Lake. Draws in sightseers
for refreshing drinks, baguettes,
cakes, and ice creams.

Vine $$$
International   Map 2 D1
1A Xuan Dieu
Tel *(04) 3719 8000*
A delight for wine connoiseurs,
with its walls lined with
wine racks. Good meal options
from a menu consisting
mostly of Italian and Mexican
cuisine. Excellent preparation
and service.

Northern Vietnam

BAC HA: Cong Fu $
Vietnamese   Map A1
Cong Fu Hotel
Tel *(020) 388 0254*
Tiny Bac Ha has few dining
options. Cong Fu, in the center
of town, may not be gourmet
dining, but the food served is
tasty and cheap.

CAT BA ISLAND:
Green Mango $$
Vietnamese/International Map C1
231, 1 Thang 4
Tel *(031) 388 7151*
Classy place serving a fantastic
range of food, from muesli and
yogurt to pan-roast salmon and
smoked duck rolls. Prices are a bit
steep, but service and quality are
top-notch.

DIEN BIEN PHU: Lien Tuoi $
Vietnamese   Map A1
Hoang Van Thai
Tel *(023) 382 4919*
Stands out among the few
good eating establishments
in Dien Bien Phu, and has a
menu in English. Offers decent
Vietnamese and Chinese dishes
at cheap prices.

HAIPHONG: Com Vietnam $
Vietnamese   Map B1
4 Hoang Van Thu
Tel *(031) 384 1698*
A simple, welcoming eatery near
the town center that serves a
wide range of Vietnamese
staples, including spring rolls,
noodle soups, and fried rice.

HAIPHONG: Nam Phuong $$
Vietnamese   Map B1
12 Tran Phu
Tel *(031) 382 7827*
This elegant restaurant in the
Harbour View is only open for
dinner, but is worth visiting for its
excellent preparation of classic
Vietnamese dishes. Try the grilled
sea bass with lemongrass.

HALONG CITY:
Asia Restaurant $$
Vietnamese   Map C1
24 Vuon Dao, Bai Chay
Tel *(033) 364 0028*
Perhaps the best of the many
restaurants near the pier in
Halong City. The menu features
a wide range of Vietnamese
dishes and the service is
generally efficient.

HALONG CITY: Bien Mo
Floating Restaurant $$
Vietnamese   Map C1
35 Ben Tau, Hong Gai
Tel *(033) 382 8951*
Most visitors to Halong Bay
hope to eat great seafood
while floating on the water,
and this upscale place provides
the perfect opportunity.

NINH BINH: Hoang Hai $$
Vietnamese   Map B2
36 Truong Han Sieu
Tel *(030) 387 5177*
Located at the Hoang Hai
Hotel, this is probably the
best spot to eat in down-
town Ninh Binh. The specialty
is goat meat cooked in
different ways.

DK Choice

SAPA: Nature Bar & Grill $
Vietnamese   Map A1
24 Cau May
Tel *(091) 227 0068*
Set in a huge Alpine-style loft
with fireplaces glowing in
winter, Nature Bar & Grill
specializes in grilled food
served on hot, stone plates.
Go for the beef or venison
dishes, accompanied by spring
rolls and maybe a steamboat to
warm the insides. The service
is very attentive and the
owner is usually on hand
with recommendations.

SAPA: Baguette & Chocolat $$
International   Map A1
Thac Bac
Tel *(020) 387 1766*
Part of the Hoa Sua School,
this stylish café trains disadvantaged youth for a career
in catering. It is a real find, with
comfortable seating, great
coffee and cakes, as well as
main meals.

SAPA: Delta $$
Italian   Map A1
33 Cau May
Tel *(020) 387 1799*
Follow up a walk in the hills round
Sapa by gorging on wood-fired
oven pizzas, pastas, Australian
steaks, or lasagna at this lovely
place in the town center.
The wine bar upstairs has an
extensive collection.

SAPA: Viet Emotion $$
International   Map A1
27 Cau May
Tel *(020)387 2559*
Has something for everyone –
from tapas to big breakfasts,
home-made soups to tasty mains

Walls stacked with bottles of wine at Vine

Garden terrace of Nest Angkor, roofed with stylish canvas

like salmon with sticky rice. There is Wi-Fi and books to browse as well.

Angkor

SIEM REAP: Café Central $
International   Map A5
Cnr of sts 9 and 11
Tel (017) 692 997
Right in the town center, a good spot either for a quick coffee and cake, or a meal of fish and chips or a burger. Kid's menu and Wi-Fi available.

SIEM REAP: Common Grounds $
International   Map A5
719–721 St 14
Tel (063) 965 687
With a mission to fund humanitarian relief schemes in the country, this American-style café not only serves tasty fare but also supports a good cause. Great breakfasts, home-made soups, and juices.

SIEM REAP: Khmer Kitchen $
Khmer   Map A5
Pub St
Tel (063) 964 154
A great place to get to know Khmer cuisine, from amok (a thick, mild curry with steamed fish) to beef lok lak (a spicy marinade) and baked pumpkin. They offer cooking classes too.

SIEM REAP: The Soup Dragon $
Fusion   Map A5
369 St 8
Tel (063) 964 933
Simple place covering three floors, with some of the cheapest and tastiest food in Siem Reap on offer. Famous for its pho

(Vietnamese noodle soup) and its amok – a thick curry with steamed fish or meat.

SIEM REAP: El Camino Taqueri $$
Mexican   Map A5
The Passage
Tel (092) 207 842
Right in the heart of Siem Reap, El Camino typifies the global nature of this tourist town. Tuck into tacos, fajitas, enchiladas, and burritos, and wash them down with a margarita.

SIEM REAP: FCC Angkor $$
International   Map A5
Pokambor Ave
Tel (063) 760 283
One of Siem Reap's more upscale restaurants, set in the ultra-modern FCC Hotel. Serves international favorites like steak and pasta, as well as some local dishes.

SIEM REAP: Red Piano $$
International   Map A5
Pub St
Tel (063) 963 240
Patronized by Angelina Jolie during the making of 'Tomb Raider', a popular bar and restaurant located on two floors of a corner property. The menu includes steaks and sandwiches as well as Thai and Indian curries.

SIEM REAP: Sugar Palm $$
Khmer   Map A5
Ta Phul Rd
Tel (063) 964 838
For those wondering where restaurant owners go to eat in Siem Reap, this is the answer. Serves superb Khmer dishes like fish amok and chargrilled eggplant with pork on a breezy terrace.

SIEM REAP: Terrasse des Elephants $$
International   Map A5
Sivatha Rd
Tel (063) 965 570
Named after one of the main sights at Angkor, Terrasse des Elephants enjoys great views from an elevated terrace. Offers Western dishes and Khmer food.

SIEM REAP: Viroth's $$
Khmer   Map A5
246 Wat Bo Rd
Tel (012) 826 346
With its lovely setting, surrounded by bamboo and greenery, this is the perfect spot to sample Khmer food at its best. Try the pineapple and shrimp salad or the Khmer sour soup.

SIEM REAP: Cuisine Wat Damnak $$$
Fusion   Map A5
Wat Damnak Village
Tel (077) 347 762 **Closed** Sun & Mon
The French chef here hunts out unusual ingredients to prepare modern takes on traditional Cambodian dishes. Also offers a degustation menu. Dinner only.

DK Choice

SIEM REAP: Nest Angkor $$$
International/Khmer   Map A5
Sivatha Rd
Tel (063) 966 381
The menu at this striking restaurant is refreshingly different and offers items such as beef tenderloin with river lobster and grilled honey duck breast. There are also sushi and noodle dishes, plus a comprehensive range of cocktails. The garden terrace is roofed with a stylish canvas.

For more information on types of restaurants see page 242

SHOPPING IN VIETNAM

Until a few decades ago, the most memorable thing about a Vietnamese store was the emptiness of its shelves. Today, the scene has changed dramatically, as shops all across the country are overflowing with a variety of products, including distinctive conical hats, fine silk, designer clothes, colorful lamps, delicate ceramic ware, and elegantly carved bamboo furnishings – all available at affordable rates. Perhaps the most coveted of all goods are the traditional wares, such as exquisitely embroidered textiles, handicrafts, and jewelry made by Vietnam's ethnic minorities. While upmarket malls are present in major cities, the local markets and the shopping streets and districts of Hanoi and Ho Chi Minh City are the best places to shop. However, Hoi An, with its amazing array of lacquerware, apparel, and crafts is the ultimate shopper's paradise.

Textiles for sale in a White Thai village, Mai Chau

Opening Hours

Most city shops open at about 8am and do not close until late in the evening at 8pm or 9pm. The newer malls and department stores in big cities open by 10am and close as late as 10pm. Keep in mind that staff tend to start shutting down an hour before the posted closing time. The traditional markets, such as Ben Thanh *(see p70)* in Ho Chi Minh City and Dong Xuan *(see p162)* in Hanoi, generally operate from sunrise to sunset. Some of these offer a thriving night market on the street outside as well, which runs until midnight. Virtually all retail operations operate seven days a week. However, during Tet *(see pp32–3)*, some shops shut for a few days, while others open later than usual.

How to Pay

Though the Vietnamese *dong* (VND) is the only legal tender in the country, nobody would refuse a US dollar. In areas that are very popular with visitors, especially the more expensive districts, most shops prefer to quote prices in dollars rather than *dong*. The reason being that dollars are more profitable for sellers than the *dong* because of its fluctuating exchange rate. Hence, as the buyer, always try and pay in *dong* as it will be cheaper.

Major credit cards are accepted in high-end shops, hotels, and restaurants in big cities and major resort towns. However, in small towns and villages, as well as at local bus stations, markets, street food stalls, and other such places, only cash is accepted.

Rights and Refunds

As a rule, all sales are final. Though some department stores in big cities may offer a return policy, by and large, once money, goods, or any services have changed hands, there is no going back. Some goods, especially electronic items such as cell phones, do come with a guarantee. But even here, it covers replacement, not refund.

Bargaining

Unless you are in an upscale shop, mall, or national bookstore chain, the asking price of goods is not necessarily the final price. Except for food and drink, which have smaller margins, the rate quoted is twice or even more than what the merchant is willing to settle for. As such, be prepared to bargain.

Effective negotiation requires three things. First and most importantly is a pleasant attitude, even a sense of humor. Remember that this is not just a commercial transaction, it's a social encounter. Secondly, be ready to spend some time. You cannot get the price down from US$50 to US$25 easily. A transaction of that magnitude can take up to ten minutes. And lastly, try walking away. At times, this prompts a drastic reduction in price.

Huge selection of handbags at a shop in Binh Tay Market, Ho Chi Minh City

Gleaming exterior of the exclusive Diamond Plaza, Ho Chi Minh City

Department Stores and Malls

Luxury shopping malls and department stores are now present in most big cities. **Vincom Shopping Center**, in Ho Chi Minh City, is one of the country's largest retail centers, with international brands and foreign fast-food chains. Another high-end shopping mall is **Diamond Plaza**, which also boasts a movie theater and bowling alley.

Nearby is **Parkson**, a classy, four-story department store, boasting brands such as Nike, Guess, Estée Lauder, and Mont Blanc among others. It also has a supermarket and several eateries. The centrally located **Tax Trading Center** hosts numerous stores, and offers better prices than most, and **Zen Plaza**, with six floors of outlets and cafés, is ideal for anything from clothing to furniture and artifacts. Close by is **Saigon Shopping Center**, with a supermarket, book store, and numerous toy and electronics stores. In the Cholon district, **An Duong Plaza** has many stores offering a range of goods, including a wide variety of Asian items.

In Hanoi, **Trang Tien Plaza** is an international level shopping center, hosting several brands, both foreign and local, while **Big C Thang Long** supermarket is not just a great place to buy quality foodstuffs. This two-story mall has goods ranging from fresh food to appliances, garments, home decorations, and electronics. However, the biggest of all is the **Vincom Mega Mall** at Royal City,

which boasts an indoor water park and skating rink as well as a bowling alley and cinemas.

Markets and Street Vendors

While modern malls are cropping up in large cities, the traditional markets are still the best places to shop. They are considerably cheaper, and ideal stopping points to absorb the city's atmosphere. The biggest markets in Ho Chi Minh City are Ben Thanh (see p70) in District 1 and Binh Tay (see p75) in Cholon. Both carry an amazing selection of products, from clothing and groceries to appliances and furnishings. For imported foods, drinks, personal items, accessories, and much more, the **Old Market** is worth a visit.

In Hanoi, Dong Xuan Market (see p162) is a favorite among visitors, and carries a vast array of household goods, as well as clothing, souvenirs, and more. For a great selection of fabrics, visit **Hang Da Market**. You can also get clothes tailored here.

One of the most charming markets in Vietnam is in Hoi An (see p132). While the day market teems with clothes, lacquer and ceramic ware, silk, footwear, and handicrafts, the night market is ideal for a fascinating evening stroll.

In addition to local markets, the streets are overflowing with shops selling souvenirs, kitchenware, counterfeit goods, and clothes.

Colorful lamp shop, Dong Khoi, Ho Chi Minh City

Shopping Streets and Districts

All the streets in Hanoi's Old Quarter (see pp160–61) are named after the products once sold there. For example, Ma (paper) Street offers paper goods, Hon Gai (hemp) Street has rows upon rows of silk shops, Chieu (mats) Street has rush mats and bamboo blinds, and Thiec (tin) Street offers tin and glass items, as well as mirrors. Although the placement of products on these streets is not so strict today, they remain excellent places to browse the wide range of goods at bargain prices.

The main shopping area in Ho Chi Minh City is Dong Khoi (see pp60–61), with a huge selection of outlets selling clothing, antiques, arts and crafts, and home furnishings.

Counterfeit Goods

Counterfeit goods can be bought on almost any street corner in Vietnam. Articles for sale include Rolex watches, army dog tags, Zippo cigarette lighters with regimental markings, and DVDs, CDs, and video games.

Coffee and Tea

Vietnamese coffee is unique, and comes in a wide selection of flavors, including vanilla, anise, and chocolate. There are three varieties of coffee – Arabica, Robusta, and Weasel. While Arabica is the most expensive and richest, Robusta is cheaper. Weasel is also expensive and is made from coffee cherries eaten and defecated by chon, Vietnamese weasels. Vietnamese tea is a green tea scented with lotus flower. The best place to buy coffee or tea is at markets such as Ben Thanh in Ho Chi Minh City or Dong Xuan in Hanoi. Street vendors also sell them but overcharge.

Collection of bright and colorful crafts and artifacts, Hoi An

Arts and Crafts

Traditional arts and crafts are produced almost everywhere in Vietnam. Exquisitely embroidered linen, intricately carved artifacts and figurines, colorful silken lanterns, as well as stylized paintings are just some of the specialties available. For fine textiles, especially good quality, hand-embroidered silk by French and Japanese artists, visit **Chi Vang** in Hanoi. Also check out **Tan My** for gorgeous, hand-embroidered tablecloths, throws, and quilts. **Lan Handicrafts** also carries fine textiles, made by people with disabilities specifically for this non-profit outlet. A similar operation in Hoi An is at Hoa-Nhap Handicrafts. Dong Khoi district in Ho Chi Minh City is home to many silk merchants, such as **Bao Nghi**, which also carries linen and other fabrics.

Hill-tribe handicrafts made by ethnic minorities are available in Ho Chi Minh City at **Sapa** outlet, which offers a range of handwoven clothing, embroidered silks, and footwear. In Hanoi, **Craft Link**, **Viet Hien**, and **Craft Window** offer a wide selection of handicrafts, while in Hoi An, **House of Traditional Handicrafts** and Handicraft Workshop (see p132) are good. For pottery, tableware, and silk lamps, walk through Hoi An's streets, which are lined with many shops selling such items. Some great ceramics – tea sets, vases, and bowls – are available at **Em Em** in Ho Chi Minh City. **Hanoi Gallery** is a good place

to buy modern art. In Ho Chi Minh City's District 1, **Dogma** carries political art and **Galerie Quynh** showcases contemporary works by leading local and foreign artists. **Hoi An Art Gallery** in Hoi An is worth visiting.

Decorative souvenir statue

Clothing

Hoi An is the most popular place to buy clothes in all of Vietnam. Boutiques here can copy any outfit from any international fashion magazine in a few hours, and at one-third of the cost at home. The most stylish outlet, with extremely high quality goods and service, is **Yaly Couture**. They can also make a range of shoes, mostly women's. For cloth purchases and simple tailoring, check out the **Hoi An Cloth Market**. For silk outfits, try **Bibi Silk**, while **Bao Khanh Tailors** specialize in custom-made formal wear. You can also visit **Gia Thuong** for clothes, and **Thang** for shoes.

Dressmaker taking measurements of a client at a shop in Hoi An

In Hanoi, **Khai Silk** gets rave reviews, especially for formal attire, while **Ha Noi Silk** can tailor suits in 24 hours. For an excellent row of silk shops, walk down Hang Gai Street. For larger sizes, check out **Things of Substance**. In Ho Chi Minh City, **H&D Tailors** make outfits for men, and women can get an *ao dai*, a traditional Vietnamese dress, made at **Ao Dai Minh Thu**. Check out **Creations** for custom-made outfits.

Furniture

Furniture is regarded as an art form in Vietnam. Most of what is available is finely wrought hardwood, often inlaid with mother of pearl or richly carved. Special orders are gladly taken, and most shops also arrange to ship your purchases home. In Ho Chi Minh City, **Furniture Outlet** offers some of the best pieces and prices, while **Tien An** carries light furniture, specializing in bamboo chairs, cabinets, and grass mats. **The Lost Art** offers antique pieces and reproductions. In Hanoi, **Viet Hien** carries a range of furnishings. And in Hoi An, **Mosaique** offers not only furnishings but items of home decor as well.

Lacquerware and Ceramics

Vietnam is famous for its lacquerware and ceramics, such as decorative pieces, tea sets, vases, bowls, plates, trays, and paintings to name a few. Some lacquer products feature an amazingly delicate inlay of eggshells or mother of pearl, while several ceramic pieces bear intricate designs. Jewelry boxes are also commonly rendered in lacquer. In Ho Chi Minh City, the note-worthy **Gaya** carries works by renowned designer Michele de Alberts. **Quang's Ceramics** in Hanoi has a splendid collection, and Le Duan Street also has some good shops. In Hoi An, there are many such shops selling traditional Vietnamese goods.

DIRECTORY

Department Stores and Malls

An Duong Plaza
18 An Duong Vuong St,
Cholon, HCMC.
Map 4 F4.
Tel (08) 3832 3288.

Big C Thang Long
222 Tran Duy Hung St,
Hanoi.

Diamond Plaza
34 Le Duan St, Dist. 1,
HCMC. **Map** 2 E3.
Tel (08) 3825 7750.
W diamondplaza.
com.vn

Parkson Plaza
35-45 Le Than Ton St,
Phuong Ben Nghe,
HCMC. **Map** 2 E3.
Tel (08) 3827 7636.

Saigon Center
65 Le Loi St, Dist. 1, HCMC.
Map 2 E4.
Tel (08) 3829 4888.

Saigon Tax Trading Center
135 Nguyen Hue St,
Dist. 1, HCMC. **Map** 2 F4.
Tel (08) 3821 3849.
W thuongxatax.com.vn

Trang Tien Plaza
Hang Bai, Hanoi. **Map** 2
E4. **Tel** (04) 3934 9734.
W trangtienplaza.vn

Vincom Center
72 Le Thanh Ton St, Dist.
1, HCMC. **Map** 2 E3.
Tel (08) 3936 9999.

Vincom Mega Mall
72A Nguyen Trai, Thanh
Xuan, Hanoi. **Map** off
map. **Tel** (04) 3974 3550.
W vincomjsc.com

Zen Plaza
54 Nguyen Trai St, Dist. 1,
HCMC. **Map** 2 D5.
Tel (08) 3925 0339.

Markets

Hang Da Market
Cnr of Hang Ga and
Doung Thanh Sts, Hanoi.
Map 2 D2.

Old Market
Cnr of Ham Nghi and Ton
That Dam Sts, Dist. 1,
HCMC. **Map** 2 F4.

Arts and Crafts

Bao Nghi
127 Dong Khoi St, Dist.1,
HCMC. **Map** 2 F4.
Tel (08) 3823 4521.

Chi Vang
27 Trang Tien, Hanoi.
Map 2 F4.
Tel (04) 3828 6576.

Craft Link
43 Van Mieu St, Hanoi.
Map 1 B4.
Tel (04) 3733 6101.
W craftlink.com.vn

Craft Window
99 Nguyen Thai Hoc St,
Hanoi.
Map 1 C3.

Dogma
43 Ton That Thien St, Dist.
1, HCMC. **Map** 2 E4.
Tel (08) 3021 8272.

Em Em
38 Mac Thi Buoi St, Dist. 1,
HCMC. **Map** 2 F4.
Tel (08) 3829 4408.

Galerie Quynh
65 De Them St, Dist. 1,
HCMC. **Map** 2 D5.
Tel (08) 3836 8019.
W galeriequynh.com

Hanoi Gallery
110 Hang Bac St, Hanoi.
Map 2 E3.

Hoi An Art Gallery
6 Nguyen Thai Hoc, Hoi
An. **Tel** (0510) 386 1792.

House of Traditional Handicrafts
41 Le Loi St, Hoi An.
Tel (0510) 386 2164.

La Gai Handicrafts
103 Nguyen Thai Hoc
St, Hoi An.
Tel (0510) 391 0496.

Lan Handicrafts
38 Au Trieu, Hanoi. **Map** 1
E3. **Tel** (04) 3828 9278.

Sapa
223 De Tham, Dist. 1,
HCMC. **Map** 2 D5.
Tel (08) 3836 5163.

Tan My
66 Hang Gai St,
Hanoi. **Map** 2 E3.
Tel (04) 3825 1579.
W tanmyembroidery.
com.vn

Viet Hien
8B Ta Hien St,
Hanoi. **Map** 2 E2.
Tel (04) 3826 9769.

Clothing

Ao Dai Minh Thu
129 De Tham, Dist. 1,
HCMC. **Map** 2 D5.
Tel (08) 3836 1947.
W aodaiminhthu.com

Bao Khanh Tailors
101 Tran Hung Dao
St, Hoi An.
Tel (0510) 386 1818.

Bibi Silk
13 Phan Chu Trinh,
Hoi An.
Tel (091) 343 3260.

Creations
105 Dong Khoi St, Dist. 1,
HCMC. **Map** 2 F4.
Tel (08) 3829 5429.
W creations.vn

Gia Thuong
41 Nguyen Thai Hoc St,
Hoi An.
Tel (0510) 386 1816.

H&D Tailors
New World Hotel,
Pham Hong Thai St,
Dist. 1, HCMC. **Map** 2 E4.
Tel (08) 3824 3517.

Ha Noi Silk
Thankg Long Opera
Hotel, 1 Tong Dan St,
Hanoi. **Map** 2 F4.
Tel (04) 3926 3469.
W hanoisilkvn.com

Hoi An Cloth Market
Cnr of Tran Phu and
Hoang Dieu Sts, Hoi An.

Khai Silk
26 Nguyen Thai Hoc St,
Hanoi. **Map** 1 C3.
Tel (04) 3928 9883.
W khaisilkcorp.com

Thang
352 Nguyen Duy Hieu.
Tel (0510) 391 0076.

Things of Substance
5 Nha Tho, Hanoi.
Map 2 E3.
Tel (04) 3828 6965.
W prieure.com.vn

Yaly Couture
358 Nguyen Duy
Hieu, St, Hoi An.
Tel (0510) 391 4995.
W yalycouture.com

Furniture

Furniture Outlet
2C Nguyen Thanh St, Dist.
1, HCMC. **Map** 2 D1.
Tel (08) 2243 7955.

The Lost Art
45 Nguyen Huu Canh,
Binh Thanh Dist., HCMC.
Map off map
Tel (08) 3514 6080.
W saigonlostart.com

Mosaique
61A Phan Chu Trinh
St, Hoi An.
Tel (0510) 850 5000.
W mosaique
decoration.com

Viet Hien
See Arts and Crafts.

Lacquerware and Ceramics

Gaya
1 Nguyen Van Trang St,
Dist. 1, HCMC. **Map** 2 D5.
Tel (08) 3925 1495.
W gayavietnam.com

Quang's Ceramics
95 Ba Trieu St, Hanoi.
Map 2 E5.
Tel (04) 3945 4235.

What to Buy in Vietnam

Sprawling traditional markets, sidewalk hawkers, and even the odd shopping mall in Vietnam offer a wide range of attractive and unique items. Almost anything wearable is usually a good bargain, be it clothing, footwear, or jewelry, while handicrafts such as ceramics, basketry, lacquerware, and even paintings by local artists make splendid souvenirs. The most distinctive items on sale are the exquisite hand-embroidered goods and silver jewelry of the hill peoples. In direct contrast, but just as tempting, are the surfeit of counterfeit products found just about everywhere.

Hand-dyed silks of the White Tai decorated with distinctive patterns

Clothes, Shoes, and Accessories

The traditional *ao dai* is surely the best pick for women. The two-piece is available in cotton, silk, and synthetics in a variety of colors. Vietnam also offers affordable clothing ranging from cotton T-shirts to silk dresses and designer wear – often good value compared to the West. Vietnamese-style silk shirts and trousers are also tailored cheaply and quickly. Stoles and scarves embroidered or woven by hill peoples are well worth every *dong*.

Richly embroidered bags of the Red Dao minority

Finely woven stoles with beaded tassels

Flip-flops with bright designs

Tailored silk dress with a Chinese collar

Lacquerware

Bowl glazed with brightly dyed lacquer

The Viets learned to harvest lacquer from sumac trees about 2,000 years ago, and even today, the country offers the most beautiful lacquer souvenirs. Even the simplest boxes, vases, and jewelry are transformed into exquisite objets d'art once they have been covered in lacquer – a process that takes months to complete. The lacquer is generally applied on a wooden base, and is usually painted or embellished with intricate inlay work.

Pencil case with mother-of-pearl inlay work

Spice jars painted with traditional motifs

Lacquerware inlaid with eggshells

Mariners' compass set with zodiac symbols

Lacquered jewelry box, with carvings of birds and leaves

Ceramics

From giant pots to tiny teacups, Vietnamese potters create beautiful and useful ceramic artifacts, which are sold throughout the country. Most renowned are the items created by the artisans in Bat Trang near Hanoi. The area is known for the quality of its white clay, and the unique glazing styles, such as "ancient pearl glaze" and "indigo-blue flower glaze," which evolved here over the centuries.

Hand-painted
ceramic elephants

Chinese-style, blue-and-white
porcelain jar

Huge vases with swirling floral designs
over ivory glaze

Paintings

Vietnam is fast becoming a draw for art collectors. Watercolors and oils are found almost everywhere, but most exquisite are the unique lacquer and silk paintings. The finest art is found in the cultural hubs of Hanoi, Hoi An, and Hue.

Silver Jewelry of the Hill Peoples

Silver is a traditional symbol of wealth among many hill peoples. Antique earrings, chunky pendants, and bangles are commonly available in shops in major towns and villages. Ornate silver belts worn by women are especially attractive.

A colorful painting by a contemporary artist

Traditional Red Dao panel

Selection of silver earrings

Rattan trays used for
serving

Wooden fruit bowls

Traditional Vietnamese
conical hat

Wicker serving tray with ceramic
handles

Painted cosmetic box

Bamboo, Rush, Leaves, and Grass

Woven with great skill into interesting shapes and sizes, grass and rush mats are used as mattresses, seating, and curtains in Vietnam. Wicker trays and bowls are popular, as are embroidered bamboo window blinds and kitchenware. The traditional *non la* or conical hats are found everywhere, often made from thick dried palm leaves. In Hue, the hats often reveal subtly painted designs when held up to the light.

Brightly painted wicker
Tet mask

ENTERTAINMENT IN VIETNAM

The cultural climate in Vietnam is more vibrant, exciting, and promising than ever. Traditional music and theater, first performed centuries ago, are being strongly promoted through cultural festivals held all around the country. Although the nation's rich artistic heritage draws international audiences, major cities also offer night clubs and modern multiplexes. Stately concert halls stage opera recitals, even as local pop stars belt out the latest ballads on makeshift stages. Ho Chi Minh City's midnight curfew is over, and a surfeit of bars and nightclubs tempt with live music and expertly mixed cocktails until the early hours of the morning. Water puppetry thrives in Hanoi, and so does jazz. Turntables and techno beats are common in small cities. Betting is legal but only on greyhounds and horses. With its many contrasts and contradictions, Vietnam offers a heady mix of entertainment options to all.

Information

The official monthly magazine of the National Administration of Tourism, *Travellive* is packed with travel and lifestyle news from around the country, as is Vietnam Airlines' in-flight magazine *Heritage*. For maximum coverage of leisure and lifestyle issues and events, as well as up-to-date listings, pick up *The Word* and *Asia Life* monthly magazines. Found free of charge in many restaurants, bars, and hotels, *Vietnam Pathfinder* has reviews and travel and culture stories from around the country. The national English-language newspaper, *Viet Nam News*, and the monthly *Saigon Times* feature sections dedicated to upcoming events in both Ho Chi Minh City and Hanoi.

Booking Tickets

Buying tickets in advance is not yet the norm in Vietnam, but most hotels are very helpful, and will either book your tickets or purchase them in advance for you. Online booking is rare but some cinemas are adopting the practice. It is usual for most Vietnamese and visitors to buy tickets on arrival at the show's venue.

Traditional Theater, Music, and Dance

Traditional music, dance, and theater are inextricably linked in Vietnam, and one is usually incomplete without the other. Even as the nation races headlong toward modernization, these performing arts have been given great impetus by tourism and still thrive.

Hanoi is regarded as the cultural heart of Vietnam. Among other things, it is the birthplace of the nation's most delightfully idiosyncratic theatrical format, water puppetry *(see p163)*. The best place to see this unique art form, where marionettes enact wildly colorful tales on a watery stage, is the Thang Long Water Puppet Theater *(see p162)* at the **Kim Dong Theater** in Hanoi. The Golden Dragon Water Puppet Theater in Ho Chi Minh City holds daily performances, and **Binh Quoi Tourist Village** also includes water puppet shows in its range of cultural events. Various forms of theatrical arts are popular in Vietnam. The nation's traditional theater *(see pp28–9)* can be categorized into three primary dramatic modes, *hat boi, hat cheo,* and *cai luong*. All three types are sung – *hat* means sing – and are distinctly operatic in form. Characterized by extravagant costumes and makeup, as well as highly stylized acting, *hat boi* or *tuong* is clearly influenced by Chinese theater but is Vietnamese in flavor.

A pared-down and simplified version of *hat boi* is *hat cheo*. Similar to operetta, this also focuses on high drama and tragedy, but is leavened with humor. *Cai luong*, in contrast, originated in the early 20th century and is somewhat like a Broadway musical. The stage is elaborately decorated, and every scene is rife with melodrama. Regardless of the story or song lyrics, it features a set number of tunes representing emotions such as happiness, sadness, suspicion, and so on. Avid theatergoers know all the melodies by heart.

Today, traditional theater enjoys more widespread popularity in Hanoi than anywhere else in the country. *Hat cheo* performances are staged regularly in **National Cheo Theater**,

Elaborately costumed puppets, Water Puppet Theater, Hanoi

while the **Golden Bell Theater** features performances from various regions of the country in an hour-long show. On weekends, Den Ngoc Son (see p164) presents excerpts from hat cheo plays. Also check the local listings for theater performances at the Temple of Literature (see pp170–71).

Apart from opera, Vietnam's classical music features both vocal and instrumental compositions. Once subject to the strict regulations and conventions of Hue's imperial court, formal music got a new lease of life under French-colonial rule. Three styles – bac (northern), trung (central), and nam (southern) – eventually emerged. Vietnamese chamber music employs string, percussion, and wood-wind instruments, creating a distinctive sound. When used for traditional theater, brass is included in the orchestra to add dramatic resonance to the sound. Musicians play often in Ho Chi Minh City's Reunification Palace (see p63) but their performances do not follow a set schedule.

Like Hanoi and Ho Chi Minh City, most cities and towns have prominent cultural centers and theaters. In Hoi An, the **Traditional Arts Theater** hosts musical recitals and plays almost every night. **Classical Opera Theater** in Danang and Hue's Biennial Arts festival, held in June every even numbered year, keep ancient Vietnamese drama, dance, and music alive. Also in Hue, the Hon Chen Temple (see p152) presents music and dance performances and recitals in the third and seventh lunar months. Nha Trang's **Vien Dong Hotel** has a nightly program showcasing ethnic minority music and dance.

Traditional music performance in Ho Chi Minh City

Contemporary Music and Concerts

Vietnam's most celebrated concert halls are the Opera House (see p166) in Hanoi and the Municipal Theater (see p62) in Ho Chi Minh City. They present orchestral music, Western and Asian opera, as well as pop music concerts. The **Conservatory of Music** in Ho Chi Minh City is home to the local symphony, and hosts classical music, opera, and Jazz recitals regularly.

Given the country's balmy weather, the Vietnamese are extremely fond of outdoor concerts. In Ho Chi Minh City, the scenic **Van Hoa Park** is very popular, while Hanoians enjoy their favorite croon-ers around Hoan Kiem Lake (see p164). Most of these shows feature Vietnamese pop music, and on occasion, a chorus line dance by women in their traditional ao dai. Although these performances may be an acquired taste for most foreigners, the festive atmosphere is extremely infectious. Sports stadiums, such as Ho Chi Minh City's **Military Region 7 Stadium**, are also common concert venues. Young Vietnamese turn up in great numbers to watch the local stars perform live. Certain restaurants, bars, and fashion houses in Ho Chi Minh City and

Actor in full cai luong regalia

Hanoi also present lively concerts fairly often. These events are announced in the local media, but hotel concierges are also good sources of information. **Maxim's Dinner Theater**, one of the oldest such venues in Ho Chi Minh City, can be relied on for a fine meal and an enjoyable show. It showcases everything from string quartets and pop music to Vietnamese folk songs and the latest local rock acts.

Modern Theater

Although there are many fine and ambitious playwrights producing insightful dramas and comedies, modern theater is a connoisseur's art in this country. Plays, usually in Vietnamese, are generally staged in small, tucked-away theaters. One good venue for foreigners is the **Ho Chi Minh City Drama Theater**, where local works are presented with English subtitles. Hanoi's **Youth Theater** is one of the best theater operations in the country. Its director, Le Hung, studied his craft in Moscow where he was inspired by Stanislavsky and Brecht. He now brings those teachings to bear on contemporary Vietnam. Many plays performed by the repertory group have been written by Le himself, while others are adaptations of works by Vietnamese and foreign playwrights. Most interesting are the modernized versions of hat cheo, which are staged occasionally.

Open dining area of a restaurant in Ho Chi Minh City

Movies

Vietnamese movies are occasionally dubbed or subtitled for an English-speaking audience. Some movie halls in Hanoi, such as the **National Cinema Theater** and **Cinematheque**, are noteworthy venues for locally produced art and foreign-language films. In all major cities, **Megastar Cineplex** features the latest international releases. Foreign films are also very popular in smaller towns, although they are mostly seen on pirated video CDs and DVDs.

Nightclubs, Discos, and Bars

Even in the first few years of Vietnam's economic reforms or *doi moi*, it seemed that the only legal hedonistic pursuit available in Ho Chi Minh City was nursing a tepid beer in a backpacker hangout. Today, the city's nightlife is picking up at an encouraging pace. **Hien and Bob's Place**, one of the oldest bars around, set an example for a slew of other intimate little watering holes.

While many bars in Ho Chi Minh City seem to come and go almost on a weekly basis, some old favorites such as **Apocalypse Now** are still going strong. This is the most famous nightclub in Vietnam. Ho Chi Minh City's backpacker district, in and around Pham Ngu Lao Street, boasts a string of dingy bars and lively clubs. Among them, **163 Cyclo Bar** is the most upscale, with a great view of the street. For a quiet drink one can head for **La Fenetre Soleil**, a cool spot to sip a cocktail or smoke a shisha pipe. Both **Vasco's** and **O'Brien's** provide cold beers

along with filling bites to eat. Also worth a look is **Blue Gecko**, a popular bar, complete with a pool table and dart board. **The Spotted Cow** allows you to watch sports on its large screen as you down your beer. **Carmen Bar** is famous for its Latin and flamenco music, while **Lush** is the place to party with the city's top DJs.

Greater sophistication can be found at rooftop bars in Dong Khoi Street's posh hotels such as Rooftop Garden at the Rex *(see p64)*. Live bands play music as guests watch the city go by below. The same goes for Saigon Saigon in the Caravelle *(see p62)*, **Breeze Sky Bar**, and **Level 23**. **ZanZBar**, located on the city's main street, Dong Khoi, is a trendy and happening spot, while for an evening of mellow live jazz, few venues can match the atmospheric **Sax n Art**.

Hanoi may not be quite as glamorous as Ho Chi Minh City but its inhabitants know how to enjoy themselves. Tiny places where the local beer *bia hoi (see p243)* is the specialty are very popular. For those who want to avoid the rough and ready, **Restaurant Bobby Chinn** is a hip hangout with great wine, *shisha*, and the celebrity chef himself. Classical music on piano and violin is played at **Ly Club**, while **Seventeen Cowboys** is all about the Wild West. **Le Pub** is a great spot to spend your time relaxing.

Most interesting, though, is Hanoi's thriving jazz scene. A shifting network of clubs can be tracked through the local media, but the top spot is the superb **Binh Minh Jazz Club** where local sax master Quyen Van Minh jams almost every night.

In Hoi An, **Tam Tam Café & Bar** *(see p250)* has a decor redolent of old Indochina, but a hip DJ spins at night. **White Marble** serves the town's widest range of wines.

Nha Trang's **Louisiane Brewhouse** is a great place to spend an afternoon or evening, while **La Bella Napoli** serves the only glass of *grappa* in town. One of the best hangouts here is the **Sailing Club**, a laid-back bar by day and hip dance club by night. In Hue, the **DMZ Bar** oozes old-world charm, while the **Why Not Bar** is perfect for a long cocktail.

Karaoke clubs are generally fronts for prostitution and are best avoided as the government is currently cracking down on these bars.

Spectator Sports

Without doubt, football is the national passion. Local teams and leagues are revered, and the country seems to come to a halt for the World Cup. Most major matches take place at **Thong Nhat Stadium** in Ho Chi Minh City and **My Dinh National Stadium** in Hanoi. Following a close second is badminton, which the Vietnamese enjoy playing even more than they like to watch the national champions.

Gambling is an integral part of Vietnamese customs and culture but is mostly illegal in the country. However, the state-run lottery, the **Saigon Racing Club**, and **Lam Son Stadium**, where greyhounds race, are above board.

A horse race in progress at the famous Saigon Racing Club

DIRECTORY

Traditional Theater, Music, and Dance

Binh Quoi Tourist Village
1147 Xo Viet Nghe Tinh St, Binh Thanh Dist, HCMC. **Tel** (08) 3898 6696.

Classical Opera Theater
155 Phan Chu Trinh St, Danang.
Tel (0511) 356 1291.

Golden Bell Theater
72 Hang Bac St, Hanoi. **Map** 2 E3.
Tel (098) 830 7272
W goldenbellshow.vn

Golden Dragon Water Puppet Theater
55B Nguyen Thi Minh Khai St, Dist 1, HCMC. **Map** 2 D4.
Tel (08) 3827 2653
W goldendragon theatre.com

Kim Dong Theater
57B Dinh Tien Hoang St, Hanoi. **Map** 2 E3.
Tel (04) 3824 9494.

National Cheo Theater
15 Nguyen Dinh Chieu, Hanoi. **Tel** (04) 3934 7361.

Traditional Arts Theater
75 Nguyen Thai Hoc St, Hoi An.
Tel (0510) 386 1159.

Vien Dong Hotel
1 Tran Hung Dao St, Nha Trang.
Tel (058) 352 3608.

Contemporary Music and Concerts

Conservatory of Music
112 Nguyen Du St, Dist. 1, HCMC. **Map** 2 D4.
Tel (08) 3822 5841.
Maxim's Dinner Theater
13,15,17 Dong Khoi St, Dist. 1, HCMC. **Map** 2 F4.
Tel (08) 3822 5554.

Military Region 7 Stadium
2 Pho Quang St, Tan Binh, HCMC.

Van Hoa Park
115 Nguyen Du St, Dist. 1, HCMC. **Map** 2 D3.

Modern Theater

Ho Chi Minh City Drama Theater
30 Tran Hung Dao St, Dist. 1, HCMC. **Map** 2 E5.
Tel (08) 3836 9556.

Youth Theater
11 Ngo Thi Nham St, Hanoi. **Map** 2 E5.
Tel (04) 3943 8020.
W nhahattutuoitre.com

Movies

Cinematheque
22A Hai Ba Trung St, Hanoi. **Map** 2 F4.
Tel (04) 3936 2648.

Megastar Cineplex
W megastar.vn

National Cinema Theater
87 Lang Ha St, Hanoi.
Map 1 A3.
Tel (04) 3514 2278.

Nightclubs, Discos, and Bars

163 Cyclo Bar
163 Pham Ngu Lao St, Dist. 1, HCMC. **Map** 2 D5.
Tel (08) 3920 1567.

Apocalypse Now
2 C Thi Sach St, Dist. 1, HCMC. **Map** 2 F3.
Tel (08) 3825 6124.

Binh Minh Jazz Club
65 Quan Su, Hanoi.
Map 2 D4.
Tel (04) 3942 0400.
W minhjazzvietnam.com

Blue Gecko
31 Ly Tu Trong, Dist. 1, HCMC. **Map** 2 E3.
Tel (08) 3824 3483.

Breeze Sky Bar
Majestic Hotel, 1 Dong Khoi St, Dist. 1, HCMC.
Map 2 F4.
Tel (08) 3829 5517.
W majesticsaigon.com

Carmen Bar
8 Ly Tu Trong St, Dist. 1, HCMC. **Tel** (08) 3829 7699.

DMZ Bar
60 Le Loi St, Hue.
Tel (054) 382 3414.
W dmzbar.com.vn

Hien and Bob's Place
43 Hai Ba Trung St, Dist. 1, HCMC. **Map** 2 F3.
Tel (08) 3823 0661.

La Bella Napoli
60 Hung Vuong St, Nha Trang. **Tel** (058) 352 7299.

La Fenetre Soleil
44 Ly Tu Trong, Dist 1, HCMC. **Tel** (08) 3824 5994.

Le Pub
25 Hang Be, Hanoi. **Map** 2 E3.
Tel (04) 3926 2104.

Level 23
Sheraton Hotel, 88 Dong Khoi St, Dist. 1, HCMC. **Map** 2 F4.
Tel (08) 3827 2828.
W sheratonsaigon.com

Louisiane Brewhouse
Lot 29, Tran Phu St, Nha Trang. **Tel** (058) 352 1948.

Lush
2 Ly Tu Trong, Dist. 1, HCMC. **Map** 2 F2.
Tel (08) 3824 2496.
W lush.vn

Ly Club
4 Le Phung Hieu, Hanoi. **Map** 2 F4.
Tel (04) 3936 3069.
W qbarsaigon.com

O'Brien's
74A2 Hai Ba Trung, Dist. 1, HCMC. **Map** 2 F3.
Tel (08) 3829 3198.

Restaurant Bobby Chinn
77 Xuan Dieu St, Hanoi. **Map** 2 E4.
Tel (04) 3719 2460.
W bobbychinn.com

Sailing Club
72 Tran Phu St, Nha Trang.
Tel (058) 352 4628.
W sailingclubvietnam. com

Sax n Art
28 Le Loi, Dist. 1, HCMC. **Map** 2 E3.
Tel (08) 3822 8472.
W saxnart.com

Seventeen Cowboys
98B Tran Hung Dao St, Hanoi. **Map** 2 D4.
Tel (090) 443 8883.

The Spotted Cow
111 Bui Vien, Dist. 1, HCMC. **Map** 2 D5.
Tel (08) 3920 7670.

Tam Tam Café and Bar
110 Nguyen Thai Hoc, Hoi An. **Tel** (0510) 386 2212.

Vasco's
74/7d Hai Ba Trung, Dist. 1, HCMC. **Map** 2 F3.
Tel (08) 3824 2888.

Why Not Bar
26 Pham Ngu Lao St, Hue.
Tel (054) 393 8855

White Marble
98 Le Loi St, Hoi An.
Tel (0510) 391 1862.

ZanZBar
19 Dong Khoi, Dist 1, HCMC. **Map** 2 F4.
Tel (04) 6291 3686.
W zanzbar.com

Spectator Sports

Lam Son Stadium
15 Le Loi St, Vung Tau.
Tel (064) 351 3555.

My Dinh National Stadium
Hoa Lac St, Tu Liem Dist, Hanoi.

Saigon Racing Club
2 Le Dai Hanh St, Dist. 11, HCMC. **Map** 3 C2.
Tel (090) 366 6433.

Thong Nhat Stadium
138 Dao Duy Tu St, Dist. 10, HCMC.
Map 4 E3.
Tel (08) 3855 7865.

OUTDOOR ACTIVITIES AND SPECIAL INTERESTS

With its misty mountain tops, tropical forests, gushing rivers, and increasingly cosmopolitan cities, Vietnam today is a playground for a range of activities. The country's relatively undeveloped coastline stretches for hundreds of miles, and is a water lover's dream, with secluded beaches, pristine bays, and untrammeled surf. Trekkers and nature enthusiasts are drawn to the impressive network of national parks, mountain trails, and nature walks, while cyclists embrace the opportunity to explore the terrain or ride on uncrowded roads all the way from Hanoi to Ho Chi Minh City. Catering to the needs of millions of international visitors, luxury golf clubs have cropped up in all the major cities and resort towns. Food lovers can exercise their palates on one of the many culinary holidays, savoring the imperial cuisine of Hue and the exotic fruit of Mekong Delta as they go along. With so many activities to choose from, Vietnam is a multifaceted country with something that fits the interests and budget of most visitors traveling here.

Divers preparing to go under, Nha Trang

Diving, Snorkeling, and Swimming

The best developed location for diving in Vietnam is the resort town of Nha Trang (see pp112–15), which is home to several competent specialists offering equipment, boats, and instructors for crash courses. **Rainbow Divers** is the oldest and most trusted operation for aquatic activities here, and has a number of branches in diving locales throughout the country. Nha Trang has many other reliable outfits in operation, including **Sailing Club Divers**. About 37 miles (60 km) north of town, **Whale Island Resort** is an increasingly popular location for both diving and snorkeling. Located farther south, Phu Quoc Island (see p105) and Con Dao Islands (see p102) are blessed with shallow coral reefs, and are primed to become serious competitors to Nha Trang. At the moment, Phu Quoc and Con Dao are relatively unspoiled, though developing fast. Rainbow Divers is the sole operator in these places. Hoi An (see pp128–33), with its string of fishermen's islands about an hour's boat ride from shore, provides excellent diving opportunities in Central Vietnam. One-, two-, and three-day trips to these islands can be organized by **Cham Island Diving Center**.

Most beaches along the coast from Danang (see p138) to Nha Trang offer stretches of water ideal for swimming. Among the safest is Mui Ne Beach (see p110), where the undercurrents are weakest. Swimming facilities are also available in cities, as most hotels allow the use of their pools for a small sum. In Ho Chi Minh City, Grand Hotel (see p236) offers one of the cheapest rates for a day at its pool, while the International Club has a pool, sauna, steam room, and gym available for less than US$10 per day. In Hanoi, the swimming pools in **Army Hotel** and **Thang Loi Hotel** are affordable to use. Water parks such as Dam Sen (see p75) in Ho Chi Minh City, **Ho Tay Water Park** in Hanoi, as well as the **Phu Dong Water Park** in Nha Trang are all good for a nice dip.

Surfing, Kitesurfing, and Windsurfing

Although few Vietnamese surf, many foreign visitors take advantage of the superb, if not terribly huge waves at China Beach (see p137). Surfing boards can be rented locally.

Kitesurfing has caught on in a big way at Mui Ne, which is now the site of an annual international competition in the sport. The calm sea and strong winds provide perfect conditions. **Jibe's Beach Club** offers kitesurfing package holidays. The popularity of windsurfing is also escalating. Two operations for both kite-surfing and windsurfing are **Sailing Club Kite School** and **C2Sky Kitecenter**.

Windsurfers riding the gentle waves of the South China Sea, Mui Ne

Kayaking

Kayaks, still something of a novelty in Vietnam, were first introduced at Halong Bay *(see pp186–88)*, and soon proved to be ideal for exploring the islands, coves, and caves of the area. While visitors are free to wander the waters on their own, it is wise to contract with a specialist tour agency. Reliable outfits include old favorites the Sinh Tourist *(see p273)* and **Buffalo Tours**, both of which arrange kayaking holidays. Also recommended is **Handspan Adventure Travel**, known for keeping to small groups and using its own vehicles and guides. **Green Trail Tours** organizes kayaking tours in Halong Bay as well as at Ba Be Lake *(see p204)* and the Mekong Delta.

Kayaking in the crystal clear waters of Halong Bay

Golf

Once regarded by Communist Party stalwarts as a decadent and bourgeois pastime, golf is becoming popular in Vietnam. Once the domain of the expatriate community, golf clubs are now frequented by a growing number of local Vietnamese enthusiasts. While club memberships are quite expensive, guest fees are not so steep.

Courses are clustered around Ho Chi Minh City, Mui Ne, Danang, Dalat, and Hanoi. **Rach Chiec Driving Range** is about a 10-minute drive north of the city center, and is more economical than most venues. **Vietnam Golf Country Club** is a top-class facility, with two floodlit 18-hole courses that enable guests to play at night.

In Hanoi, you can practice your swing at **Lang Ha Driving Range**, while an hour west of

The luxuriant expanse of the beachside Ocean Dunes golf course, Phan Thiet

the city is the exclusive **King's Island Golf Course**. The most popular courses, though, are in and around Dalat *(see p118–20)*. Two extremely stylish golf clubs are **Dalat Palace**, established during the French-Colonial era, and Phan Thiet's **Ocean Dunes**, designed by Nick Faldo. **Sea Links** in Mui Ne is one of the country's most luxurious courses.

Trekking

The sheer topographic variety found in Vietnam makes it an ideal terrain for trekkers. You can choose between nature walks on national park trails or go on a hike on mountain slopes, adventurous romps through densely foliaged forests, and long strolls along the beaches.

The northern mountainous area around Sapa *(see pp200–201)* is one of the most popular trekking areas with visitors and locals alike, served by many tour agencies such as **Topas Adventure**, **Exotissimo**, and **Footprints**. Both take pride in their hands-on style, and provide local guides, who make useful ambassadors when approaching ethnic villages.

National parks are also ideal for trekking expeditions, with tended trails and some basic infrastructure. Cat Ba National Park *(see p193)* has one of the most challenging hiking trails in the park system. It winds its way through 29 miles (47 km) of jungle, right up to the summit of one of the park's highest hills. Sturdy shoes, a plastic raincoat, and plenty of water are essential. It is advisable to hire a guide. Any nearby hotel can make the

necessary arrangements. Not all trails in Cuc Phuong National Park *(see p197)* are marked, so it is best to take a guide. The longest walk here is a five-hour trek to the village of Kanh, where one can stay the night and go rafting on Buoi River. A 5-mile (8-km) trek takes hikers deep into the forest to a huge tree said to be 1,000 years old. Shorter hikes include a nice walk through the botanical garden and to the Primate Rescue Center, while another leads to a cave where prehistoric artifacts were discovered.

Some of the most impressive trails are in Bach Ma National Park *(see p140)*. Summit Trail leads to the top of Bach Ma Mountain or White Horse Mountain, so named for the streaks of white cloud often seen at its summit. The stunning views are well worth the steep climb. The Five Lakes Cascade Trail takes hikers by a series of enchanting waterfalls through the park, and is filled with rare flora and fauna. Alternatively, the Rhododendron Trail lives up to its name during spring when it is cloaked in flowers.

A section of the Five Lake Cascade Trail, Bach Ma National Park

Cycling

The best way to get a feel of the real Vietnam is on a bicycle. The route between Hanoi and Ho Chi Minh City has become the Holy Grail for many cyclists. Highway 1 has become congested and is also susceptible to flooding, so the preferred route these days is Highway 14. While it lacks the ocean breeze of the coastal route, it is still very picturesque.

The Mekong Delta region offers easy riding on flat roads. Views here are beautiful, especially at rice harvest time. In the Central Highlands, mountain cycling is taking off, though there are no dedicated trails at present. The condition of the roads along the southern route can vary; however, the many rivers and bridges on the way provide scenic stopovers. **Veloasia** organizes customized cycling tours to remote parts of the country, as does the excellent Bangkok-based **SpiceRoads**. However, try to avoid long-distance tours in the northern mountains in winter as the roads can be slippery and quite dangerous. For cycling in Dalat and the South Central Highlands, try **Phat Tire Ventures**.

Cyclists planning to travel independently should bring their own gear – rented bikes can be unreliable. If the bike breaks down, there are several bicycle repair shops along the way. You will also have to be vigilant of your possessions.

Martial arts instructor practising in a park, a common sight

Martial Arts

Martial arts are an important part of the cultural, athletic, and social mix in Vietnam. Many forms are practised here, including the indigenous *vo dao*, the origins of which go back around 2,000 years. Like judo, it turns the opponent's strength against him or her, and like kung fu, includes a wide vocabulary of blows. Weapons such as cudgels, swords, and axes can also be incorporated into the practitioner's repertoire. You can take a course at **Nam Huynh Dao School** in Ho Chi Minh City. Another martial art that is indigenous to Vietnam is *sa long cuong*. It stresses the principles of mind over matter, and flexibility over rigidity. Lessons are given at the **Youth Culture House of HCMC** in Ho Chi Minh City.

Various other combative arts such as judo, aikido, and kung fu can be practised at **Saigon Sports Club** in Ho Chi Minh City for a fee. Those who are only interested in watching the art can do so for free as well. In some of the city's parks, particularly in the Cholon district, it is common to see martial arts instructors practising in full-swing. In Hanoi, taekwondo – a style of unarmed combat for self-defence – is the most popular martial art, and the renowned **GTC Club** in Hanoi is one of the best places to practice.

Bird-Watching

With over 800 species recorded in the country, Vietnam is a prime destination for bird-watching enthusiasts. The country is also an important breeding ground for many migratory birds, and the more common birds can be spotted everywhere. Tour agencies are beginning to include specialized tours in their itineraries, and information is easy to come by in tourist offices. In the last decade, Vietnam has been subject to outbreaks of bird flu, but currently, the situation is under control.

Fresh ingredients and spices awaiting preparation, Hue

Culinary Holidays

Vietnam is home to one of the most interesting cuisines in the world. While culinary tours can be expensive, most epicures swear by them. New York-based **Absolute Travel** offers a luxury tour that starts in Ho Chi Minh City, moves on to Hoi An *(see pp128–32)* and Hue *(see pp142–8)*, and wraps up in Hanoi. In little more than a week, it lets you sample the basic styles of Vietnamese cooking. Cookery classes can be another option. Many hotels offer courses, one of the best being Madame Thi Kim Hai's at the Sofitel Legend Metropole Hotel *(see p166)* in Hanoi. This half-day course takes you on a trip to the market and then back to the kitchen to prepare the ingredients in northern style. Another interesting course to take a look at is **Miss Vy's Cooking Class** in Hoi An.

Cyclists exploring the streets of Hoi An

Spas

Some of Vietnam's best spas are part of luxurious hotel complexes, like the Six Senses Hideaway Ninh Van Bay *(see p238)* in Ninh Hoa. However, other, smaller spas are also making a mark, such as the **Thap Ba Hot Springs** *(see p114)* in Nha Trang, and **Tam Spa** and **Forester Spa** in Mui Ne.

Water villas on the beach at the Six Senses Hideaway Ninh Van Bay, Ninh Hoa

DIRECTORY

Diving, Snorkeling, and Swimming

Army Hotel
33C Pham Ngu Lao St, Hanoi. **Map** 2 F4.
Tel (04) 3826 5541.

Cham Island Diving Center
88 Nguyen Thai Hoc St, Hoi An.
Tel (0510) 391 0782.

C2Sky Kitecenter
82 Nguyen dinh Chieu St, Mui Ne.
Tel (091) 665 5241.
[W] c2skykitecenter.com

Ho Tay Water Park
614 Lac Long Quan St, Hanoi. **Tel** (04) 3718 4222.

Phu Dong Water Park
Tran Phu St, Nha Trang.

Rainbow Divers
90A Hung Vuong St, Nha Trang.
Tel (058) 352 4351.

Sailing Club Divers
72–74 Tran Phu St, Nha Trang.
Tel (058) 352 2788.

Thang Loi Hotel
200 Yen Phu St, Ho Tay, Hanoi. **Tel** (04) 3289 4211.

Whale Island Resort
2 Me Linh St, Nha Trang.
Tel (058) 351 3871.

Surfing, Kite-surfing, and Windsurfing

Jibe's Beach Club
90 Nguyen Dinh Chieu St, Mui Ne, Phan Thiet.
Tel (062) 384 7008.

Sailing Club Kite School, Mia Resort
24 Nguyen Dinh Chieu St, Mui Ne, Phan Thiet.
Tel (062) 384 7442.
[W] stormkiteboarding.com

Kayaking

Buffalo Tours
Hanoi. **Tel** (04) 3828 0702.
[W] buffalotours.com

Green Trail Tours
Hanoi. **Tel** (04) 3754 5260 (ext. 101). [W] greentrail-indochina.com

Handspan Adventure Travel
Hanoi. **Tel** (04) 3926 2828.
[W] handspan.com

Golf

Dalat Palace
Phu Dong Thien Vuong St, Dalat.
Tel (063) 382 1201.

King's Island Golf Course
Dong Mo Lake, Son Tay.
Tel (034) 3368 6555.

Lang Ha Driving Range
6 Lang Ha St, Hanoi.
Tel (04) 3835 0909.

Ocean Dunes
1 Ton Duc Thang St, Phan Thiet. **Tel** (062) 382 3366.

Rach Chiec Driving Range
An Phu Village, Dist. 9, HCMC. **Tel** (08) 3986 0756.

Sea Links Golf & Country Club
Nguyen Dinh Chieu St, Mui Ne, Phan Thiet.
Tel (062) 374 1741.
[W] sealinkscity.com

Vietnam Golf Country Club
Long Thanh My Village, Thu Duc, HCMC.
Tel (08) 6280 0103.

Trekking

Exotissimo
26 Tran Nhat Duat St, Hanoi. **Map** 2 E2.
Tel (04) 3828 2150.
[W] exotissimo.com

Footprints
10 Ly Nam De St, Hanoi. **Map** 2 D2.
Tel (04) 3933 2844.
[W] footprintsvietnam.com

Topas Adventure
52 To Ngoc Van St, Hanoi.
Map 1 C1. **Tel** (04) 3715 1005. [W] topastravel.vn

Cycling

Phat Tire Ventures
109 Nguyen Van Troi St, Dalat. **Tel** (063) 382 9422.
[W] phattireventures.com

SpiceRoads
[W] spiceroads.com

Veloasia
283/20 Pham Ngu Lao St, Dist. 1, HCMC. **Map** 2 D5.
Tel (08) 3837 6766.
[W] veloasia.com

Martial Arts

GTC Club
A3 Ngoc Khanh St, Hanoi.
Tel (04) 3846 3095.

Nam Huynh Dao School
29 Tran Quang Khai St, Dist. 1, HCMC. **Map** 1 C1.

Saigon Sports Club
514B Huynh Tan Phat St, Dist. 7, HCMC.
Tel (096) 633 0089.

Youth Culture House of HCMC
4 Pham Ngoc Thach St, Dist. 1, HCMC.
Map 2 E3.
Tel (08) 3829 4345.

Culinary holidays

Absolute Travel
[W] absolutetravel.com

Miss Vy's Cooking Class
Cargo Club, 107 Nguyen Thai Hoc St, Hoi An.
Tel (0510) 391 1227
[W] restaurant-hoian.com

Spas

Forester Spa
82 Nguyen Dinh Chieu St, Mui Ne, Phan Thiet.
Tel (062) 374 1317.

Tam Spa
9A Nguyen Dinh Chieu St, Mui Ne, Phan Thiet.
Tel (062) 374 1899.

Thap Ba Hot Springs
15 Ngoc Son St, Nha Trang. **Tel** (058) 383 5345.
[W] thapbahotspring.com.vn

SURVIVAL GUIDE

PRACTICAL INFORMATION

Vietnam today is a popular tourist destination, drawing an ever increasing number of visitors each year. Although the country opened up to tourism during the mid-1990s, since then, infrastructure and related facilities have gradually improved for the millions of tourists visiting each year. All major cities offer accommodations ranging from budget guesthouses to five-star hotels. Most towns and cities also have a range of restaurants catering to varying tastes and budgets. Almost the entire coastline is now open to tourist development and new resorts continue to crop up all the time. The white sand beaches and the spectacular coral reefs add to the beauty. Remote areas such as the northern mountains are still relatively undeveloped – a virtue perhaps – but not too difficult to access given the proliferation of travel agencies in most cities. Government-run outfits are not known for their helpfulness, but there are several reliable private tour operators who can arrange organized trips in most parts of this scenic and beautiful country.

When to Go

The temperature and rainfall patterns in Vietnam fluctuate widely from region to region (see pp38–9). Hence, visitors should make their itineraries according to the area they plan to visit, taking care to avoid the worst of the monsoon. The south gets its heaviest rainfall between May and November, while in the north, May to August are the wettest months. However, as these rainy months are in the off-season, it can work out much cheaper to visit. But bear in mind it can be uncomfortable and inconvenient due to flooding and low visibility.

If you want to participate in major holidays such as Tet (see pp32–3), the period from December to February is best, although prices are higher. For better weather and fewer crowds, the period from March to May is the best time to visit.

A balmy January afternoon at Phan Thiet (see p110)

What to Take

There is very little that cannot be bought in Vietnam's towns and cities, and at cheaper rates than back home. Villages and more remote areas are not likely to offer the same range of options though. In general, it is advisable to wear a wide-brimmed hat and carry lots of sunblock, while a collapsible umbrella is a must for rainy months. It is also a good idea to keep a Swiss army knife, a torch and batteries, and a mosquito repellent handy.

The best clothing for the south's warm, tropical climate is pale, lightweight colored cotton or silk. Shoes should be light in weight as you will probably need to walk a lot. In the north, especially in the highlands, nights are cold and day temperatures can fall quite low. Travelers should wear layers to trap body heat in order to keep warm.

Advance Booking

The peak flying season to Vietnam is from December to February. During this time, thousands of Viet Kieu or overseas Vietnamese flock back to their homeland to spend Christmas and Tet with their families. Make reservations for this period at least three months in advance. Some travelers avoid this crush by entering overland from either Laos or Cambodia, but most countries in Southeast Asia experience the same holiday rush. Several reliable travel agencies can take care of the bookings (see p273 & p283). It is also wise to book your accommodation well in advance during this period, especially if you plan to stay in a high-end hotel. However, budget accommodations usually present no problem.

Posters advertising specialized tours offered by a travel agency

Visas and Passports

Most travelers to Vietnam must possess a valid passport and visa, whether entering by air, land, or sea. Citizens from a number of surrounding countries may receive visa waivers on arrival, of varying

◀ Woman riding a bicycle through the green fields of Tam Coc, Ninh Binh area

A trader passport being inspected at the Chinese border

lengths. Visas to Vietnam are issued only by Vietnamese embassies and are best applied for through a travel agency. A procedure is now in place for granting visas on arrival. This process is easily done online and saves a trip to the embassy. Though there is a stamping fee (currently US$45) to be paid at the airport on top of the visa fee.

A standard tourist visa is valid for one month, though a three-month visa costs only a little more. Visitors can also apply for a single- or multiple-entry visa. Business visas can also be obtained for one to three months, though a letter of sponsorship or invitation from a Vietnamese business partner is required for this.

Immunization

Several vaccinations have been recommended by the World Health Organization (WHO) for anyone traveling in Southeast Asia. The list of diseases that one needs to be immunized against includes hepatitis A and B, tetanus, rubella, measles, mumps, diphtheria, and typhoid. Malaria has been eradicated from most of the country, but there is still a slight risk on Phu Quoc Island and Highland areas. Drug recommendations for malaria can vary depending on time, terrain, weather, and even the breed of mosquito. It is best to consult your family doctor or the WHO in advance when traveling to this region.

Dengue fever is now a serious problem in Vietnam, as in many of the surrounding countries. Unfortunately, there is currently no vaccination to protect against it. The virus is transmitted by mosquito and the best form of prevention is the use of repellent and nets.

Be aware that the quality of medical facilities and other healthcare in Vietnam, especially in smaller towns and rural areas, can be very poor. Patients may also be refused treatment if they are unable to provide proof in advance that they can pay their medical fees. For further information on personal health, *see pages 274–5.*

Customs Information

Customs regulations for tourists are normally straight-forward in Vietnam. Visitors are allowed to bring in 1.5 liters of alcoholic beverages and 400 cigarettes with them. Gold over 11 oz (300 g) and cash over US$5000 must be declared.

Upon arrival, a customs form has to be filled in, a yellow copy of which will be handed back to you. While few foreign visitors are searched, items deemed politically offensive or otherwise sensitive can be seized, including pornography, CDs, video tapes, and any material considered critical of the government. The website of **Vietnam Customs** in the United States is a useful source of up-to-date information on customs regulations.

DIRECTORY

Embassies

Australia
8 Dao Tan St, Hanoi.
Map 2 F3.
Tel (04) 3774 0100.
W vietnam.embassy.gov.au

Cambodia
71 Tran Hung Dao St, Hanoi.
Map 2 D5.
Tel (04) 3942 4789.

Canada
31 Hung Vuong St, Hanoi.
Map 1 B3.
Tel (04) 3734 5000.
W canadainternational.gc.ca/vietnam

France
57 Tran Hung Dao St, Hanoi.
Map 2 E5.
Tel (04) 3944 5700.
W ambafrance-vn.org

Laos
22 Tran Binh Trong St, Hanoi.
Map 1 D5.
Tel (04) 3942 9746.

United Kingdom
31 Hai Ba Trung St, Hanoi.
Map 2 F4
Tel (04) 3936 0500.
gov.uk/government/world/vietnam

United States
7 Lang Ha St, Hanoi.
Tel (04) 3831 4590.
W http://vietnam.usembassy.gov

Customs information
W customs.gov.vn

Group of tourists posing before Ho Chi Minh Mausoleum *(see p169)*

Neon-lit sign and logo of Saigon Tourist, Ho Chi Minh City

Tourist Information

Vietnam's hospitality industry is still developing. The two official sources of information and assistance, **Saigon Tourist** and **Vietnam Tourism**, are state-owned enterprises that make a profit by operating hotels and arranging tours. They also have very useful and informative websites. Independent travel agents and tour operators *(see also p283 & p285)* are better and more service-oriented if you need help in planning your own itinerary, or if you want the benefits of a customized package tour. While there are several dubious tour operators offering inferior service, most service providers are reliable and knowledgeable.

Admission Charges

Most museums, zoos, and botanical gardens charge a modest entry fee, which is usually US$1 or less. Until recently, a two-tiered pricing system was enforced, in which the price for foreigners could be five times that paid by the locals. This practice has been done away with officially, but is still prevalent in places. Most pagodas do not charge an admission fee, though a donation box is always prominently displayed.

Facilities for the Disabled

Unfortunately, facilities for the disabled are quite rare in this country, especially for those who use a wheelchair. Though the sidewalks are wide, it is quite difficult to maneuver a wheelchair along them as many street vendors have set up shop there, while others use them for parking their two-wheelers.

There appear to be wheelchair ramps on every block, but these are actually meant for motorbike access. Elevators are not very common, and toilets for the disabled are virtually unheard of. Nonetheless, even though they should be ready for some discomfort, disabled travelers with special needs should not be deterred by these infrastructural short-comings. Many high-end hotels and resorts are now well equipped to accommodate the dis-abled, while travel agents can hire an assistant, albeit not always a qualified one, for those who require one. With planning and the help of specialist agencies such as **Accessible Journeys** and **Society for Accessible Travel and Hospitality**, incon-veniences can be minimized.

Facilities for Children

Children are adored by all and welcomed almost everywhere in this family-oriented nation. The sight of parents traveling with small children is common here, and diapers, baby food, and other child-care products are readily available, especially in bigger cities. All restaurants are child friendly; however, most do not offer any special menus.

Pagoda sign asking visitors to dress modestly

Some foods may be spicy for kids, but ice cream, yogurt, and fresh fruit are always on offer. There is little in the way of special accommodation for children, but many hotels have rooms furnished with three or more single beds.

Language

With its range of tonal variations, Vietnamese can be a very hard language to learn. Fortunately, many people, espe-cially those who want to sell goods or services to foreigners, speak a smattering of English. It is often fractured, and, at times, difficult to understand, but since Vietnamese is written in the Roman alphabet, most ven-dors can write what they need to say. All the major airlines, banks, and hotels have some staff that speak adequate English. In rural areas, it is wise to travel with an interpreter or guide who can be hired for around US$20 to US$40 a day.

Multilingual sign at a temple

Etiquette

Vietnamese etiquette is strict but generally easy to comply with. As a rule, smile a lot, do not raise your voice, and never point at people. If you need to beckon or attract someone's attention, make sure that your palms are facing downwards before you gesture to them. It is also important to remember that losing your temper is coun-terproductive. The Vietnamese are more likely to respond to your grievances when they are addressed politely.

When meeting and greeting, shaking hands is customary. Do not touch anybody on the head as that is consi-dered the repository of the soul. That said, most Vietnamese are tactile individuals. People of the same sex walk arm in arm, pat each other on the shoulder, and hold

Travelers relaxing and enjoying a meal at a pavement café

hands. This does not extend to people of the opposite sex unless the couple is married. It is very common for locals to swoop down on foreign babies, often pinching their cheeks or even cuddling them. Some visitors may find this perturbing, but there is only affection behind such spontaneous displays. In apparel, it is not unusual to see a man wearing just a pair of loose-fitting shorts. Most women dress modestly. Always keep in mind that the Vietnamese are very particular about propriety, especially in places of worship. At such sites, you should dress appropriately, with arms and legs covered.

At the table, it is good manners to wait for the oldest person there to start the meal, unless you are the guest of honor. Never stab food with chopsticks or set them upright in a bowl of food, as that is a funerary practice. It is normal to eat with noisy gusto as an expression of appreciation for the food. Note that although you may be invited to dine in someone's home, guests are usually entertained in restaurants. *See page 243* for additional advice on table manners and customs, as well as tipping.

Photography

Most places in Vietnam are photogenic. Good-quality camera equipment, and memory cards are easily and cheaply available in Ho Chi Minh City, Hanoi, and other large cities. Note that photography is restricted in military areas and around police stations. It is also safer to request permission before taking pictures of religious sites or of people, especially the ethnic minorities.

Time and Calendar

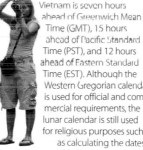
Tourist taking a photograph

Vietnam is seven hours ahead of Greenwich Mean Time (GMT), 15 hours ahead of Pacific Standard Time (PST), and 12 hours ahead of Eastern Standard Time (EST). Although the Western Gregorian calendar is used for official and commercial requirements, the lunar calendar is still used for religious purposes such as calculating the dates of festivals.

Measurements

The metric system has been in use since the French era. Some basic conversions from the US Standard to metric are:
1 inch = 2.54 centimeters
1 foot = 30 centimeters
1 mile = 1.6 kilometers
1 ounce = 28 grams
1 pound = 454 grams
1 US quart = 0.947 liter
1 US gallon = 3.6 liters

Electricity

As is common throughout the region, the electrical current in Vietnam is 220 volts. Most wall sockets accommodate French-style rounded pins as well as American-style flat pins. Hotel staff usually have adaptors on hand but they can also be found at any shop carrying domestic goods. Still, to be on the safe side, it is a good idea to bring along your own adapter. Charge your laptop and cell phone batteries daily as power outages are not uncommon, especially in small and remote towns.

DIRECTORY

Travel Agencies and Tourist Information

Ann Tours
77 Pham Hong Thai, Hanoi.
Map 2 D1. **Tel** (04) 3715 0950.
58 Ton That Tung St, Dist. 1,
HCMC. **Map** 1 C5.
Tel (08) 3833 2564.
W anntours.com

Saigon Tourist
45 Le Thanh Ton St, Dist. 1, HCMC.
Map 2 E3.
Tel (08) 3827 9279.
W saigontourist.net

The Sinh Tourist
52 Luong Ngoc Quyen St, Hanoi.
Map 2 E2. **Tel** (04) 3926 1568.
246 De Tham St, Dist. 1, HCMC.
Map 2 D5. **Tel** (08) 3836 9597.
W the sinhtourist.vn

TNK Travel Vietnam
220 De Tham St, Dist. 1, HCMC.
Map 2 D5.
Tel (08) 3920 4766.
W tnktravelvietnam.com

Tuan Travel
32 Bui Vien, Dist. 1, HCMC.
Map 2 D5. **Tel** (08) 3837 9667.
W tuantravel.com

Vietnam Tourism
80 Quan Su St, Hanoi.
Map 2 D4. **Tel** (04) 3942 2070.
W vietnamtourism.com

Disabled Services

Accessible Journeys
W disabilitytravel.com

Disability World
W disabilityworld.com

Mobility International USA
W miusa.org

Society for Accessible Travel & Hospitality
W sath.org

Personal Security and Health

Vietnam is one of the safest places to travel in the world. In addition to a very authoritarian government, the country boasts a generally law-abiding society. Visitors can go about their activities in relative safety, although common-sense rules do apply. Sadly, petty crime is on the increase in big cities. Although violent crime is rare, it does happen. The Vietnamese establishments are generally clean, and while street food is safe enough, it is better to stick to bottled water. Healthcare facilities are still lacking. With few ambulances or well-equipped emergency rooms, it is wise to carry travel insurance with a good medevac (medical evacuation) provision.

General Precautions

Though traveling in Vietnam is considered to be quite safe, there are some basic precautions that should be followed. Since petty crimes such as bag-snatching and pick-pocketing are prevalent in larger cities such as Ho Chi Minh City and Nha Trang, avoid carrying large sums of money or wearing much jewelry. It is advisable to keep part of your cash, and passport in a hidden money belt, and leave a portion of your valuables in your hotel's safe. Secure your cameras and purse when out walking or on a motorbike ride, as motorbike-mounted thieves have been known to pull up alongside, snatch such items, and drive on.

Another basic safety rule is to avoid venturing into unfamiliar areas at night. Do not accept coffee invitations from stangers in Downtown Saigon as Filipino Mafia prey upon tourists in this way. It is also important to make photocopies of your passport, travel insurance, and other relevant documents. In case of theft or loss, these copies will aid replacement.

There is an HIV problem in Vietnam, and sexual transmission has taken over intravenous transmission as the main cause of its spread. In 2012, UNAIDS estimated that there were 260,000 HIV-positive people in the country; the number has not increased in recent years.

Traffic policeman (*left*) and general policeman (*right*) in uniform

Tourist Police

In addition to the traffic and general police forces, Vietnam's tourist police are stationed at popular tourist sites. However, their presence is generally just for show, and they may not be able to help in an emergency. Generally, the police presence is unobtrusive and scant. In any dealing with the police, be polite. If you are robbed, the police might help you file a report for insurance purposes, but they often refuse. You may need an interpreter.

Hospitals and Medical Facilities

Most Western-operated and up-to-date medical facilities in the country are located in Ho Chi Minh City and Hanoi. If you fall ill in a small town, do try and get to one of these two cities. However, though the hospitals and clinics here are sufficient for daily needs and minor surgery, they might lack the drugs, equipment, or expertise for more complicated cases. The same holds true for dental care. If you are seriously injured, then it is better to leave Vietnam and go to major destinations such as Bangkok, Hong Kong, or even Singapore. Most pharmacies in Hanoi and Ho Chi Minh City now stock a wide variety of drugs, but do check the expiry date before buying. If you require some specific medicine, do remember to carry a sufficient supply from home.

Travel Insurance

A general travel insurance policy is a good idea in most places, but especially in this part of the world. Make sure that in addition to illness and injury, it covers theft as well. Most importantly, it should cover medical evacuation in case of an emergency.

Food- and Water-borne Diseases

The most common ailments are diarrhoea, dysentery, and giardiasis, all of which are food-related. Each of these is treatable with antibiotics, and

One of the many well-stocked fresh fruits stalls found throughout Vietnam

preventable by following some general safeguards. Wash your hands thoroughly before each meal, eat only at clean places, which offer well-cooked food or prepare the food in front of you, and peel fresh fruit yourself. Street food isn't always risky, although due caution as well as judgement should be used. Care is also needed when eating at a buffet or using room service even in five-star hotels. If your normal diet is bland, do keep in mind that food in Vietnam can be rather spicy. This simple change of diet can lead to an upset stomach for some. Always carry pills such as Tums and Pepto Bismol for indigestion. To prevent water-borne diseases such as typhoid and cholera, stick to bottled water, easily available everywhere, or well-boiled water. Drinking tea is usually safe as the water is traditionally brought to a full boil at the time of preparation.

Heat

During summer, it can become exceedingly hot in Vietnam. It is important to stay hydrated if you are traveling in this warm and humid weather. Always carry plenty of water, and remember to drink it at regular intervals. To protect yourself from heatstroke, wear a hat, sunglasses, and loose-fitting clothes. Use a good sunscreen to avoid getting sunburns.

Insect Bites & Infections

A mosquito bite may lead to dengue or, less frequently, malaria, two potentially serious diseases that a few precautions can prevent. The disease-carrying mosquitos are more active at dusk or dawn, and to avoid getting bitten, apply a repellent and sleep under a mosquito net. Rooms with fans or air-conditioning usually don't have mosquitoes. Take a prophylactic for malaria if visiting jungle areas or the Mekong, but seek advice from a doctor first. Carry your own disinfectant ointment and bandages as

wounds can become infected relatively easily in this climate, and should be kept clean.

Epidemics

Bird flu, swine flu, and hand, foot and mouth disease (a concern for children) have all been significant recurring issues since 2005, so, it may be best to avoid public child-care facilities. Temples keep caged birds, often wild, for release as a form of prayer. These birds are best avoided.

Undetonated Explosives

Leftover or unexploded bombs and artillery shells are still a matter of some concern in areas such as the DMZ *(see p153)*. All major tourist areas have been cleared of these dangers. Should you go off-the-beaten path and see anything that looks like a rocket or bomb, do not touch it. Walk away carefully and inform the authorities

A female visitor strolling along Vietnam's streets with a child

Women Travelers

It is not at all unusual to see a foreign woman traveling alone. They may be stared at in some rural areas, more out of curiosity than hostility or predation. The Vietnamese are hospitable people, and female tourists can find themselves invited home to dinner or even a sleepover with the family. Avoid skimpy clothes as they attract unwanted attention. Normal precautions should be taken at night.

Men's public toilet sign

DIRECTORY

Emergency Numbers

Ambulance, nationwide
Tel 115.

Fire, nationwide
Tel 114.

Police, nationwide
Tel 113.

Medical Resources

Centers for Disease Control
W cdc.gov

Vietnam Family Medical Practice
W vietnammedicalpractice.com

World Health Organization
W who.int/ith

Gay and Lesbian Travelers

Utopia
W utopia-asia.com

Gay and Lesbian Travelers

Vietnam's societal attitudes towards homosexuality have changed drastically over the last decade. An influx of Western culture has led to a more tolerant attitude and Ho Chi Minh City now has a thriving gay scene. For more information, consult websites such as **Utopia**.

Public Toilets

Public toilets are rare. Even in Ho Chi Minh City, only the central part of town has attended pay toilets, costing about US 10 cents. Hoi An has the largest number of public toilets per capita. Occasionally you will find squat toilets, often squalid, with little privacy. Bring your own toilet paper but don't flush it or you will block the plumbing.

Banking and Currency

In all major Vietnamese cities, as well as towns of appreciable size, financial services are abundant. Traveler's checks can be cashed at banks, and well-established hotels accept them as payment. Shopkeepers are also happy to accept US dollars. While currency exchanges and Automatic Teller Machines (ATMs) are common in most towns and cities, this is not yet the case in remote areas. Remember to carry a sufficient amount of Vietnamese currency when traveling to such places, although you will never be more than a few hours' journey from a banking facility of some kind.

Withdrawing money from an ANZ Automatic Teller Machine

Banks and Banking Hours

Vietnam's leading banks are **Vietcombank** and **Sacombank**, while the most common international banks are **ANZ** and **HSBC**. All maintain offices and ATMs throughout the country, and are connected to the Plus ATM network. Going to a bank for currency exchange or credit-card withdrawal is more time consuming than an ATM or private exchange.

While it can vary marginally in different cities and banks, banking hours are generally from 8am to 5pm, Monday to Friday, with some banks closing at midday for lunch. Most private currency exchanges set their own hours.

ATM Services

In 1999, there were only two ATMs in the country, both in Hanoi. Now they are found virtually everywhere there is a bank. All provide instructions in Vietnamese and English, and are available 24 hours a day. Money is issued only in the Vietnamese currency, calculating dollar withdrawals at the daily official rate of exchange. An unlimited number of withdrawals may be made in a day, but each is between two and five million *dong*, with a fee for each withdrawal, usually between US$2 and US$5. Larger withdrawals can be arranged with a bank teller. If you are planning to stay in Vietnam for more than a few months, consider opening your own account. Though the red tape involved can be daunting, it will make financial transactions smoother for you.

Changing Money

The process of changing cash has improved over the past few years, but a long wait at banks is still the norm. The process is faster at a private exchange, although the rates are not as good. In fact, the best rates are given by gold and jewelry shops, but they offer no security against shortchanging or counterfeit bills. With the proliferation of ATMs in most cities, however, many travelers opt simply to use their debit cards instead.

Credit and Debit Cards

Although credit and debit cards are not widely accepted in Vietnam's smaller towns, plastic is almost as useful as dollars and *dong* in larger cities, especially Ho Chi Minh City and Hanoi. Airlines, travel agents, upmarket hotels and restaurants, as well as upscale shops catering to tourists, are all glad to accept major credit cards such as MasterCard and Visa. If needed, you can also get a cash advance at the bank drawn on your credit card.

Currency

The *dong*, abbreviated to VND or d, is the Vietnamese unit of currency. Though it is not "official," US dollars are accepted almost everywhere, especially in tourist zones. Always ensure that these notes are in mint condition. It is also advisable to always keep some *dong* notes (preferably in smaller denominations) at hand for day-to-day expenditure. Bear in mind that the *dong* cannot be converted outside Vietnam.

Traveler's Checks

Encashing and using traveler's checks is not the best option in Vietnam, though it is a good idea to carry a few in case of an emergency. They can be cashed in at leading banks and exchanges, as well as at airlines and high-end hotels for a small commission. If lost, it is likely that you will need to go to a major city to have them replaced.

A branch of Vietcombank, a reliable option for currency exchange

Banknotes

Vietnamese banknotes are circulated in denominations of 500d, 1,000d, 2,000d, 5,000d, 10,000d, 20,000d, 50,000d, 100,000d, 200,000d, and 500,000d. All notes bear Ho Chi Minh's visage, and notes from 10,000d upward are made of polymer. Denominations under 1,000d are being phased out.

500,000 *dong*

100,000 *dong*

50,000 *dong*

200,000 *dong*

20,000 *dong*

10,000 *dong*

5,000 *dong*

200 *dong*

500 *dong*

1,000 *dong*

2,000 *dong*

Coins

In 2004, the Vietnamese government introduced 200d, 500d, 1,000d, 2,000d, and 5,000d coins in order to facilitate the phasing out of banknotes of the same denomination. Perceived by many as merely a gimmick, some shops and street vendors won't accept them because they are heavy and easily lost.

5,000 *dong*

DIRECTORY

Banks

ANZ Bank
2 Ngo Duc Ke St, Dist. 1, HCMC.
Map 2 F4. **Tel** (08) 3829 9319.
14 Le Thai To St, Hanoi. **Map** 2 F3.
Tel (04) 3825 8190. **W** anz.com

HSBC Bank
235 Dong Khoi St, Dist. 1, HCMC.
Map 2 F4. **Tel** (08) 3829 2288.
W vn.hsbc.com

Sacombank
278 Nam Ky Khoi Nghia St, Dist. 3,
HCMC. **Map** 1 C2.
Tel (08) 3932 2585.
W sacombank.com

Vietcombank
37 Ton Duc Thang St, Dist 1,
HCMC. **Map** 2 E2.
Tel (08) 3910 1993.
2 Hang Bai St, Hanoi.
Map 2 E4. **Tel** (04) 3934 3472.
W vietcombank.com.vn

Communication

Once considered archaic and mostly unreliable, the communications network in Vietnam has improved dramatically over the years. It is now possible to make an international call or send an e-mail or a fax from all but the most remote of locations. Nearly everybody has a cell phone. Public phones, on the other hand, are quite limited. The country also provides easy access to the Internet, with hotels and cafés offering the service. Major international publications are available in all big cities, and locally published English magazines and newspapers are growing in number. The postal system is efficient and staffed by helpful people, though courier services are generally preferred for faster delivery. The post office remains strictly censored, however, and all parcels are inspected before being sent.

Small yet reliable cyber café found all over Ho Chi Minh City

Public telephone booth at a street corner in Ho Chi Minh City

International and Local Telephone Calls

International calls can easily be made from most hotels, but are usually very expensive, as are local calls, though to a lesser extent. The best place to make international calls is from the post office. Callers also have the option of reversing the charges to major destinations.

Another option for making international calls is to use the budget-friendly Voice Over Internet Protocol (VoIP). This economic service enables users to make calls via the Internet. Dial 1717 plus 00, followed by the country code, the area code, and then the telephone number. A prepaid option using the 1717 calls facility is also available, for which you need to purchase a 1717 card, which is available at

most telecommunication outlets. In contrast, domestic calls are much more affordable. Vietnam made changes to its phone system in 2008, adding an extra digit (usually a 3) to all landlines. Most places now have seven-digit numbers, plus a three- or four-digit area code. Exceptions include Ho Chi Minh City, Haiphong, and Hanoi. The landline service is usually reliable, but a long-distance connection can have much disturbance and static. Most shops offer a cheap telephone service. Look out for a blue sign: *dien thoai cong cong* (public telephone).

Cell phones are very popular in Vietnam, and they are cheaper than in the West. Network services and sending text messages is also cheap. If you are staying for more than a few weeks, the best option is to purchase a SIM card from VinaPhone or MobiFone for your cell phone. All cell numbers have a 10-digit number provided by the operating company.

Pair of colorful Vietnamese stamps

Internet Facilities

Today, even the smallest towns in Vietnam boast Internet facilities. In fact, at places where foreigners congregate, Internet

facilities are ubiquitous. Most modern hotels provide Wi-Fi (Wireless Internet connection) in their rooms and so do most backpacker hostelries as well. Many bars and restaurants also offer Wi-Fi, which is useful for laptop and cellphone users. Dedicated Internet cafés are available but not as popular as a few years ago.

Vietnam permanently blocks a number of websites, and others are blocked intermittently. These include social networking sites, BBC, and a variety of blogs and news services critical of the government.

Postal Services

No matter where you are in Vietnam, you will not be far from a post office. The Vietnamese are enthusiastic letter writers and gift senders, so the postal service plays an important role in daily life. Most post offices are open until late, typically from 8am to 9pm, seven days a week. The staff are usually very helpful and willing clerks help wrap parcels and fill out customs forms, and will even stick stamps for you. Vietnamese stamps do not always have adhesive backs, and a pot of glue and a brush is needed. The postal delivery process is not very speedy. However, be aware that all parcels will be opened and inspected before they are mailed. Letters posted from

Hanoi or Ho Chi Minh City usually take ten to fourteen days to reach the US and other Western nations, while parcels can take a few months due to government inspection. Post from a small town bound for foreign shores can take even longer to reach the international departure system. Postal rates more or less match what they are in the rest of the world. A postcard to the US or Europe will cost just about half a dollar. *Poste restante* is available in major cities such as Hanoi and Ho Chi Minh City at a nominal charge. For faster delivery, well-known courier companies such as **DHL**, **Federal Express**, and **UPS** are available. However, parcels sent by courier can be detained and searched by the authorities. The same is true for packets with CDs and photographs, which may be intercepted for further scrutiny.

Some international and national newspapers available in Vietnam

Newspapers and Magazines

A selection of international publications, both English and French, are available in most prominent hotels and at news-stands in major cities. These include newspapers such as the *New York Times*, *Le Monde*, and *Bangkok Post*, as well as magazines such as *Time* and *Newsweek*. Many bars in Ho Chi Minh City and Hanoi stock newspapers for use by their patrons. The most widely read English language newspaper is *Viet Nam News*. It is a useful paper for cultural happenings, and the Sunday

edition has a leisure magazine. For further information on upcoming events and up-to-date listings, you can check publications such as *Word* and *Asia Life*.

All media is censored by the government, and journalists who have criticized the authorities are occasionally imprisoned for "abusing freedoms."

Television and Radio

Vietnamese television and radio – VTV and Voice of Vietnam respectively – are both government operated, consisting mainly of news, soap operas, Viet Pop music, and films. However, most of the hotels now offer a range of popular international TV channels including Cinemax, CNN, HBO, BBC, ESPN, MTV and Singapore's News Asia. Sports stations are also favored, especially during the soccer season.

Vietnamese Addresses

Addresses in Vietnam are quite straightforward: number, street, and city. In Ho Chi Minh City, the district number is also added after the street. Addresses with a slash, such as 120/5 Nguyen Trai Street, means that you have to go to No. 120 on this street, and then find building No. 5 in the alley next to it. Also note that the

same street begins new numbering upon entering a new district, and that the Vietnamese word for street, *pho* or *duong*, comes at the start of the street name.

Useful Dialing Codes

- For international calls, dial 00, then the country code, the area code, and then the number.
  Some country codes are: USA and Canada 1; Australia 61; UK 44; New Zealand 64; and France 33.
- To call Vietnam from abroad, dial 011, then 84, followed by the city code and the number.
- To speak to the international operator, just dial 00.
- For any kind of directory assistance, call 1080.
- To speak to the domestic operator, dial 0. This number may change according to the service provider for your cell phone. Customer assistance is available in English as well as Vietnamese. You may have to wait for some time to get to the instructions in the English language.

Cell phone calling cards by VinaPhone

TRAVEL INFORMATION

Most visitors fly to Vietnam. The country's domestic air transport system is good and getting better. The safety record is admirable, while the flights are mostly on time, and well connected to the main tourist destinations. Visitors from the US and Europe usually arrive via Bangkok or Hong Kong. From Cambodia, traveling by boat along the Mekong River is a scenic option. With the opening of several border crossings, many travelers opt to enter Vietnam by train, car, or bus from China, Laos, or Cambodia. The cheapest, often the quickest, and the most convenient way to get around the country is by the long haul bus system and the Open Tour bus. And for the independent traveler, a car with a driver is relatively inexpensive. Locally, metered and motorcycle taxis are the preferred modes of transport.

New arrivals outside Ho Chi Minh City's busy Tan Son Nhat airport

Arriving by Air

Of all three international airports in Vietnam, Ho Chi Minh City's Tan Son Nhat is by far the busiest. Hanoi's Noi Bai Airport and Danang International are also major airports. **Vietnam Airlines**, the country's official international carrier, operates direct flights from many destinations across the world, such as Paris, Beijing, San Francisco, Sydney, Siem Reap, Bangkok, and Singapore. Many prominent international airlines also service Vietnam, including **Air France**, **Cathay Pacific**, **Thai Airways**, **Malaysia Airlines**, **Qantas**, **Lufthansa**, **Japan Airlines**, and **Singapore Airlines** to name a few. A trans-Pacific journey from the USA takes over 20 hours, while from Europe, the trip takes less time. It's worth checking whether a transit or tourist visa is required for any stopover to Vietnam.

Air Fares

The cost of flying to Vietnam varies with airline, the season, and your travel agent. The average cost from the North American West Coast is about US$1,500 return fare; prices are equivalent from Europe. The busiest and most expensive time to travel to Vietnam is from December to February, when many families are flying in to celebrate Tet (see pp32–3). Discounted tickets are usually available during the off-season.

On Arrival

The arrival system in Vietnam is now more efficient and streamlined. While on the plane, passengers are handed an immigration form to fill out. This needs to be submitted, along with your passport, at the airport's immigration counter. Those who have applied for a visa online must pay the fee and get their visa before passing through immigration.

Getting from the Airports

Ho Chi Minh City's Tan Son Nhat is one of the best-equipped airports in Vietnam. Both arrivals and departures are handled in a quick and efficient manner. Note that at this airport, you must go through security checks during arrival and departure. The airport is 3 miles (5 km) from the center of the city. A metered taxi can be hired from the authorized taxi service, which is located near the currency exchange counter at the airport. Avoid any drivers offering flat rates. Minibuses are also available for transport to the city as are shuttle pick-ups, which can be provided by the hotels on request. Be prepared for large crowds outside the terminal as people come not only to pick up their family members, but

Airport taxi, a convenient mode of transport

Airports	Ⓘ Information	Distance from City Center	Average Taxi Fare	Average Journey Time
Tan Son Nhat, Ho Chi Minh City	(08) 3848 5383	3 miles (5 km)	US$15	20 minutes
Danang International	(0511) 382 3391	1 mile (1.6 km)	US$2	5 minutes
Noi Bai Airport, Hanoi	(04) 3886 5047	20 miles (35 km)	US$17	45–60 minutes

Tourists loading luggage into a bright yellow, metered Vina Taxi

also to watch passengers and planes arrive and depart.

Hanoi's brand new Noi Bai Airport is the farthest from the city center, and it can take more than 45 minutes by taxi to get into town. All transport service operators, including metered taxis and minibuses, are located outside the terminal. However, it is necessary to negotiate the fare first as most drivers refuse to use their meters. The fare to the Old Quarter amounts to about US$17. Also, watch out for drivers who try to take you to a hotel of their choice, as they stand to make a commission. The Noi Bai taxi mafia is notorious for this trick. The cheapest way to get to the city center is by taking the number 7 or 17 city bus which departs every 15 minutes. They take an hour and a half to reach the city, and stop when requested on the way to Hoan Kiem Lake (see p164). Another affordable option is the Vietnam Airlines shuttle bus, which costs about US$3, and is supposed to take all its passengers to the

airlines' office on Trang Thi Street. Some drivers also drop off passengers at their hotels if requested. Note that you are not required to pay any toll taxes on the way to or from the airport. Located at the western edge of town, Danang International is the smallest of the three international airports. There is only one terminal, with a small part of it dedicated to international flights. The taxi service outside the terminal offers fixed and inexpensive rates for a ride into the city.

Arriving via Land or Water

Vietnam shares land borders with three countries – China, Laos, and Cambodia. With new border crossings opening to foreigners (presently there are three with China, seven with Laos, and seven with Cambodia), more independent travelers are taking the land route.

From China, you can enter Vietnam by car, bus, or train. The popular Friendship Pass, located at Dong Dang, is open to rail and road traffic, and is the busiest crossing between the nations. A bi-weekly train, connecting Beijing to Hanoi, makes a brief stop at this pass. The other two border crossings are at Lao Cai (see p201) and Mong Cai. Open only to motor vehicles, they are less popular routes.

The crossings from Laos are Lao Bao, west of Dong Ha; the popular Cau Treo; Nam Can; Cha Lo; Na Meo; Tay Trang and Bo Y. The first three are open only to motor vehicles. Crossing by bus can be extremely

time-consuming. Visitors are advised to fly in from Laos.

Entry from Cambodia is easy and usually hassle free (see pp226–7). The Moc Bai crossing is the busiest, being only about two hours from Ho Chi Minh City. Many buses run daily between the two countries. The Vinh Xuong border near Chau Doc offers a more scenic approach to Vietnam. Tourists can travel along the Mekong River, taking in the view from a boat or a luxury ship. Five other, more remote, crossings are less often used.

DIRECTORY

Airlines

Air France
1 Ba Trieu St, Hanoi.
Map 2 E4.
Tel (04) 3824 7066.
🔲 airfrance.com.vn

Cathay Pacific
49 Hai Ba Trung St, Hanoi.
Map 2 D4 **Tel** (04) 3826 7298.
🔲 cathaypacific.com

Japan Airlines
36 Le Duc Tho St, Tu Liem District, Hanoi. **Tel** (04) 3826 0093.
🔲 jal.co.jp

Lufthansa
19–25 Nguyen Hue St, Dist. 1, HCMC. **Map** 2 F4.
Tel (08) 3829 8529.
🔲 lufthansa.com

Malaysia Airlines
49 Hai Ba Trung St, Hanoi.
Map 2 D4. **Tel** (04) 3826 8820.
🔲 malaysiaairlines.com

Qantas
186-188 Le Thanh Ton, Dist. 1, HCMC. **Map** 2 E4. **Tel** (08) 3910 5373. 🔲 qantas.com

Singapore Airlines
17 Ngo Quyen St, Hanoi.
Map 2 F4. **Tel** (04) 3826 8888.
🔲 singaporeair.com

Thai Airways
28 Thanh Nien St, Tay Ho District, Hanoi. **Map** off map.
Tel (04) 3826 7921.
🔲 thaiair.vn.com

Vietnam Airlines
25 Trang Thi St, Hanoi.
Map 2 E4.
Tel (04) 3832 0320.
🔲 vietnamairlines.com

An airport bus traveling through the streets of Ho Chi Minh City

Getting Around Vietnam

With the rapid development of Vietnam's infrastructure, the country's internal transport system is improving at a fast pace, and becoming more convenient and affordable. Railway lines run from Ho Chi Minh City to Hanoi, connecting several cities en route, before passing on into China. Reasonably comfortable and inexpensive trains are the most efficient mode of transport. Long-distance buses are popular with backpackers, but can be uncomfortable after a few hours, although the more expensive express buses are comparatively luxurious. Most popular is the Open Tour bus system, which links major centers. For quick travel between major cities, the airline system is great, while ferries and hydrofoils connect some ports. Travelers can also hire a motorbike or a car and driver.

Passengers boarding a train at Ho Chi Minh City's railway station

Domestic Airlines

The four domestic airlines are Vietnam Airlines (see p281), **Jetstar Pacific Airlines**, **Vietnam Air Service Company (VASCO)**, and **Vietjet Air**. Vietnam Airlines and VASCO are owned by the state. The former is the major carrier, servicing the entire nation; VASCO operates in much of southern Vietnam. Jetstar Pacific is partly owned by the state and serves the six largest cities. Vietjet Air, the country's first privately-owned airline, also serves several major cities.

Plane Tickets, Fares, and Reservations

Tickets can be purchased online or at the airlines' booking offices in major cities or at the reservation counter at the airport. An English-speaking attendant is usually on duty. Any of the many travel agents throughout Vietnam can also arrange air travel, and their prices are usually no more than what you would pay at the airline office.

You can also book tickets at the travel desk of some of the better hotels, or even through some diving operators and select souvenir shops.

Domestic fares are usually under US$150 excluding baggage fees. It is a good idea to make advance reservations if planning to travel during the peak season, from mid-November to mid-March.

Railroad Network

The railroad network services almost the entire length of the country. It mainly follows the coast from Ho Chi Minh City to Hanoi, with stops at several big cities along the way. From Hanoi, a few lines connect to Halong Bay (see pp186–8), Sapa (see pp200–201), and China. The running times vary, but the fastest transit between Ho Chi Minh City and Hanoi is about 33 hours. Trains commonly run late but, curiously, can also sometimes arrive early. Even-numbered trains run from north to south, while odd-numbered trains run in the opposite direction. Although trains connecting Hanoi to Ho Chi Minh City are called Reunification Expresses, no train is actually named so.

Trains

Most passenger trains in Vietnam are fairly affordable, clean, and reasonably comfortable, if not really luxurious. Some of the carriages are air-conditioned. Four classes of tickets are on offer here: Hard Seat, which is basically a wooden bench; Soft Seat, a cushioned recliner in a carriage with a TV; Hard Sleeper, which is a compartment with six bunks; and Soft Sleeper, a private compartment with four bunks and a lockable door. Meals and snacks are available in all classes for an extra charge. Passengers may also alight at stops to buy food. Long-distance trains have a dining car, and vendors bearing a variety of drinks and snacks roam the trains.

Train Tickets, Fares, and Reservations

Tickets can be purchased at the stations, as well as through travel agents (see p273) and good hotels. Note that some travel agents are limited to single destination tickets, and cannot take you beyond certain points. Other agents may have more ticket options. Check the stations, the **Vietnam Railways** website, and with travel agents for up-to-date schedules. Train fares range from a few dollars to over US$100, with the most expensive being the private Victoria Service from Hanoi to Sapa. Be sure to make advance bookings if traveling during popular Vietnamese holidays.

A long-distance bus awaiting departure, Mien Tay bus terminal

Travelers buying tickets at Mien Tay bus terminal, Ho Chi Minh City

Buses

The advent of new and clean express buses has made bus travel the preferred means of getting around for visitors traveling between major cities. The vehicles are more expensive than their non-express counterparts and local mini-buses, but are faster, safer, and more comfortable. Their chief disadvantage, however, is the karaoke machine most of them carry. In addition to the regularly scheduled buses, another viable option is the chartered minibus. Most travel agents and hotels can arrange one to carry up to 18 passengers for out-of-town trips.

The Open Tour bus or coach travels between major destinations and is a popular and quick method of transportation for tourists. Many tourist cafés such as The Sinh Tourist (see p273) run these services. Tickets are one-way, cheap and flexible, and allow stop-offs as well.

Bus Tickets and Fares

Bus fares are low, with the Ho Chi Minh City–Hanoi routes ranging from US$45 to US$60. The ticketing and scheduling system, however, can be maddeningly complex. Tickets can be bought on the day of travel or before, but a station can sell tickets only to certain destinations, and connecting routes complicate the matter even more. It is usually best to make arrangements via an agent or hotel.

Renting a Car or Motorbike

If you choose to rent a car, you must also hire a driver licensed in Vietnam. A car plus driver costs between US$65 and US$120 per day. The price varies with the distance you expect to cover and the amount of fuel needed. The driver takes care of his own meals and lodgings on trips lasting more than a day.

Legally, a license is required to rent a motorbike but is rarely asked to be shown. If you want to get around by motorbike, it is best to hire a motorcycle taxi, locally called xe om or a Honda om. Depending on the distance you expect to travel, it should cost upward of US$10 per day. A helmet is required by law.

Boats and Ferries

Boats sail all the way from Ho Chi Minh City to Chau Doc at the Cambodian border on the Mekong. The river trip takes two days on a slow boat, and one day on a fast boat. There are also some ferries to Phu Quoc Island (see p105) from Rach Gia, and to many points among the Islands of Halong Bay. Hydrofoils, which are run by reliable companies such as **Vina Express**, operate regular services between Ho Chi Minh City and Vung Tau (see p80).

Cruise liner moored at a Saigon River harbor

DIRECTORY

Airlines

Jetstar Pacific Airlines
w jetstar.com

VASCO
w vasco.com.vn/en

Vietjet Air
w vietjetair.com

Train Stations

Danang Station
202 Haiphong St, Danang.
Tel (0511) 382 3810.

Hanoi Station
120 Le Duan St, Hanoi.
Map 1 C4.
Tel (04) 3942 3697.

Saigon Station
1 Nguyen Thong St, Dist. 3, HCMC. **Map** 1 A3.
Tel (08) 3343 6528.

Vietnam Railways
w vr.com.vn/english

Bus Stations

Cholon Station
86 Trang Tu St, Cholon, HCMC. **Map** 3 C5.
Tel (08) 3855 7719.

Gia Lam Station
Gia Thuy Long Bien St, Hanoi.
Tel (04) 3827 1569.

Giap Bat Station
6 Giai Phong St, Hanoi.
Tel (04) 3864 1467.

Kim Ma Station
Cnr. of Nguyen Thai Hoc & Giang Vo sts, Hanoi.
Map 1 A3.
Tel (04) 3845 2846.

Mien Dong Station
292 Dinh Bo Linh, Binh Thanh Dist, HCMC.
Tel (08) 3899 4056.

Mien Tay Station
395 Kinh Duong Vuong St, Binh Chanh Dist, HCMC.
Tel (08) 3825 5955.

Boat and Ferry Terminals

Danang Port
26 Bach Dang St, Danang.
Tel (0511) 382 2513.

Haiphong Port
8A Tran Phu St, Haiphong.
Tel (031) 385 9456.

Vina Express at Bach Dang Jetty
Ton Duc Thang St, Dist. 1, HCMC. **Map** 2 F4.
Tel (08) 3829 7892.

Travel Agencies

Kangaroo Café
22 Bao Khanh St, Hanoi.
Map 2 E3.
Tel (04) 3828 9931.

Sinhbalo Adventure Travel
283/20 Pham Ngu Lao St, Dist.1, HCMC. **Map** 2 D5.
Tel (08) 3837 6766.

Local Transportation

The public transport system in Vietnam is still in its nascent stage, although it does vary from city to city. The most convenient and safest mode of transport for travelers is by metered taxis. The local bus network is not a viable or reliable option as the buses are crowded, noisy, unsafe, and highly erratic. Probably the quickest and cheapest way to get around is by motorbike taxis, known as *xe om* or Honda *om*. The streets of Ho Chi Minh City especially are overflowing with them. Foreign visitors may rent both motorbikes and cars to drive. Though banned in 2009 and not very safe in busy streets, cyclos still service tourist areas in Ho Chi Minh City and Hanoi.

pillion, and can be found in large numbers throughout the cities. In major tourist areas, men on motorbikes offer their services at almost every corner. If you are not approached, simply stand on the sidewalk and try to wave down a passing bike. Sooner or later, one will stop for you. A typical fare is about US 70 cents per half-a-mile (1 km). Fares, however, vary from district to district, and will depend largely on your negotiating skills.

Tam Hanh, a reputable intercity bus company operating in South Vietnam

Getting Around Hanoi and Ho Chi Minh City

The best way to explore both Ho Chi Minh City and Hanoi – the latter especially so – is on foot. Though Ho Chi Minh City is a great urban sprawl spread across many miles, each of its districts is walkable in itself. Hanoi's Old Quarter, on the other hand, is a charming little neighborhood, the length and breadth of which can be easily walked in a day.

A cyclo is a bicycle-like contraption where passengers sit in front of the driver, who pedals them through alleys and city streets. A popular mode of transport for visitors wishing to explore Ho Chi Minh City, Hanoi, Hue, and other centers of tourism, cyclos were also engrained in Vietnamese culture. They were used to transport both passengers and heavy loads of goods between markets, shops, and homes throughout Vietnam's colonial and modern

history. Unfortunately, in modern-day Vietnam, the streets are crowded with speeding motorbikes and automobiles, and the cyclo has become a traffic hazard. It is still possible to ride cyclos in some tourist areas, but not necessarily advised.

A faster yet affordable way of getting around, especially in Ho Chi Minh City, is on a Honda *om*, known as *xe om* in Hanoi. These are motorbike taxis on which the passenger rides

Buses and Minibuses

City buses in Vietnam are not only uncomfortable to ride, but also woefully inadequate, a fact acknowledged even by the government. Although they are an inexpensive form of transport, the number of buses servicing the cities is insufficient. In addition, most are slow and lack facilities such as air-conditioning.

Minibuses are available for hire at affordable rates, and can be arranged for by most hotels and travel agencies. Small groups of tourists or families can easily hire one for day trips, and even for a one- or two-day excursion out of town.

Metered Taxis

Until recently, taxis were a rarity on the streets of Vietnam's cities. Where they did exist, they were privately owned, borrowed, or rented cars with negotiable fares. Today, taxis are everywhere in most cities, and virtually all are metered. The government acknowledges that

Driver walking past parked taxis in the Old Quarter, Hanoi

Heavily congested streets of Ho Chi Minh City

even the most reputable taxi companies rig their meters or cheat customers by taking longer routes. Fares generally start at just under US$1 but vary according to company and location. Always watch the meter closely and try to pay the exact fare, as many drivers falsely claim they have no change.

Rules of the Road

The number one rule of the road is never yield to the temptation to rent a car and drive it yourself. It is simply not advisable for foreigners to rent self-drive cars as the traffic can get very chaotic at times. Renting a motorbike for getting around is relatively safer, although it would be wise to observe and familiarize yourself with the general flow and movement of traffic, usually erratic, for a few days first. Also keep an eye out for livestock on the road.

For the average tourist, the main consideration is how to cross the street. There are few traffic lights, and those that do exist are often considered to convey an advisory rather than a compulsory message. Watch the locals step out into traffic and follow their lead, first waiting for four-wheeled vehicles to pass, and then walking slowly and steadily through a sea of two-wheelers. Don't hesitate or stop suddenly as drivers will not be able to predict your movement and you will risk a collision.

Motorbike riders are required to wear helmets at all times.

Only two people are allowed to ride on a motorbike. However, this law is enforced somewhat inconsistently and, at times, blatantly ignored.

Honda om or xe om motorbikes available for rent

Organized Tours

Organized day trips, as well as one- and two-day group tours are very common. In addition to being convenient, they can also, at times, work out cheaper depending on the size of your group. There are numerous companies in both Hanoi and Ho Chi Minh City offering such tours. Since costs can vary extensively, it would be a good idea to check with a few tour companies for the best deal available. Most trips from Ho Chi Minh City are to the Cu Chi

Tunnels (see p76) and Mekong Delta, while from Hanoi, tours frequently lead to Halong Bay (see pp186–8) and Sapa (see pp200–201).

DIRECTORY

Taxi services – Hanoi

Airport Taxis
Tel (04) 3873 3333.

Hanoi Taxis
Tel (04) 3853 5353.

Mai Linh Taxi
Tel (04) 3861 6161.

Taxi services – Ho chi minh city

Airport Taxis
Tel (08) 3844 6440.

Mai Linh Taxis
Tel (08) 3838 3838.

Vina Taxi
Tel (08) 3811 1111.

Tour Companies

Buffalo Tours
See p275.

Kim Travel
189 De Tham St, Dist. 1, HCMC.
Map 2 D5. Tel (08) 3920 5552.

Queen Travel
65 Hang Bac St, Hanoi.
Map 2 E3. Tel (04) 3826 0860.

Saigon Tourist
See p281.

The Sinh Tourist
See p281.

TNK Travel
See p273

Vientindo Travel
S-239/71 Bo De St, Long Bien District, Hanoi.
Tel (04) 3872 7754.

Tour bus making a stop in front of the Thang Long Water Puppet Theater

General Index

Acknowledgments

Dorling Kindersley would like to thank the many people whose help and assistance contributed to the preparation of this book.

Contributors

Andrew Forbes has a BA in Chinese and a PhD in Chinese History. He has lived in Chiang Mai, Thailand, for the past 20 years, where he is editor of CPA Media (www.cpamedia.com). He has visited Vietnam on an annual basis over the past decade.

Richard Sterling is a travel writer of long standing in the greater San Francisco area. He holds the Lowell Thomas Award for travel literature. He has written extensively on Vietnam and travels annually in the region.

Fact Checkers
Adam Bray, Nam Nguyen, Nick Ray

Proofreader
Shahnaaz Bakshi

Indexer
Jyoti Dhar

DK London
PUBLISHER Douglas Amrine
PUBLISHING MANAGERS Jane Ewart,
Scarlett O'Hara, Kate Poole
MANAGING EDITOR Kathryn Lane
PROJECT EDITOR Ros Walford
PROJECT ART EDITORS Gadi Farfour, Kate Leonard
REVISIONS AND RELAUNCH TEAM Judith Bamber, Ron Emmons, Alexandra Farrell, Emer FitzGerald, Fay Franklin, Anna Freiberger, Rhiannon Furbear, Camilla Gersh, Kaberi Hazarika, Jacky Jackson, Claire Jones, Sumita Khatwani, Priya Kukadia, Maite Lantaron, Anwesha Madhukalya, Hayley Maher, Alison McGill, Vikki Nousiainen, Catherine Palmi, Susie Peachey, Marianne Petrou, Khushboo Priya, Ellen Root, Lokamata Sahoo, Azeem Siddiqui, Sands Publishing Solutions, Priyansha Tuli, Janis Utton, Ajay Verma
SENIOR CARTOGRAPHIC EDITOR Casper Morris
DTP DESIGNER Natasha Lu
PICTURE RESEARCH ASSISTANT Rachel Barber
DK PICTURE LIBRARY Romaine Werblow
DIGITAL MEDIA TEAM Fergus Day
PRODUCTION CONTROLLER Louise Daly

Additional Photography
Simon Bracken, Adam Bray, Demetrio Carrasco, Eric Crichton, Tim Draper, Robin Forbes, Ken Findlay, Frank Greenaway, Colin Keates, Dave King, David Mager, Ian O'Leary, David Peart, Rough Guides / Tim Draper, Roger Smith, Kavita Saha, Kim Taylor, Álvaro Velasco, Jerry Young.

Special Assistance
Dorling Kindersley would like to thank the following for their assistance: Ton Sinh Thanh, and Nguyen Luong Ngoc, Embassy of the Socialist Republic of Vietnam in New Delhi, India; Pham Ngoc Minh, Buffalo Tours Vietnam; and all the other museums, churches, hotels, restaurants, shops, galleries and sights too numerous to thank individually.

Cartography credits
Base mapping for Ho Chi Minh City and Hanoi derived from Netmaps.

Picture Credits
a = above; b = below/bottom; c = center; f = far; l = left; r = right; t = top.

The Publishers are grateful to the following individuals, companies, and picture libraries for permission to reproduce their photographs:

4CORNERS IMAGES: Amantini Stefano 2–3.

AKG-IMAGES LTD: 53c; Amelot 6–7; François Guénet 259cr.

Alamy: A.M. Corporation 5tl, 134bl, 185tr; Arco Images 22bl; Bill Bachmann 69tc; Oliver Benn 109br, 118cl; Blickwinkel 22cb, 101crb, 205crb; Tibor Bognar 94tl, 235br; Jon Bower 219tr, 220ca, 224bl; Rachael Bowes 49bl; Paul Carstairs 27br; Rob Cousins 3c, 17b; FLPA 186tl; Glow Images 28tl, 30clb, 259br; Alex Griffiths 27cr, 196clb; Gavin Hellier 209t; Henry Westheim Photography 24tr, 205cla; Hornbil Images Pvt Ltd 23clb; Jeremy Horner 99ca; Imagebroker 103cra, 218crb; ImageState 43t, 150–51; Index Stock 170cla; Ingo Jezierski 36cr; Jon Arnold Images 16, 18tl, 156, 206–7, 208bl; Elmari Joubert 186bc; E.J. Baumeister Jr 29br; Christian Kober 29tr; Serge Kozak 67br; Kevin Lang 29bl, 32bl, 54crb, 103crb, 124,170br; Barry Lewis 33bl; Mary Evans Picture Library 44br, 207c; Neil McAllister 131crb, 132br, 164tl, 171tl, Chris McLennan 163c, 164cr; Nic Cleave Photography 218bl; David Osborn 22clb; Papilio 101clb; Edward Parker 196tr; Paul Thompson Images 233bl; Photobyte 203bl; Photofrenetic 23ca, 102c; Photoz.at 133bl; Pictorial Press Ltd 63crb; Christopher Pillitz 268–9; Nicholas Pitt 265tr; Popperfoto 48tr, 49crb; Royal Geographical Society 54cla; Marcus Wilson-Smith 23cra; Stephen Frink Collection 194bl; The Photolibrary Wales 94bl; Tribaleye Images/J. Marshall 183b; Ian Trower 28bc; Visual Arts Library (London) 41br; Andrew Woodley 118tr, 200bl; WorldFoto 196cla.

ARDEA.COM: Jean Paul Ferrero 205c; Masahiro Iijima 205bl; Jean Michel Labat 23br; ASIAN EXPLORERS: Timothy Tye 219tl.

ADAM BRAY ©2008: 120tr, 178ca, 284br.

The Bridgeman Art Library: Archives Charmet/Private Collection The arrival of French troops in the Bay of Haiphong in June 1884 (colour litho), Vietnamese School (19th century) 46tl; Archives Charmet/ Bibliotheque Nationale, Paris, France The Tours Congress, Ho Chi Minh (1890-1969) from 'L'Humanite', December 1920 (b/w photo) 173cra; Juliet Bui: 102tr.

Corbis: 23bc, 265cl; Asian Art & Archaeology, Inc 41c; Bettmann 47br, 48cl, 48bc, 48bl, 49tl, 49tr, 49c, 49clb, 49crb, 50bl, 50br,

155crb, 173cr, 173bl; Christophe Boisvieux 32br, 33cra, 34bl, 247c; Corbis Sygma/J.P. Laffont 50clb, /Jacques Langevin 50tl, / Les Stone 271br, /Orban Thierry 173br; Natalie Fobes 24br, 37tl; Owen Franken 78cla, 187cl; Michael Freeman 108cl, 136cl; Philippe Giraud 160cla, Robert van der Hilst 247tl; Jeremy Horner 103clb; Hulton-Deutsch Collection 46cb, 173cl; Catherine Karnow 24–5c, 32tl, 186cla, 190–91, 261cb; Charles & Josette Lenars 42tc; Luong Thai Linh/Epa 260ca, Christophe Loviny 219cr; Wally McNamee 49br; Kevin R. Morris 213tl, 222br; David A. Northcott 23c; Tim Page 35bl, 36tl, 123br; Papilio/John R. Jones 24cla, 29cla, 29cra, 45tc, Steve Raymer 17b, 25tl, 25tr, 29cr, 34tc, 170cra, 171cla, 271tl; Reuters/Dien Bien Phu Museum 47crb; Roman Soumar 76tl; Keren Su 23fcra; Luca Tettoni 267tr; Brian A. Vikander 6/tl; Nevada Wier 28cra, 31crb, 34cr, 35tl; Alison Wright 202clb; Michael S. Yamashita 103bl; Zefa/Gary Bell 194cla.

CPA Media: 26bl, 42clb, 44c, 46bc, 47tc, 48crb; Jim Goodman 28tr, 28br, 33cr; David Henley 26tl, 27cl, 27clb, 33clb, 139cl, 139c.

David J. Devine. 48tl. Flink in Maia Da Nang resort: 232bl.

Frank Lane Picture Agency Limited: Colin Marshall 182.

Getty Images: AFP 284br, AFP/Hoang Dinh Nam 28cla; Asia Images/Martin Puddy 196tr; Eternity in an Instant 51crb; Iconica/John W. Banagan 107b; Photographer's Choice/John W. Banagan 101cl; Planet Observer/Universal Images Group 15tr; River Astromujin 14til; Robert Harding World Imagery: 22cra, Robert Francis 115crb, 246cl, Occidak Ltd 203br; The Image Bank/Peter Adams 20bl, Time Life Pictures/Larry Burrows: 48–9c, Stringer 48clb; Stone/Simeone Huber 214–15.

Hotel Continental Saigon: 61tr, 232cr.

Tran Linh: 36br.

Lonely Planet Images: John Banagan 4br, 96–7, 106, 116–17, 230–31; Anders Blomqvist 52–3, 157b, 210bl; Alain Evrard 23cla; Mason Florence 88, 168tl; Kraig Lieb 122tl; Craig Pershouse 197bl; Peter Ptschelinzew 44tl; Patrick Ben Luke Syder 27cla.

Mary Evans Picture Library: 7c, 26tr, 26clb, 40, 47bl, 231c, 269c.

Masterfile: Pierre Arsenault 22cla, 89b.

Naturepl.com: Jeff Foott 22c; David Kjaer 140c; Pete Oxford 20bcr; Ngoc: 33cla; Ngoc Dong Ha Nam Co. Ltd: 259clb, 259cb, 259fclb, 259bc; Phong T. Nguyen: 28clb, 28crb, 29cl

Mick Palarczyk: 9br; Peter Pham: 202br; Photographersdirect.com: Images & Stories 202tr; Jamie Marshall Photography 203tl; Peter Schickert 19/tl; Steve MacAulay Photography 203tr; tanchouzuru.com 55cr; Tanya D'Herville Photography 9cl.

Photolibrary: Oxford Scientific Films/Mary Plage 81br.

Reuters: Larry Downing 51tc, 51bc; Kham 82tc; Nguyen Huy Kham 24clh

Rex Hotel: 64tl.

Stars & Stripes: Photograph by John Olson - "Cu Chi, South Vietnam, November, 1967: Colt .45 and flashlight in hand, wearing a gas mask, "tunnel rat" Sp4 Richard Winters of 2nd Battalion, 27th Infantry, 25th Infantry Division cautiously lowers himself into a 1,000-foot-long Viet Cong tunnel found in Vietnam's "Iron Triangle" 77cra;

swright.smugmug.com: Steven L. Wright 99bl.

Sun Group Corporation: 137t.

Terra Galleria Photography: Q.T. Luong 69br, 155tr.

Louis Vuitton: 61tl

Wikipedia.com: Public Domain 43 bc; World Pictures: Eur 188b; Stuart Pearce 105bl.

Front Endpaper: Alamy: Jon Arnold Images c, tr; Kevin Lang cla; Frank Lane Picture Agency Limited: Colin Marshall tl; Lonely Planet Images: John Banagan cr; Mason Florence bl.

Cover Picture Credits

Front - AWL Images: Keren Su; Dorling Kindersley: Demetrio Carrasco bl;
Spine - AWL Images: Keren Su.

All other images © Dorling Kindersley
For further information see: www.dkimages.com

Special Editions of DK Travel Guides

DK Travel Guides can be purchased in bulk quantities at discounted prices for use in promotions or as premiums.
    We are also able to offer special editions and personalized jackets, corporate imprints, and excerpts from all of our books, tailored specifically to meet your own needs.

To find out more, please contact:
(in the United States) **SpecialSales@dk.com**
(in the UK) **travelspecialsales@uk.dk.com**
(in Canada) DK Special Sales at **general@ tourmaline.ca**
(in Australia)
business.development@pearson.com.au

Phrase Book

Vietnamese belongs to the Mon-Khmer group in the Austroasiatic family of languages. Besides Standard Vietnamese, which is spoken in the Hanoi area, there are several other dialects, the most important being those of the central and southern regions. These differ mainly in phonetics (for example, they have fewer tones than standard Vietnamese) and lexicology, but not grammar.

For centuries, Chinese (*chu han*) was the official language for administration and education as there was no written form of Vietnamese. Later, a special script called *chu nom* was developed to record the native language. By the 17th century, a romanized script, *quoc ngu*, was devised by Roman Catholic missionaries in southeast Asia as a simple way of transcribing Vietnamese *(see p41)*. With the arrival of the French, *quoc ngu* was officially introduced. Despite early opposition to the new script, perceived to be an instrument of colonial rule, the fact that it was relatively easy to learn gradually won over its critics.

The Six Tones

Vietnamese is a complex tonal language, which means that words are pronounced at varying levels of pitch. Standard Vietnamese has six tones, which are marked by special diacritics usually positioned above the vowel.

Tone can affect the meaning of words dramatically. For example, *ma* has six meanings depending on the pitch at which it is delivered. Accents indicate the tone of each syllable in the following chart:

Ma (ghost)	High, level tone
Mà (but)	Low (falling), level tone
Mã (horse)	Rising broken tone with a glottal stop
Mả (grave)	Falling-rising tone
Má (Cheek)	Rising tone
Mạ (rice seedling)	Sharp falling tone, heavy glottal stop

Kinship Terms

Words denoting family relationships, known as "kinship terms," are used when people address each other. The choice of expression depends on gender, age, social status, and the relationship and degree of intimacy between the speakers. The most common terms are:

Anh (older brother) to address a young male.

Chị (older sister), female equivalent of **anh**.

Em (younger sibling) to address someone younger than you.

Ông (grandfather) to address an older man, formal and respectful, similar to Sir in English.
Bà (grandmother) to address an older woman, formal and respectful.
Cô similar to Madam in English.

Guidelines for Pronunciation

Most of the consonants are pronounced as in English, except the following:

d	as in Zoo (in the north); as in You (in the south)
đ	as in Down
gi	as in Zoo (in the north); as in You (in the south)
kh	aspirated K
ng	nasal n, as in learniNG
ngh	nasal n, as in learniNG
nh	as in KeNYa
r	as in Zebra
t	as in Top
th	as in Top
tr	as in CHop
x	as in See

Vowels are pronounced as follows:

a	as in bAsk
â	as in ơ but shorter
ă	as in hUt
e	as in End
ê	as in hEllo
i	as in Ink
o	as in lOng
ô	as in bAll
ơ	as in liOn
u	as in pUt
ư	as in mountAIn

Communication Essentials

Hello!	Xin chào!
Goodbye!	Tạm biệt!
Yes/no	Vâng/không
I understand	Tôi hiểu
I don't understand	Tôi không hiểu
I don't know	Tôi không biết
Thank you	Cám ơn!
Do you speak English?	Anh/chị có biết tiếng Anh không?
I can't speak Vietnamese	Tôi không biết tiếng Việt
Sorry/Excuse me!	Xin lỗi!
Not at all	Không dám
Come in please!	Mời anh/chị vào!
emergency	Cấp cứu
police	Công an
ambulance	Xe cấp cứu
fire brigade	Cứu hỏa

Useful Phrases

My name is …	Tên tôi là …
What is your name?	Tên anh/chị là gì?
How do you do/ pleased to meet you	Rất hân hạnh được gặp anh/chị
How are you?	Anh/chị có khỏe không?
What work do you do?	Anh/chị làm nghề gì?
How old are you?	Anh/chị bao nhiêu tuổi?
What nationality are you?	Anh/chị là người nước nào?
What is this?	Dây là cái gì?
Is there … here?	Ở đây có… không?
Where is …. ?	…. ở đâu?
How much is it?	Cái này giá bao nhiêu?
What time is it?	Bây giờ là mấy giờ?
Congratulations	Chúc mừng
Where is the restroom/toilet?	Phòng vệ sinh ở đâu?
Where is the British Embassy?	Đại sứ quán Anh ở đâu?

Useful Words

I	tôi
man	đàn ông
woman	đàn bà
family	gia đình
parents	bố mẹ/cha mẹ/ ba má
father	bố/cha/ba
mother	mẹ/má/mạ
younger brother	em trai
older brother	anh trai
younger sister	em gái
older sister	chị
big/small	to/nhỏ
high/low	cao/thấp
hot/cold	nóng/lạnh
good/bad	Tốt/xấu
young/old	trẻ/già
old/new	cũ/mới
expensive/cheap	đắt/rẻ
here	đây
there	kia
What?	gì?
Who?	ai?
Where?	(ở) đâu?
Why?	(tại) sao?
How? What is it like?	thế nào?

Money

I want to change US$100 into Vietnamese currency.	Tôi muốn đổi 100 đô la Mỹ ra tiền Việt.
exchange rate	tỷ giá hối đoái
I'd like to cash these travelers' checks.	Tôi muốn đổi séc du lịch này ra tiền mặt.
bank	ngân hàng
money/cash	tiền/tiền mặt
credit card	thẻ tín dụng
dollars	đô la
pounds (sterling)	bảng
Vietnamese dong	đồng (Việt Nam)

Keeping in Touch

I'd like to make a telephone call.	Tôi muốn gọi điện thoại.
I'd like to make an international phone call.	Tôi muốn gọi điện thoại quốc tế.
mobile phone	máy điện thoại di động
telephone enquiries	chỉ dẫn điện thoại
public phone box	trạm điện thoại công cộng
area code	mã (vùng)
post office	bưu điện
stamp	tem
letter	thư
registered letter	thư bảo đảm
address	địa chỉ
street	phố
town	thành phố
village	làng

Shopping

Where can I buy…?	**Tôi có thể mua …. ở đâu?**
How much does this cost?	**Cái này giá bao nhiêu?**
May I try this on?	**Tôi mặc thử có được không?**
How much?	**Bao nhiêu?**
How many?	**Mấy?**
expensive/cheap	**đắt/rẻ**
to bargain	**mặc cả**
size	**số, cỡ**
color	**màu**
black	**đen**
white	**trắng**
blue	**xanh da trời**
green	**xanh lá cây**
red	**đỏ**
brown	**nâu**
yellow	**vàng**
grey	**xám**
bookstore	**hiệu sách**
department store	**cửa hàng bách hóa**
market	**chợ**
pharmacy	**hiệu thuốc**
supermarket	**siêu thị**
souvenir shop	**cửa hàng lưu niệm**
souvenirs	**đồ lưu niệm**
lacquer painting	**tranh sơn mài**
painting on silk	**tranh lụa**
wooden statue	**bức tượng gỗ**
silk scarf	**khăn lụa**
tablecloth	**khăn trải bàn**
tray	**khay**
vase	**lọ hoa**

Sightseeing

travel agency	**công ty du lịch**
Where is the international ticket office? (plane)	**Phòng bán vé máy bay quốc tế ở đâu?**
Vietnam Airlines	**Hãng hàng không Việt Nam**
beach	**bãi**
bay	**vịnh**
ethnic minority	**dân tộc ít người**
festival	**lễ hội**
island	**hòn đảo**
lake	**hồ**
forest, jungle	**rừng**
mountain	**núi**
river	**sông**
temple	**đền**
museum	**bảo tàng**

pagoda	**chùa**
countryside	**nông thôn**
cave, grotto	**hang**

Getting Around

train station	**nhà ga**
airport	**sân bay**
air ticket	**vé máy bay**
bus station	**bến xe búyt**
ticket	**vé**
one-way ticket	**vé một lượt**
return ticket	**vé khứ hồi**
taxi	**tắc xi**
car rental	**thuê xe ô tô**
car	**xe ô tô**
train	**xe lửa**
plane	**máy bay**
motorbike	**xe máy**
bicycle	**xe đạp**
cyclo	**xích lô**
How long does it take to get to…?	**Đi …. mất bao lâu?**
Do you know …. road?	**Anh/chị có biết đường …. không?**
Is it far?	**Có xa không?**
Go straight.	**Đi thẳng.**
turn	**rẽ**
left	**trái**
right	**phải**
passport	**hộ chiếu**
visa	**thi thực**
customs	**hải quan**

Accommodations

hotel	**khách sạn**
guesthouse	**nhà khách**
room (single, double)	**phòng (đơn, đôi)**
air conditioning	**máy lạnh**
passport number	**số hộ chiếu**

Eating Out

I'd like to book a table for two.	**Tôi muốn đặt trước một bàn cho hai người.**
waiter	**người phục vụ**
May I see the menu?	**Cho tôi xem thực đơn**
Do you have any special dishes today?	**Hôm nay có món gì đặc biệt không?**
What would you like to order?	**Anh/chị muốn gọi gì?**

Can I have the bill, please?	**Anh/chị cho hóa đơn**	noodle soup beef/ chicken	**phở bò/gà**
I am a vegetarian.	**Tôi ăn chay.**	onion	**hành**
tasty/delicious	**ngon/ngon tuyệt**	papaya	**đu đủ**
spicy (hot)	**cay**	peach	**đào**
sweet	**ngọt**	pepper	**hạt tiêu**
sour	**chua**	pork	**thịt lợn, thịt heo**
bitter	**đắng**	potato (sweet potato)	**khoai tây (khoai)**
breakfast	**bữa ăn sáng**	prawn	**tôm**
chopsticks	**đôi đũa**	rambutan	**chôm chôm**
knife	**dao**	rice	**gạo**
fork	**nĩa**	rice (cooked)	**cơm**
spoon	**thìa**	glutinous rice	**gạo (cơm) nếp**
to drink	**uống**	non-glutinous rice	**gạo (cơm) tẻ**
to eat	**ăn**	salad	**xà lách**
hungry/thirsty	**đói/khát**	salt	**muối**
restaurant	**hiệu ăn, nhà hàng**	snail	**ốc**
Western food	**món ăn Âu**	spring rolls	**nem rán (chả giò)**
Vietnamese specialties	**đặc sản Việt Nam**	starter	**(món) khai vị**
		soup	**xúp**
		soy sauce	**tương**

Food

		stir fried beef with mushrooms	**bò xào nấm**
apple	**táo**	sugar	**đường**
banana	**chuối**	vegetables	**rau**
bamboo shoots	**măng**	Vietnamese noodle soup	**phở**
bean sprouts	**giá**		
beef	**thịt bò**		
bread	**bánh mì**		
butter	**bơ**		
cake	**bánh ngọt**		

Drinks

chicken	**(thịt) gà**	tea	**trà, chè**
coconut	**dừa**	coffee (white coffee)	**cà phê (cà phê sữa)**
crab	**cua**	water	**nước**
dessert	**(món) tráng miệng**	fruit juice	**nước quả, nước trái cây**
duck	**vịt**		
eel	**lươn**	mineral water	**nước khoáng**
egg	**trứng**	milk	**sữa**
fish	**cá**	soft drinks	**nước ngọt**
fish sauce	**nước mắm**	beer	**bia**
frog	**ếch**	wine	**rượu vang**
fruit	**hoa quả, trái cây**	glass	**cốc**
ginger	**gừng**	bottle	**chai**
ice	**đá**		

Health

ice cream	**kem**		
lemon	**chanh**	What is the matter with you?	**Anh/chị bị làm sao?**
lemongrass	**xả**	fever	**sốt**
lobster	**tôm hùm**	accident (traffic)	**tai nạn (giao thông)**
mandarin orange	**quít**	acupuncture	**châm cứu**
mango	**xoài**	allergy	**dị ứng**
menu	**thực đơn**	ambulance	**xe cấp cứu**
milk	**sữa**	antibiotics	**thuốc kháng sinh**
mushrooms	**nấm**	blood	**máu**
meat	**thịt**	blood pressure (high/low)	**huyết áp (cao/thấp)**
(well done, medium, rare)	**(tái, vừa, chín)**		
noodles	**mì, miến**		

cough	ho
diabetes	bệnh đái đường
diarrhea	đi ngoài
dizzy	chóng mặt, hoa mắt
doctor	bác sĩ
ear	tai
flu	cúm
food poisoning	ngộ độc thức ăn
headache	đau đầu
heart	tim
hospital	bệnh viện
hygiene	vệ sinh
insomnia	mất ngủ
illness	bệnh
injection	tiêm
malaria	bệnh sốt rét
medicine	thuốc
operate	mổ
pharmacy	cửa hàng thuốc
prescription	đơn thuốc
sore throat	viêm họng
temperature	sốt
tetanus injection	tiêm phòng uốn ván
tooth	răng
toothache	đau răng
Vietnamese traditional medicine	thuốc Nam

Time and Season

minute	phút
hour	giờ
day	ngày
week	tuần
month	tháng
year	năm
Monday	(ngày) thứ hai
Tuesday	(ngày) thứ ba
Wednesday	(ngày) thứ tư
Thursday	(ngày) thứ năm
Friday	(ngày) thứ sáu
Saturday	(ngày) thứ bảy
Sunday	Chủ nhật
season	mùa
spring	mùa xuân
summer	mùa hè/mùa hạ
fall	mùa thu
winter	mùa đông
dry season	mùa khô
rainy season	mùa mưa
rain (it is raining)	mưa (trời mưa)
wind	gió
sunny	nắng
weather	thời tiết
warm/cold	ấm/lạnh
lunar calendar	Âm lịch

solar calendar	Dương lịch
Vietnamese New Year	Tết Nguyên đán
What time is it?	Bây giờ là mấy giờ?
8:30	tám giờ rưởi
8:45	tám giờ bốn mười lăm phút/chín giờ kém mười lăm (phút)
10:15	mười giờ mười lăm phút
12:00	mười hai giờ
morning	buổi sang
midday	buổi trưa
afternoon	buổi chiều
evening	buổi tối
night	đêm

Numbers

1	một
2	hai
3	ba
4	bốn
5	năm
6	sáu
7	bảy
8	tám
9	chín
10	mười
11	mười một
12	mười hai
15	mười lăm
20	hai mươi
21	hai mươi mốt
24	hai mươi bốn/ hai mươi tư
25	hai mươi lăm
30	ba mươi
40	bốn mươi
50	năm mươi
100	một trăm
101	một trăm linh (lẻ) một
105	một trăm linh (lẻ) năm
200	hai trăm
300	ba trăm
1,000	một nghìn/ một ngàn
10,000	mười nghìn/ mười ngàn
1,000,000	một triệu

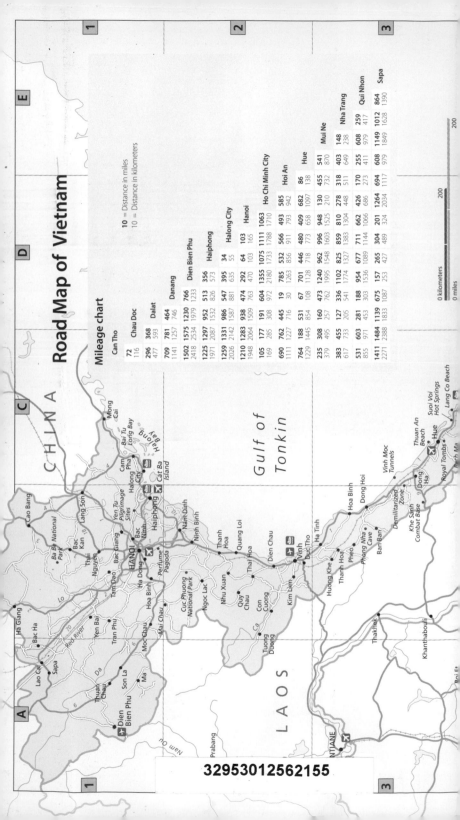

Road Map of Vietnam

Mileage chart

10 = Distance in miles
10 = Distance in kilometers

	Can Tho	Chau Doc	Dalat	Danang	Dien Bien Phu	Haiphong	Halong City	Hanoi	Ho Chi Minh City	Hue	Hoi An	Mui Ne	Nha Trang
Chau Doc	72 / 116												
Dalat	296 / 477	368 / 593											
Danang	709 / 1141	781 / 1257	464 / 746										
Dien Bien Phu	1502 / 2418	1575 / 2534	1230 / 1979	766 / 1233									
Haiphong	1225 / 1971	1297 / 2087	952 / 1532	513 / 826	356 / 573								
Halong City	1259 / 2026	1331 / 2142	986 / 1587	547 / 881	395 / 635	34 / 55							
Hanoi	1210 / 1948	1283 / 2064	938 / 1509	474 / 763	292 / 470	64 / 103	103 / 165						
Ho Chi Minh City	105 / 169	177 / 285	191 / 308	604 / 972	1355 / 2180	1075 / 1733	1111 / 1788	1063 / 1710					
Hue	764 / 1229	785 / 1263	445 / 716	67 / 108	701 / 1128	532 / 856	566 / 911	409 / 658	585 / 942				
Hoi An	682 / 1097	762 / 1227	446 / 718	19 / 30	785 / 1263	541 / 870	608 / 979	493 / 793	604 / 972	86 / 138			
Mui Ne	235 / 379	308 / 495	160 / 257	531 / 854	1240 / 1995	962 / 1548	996 / 1603	948 / 1525	130 / 210	455 / 732	403 / 649		
Nha Trang	383 / 617	455 / 733	127 / 205	336 / 541	1102 / 1774	825 / 1327	859 / 1383	810 / 1304	278 / 448	318 / 511	255 / 411	148 / 238	
Qui Nhon	531 / 855	603 / 971	281 / 453	188 / 303	954 / 1536	677 / 1089	711 / 1144	662 / 1066	426 / 686	255 / 411	170 / 273	265 / 427	259 / 412
Sapa	1411 / 2271	1484 / 2388	1139 / 1833	675 / 1087	157 / 253	265 / 427	304 / 489	201 / 324	1264 / 2034	694 / 1117	608 / 979	1149 / 1849	1012 / 1628

0 kilometers   200

0 miles   200